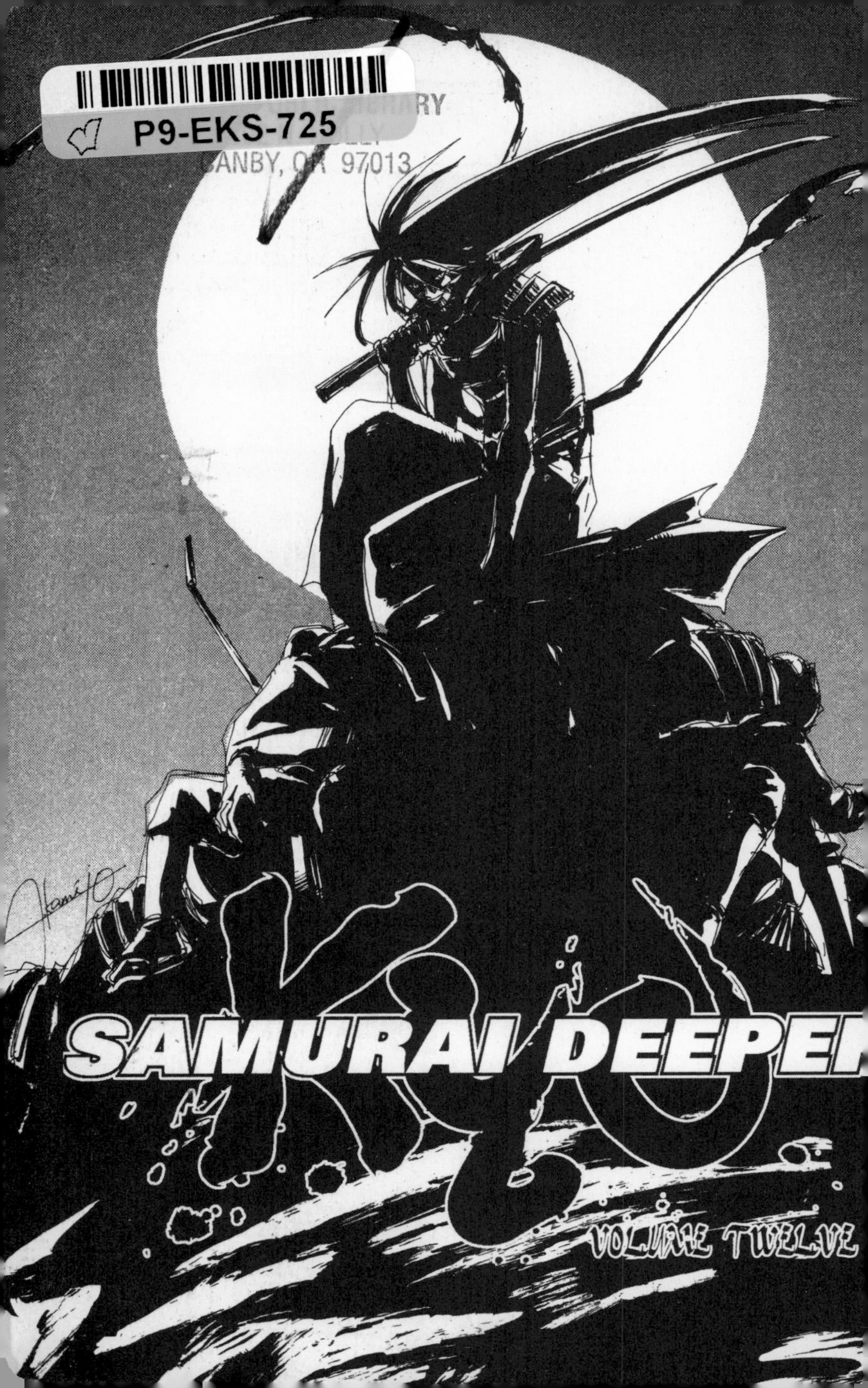
SAMURAI DEEPER
VOLUME TWELVE

Samurai Deeper Kyo Vol. 12
Created by Akimine Kamijyo

Translation - Alexander O. Smith
Script Editor - Rich Amtower
Copy Editor - Peter Ahlstrom
Retouch and Lettering - Patrick Tran
Production Artists - Eric Pineda
Cover Design - Seth Cable

Editor - Aaron Suhr
Digital Imaging Manager - Chris Buford
Pre-Press Manager - Antonio DePietro
Production Managers - Jennifer Miller and Mutsumi Miyazaki
Art Director - Matt Alford
Managing Editor - Jill Freshney
VP of Production - Ron Klamert
Editor-In-Chief - Mike Kiley
President and C.O.O. - John Parker
Publisher and C.E.O. - Stuart Levy

A  Manga

TOKYOPOP Inc.
5900 Wilshire Blvd. Suite 2000
Los Angeles, CA 90036

E-mail: info@TOKYOPOP.com
Come visit us online at www.TOKYOPOP.com

ISBN: 1-59532-452-6

First TOKYOPOP printing: April 2005
10 9 8 7 6 5 4 3 2 1
Printed in the USA

SAMURAI DEEPER Kyo

Vol. 12
by Akimine Kamijyo

HAMBURG // LONDON // LOS ANGELES // TOKYO

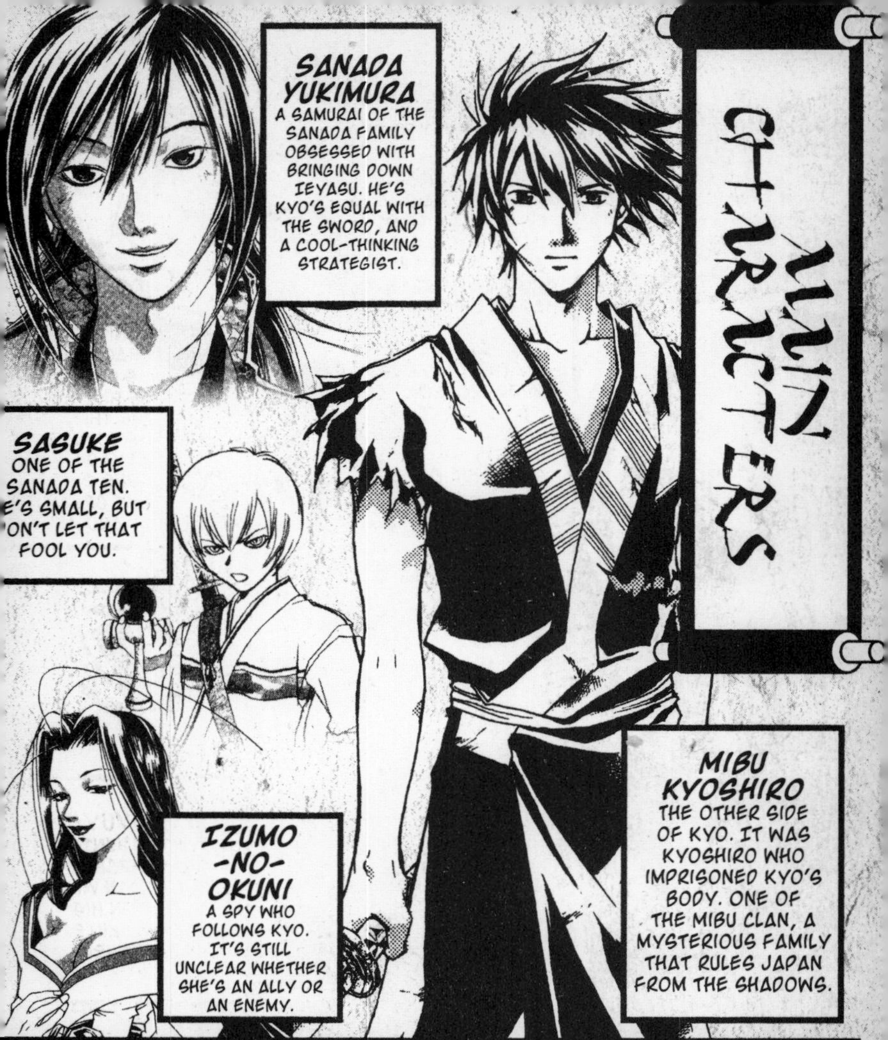
MAIN CHARACTERS
SANADA YUKIMURA
A SAMURAI OF THE SANADA FAMILY OBSESSED WITH BRINGING DOWN IEYASU. HE'S KYO'S EQUAL WITH THE SWORD, AND A COOL-THINKING STRATEGIST.
SASUKE
ONE OF THE SANADA TEN. E'S SMALL, BUT ON'T LET THAT FOOL YOU.
MIBU KYOSHIRO
THE OTHER SIDE OF KYO. IT WAS KYOSHIRO WHO IMPRISONED KYO'S BODY. ONE OF THE MIBU CLAN, A MYSTERIOUS FAMILY THAT RULES JAPAN FROM THE SHADOWS.
IZUMO-NO-OKUNI
A SPY WHO FOLLOWS KYO. IT'S STILL UNCLEAR WHETHER SHE'S AN ALLY OR AN ENEMY.

THE STORY

FOUR YEARS HAVE PASSED SINCE THE BATTLE OF SEKIGAHARA.
YUYA AND KYOSHIRO MEET AND BEGIN TO TRAVEL TOGETHER, BUT YUYA SOON LEARNS THAT KYOSHIRO HAS ANOTHER SIDE: THE CRUEL AND POWERFUL SAMURAI KYO.
AS THE TWO KYOS FIGHT FOR DOMINANCE, THEY PICK UP TWO MORE TRAVELING COMPANIONS, BENITORA AND YUKIMURA, AND LEAVE EDO, HEADING WEST. THEIR DESTINATION: THE AOKIGAHARA FOREST AT THE BASE OF MT. FUJI, WHERE KYO'S BODY LIES HIDDEN...BUT ON THE WAY, THEY ARE ASSAILED BY THE SIXTH DEMON KING, ODA NOBUNAGA, AND HIS TWELVE GOD SHOGUNS! A BATTLE ENSUES, AND BLOOD IS SPILLED UPON BLOOD. JUST AS KYO SEEMED ABOUT TO RECLAIM HIS BODY, IT WAS SNATCHED AWAY BY AN OLD FRIEND--AKIRA.
THE PARTY SETS OUT TOWARD KYOTO, HOT ON AKIRA'S TRAIL WHEN THEY ENCOUNTER BONTENMARU, ANOTHER OF THE FOUR EMPERORS. HE LEADS THEM TO THE HOME OF KYO'S MASTER, MURAMASA. THERE, A DEADLY BATTLE ENSUES BETWEEN KYO AND SHINREI, A MIBU CLAN ASSASSIN!

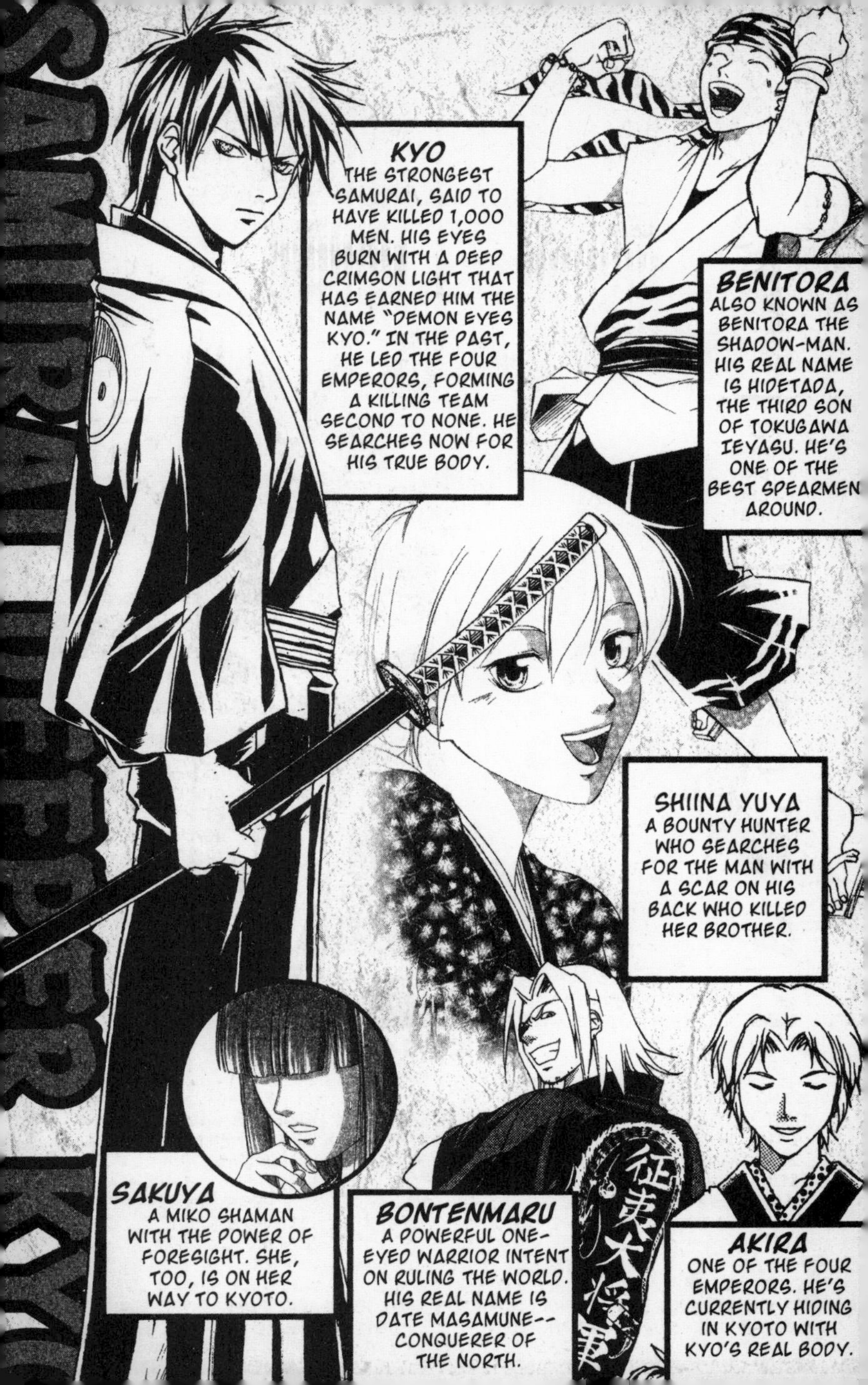
SAMURAI DEEPER KYO
KYO
THE STRONGEST SAMURAI, SAID TO HAVE KILLED 1,000 MEN. HIS EYES BURN WITH A DEEP CRIMSON LIGHT THAT HAS EARNED HIM THE NAME "DEMON EYES KYO." IN THE PAST, HE LED THE FOUR EMPERORS, FORMING A KILLING TEAM SECOND TO NONE. HE SEARCHES NOW FOR HIS TRUE BODY.
BENITORA
ALSO KNOWN AS BENITORA THE SHADOW-MAN. HIS REAL NAME IS HIDETADA, THE THIRD SON OF TOKUGAWA IEYASU. HE'S ONE OF THE BEST SPEARMEN AROUND.
SHIINA YUYA
A BOUNTY HUNTER WHO SEARCHES FOR THE MAN WITH A SCAR ON HIS BACK WHO KILLED HER BROTHER.
AKIRA
ONE OF THE FOUR EMPERORS. HE'S CURRENTLY HIDING IN KYOTO WITH KYO'S REAL BODY.
BONTENMARU
A POWERFUL ONE-EYED WARRIOR INTENT ON RULING THE WORLD. HIS REAL NAME IS DATE MASAMUNE--CONQUERER OF THE NORTH.
SAKUYA
A MIKO SHAMAN WITH THE POWER OF FORESIGHT. SHE, TOO, IS ON HER WAY TO KYOTO.

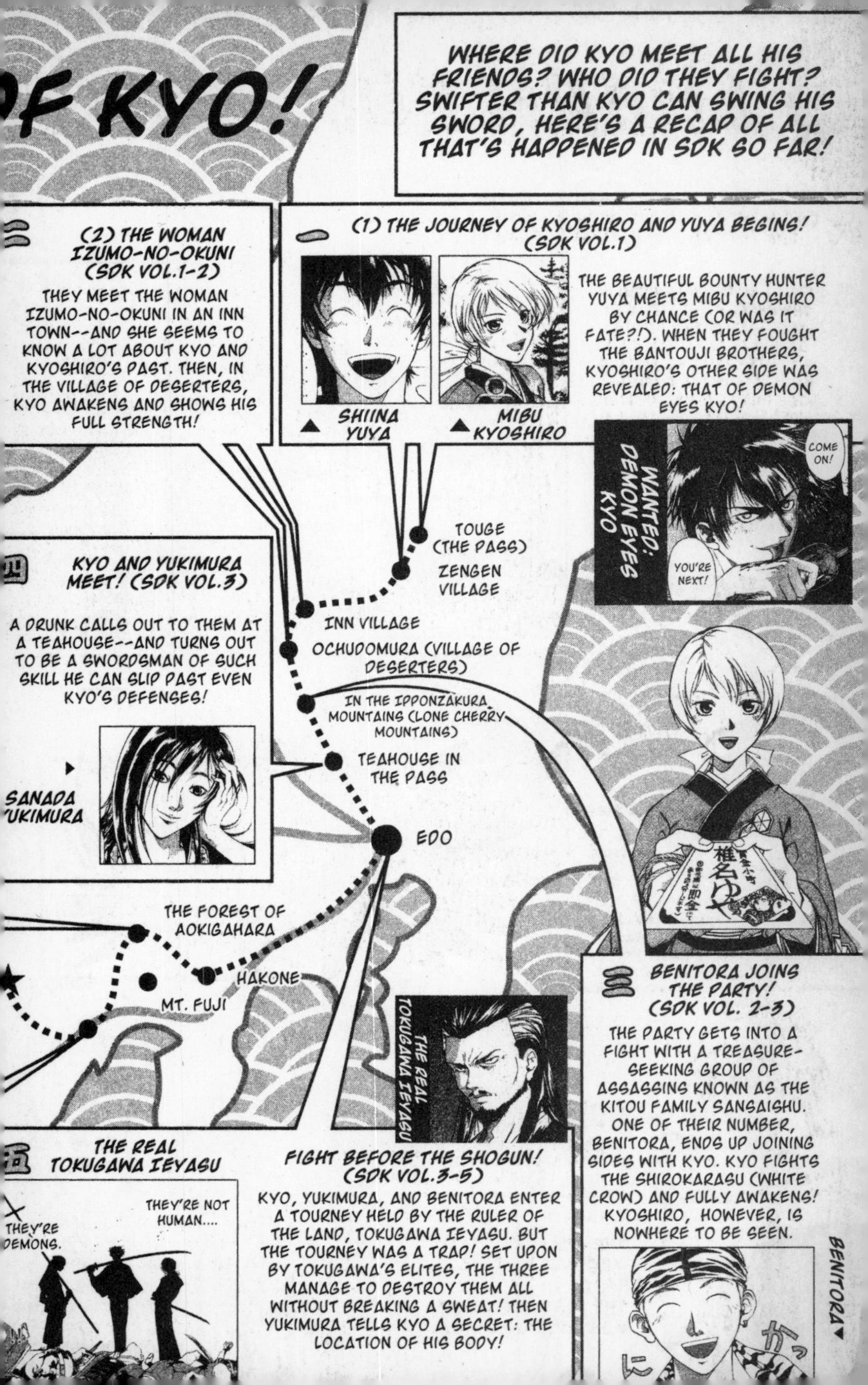

...OF KYO!
WHERE DID KYO MEET ALL HIS FRIENDS? WHO DID THEY FIGHT? SWIFTER THAN KYO CAN SWING HIS SWORD, HERE'S A RECAP OF ALL THAT'S HAPPENED IN SDK SO FAR!
(1) THE JOURNEY OF KYOSHIRO AND YUYA BEGINS! (SDK VOL.1)
THE BEAUTIFUL BOUNTY HUNTER YUYA MEETS MIBU KYOSHIRO BY CHANCE (OR WAS IT FATE?!). WHEN THEY FOUGHT THE BANTOUJI BROTHERS, KYOSHIRO'S OTHER SIDE WAS REVEALED: THAT OF DEMON EYES KYO!
▲ SHIINA YUYA
▲ MIBU KYOSHIRO
WANTED: DEMON EYES KYO
COME ON!
YOU'RE NEXT!
(2) THE WOMAN IZUMO-NO-OKUNI (SDK VOL.1-2)
THEY MEET THE WOMAN IZUMO-NO-OKUNI IN AN INN TOWN--AND SHE SEEMS TO KNOW A LOT ABOUT KYO AND KYOSHIRO'S PAST. THEN, IN THE VILLAGE OF DESERTERS, KYO AWAKENS AND SHOWS HIS FULL STRENGTH!
TOUGE (THE PASS)
ZENGEN VILLAGE
INN VILLAGE
OCHUDOMURA (VILLAGE OF DESERTERS)
IN THE IPPONZAKURA MOUNTAINS (LONE CHERRY MOUNTAINS)
TEAHOUSE IN THE PASS
EDO
THE FOREST OF AOKIGAHARA
HAKONE
MT. FUJI
BENITORA JOINS THE PARTY! (SDK VOL. 2-3)
THE PARTY GETS INTO A FIGHT WITH A TREASURE-SEEKING GROUP OF ASSASSINS KNOWN AS THE KITOU FAMILY SANSAISHU. ONE OF THEIR NUMBER, BENITORA, ENDS UP JOINING SIDES WITH KYO. KYO FIGHTS THE SHIROKARASU (WHITE CROW) AND FULLY AWAKENS! KYOSHIRO, HOWEVER, IS NOWHERE TO BE SEEN.
BENITORA▶
KYO AND YUKIMURA MEET! (SDK VOL.3)
A DRUNK CALLS OUT TO THEM AT A TEAHOUSE--AND TURNS OUT TO BE A SWORDSMAN OF SUCH SKILL HE CAN SLIP PAST EVEN KYO'S DEFENSES!
▶ SANADA YUKIMURA
THE REAL TOKUGAWA IEYASU
FIGHT BEFORE THE SHOGUN! (SDK VOL.3-5)
KYO, YUKIMURA, AND BENITORA ENTER A TOURNEY HELD BY THE RULER OF THE LAND, TOKUGAWA IEYASU. BUT THE TOURNEY WAS A TRAP! SET UPON BY TOKUGAWA'S ELITES, THE THREE MANAGE TO DESTROY THEM ALL WITHOUT BREAKING A SWEAT! THEN YUKIMURA TELLS KYO A SECRET: THE LOCATION OF HIS BODY!
THE REAL TOKUGAWA IEYASU
THEY'RE NOT HUMAN....
THEY'RE DEMONS.

IN JUST 3 MINUTES!

LEARN THE LEGEN

六 (6) MORTAL COMBAT VERSUS ODA NOBUNAGA AND THE TWELVE GOD SHOGUNS! (SDK VOL. 5-10)

KYO'S BODY LIES HIDDEN IN THE DEEPEST REACHES OF THE AOKIGAHARA FOREST AT THE FOOT OF MT. FUJI. BUT BETWEEN KYO AND HIS BODY STAND THE TWELVE--GUARDIANS OF THE MASTER, ODA NOBUNAGA. AFTER A STRING OF BLOODY BATTLES, KYO'S DEMONBLADE, MURAMASA, RELIEVES NOBUNAGA'S BODY OF ITS HEAD, BUT AKIRA MAKES HIS ESCAPE WITH KYO'S BODY!

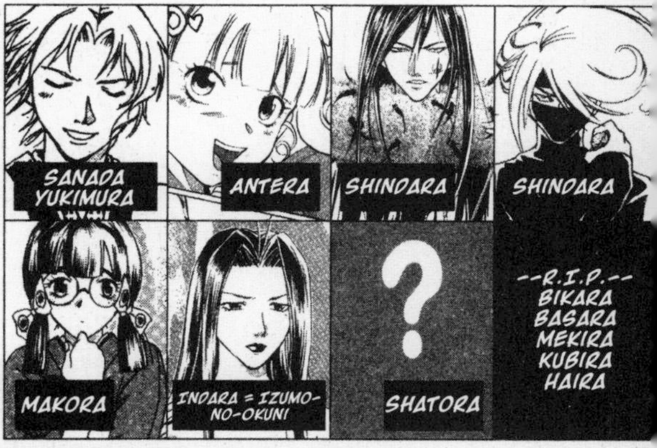
SANADA YUKIMURA
ANTERA
SHINDARA
SHINDARA
MAKORA
INDARA = IZUMO-NO-OKUNI
?
SHATORA
--R.I.P.--
BIKARA
BASARA
MEKIRA
KUBIRA
HAIRA

NOBUNAGA AWAITS THE TIME OF HIS RESURRECTION IN THE VILLAGE OF THE MIBU, DEEP WITHIN THE LAND OF THE FIRE LOTUS.

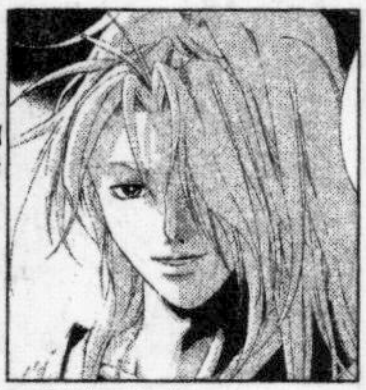

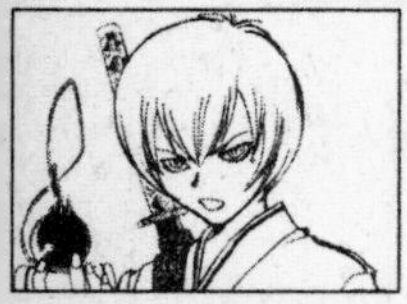

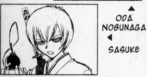

▲ ODA NOBUNAGA

◀ SASUKE

ONE OF THE SANADA TEN. HE RETURNED TO THE FOREST WHERE HE WAS BORN ON YUKIMURA'S ORDERS.

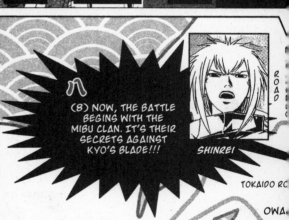

八 (8) NOW, THE BATTLE BEGING WITH THE MIBU CLAN. IT'S THEIR SECRETS AGAINST KYO'S BLADE!!!

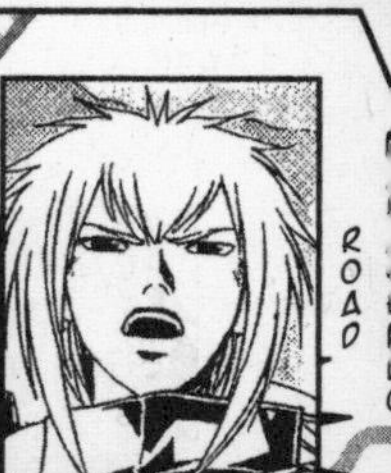

SHINREI

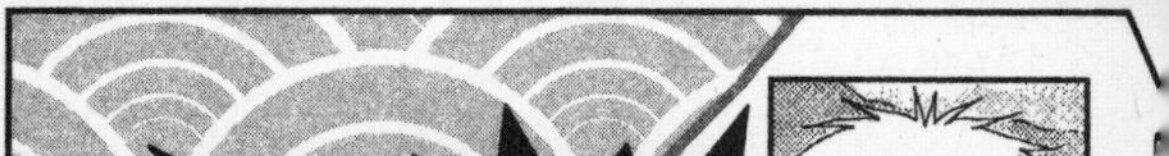
ROAD
TOKAIDO RO
OWA
KYOTO

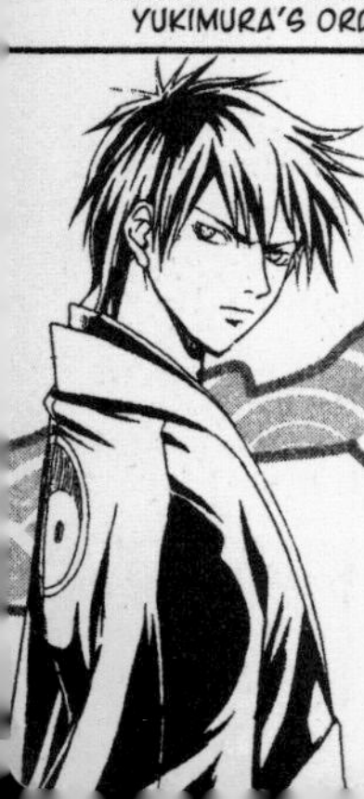

(7) ENTER BONTENMARU! (SDK VOL. 10)

THE ONE-EYED DATE MASAMUNE APPEARS BEFORE KYO AND LEADS THE PARTY TO KYO'S MASTER, MURAMASA.

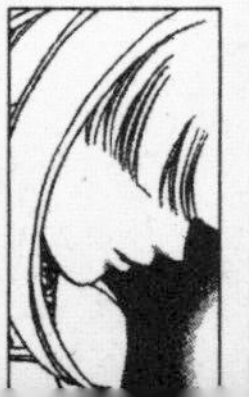

七 KYOTO: WHERE KYO'S BODY LIES!

AKIRA HAS GONE TO GROUND IN KYOTO, TAKING KYO'S BODY WITH HIM! BUT ANOTHER MAKES FOR KYOTO: KYO'S BELOVED SAKUYA HAS LEFT THE PROTECTION OF THE SANADAS!

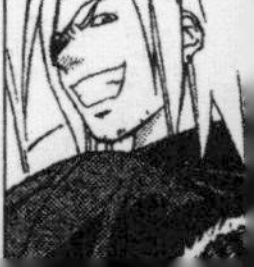

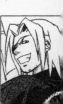

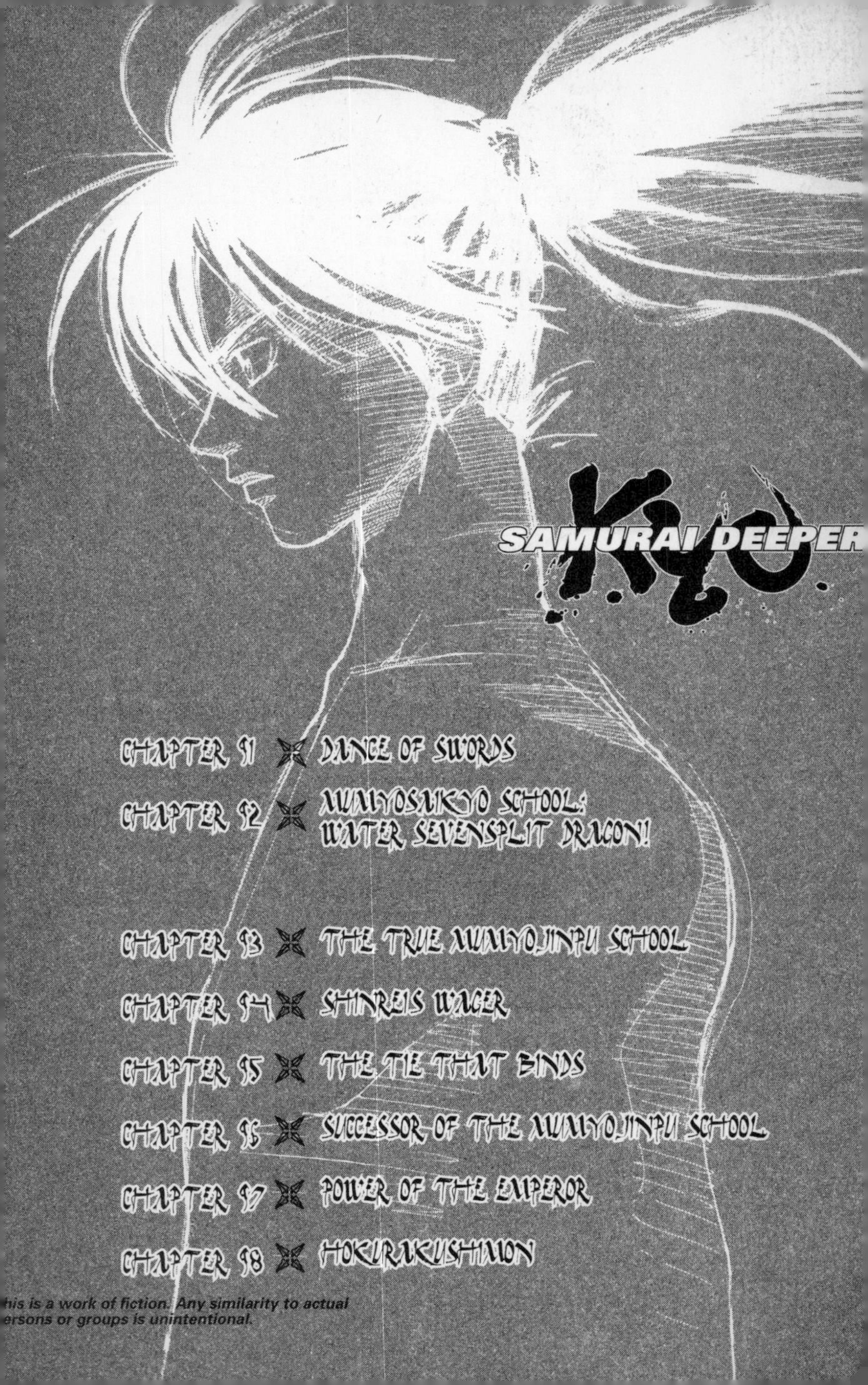

SAMURAI DEEPER KYO

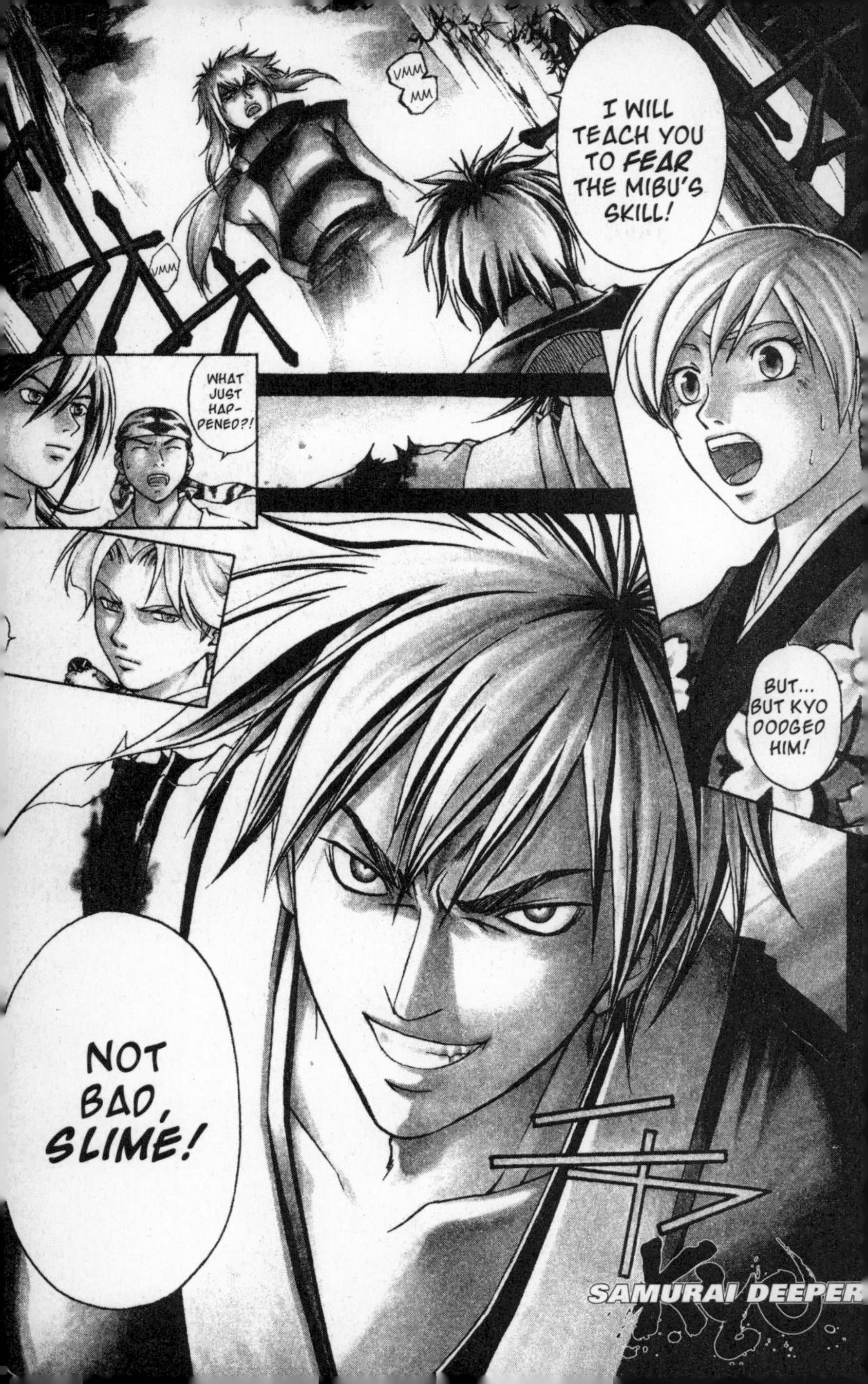
I WILL TEACH YOU TO FEAR THE MIBU'S SKILL!
VMM MM
VMM
BUT... BUT KYO DODGED HIM!
WHAT JUST HAP-PENED?!
NOT BAD, SLIME!
SAMURAI DEEPER
KYO

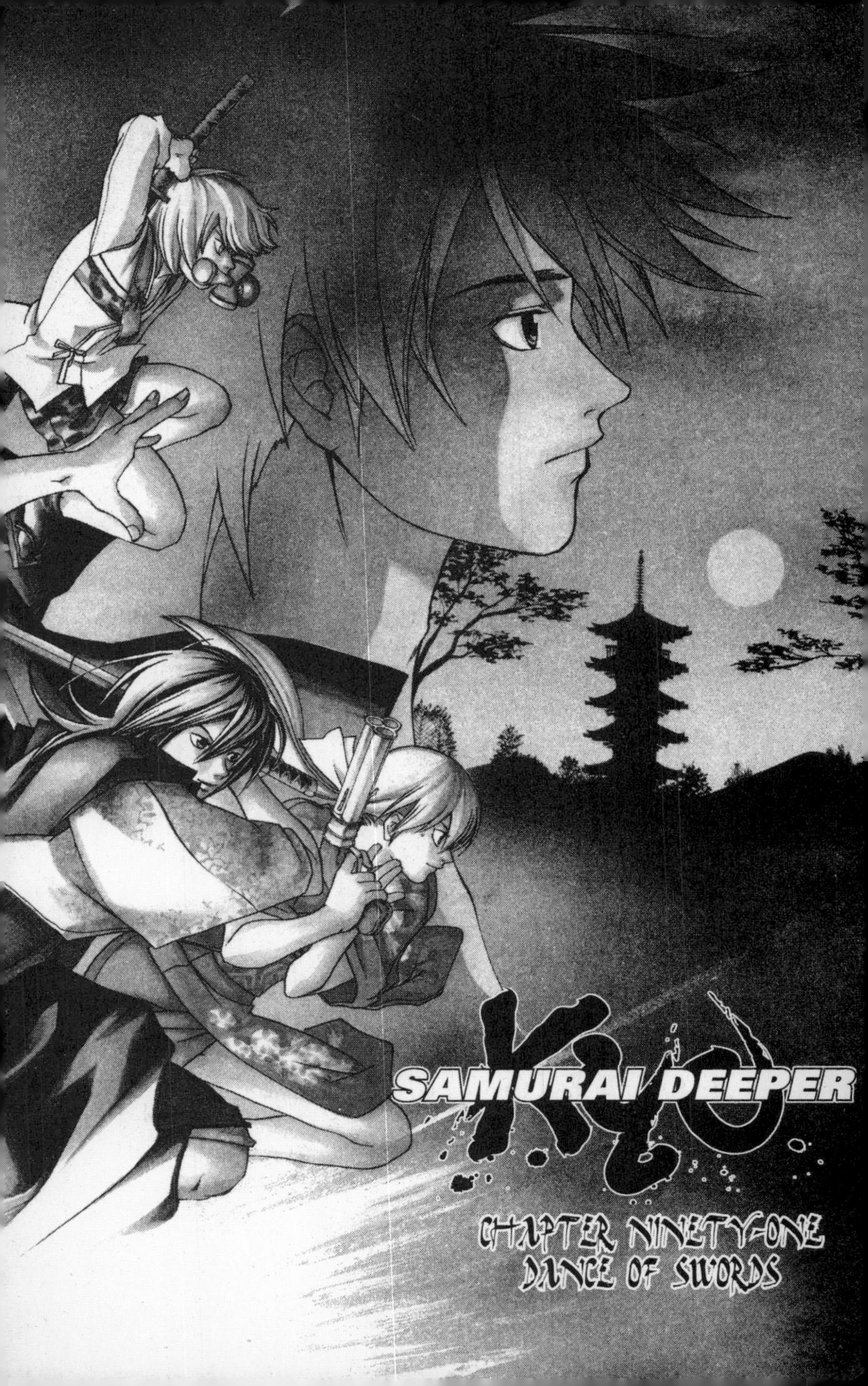
SAMURAI DEEPER KYO
CHAPTER NINETY-ONE
DANCE OF SWORDS

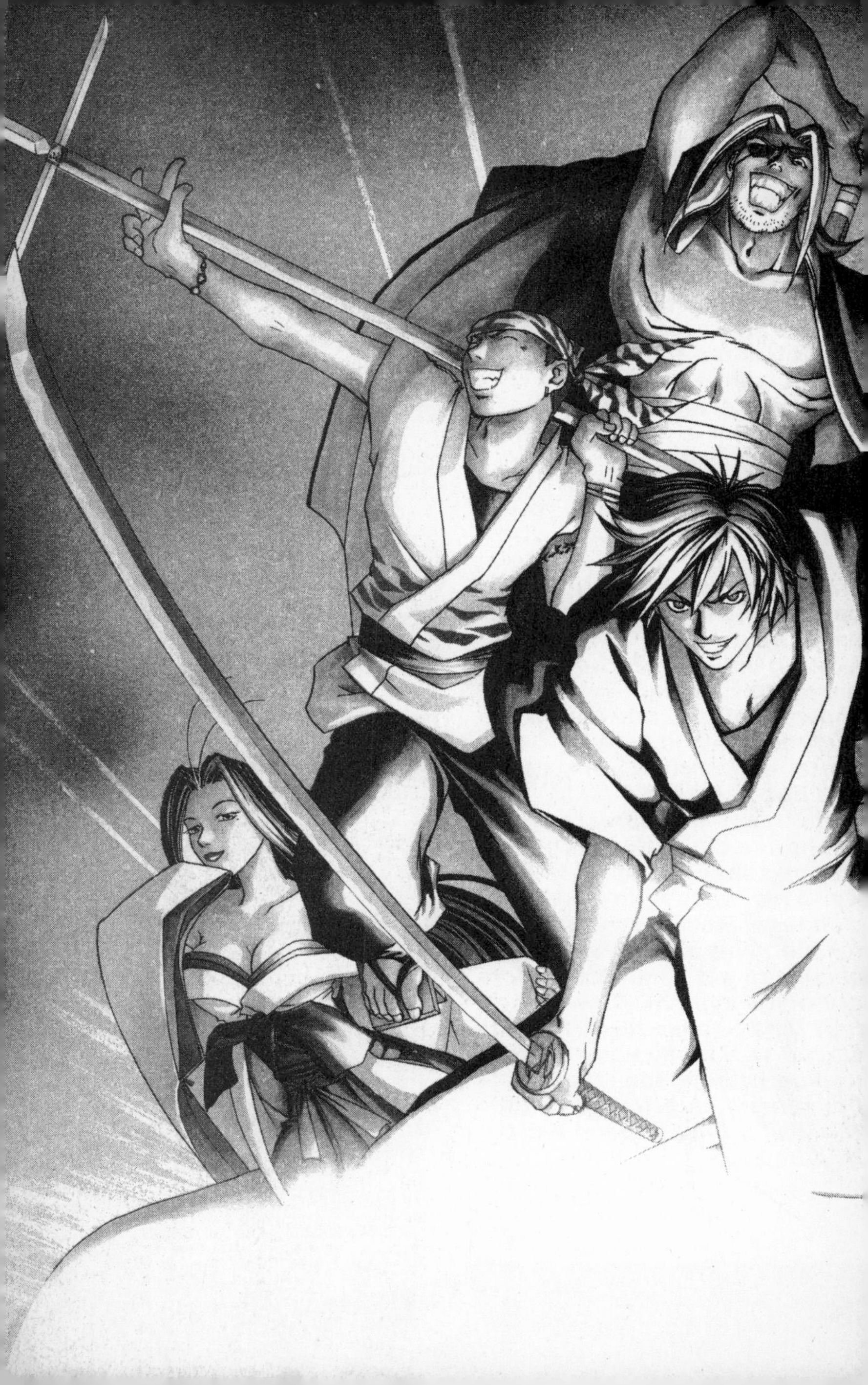

Yo! Kamijyo here! For a change, I'm using my PC to write this month. I never have the time to use my PC, nor much reason, so it just sits around...and I've got the addresses of everyone who's written to me on there... but it crashes a lot! Hope I don't lose everything!
We had a lot of room for bonus pages this issue, so we went all out! It was a real effort to put together, but seeing your letters gives me the strength I need! For one, I'm trying to answer all those questions that have been piling up. Hope you enjoy them!
Now, in volume 12, the story moves to Edo and Kyo doesn't show up much...not that he said much when he was the center of attention anyway! (lol) But to have a manga without a main character... That's like when Kyoshiro stopped showing up! Anyway, Kyo's real busy right now (for a change), so keep rooting for him. This also gives me a chance to get Sasuke and 'Tora out of my system. (This is the first time Sasuke really fights!) Of course, I really want to do Kyo again now, too...oh well, I'm sure when he comes back the wait will have been worth it! (I hope!)

MY INTERVIEW

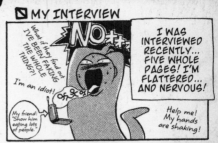

I WAS INTERVIEWED RECENTLY... FIVE WHOLE PAGES! I'M FLATTERED... AND NERVOUS!
NO
What if they find out I'VE BEEN FAKING THE WHOLE THING?!
Help me! My hands are shaking!
I'm an idiot!
My friend: "Show him eating lots of people."
When the going gets rough...
Heh heh
The tough LIE.
That was the plan ....
Of course, the interviewer was great at getting me to talk, so it was a lot of fun.
Mr. S
whirring
The tape recorder did make me a little nervous...
I said it all: the good, the bad.
I guess I was just me, Kamijyo.
Boring... Don't you have any faults at all?
Mr. H
Huh?
W- what'dya expect?!
So the real Kamijyo is, what, boring?!
...Secretly, I think he was relieved.

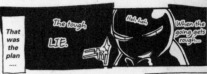

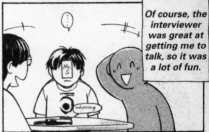

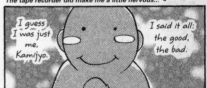

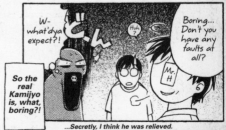

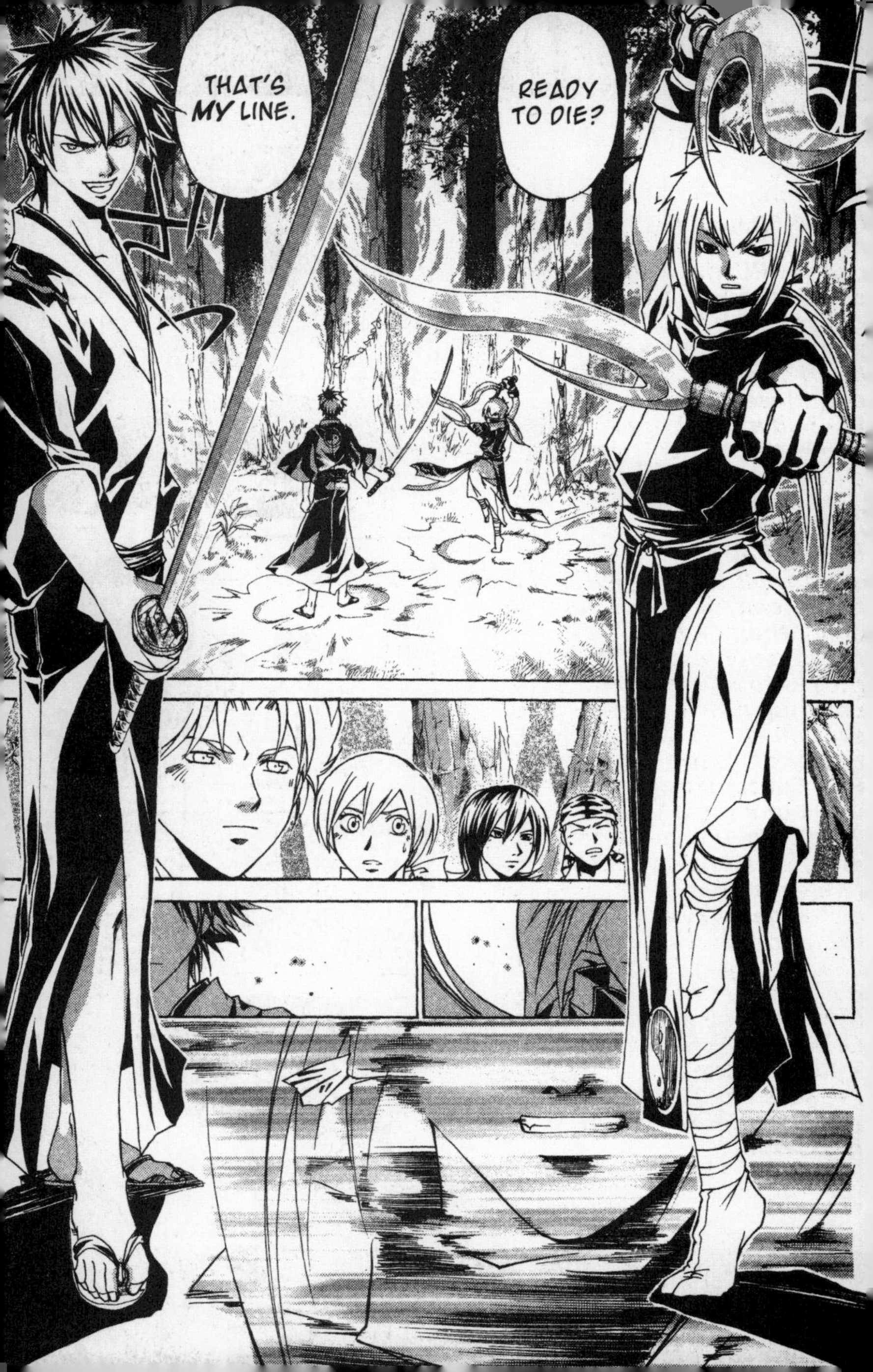
READY TO DIE?
THAT'S MY LINE.

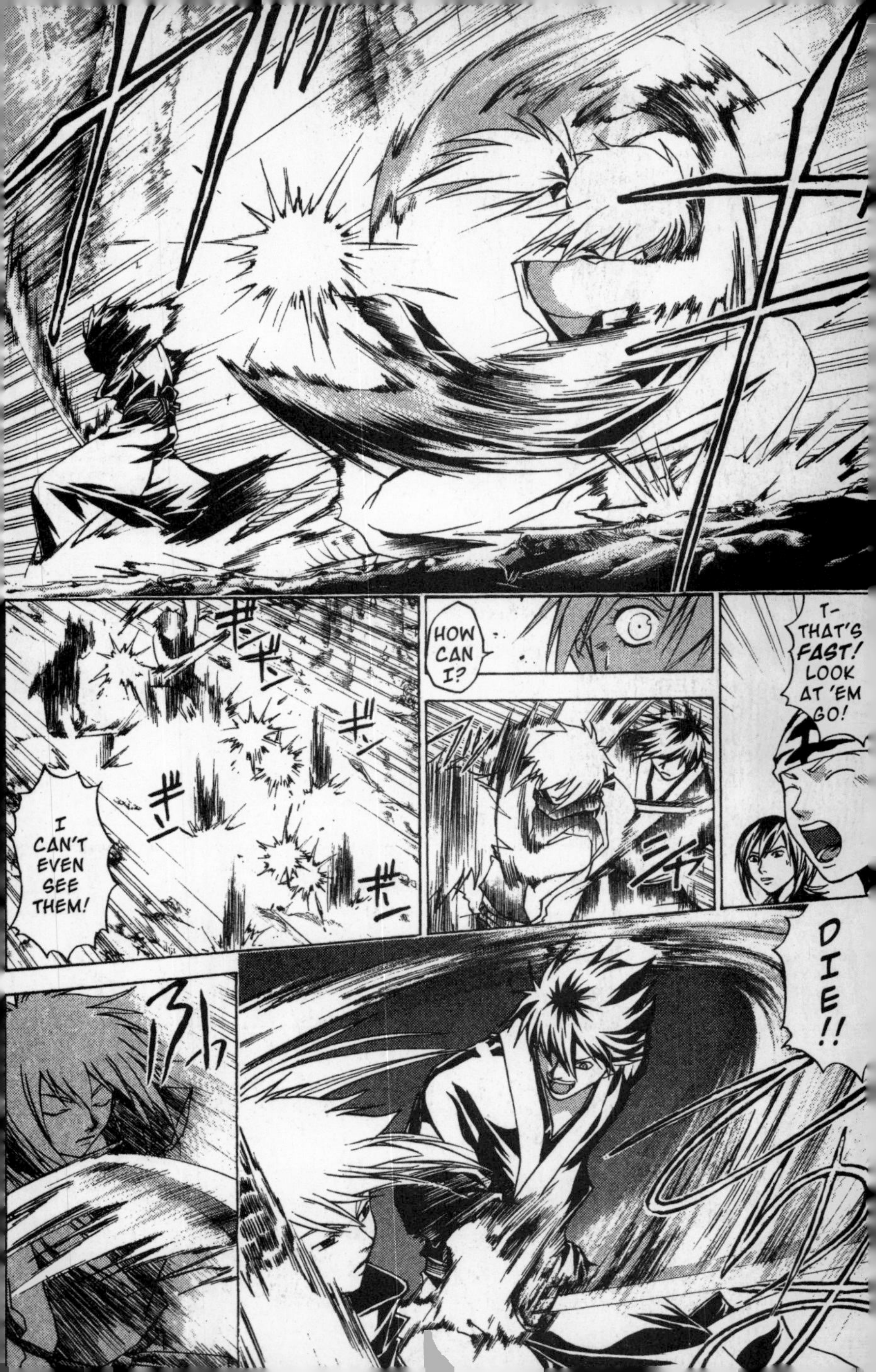
T-THAT'S FAST! LOOK AT 'EM GO!
HOW CAN I?
I CAN'T EVEN SEE THEM!
DIE!!

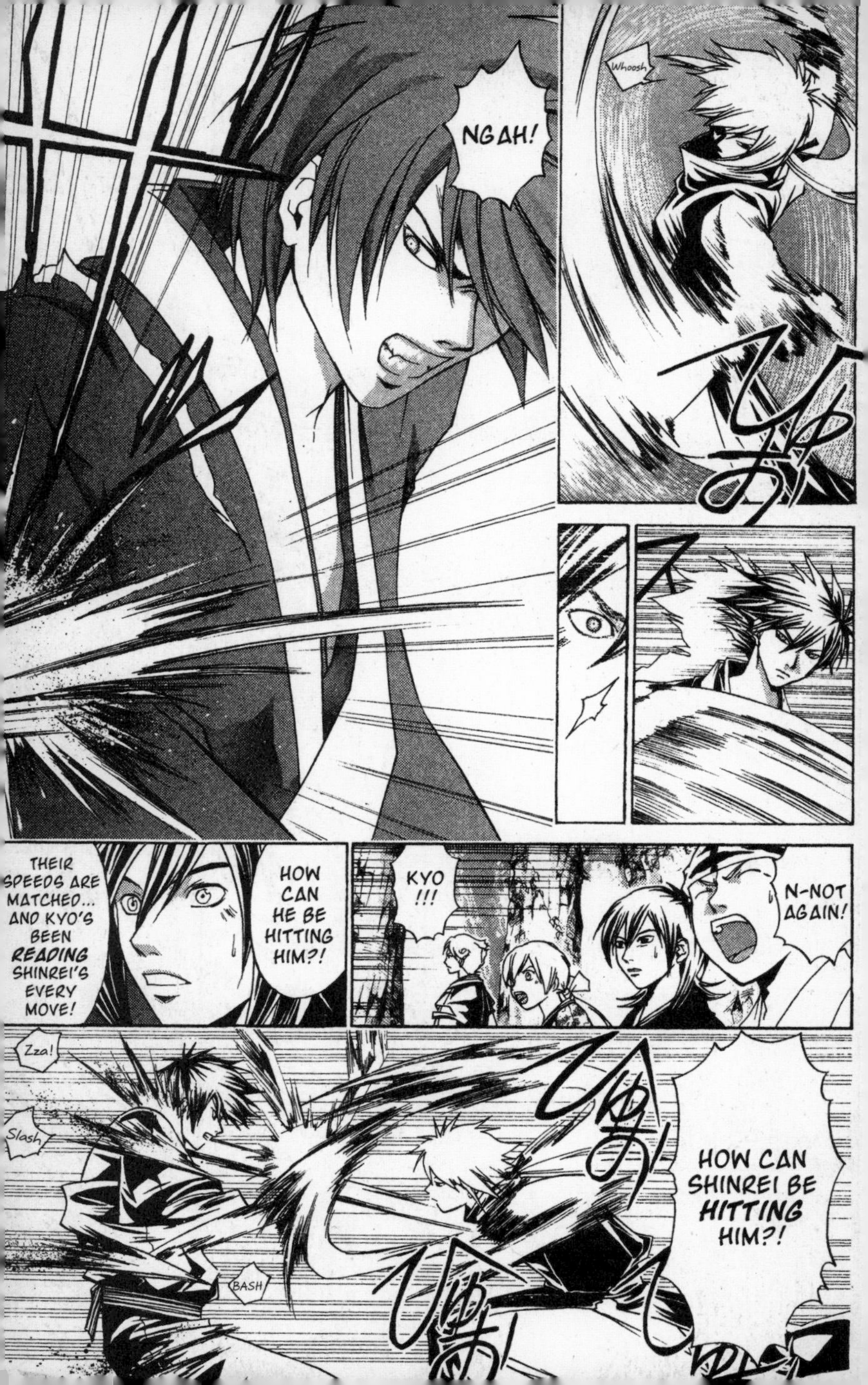
Whoosh
NGAH!
N-NOT AGAIN!
KYO!!!
HOW CAN HE BE HITTING HIM?!
THEIR SPEEDS ARE MATCHED... AND KYO'S BEEN **READING** SHINREI'S EVERY MOVE!
HOW CAN SHINREI BE **HITTING** HIM?!
Zza!
Slash
BASH

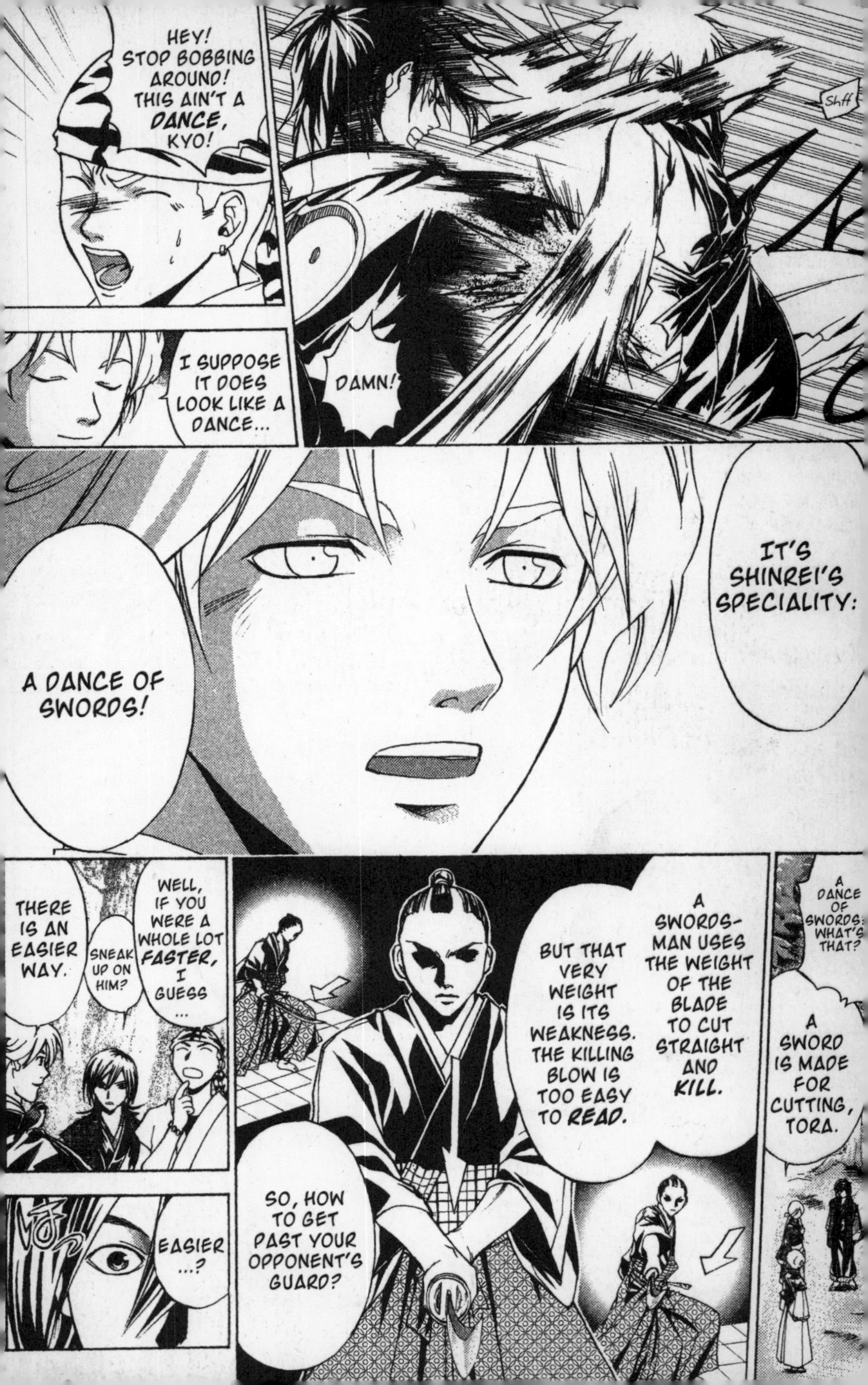
Shff
DAMN!
HEY! STOP BOBBING AROUND! THIS AIN'T A DANCE, KYO!
I SUPPOSE IT DOES LOOK LIKE A DANCE...
IT'S SHINREI'S SPECIALITY:
A DANCE OF SWORDS!
A DANCE OF SWORDS: WHAT'S THAT?
A SWORD IS MADE FOR CUTTING, TORA.
A SWORDSMAN USES THE WEIGHT OF THE BLADE TO CUT STRAIGHT AND KILL.
BUT THAT VERY WEIGHT IS ITS WEAKNESS. THE KILLING BLOW IS TOO EASY TO READ.
SO, HOW TO GET PAST YOUR OPPONENT'S GUARD?
WELL, IF YOU WERE A WHOLE LOT FASTER, I GUESS ...
SNEAK UP ON HIM?
THERE IS AN EASIER WAY.
EASIER ...?

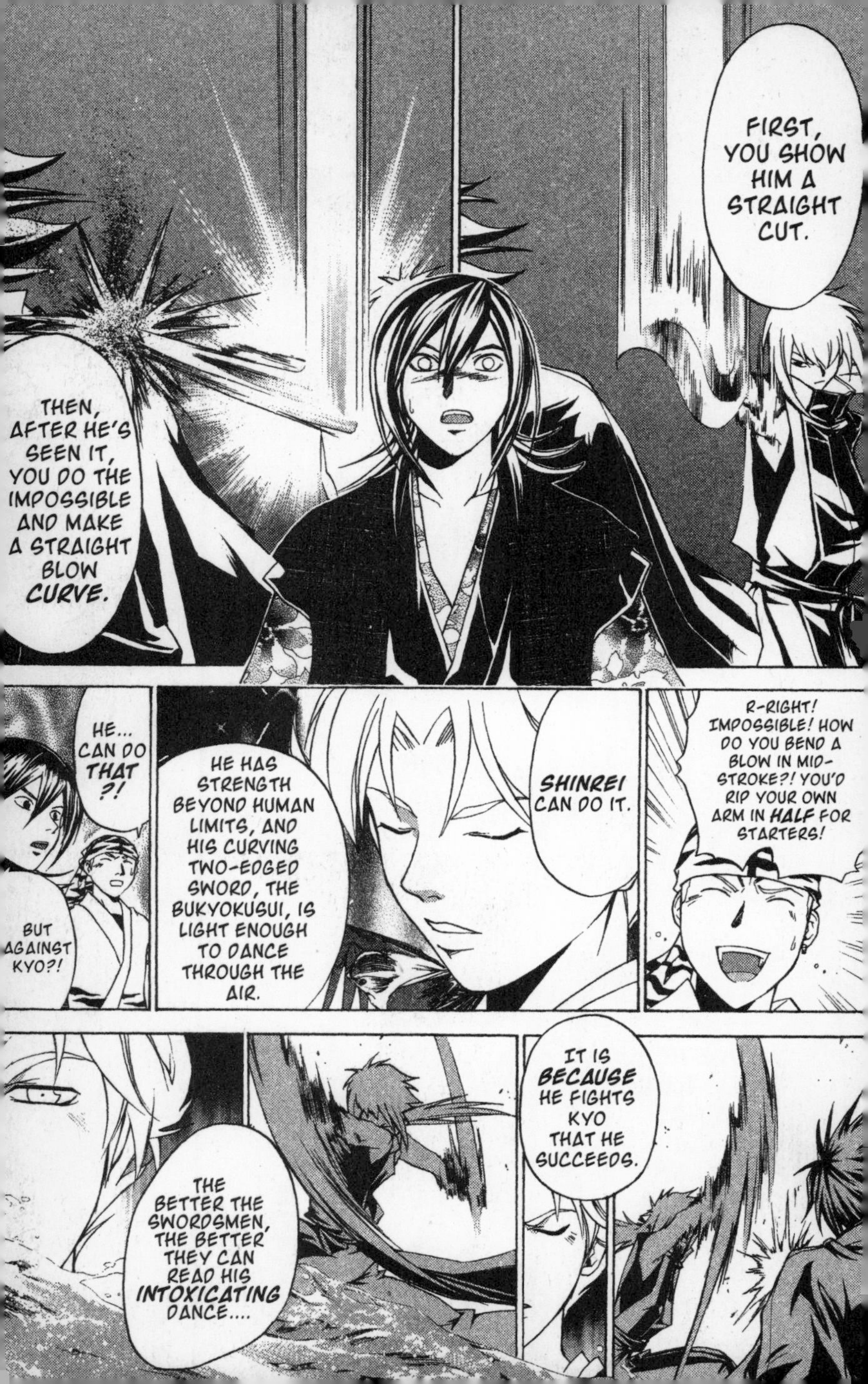
FIRST, YOU SHOW HIM A STRAIGHT CUT.
THEN, AFTER HE'S SEEN IT, YOU DO THE IMPOSSIBLE AND MAKE A STRAIGHT BLOW CURVE.
R-RIGHT! IMPOSSIBLE! HOW DO YOU BEND A BLOW IN MID-STROKE?! YOU'D RIP YOUR OWN ARM IN HALF FOR STARTERS!
SHINREI CAN DO IT.
HE HAS STRENGTH BEYOND HUMAN LIMITS, AND HIS CURVING TWO-EDGED SWORD, THE BUKYOKUSUI, IS LIGHT ENOUGH TO DANCE THROUGH THE AIR.
HE... CAN DO THAT?!
BUT AGAINST KYO?!
IT IS BECAUSE HE FIGHTS KYO THAT HE SUCCEEDS.
THE BETTER THE SWORDSMEN, THE BETTER THEY CAN READ HIS INTOXICATING DANCE....

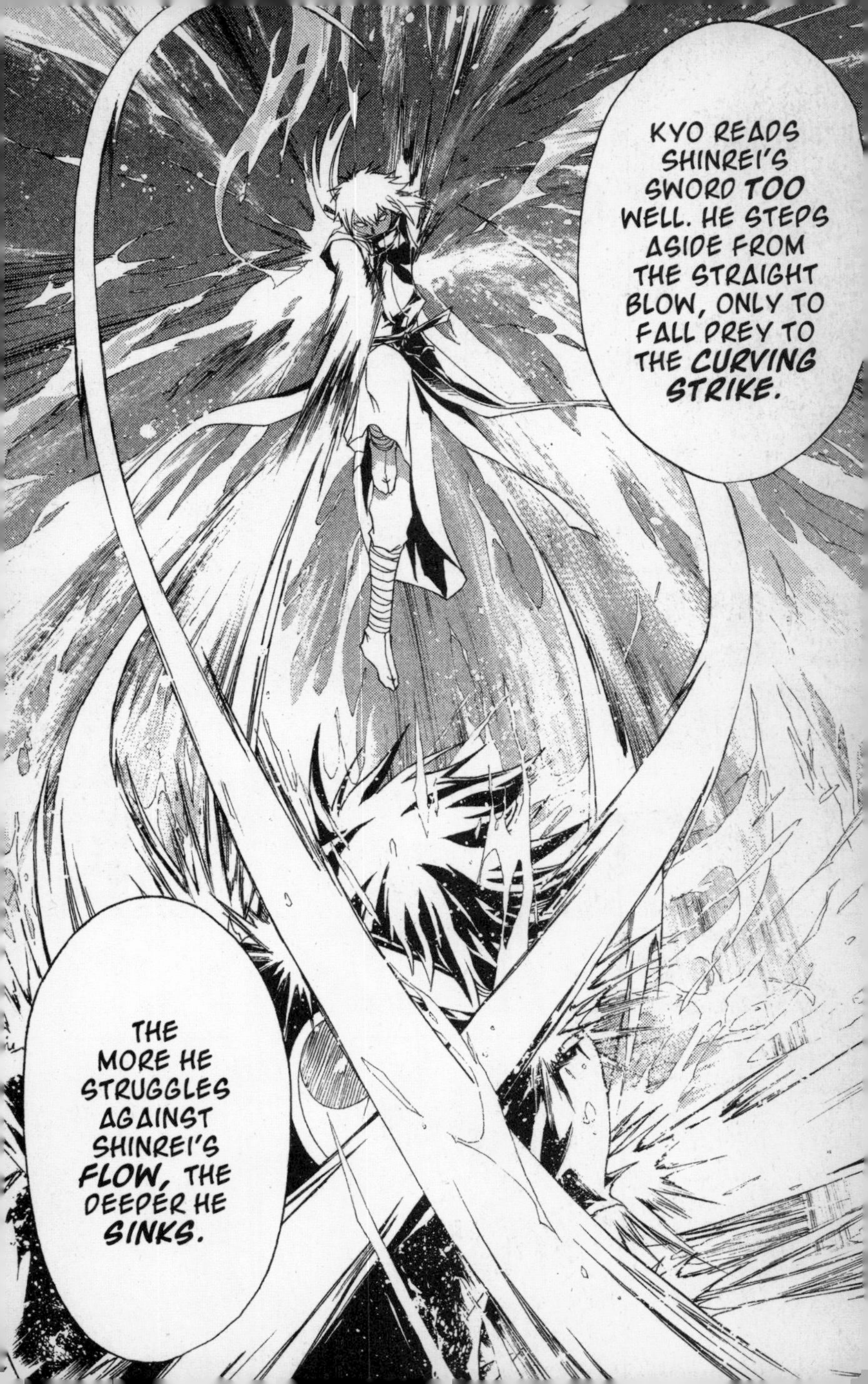
KYO READS SHINREI'S SWORD TOO WELL. HE STEPS ASIDE FROM THE STRAIGHT BLOW, ONLY TO FALL PREY TO THE CURVING STRIKE.
THE MORE HE STRUGGLES AGAINST SHINREI'S FLOW, THE DEEPER HE SINKS.

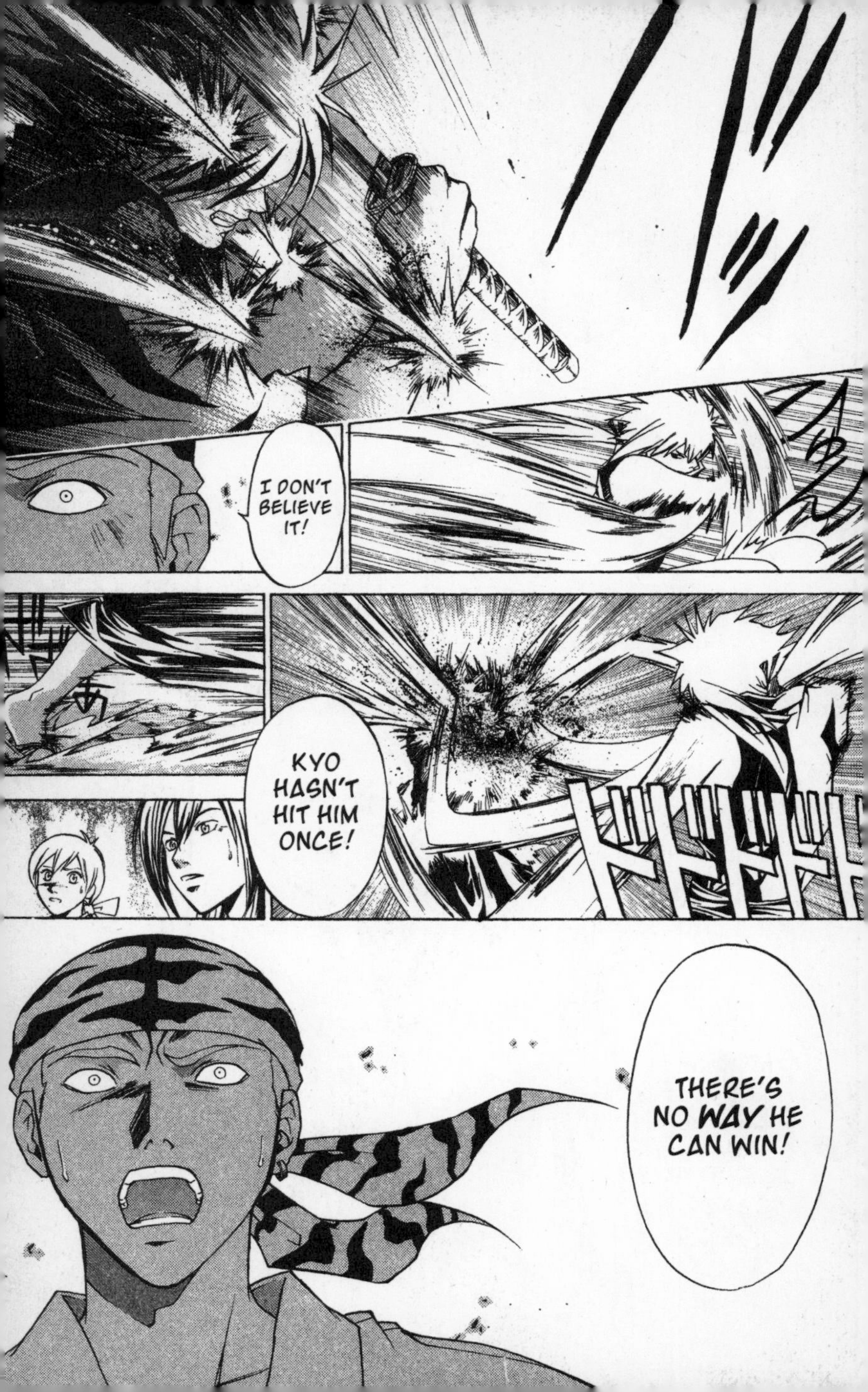

I DON'T BELIEVE IT!
KYO HASN'T HIT HIM ONCE!
THERE'S NO **WAY** HE CAN WIN!

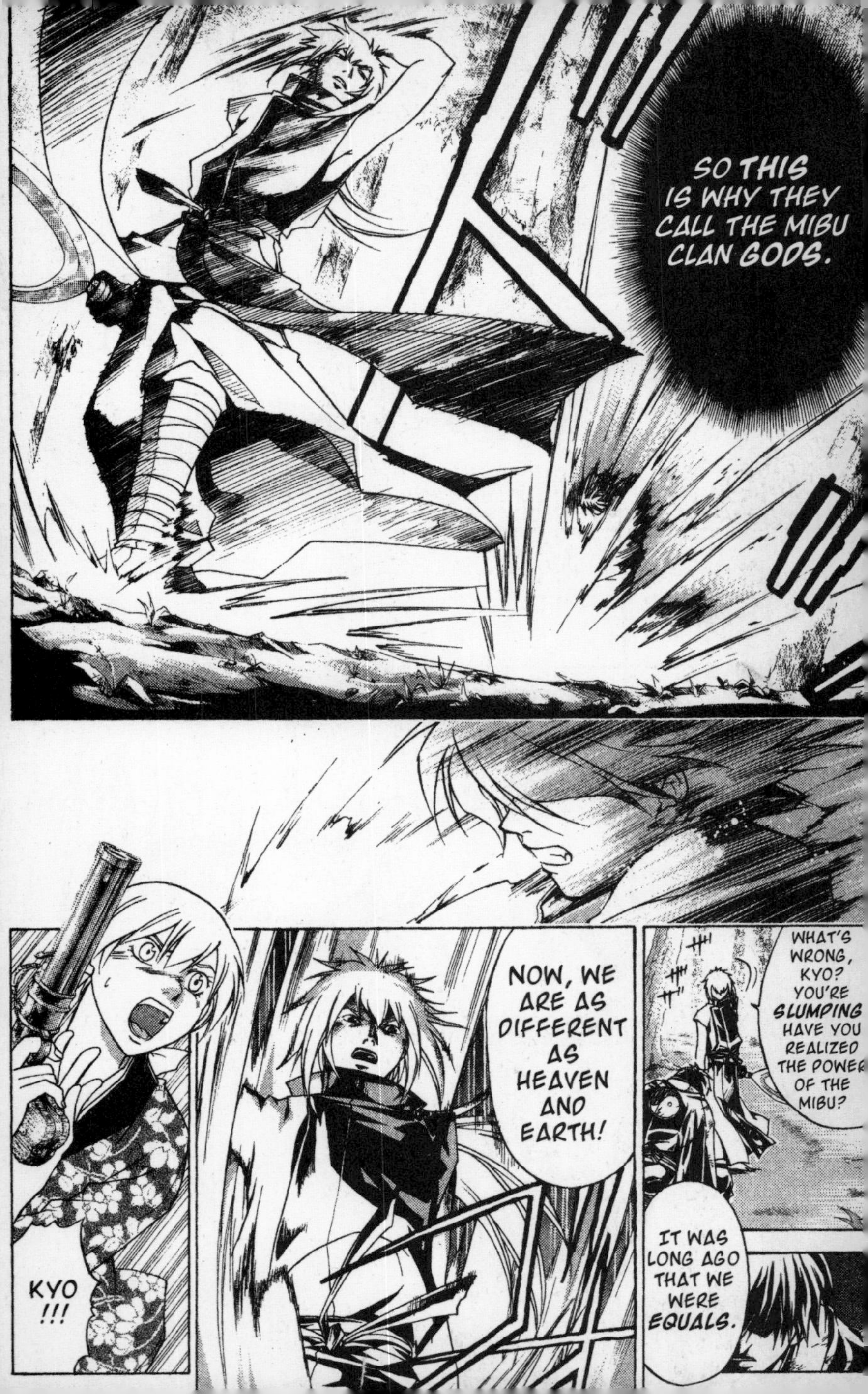
SO THIS IS WHY THEY CALL THE MIBU CLAN GODS.
WHAT'S WRONG, KYO? YOU'RE SLUMPING HAVE YOU REALIZED THE POWER OF THE MIBU?
IT WAS LONG AGO THAT WE WERE EQUALS.
NOW, WE ARE AS DIFFERENT AS HEAVEN AND EARTH!
KYO !!!

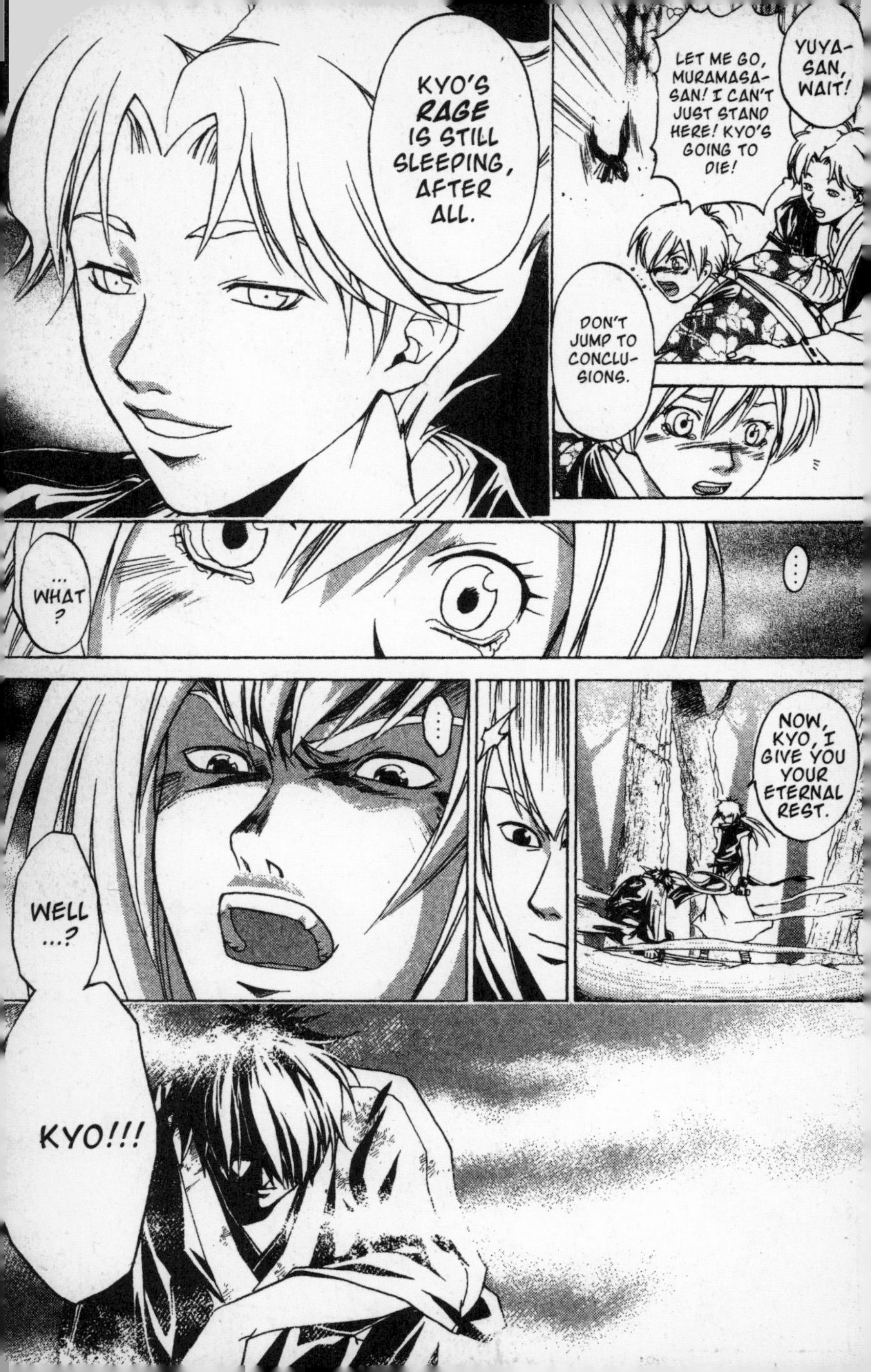
YUYA-SAN, WAIT!
LET ME GO, MURAMASA-SAN! I CAN'T JUST STAND HERE! KYO'S GOING TO DIE!
DON'T JUMP TO CONCLUSIONS.
KYO'S RAGE IS STILL SLEEPING, AFTER ALL.
...
... WHAT ?
NOW, KYO, I GIVE YOU YOUR ETERNAL REST.
....
WELL ...?
KYO!!!

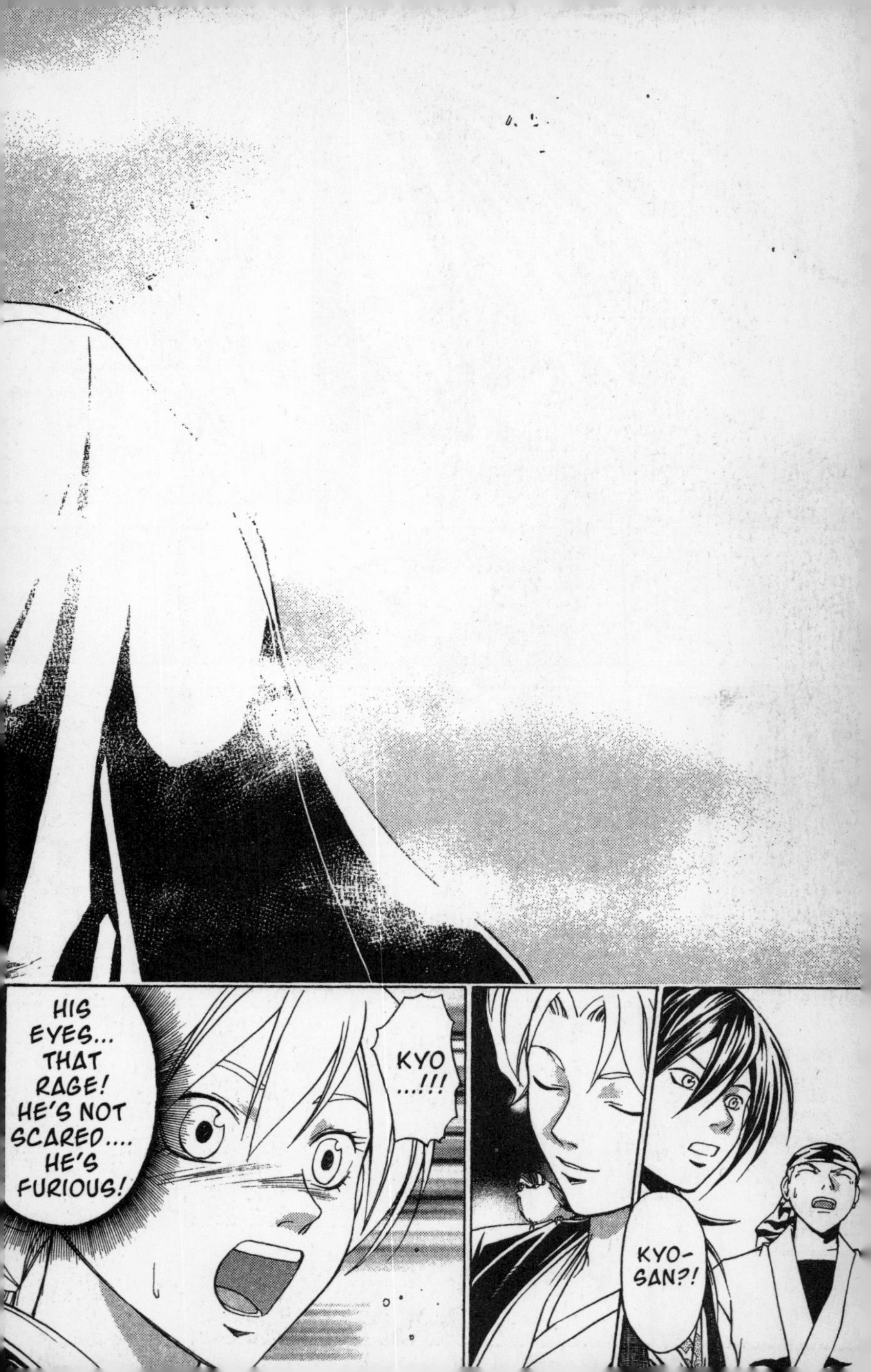
KYO-SAN?!
KYO ...!!!
HIS EYES... THAT RAGE! HE'S NOT SCARED.... HE'S FURIOUS!

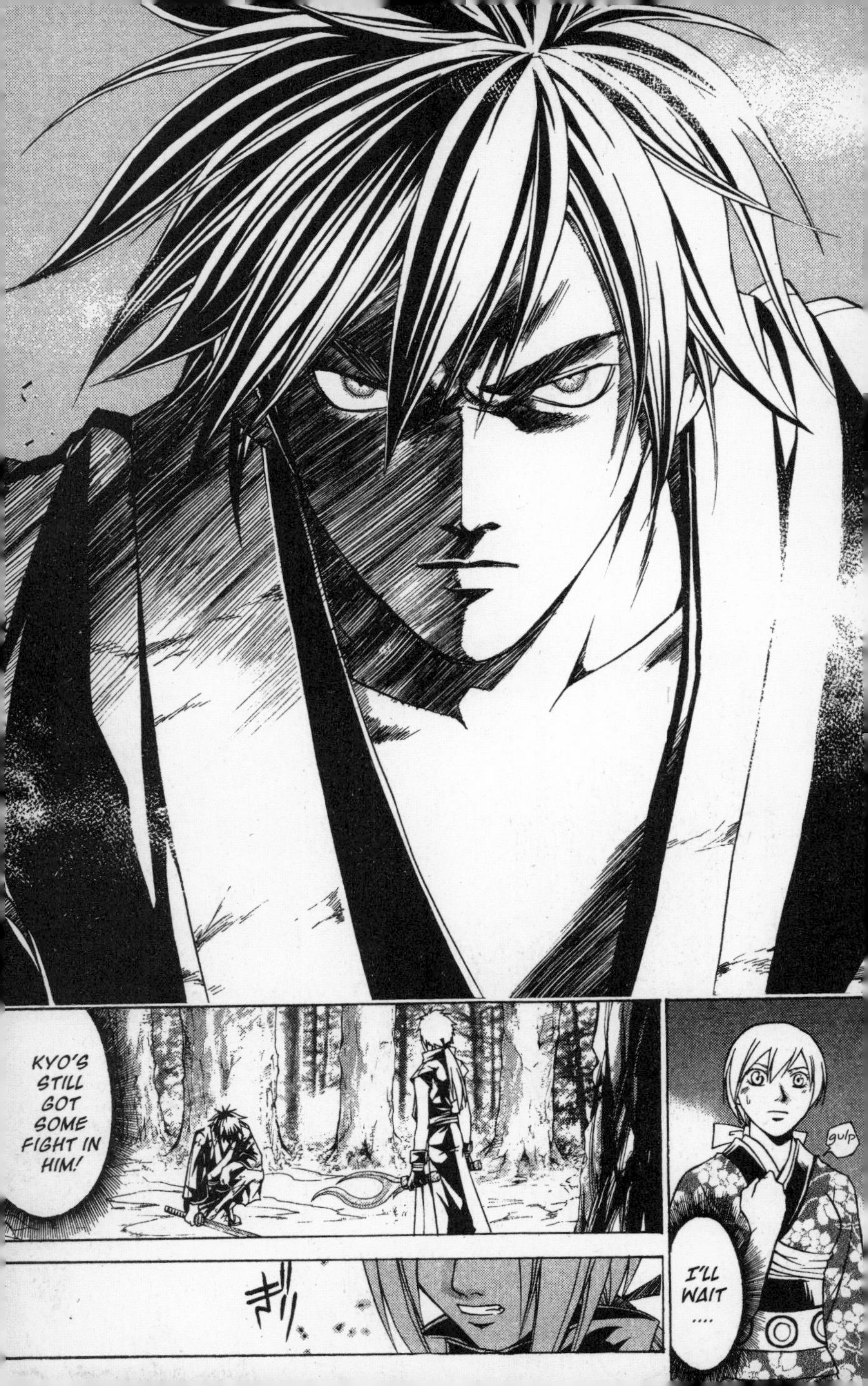
gulp
I'LL WAIT ....
KYO'S STILL GOT SOME FIGHT IN HIM!
ギリ

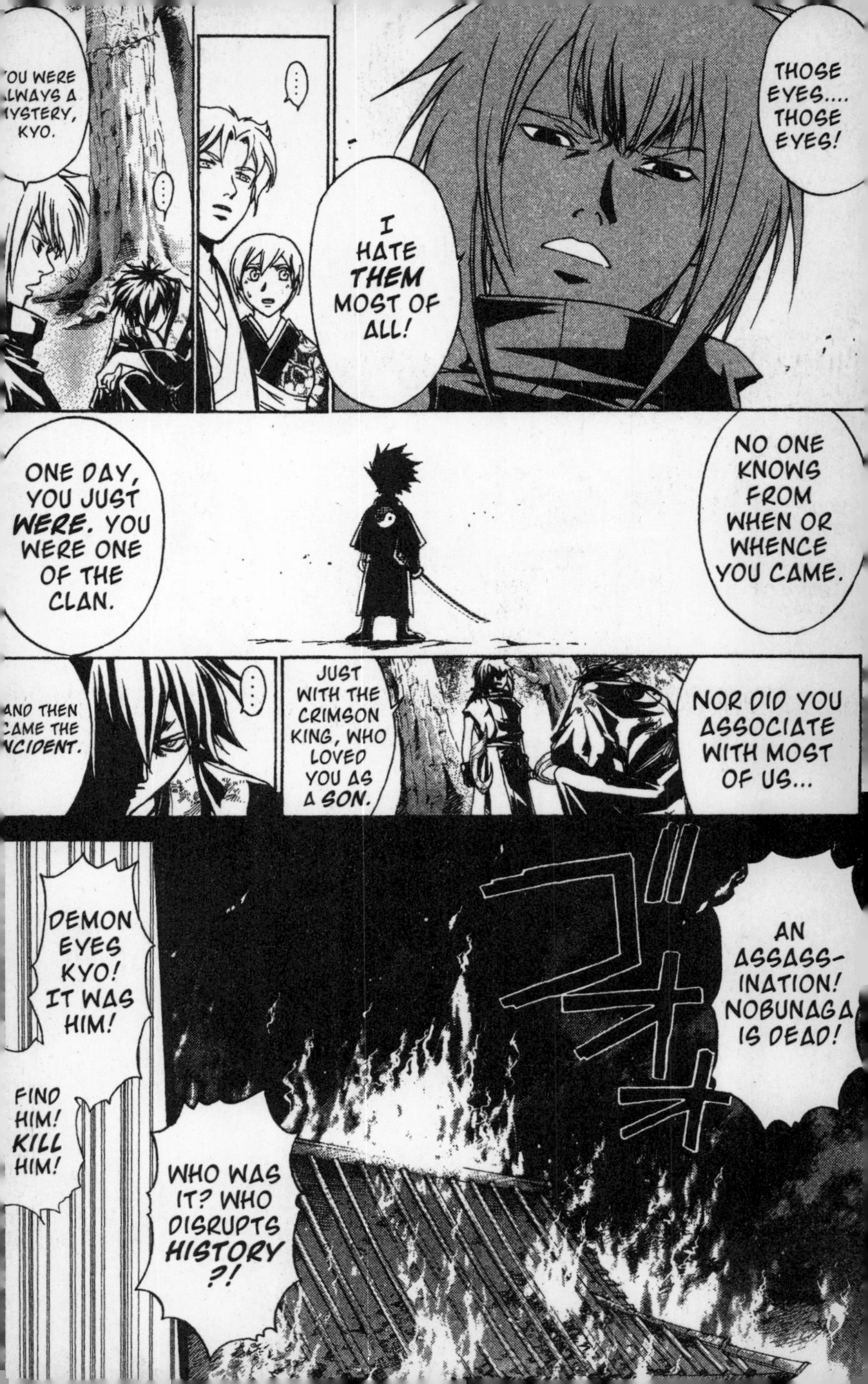
THOSE EYES.... THOSE EYES!
I HATE THEM MOST OF ALL!
...
...
OU WERE LWAYS A YSTERY, KYO.
NO ONE KNOWS FROM WHEN OR WHENCE YOU CAME.
ONE DAY, YOU JUST WERE. YOU WERE ONE OF THE CLAN.
NOR DID YOU ASSOCIATE WITH MOST OF US...
JUST WITH THE CRIMSON KING, WHO LOVED YOU AS A SON.
...
AND THEN AME THE NCIDENT.
AN ASSASS-INATION! NOBUNAGA IS DEAD!
DEMON EYES KYO! IT WAS HIM!
WHO WAS IT? WHO DISRUPTS HISTORY?!
FIND HIM! KILL HIM!

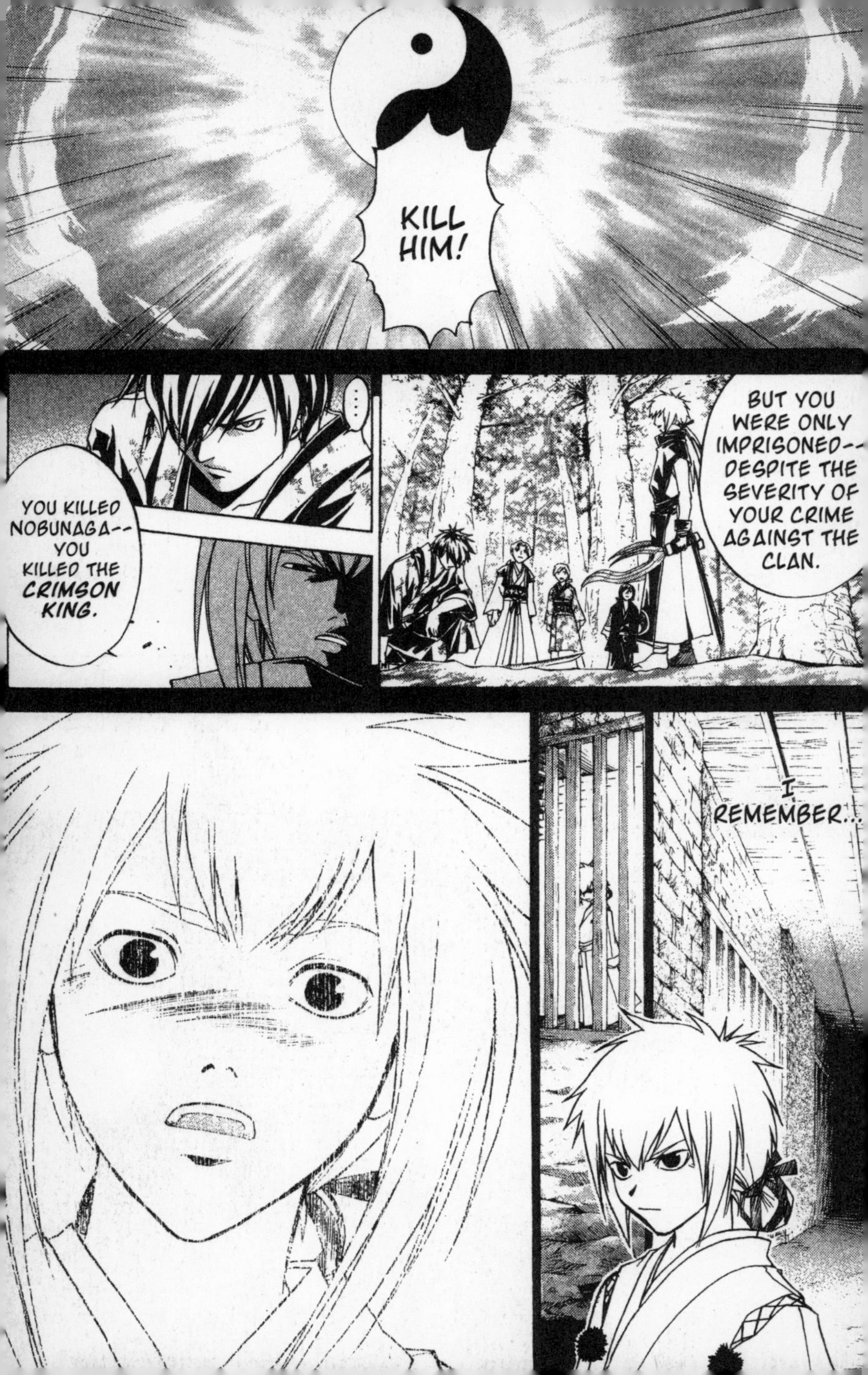
KILL HIM!
BUT YOU WERE ONLY IMPRISONED--DESPITE THE SEVERITY OF YOUR CRIME AGAINST THE CLAN.
...
YOU KILLED NOBUNAGA--YOU KILLED THE **CRIMSON KING**.
I REMEMBER...

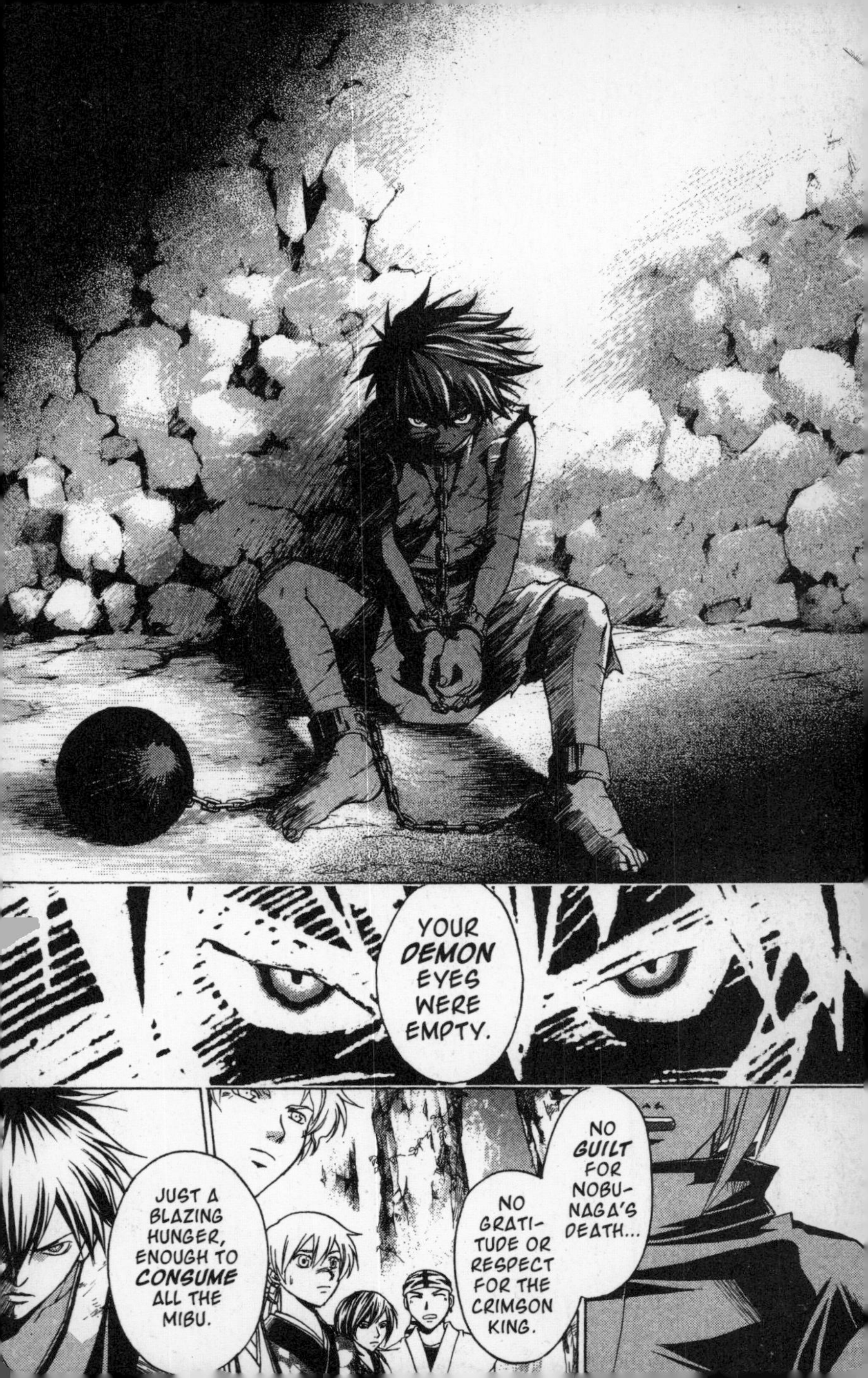
YOUR DEMON EYES WERE EMPTY.
NO GUILT FOR NOBU-NAGA'S DEATH...
NO GRATI-TUDE OR RESPECT FOR THE CRIMSON KING.
JUST A BLAZING HUNGER, ENOUGH TO CONSUME ALL THE MIBU.

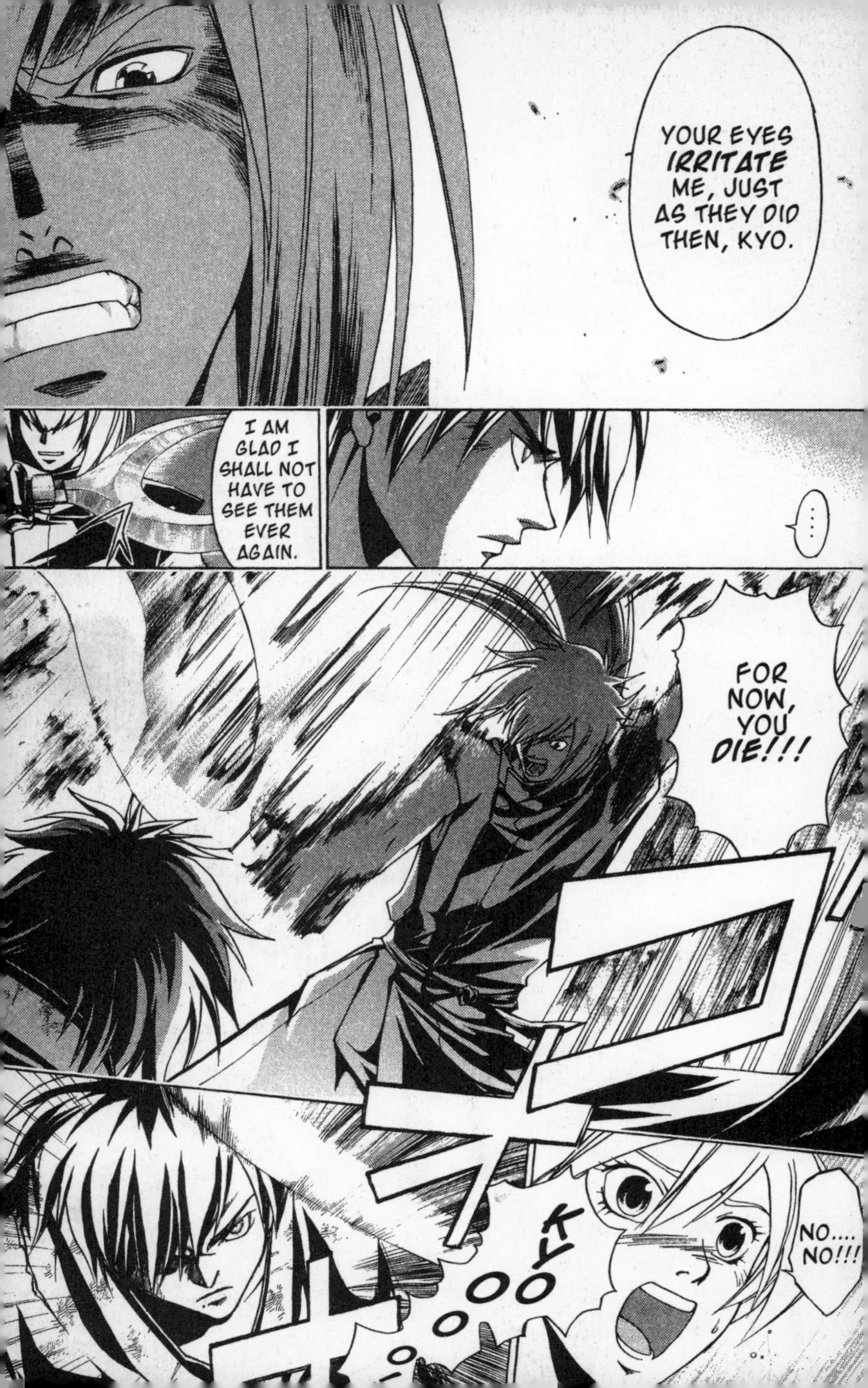
YOUR EYES IRRITATE ME, JUST AS THEY DID THEN, KYO.
....
I AM GLAD I SHALL NOT HAVE TO SEE THEM EVER AGAIN.
FOR NOW, YOU DIE!!!
NO.... NO!!!
KYOOOOO

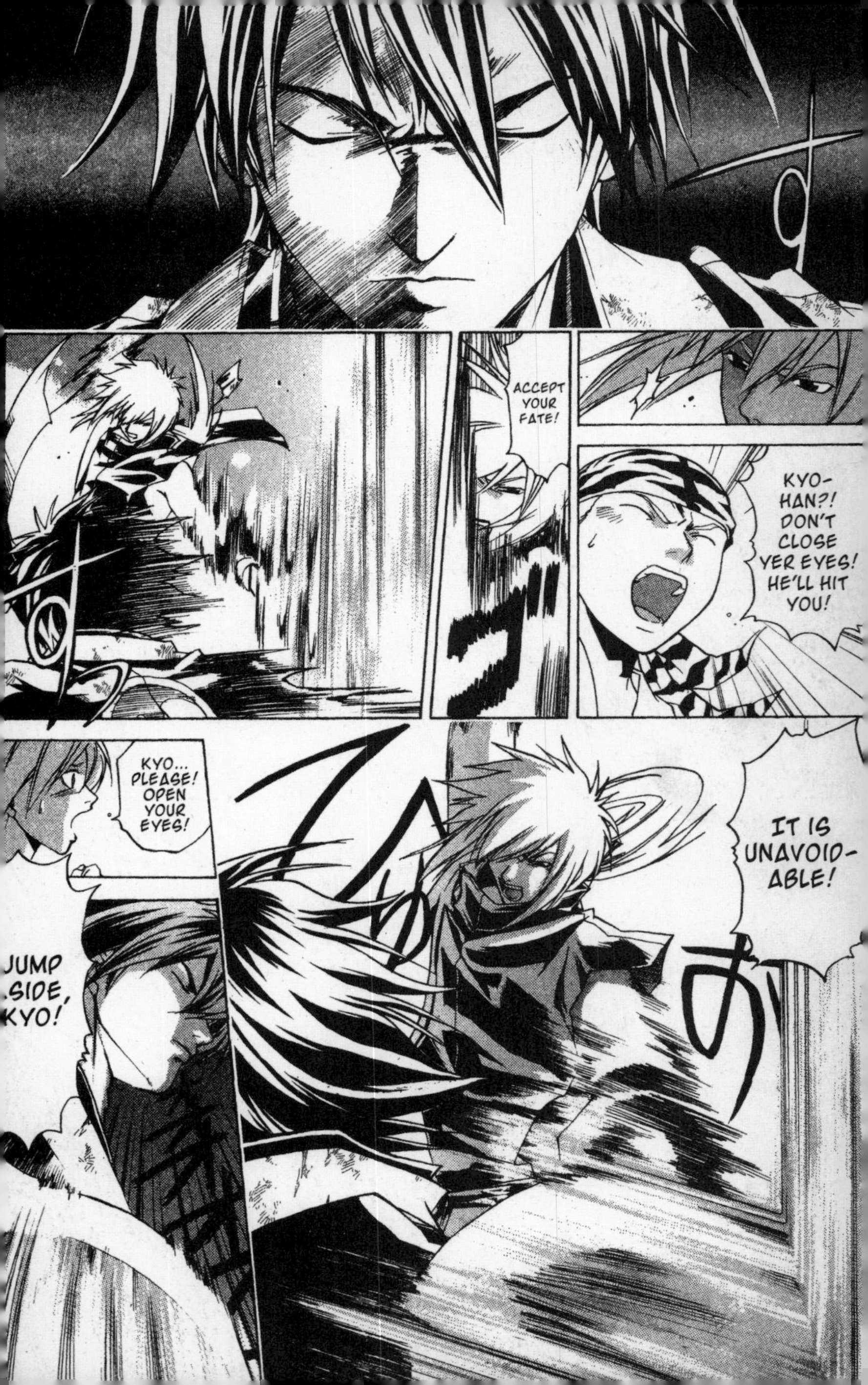
KYO-HAN?! DON'T CLOSE YER EYES! HE'LL HIT YOU!
ACCEPT YOUR FATE!
IT IS UNAVOIDABLE!
KYO... PLEASE! OPEN YOUR EYES!
JUMP
SIDE, KYO!

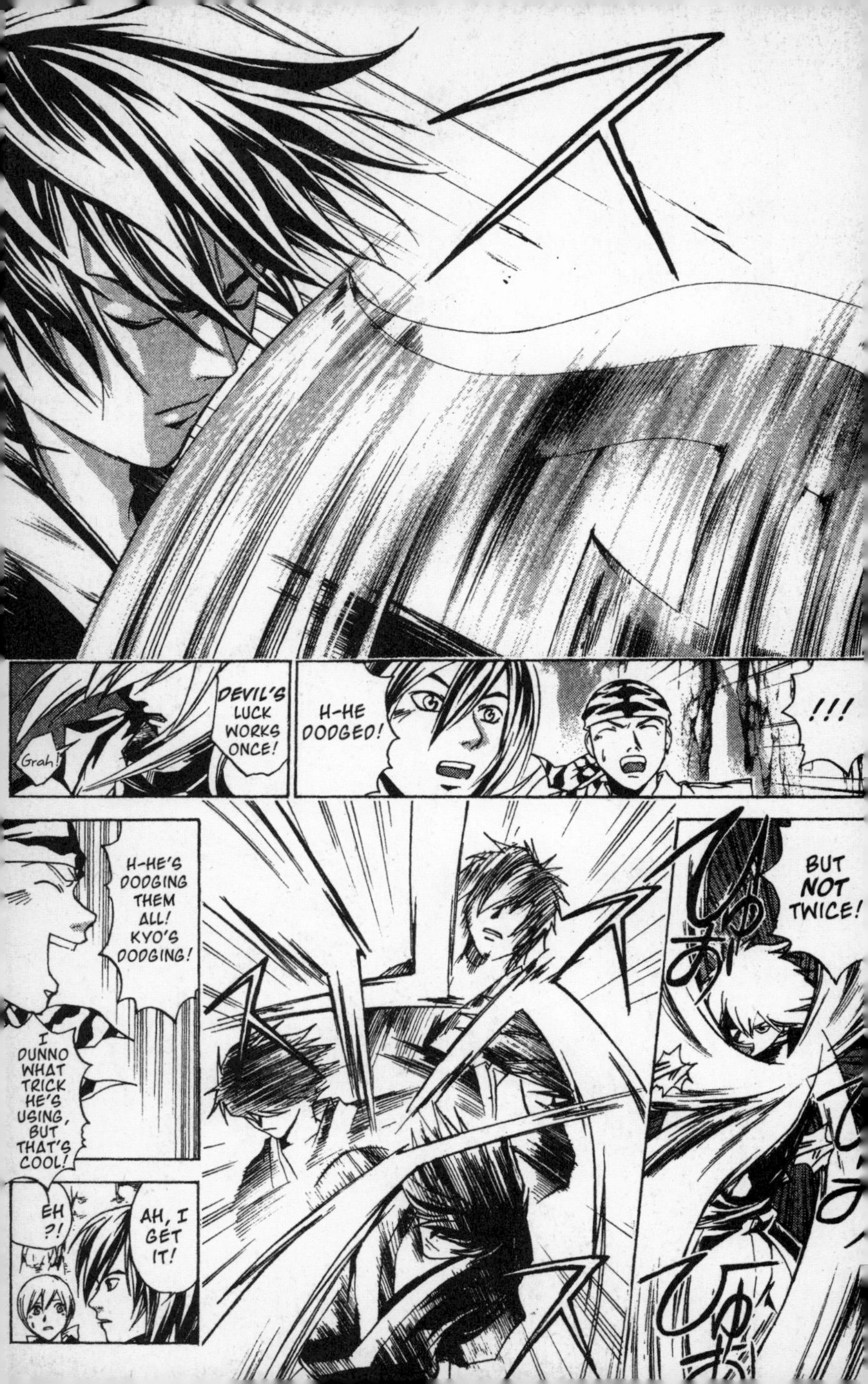
!!!
H-HE DODGED!
DEVIL'S LUCK WORKS ONCE!
Grah!
BUT NOT TWICE!
H-HE'S DODGING THEM ALL! KYO'S DODGING!
I DUNNO WHAT TRICK HE'S USING, BUT THAT'S COOL!
AH, I GET IT!
EH?!

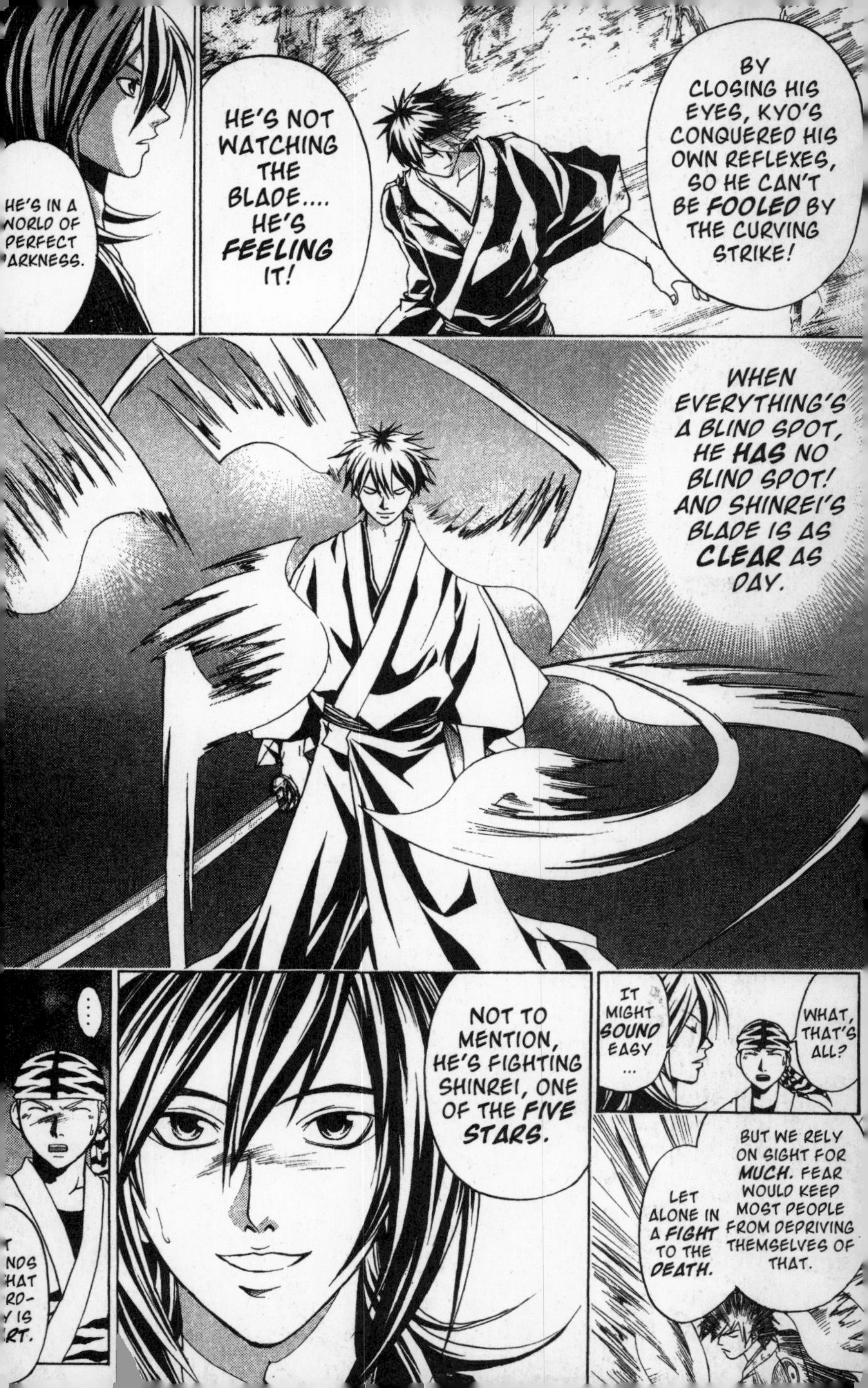
BY CLOSING HIS EYES, KYO'S CONQUERED HIS OWN REFLEXES, SO HE CAN'T BE **FOOLED** BY THE CURVING STRIKE!
HE'S NOT WATCHING THE BLADE.... HE'S **FEELING** IT!
HE'S IN A WORLD OF PERFECT ARKNESS.
WHEN EVERYTHING'S A BLIND SPOT, HE **HAS** NO BLIND SPOT! AND SHINREI'S BLADE IS AS **CLEAR** AS DAY.
WHAT, THAT'S ALL?
IT MIGHT **SOUND** EASY ...
BUT WE RELY ON SIGHT FOR **MUCH**. FEAR WOULD KEEP MOST PEOPLE FROM DEPRIVING THEMSELVES OF THAT.
LET ALONE IN A **FIGHT** TO THE **DEATH**.
NOT TO MENTION, HE'S FIGHTING SHINREI, ONE OF THE **FIVE STARS**.
...

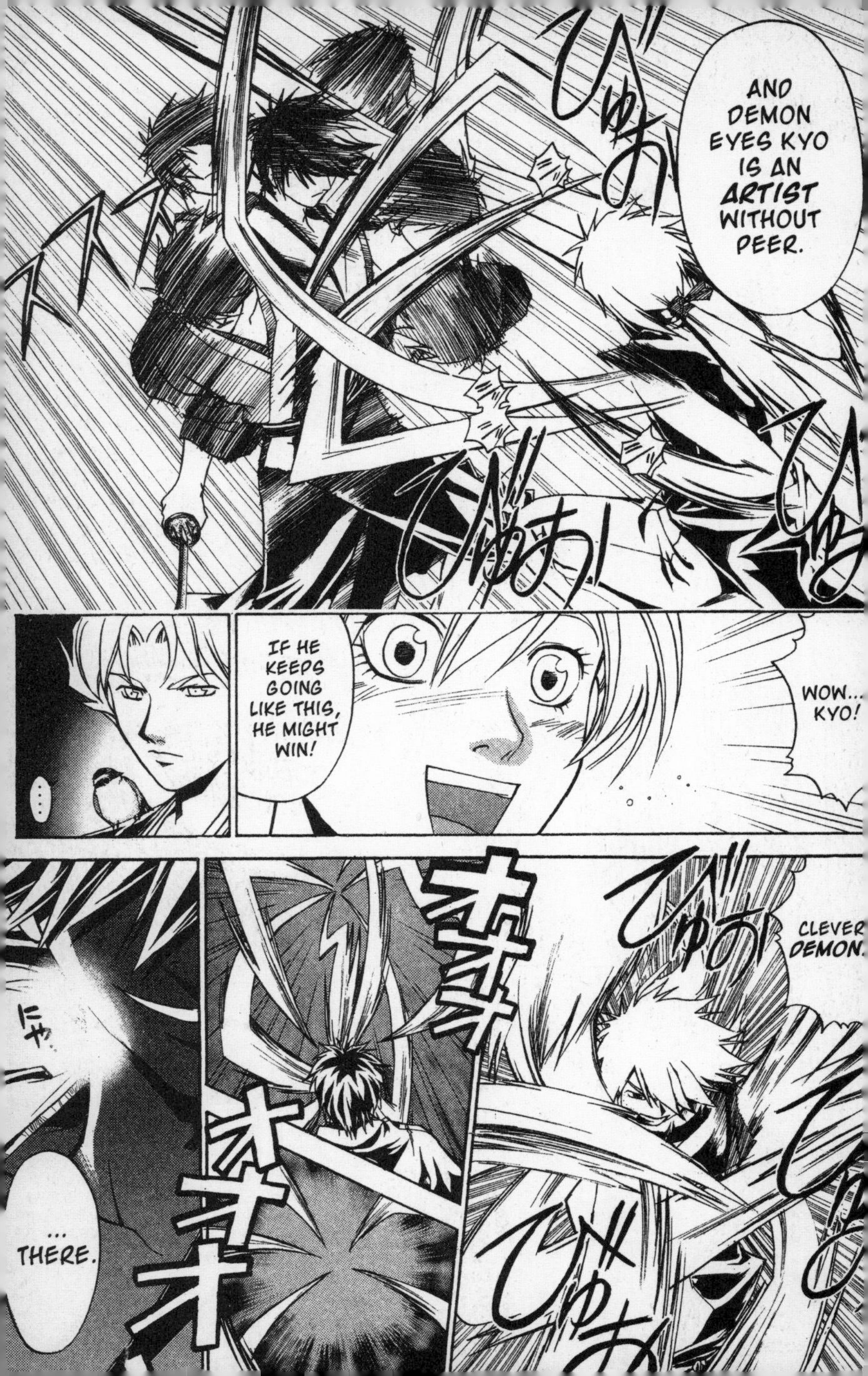
AND DEMON EYES KYO IS AN ARTIST WITHOUT PEER.
WOW... KYO!
IF HE KEEPS GOING LIKE THIS, HE MIGHT WIN!
...
CLEVER DEMON.
... THERE.

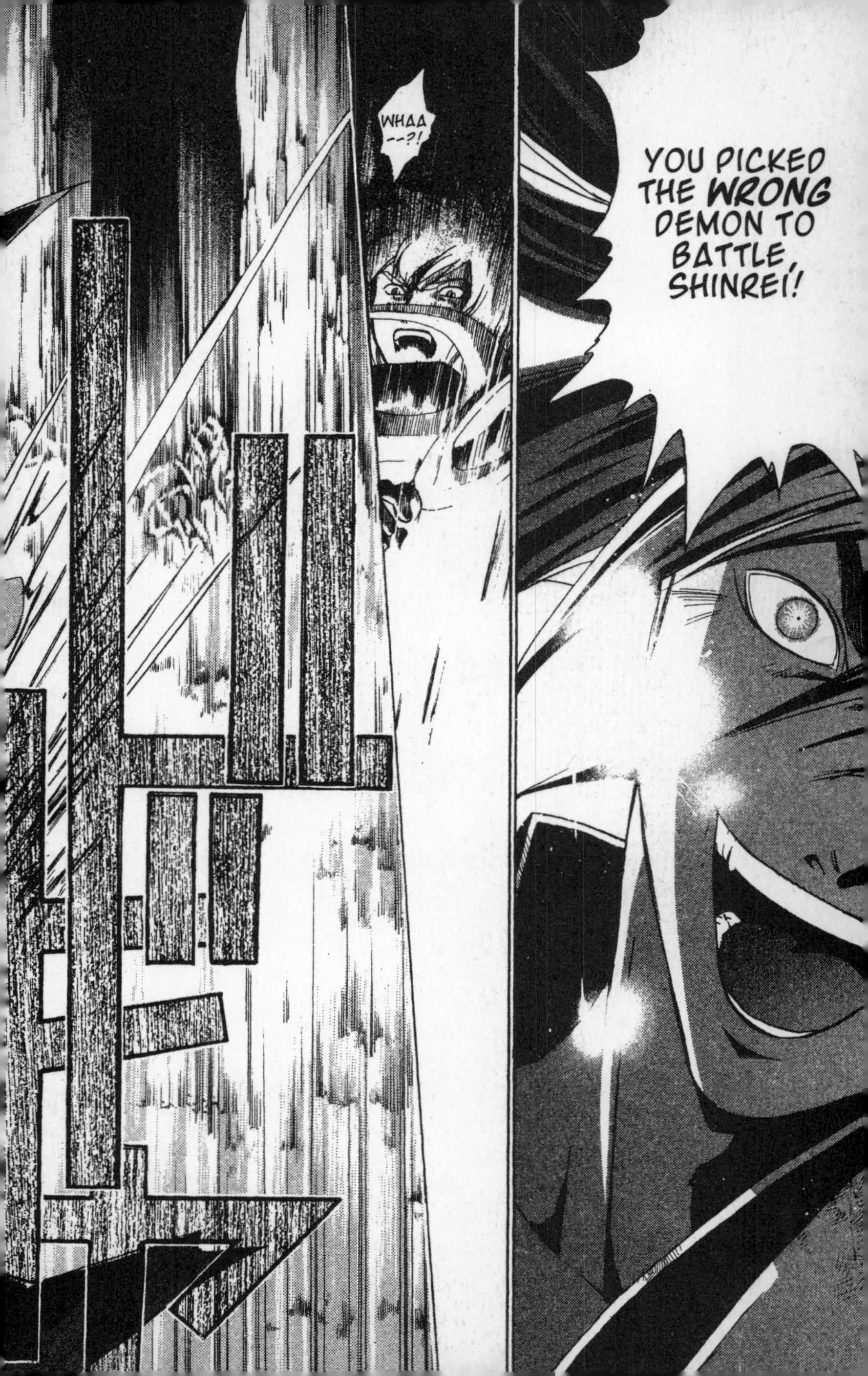
YOU PICKED THE WRONG DEMON TO BATTLE SHINREI!
WHAA--?!

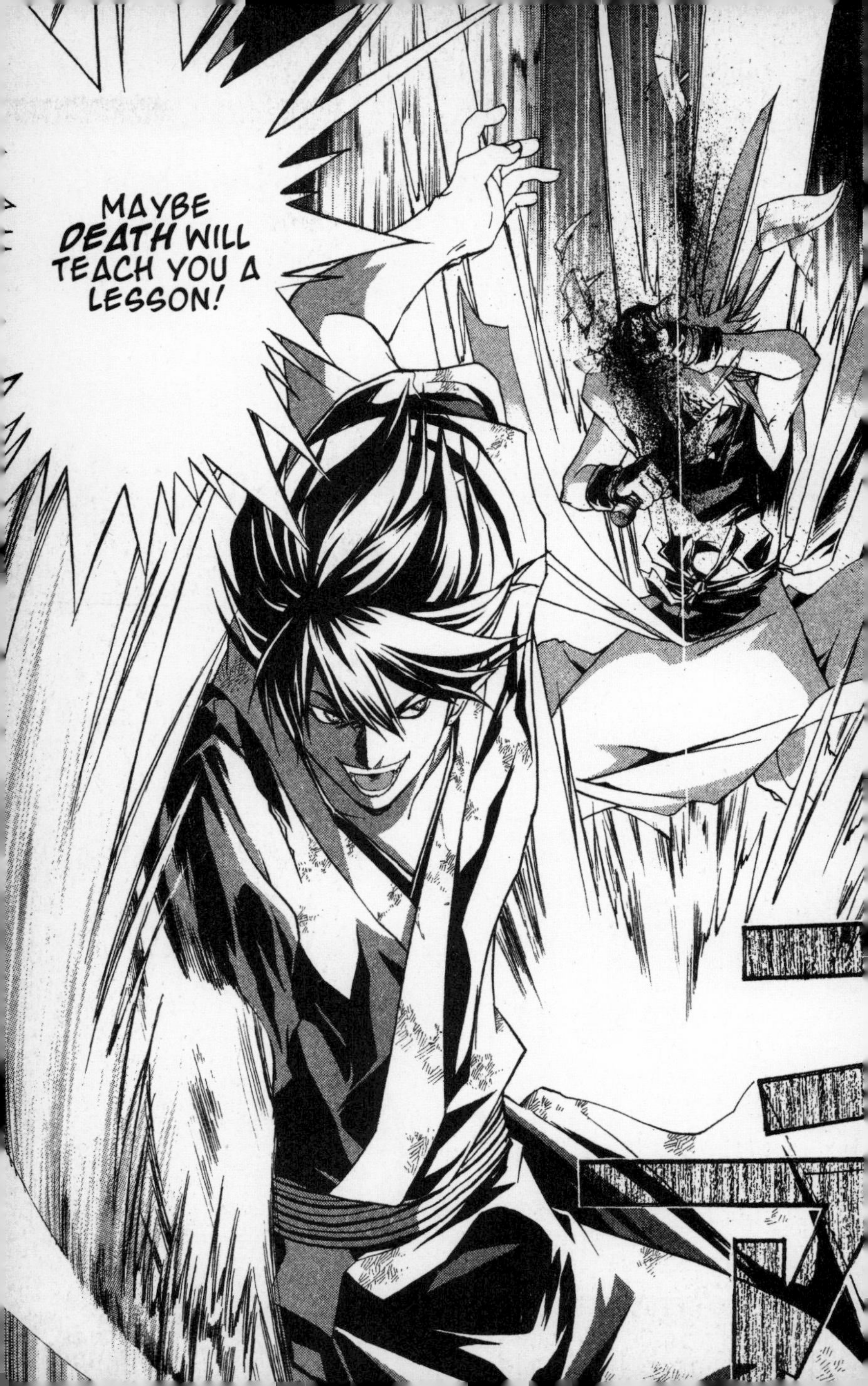
MAYBE DEATH WILL TEACH YOU A LESSON!

DEEPER 20

NOT IMPORTANT, BUT GOOD ENOUGH FOR A BONUS *PAGE!*

This Month: A Kyo by Any Other Name!

There's lots of ways to call someone: by their last name, by their first name, by a nickname.... It reveals our relationship to that person, and nowhere is this more true than in SDK! Presenting, a complete list of names SDK characters use to call each other! Check it out, you might just learn something!

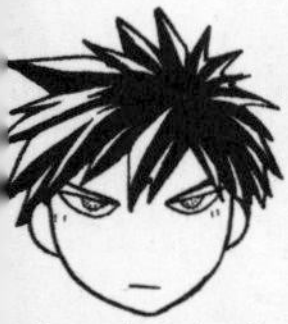

I usually jus' call 'em all "HEY YOU."

Kyo	→ Me. Me-SAMA
Kyoshiro	→ Him
Yuya	→ Dog, #1 Servant
Benitora	→ #2 Servant
Yukimura	→ Yukimura
Sasuke	→ Sarutobi (kid)
Bontenmaru	→ Bon
Okuni	→ Sly Fox
Muramasa	→ Old Man

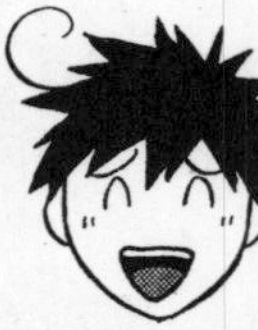

I calls 'em like I sees 'em!

Kyo	→ Him
Kyoshiro	→ Me
Yuya	→ Yuya-saaan ♥
Benitora	→ Benitora ("Tora-san" these days?)
Yukimura	→ Yukimura-san
Sasuke	→ Sasuke-kun
Bontenmaru	→ Bontenmaru-san
Okuni	→ Okuni-san

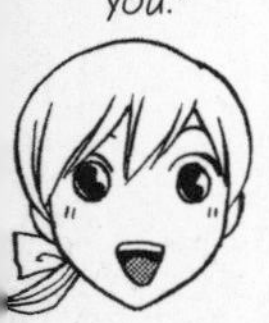

Always show respect!

Kyo	→ Kyo
Kyoshiro	→ Kyoshiro
Yuya	→ Me (myself)
Benitora	→ Tora
Yukimura	→ Yukimura-san
Sasuke	→ Sasuke-kun
Bontenmaru	→ Bontenmaru-san
Okuni	→ Okuni-san

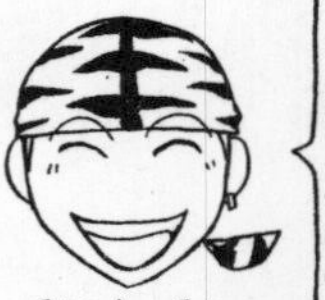

I like her, I like him NOT....

Kyo	→ Kyo-han
Kyoshiro	→ Kyoshiro-han
Yuya	→ Yuya-han ♥♥
Benitora	→ Me
Yukimura	→ Yukimura-han
Sasuke	→ Punk!
Bontenmaru	→ Bon-han
Okuni	→ Okuni-han

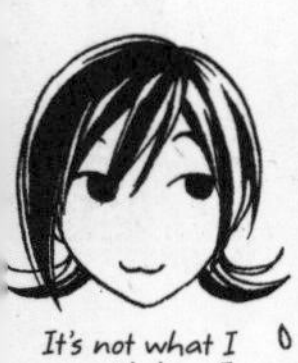

It's not what I say; it's how I say it!

Kyo	→ Kyo-san ♥
Kyoshiro	→ Kyoshiro-san
Yuya	→ Yuya-san
Benitora	→ Tora-san
Yukimura	→ Moi ♥
Sasuke	→ Sasuke ♥
Bontenmaru	→ Bon-chan
Okuni	→ Okuni-san
Muramasa	→ Niisan ♥

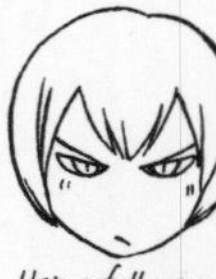

Using full names is rude.

Kyo	→ Demon Eyes Kyo
Kyoshiro	→ Mibu Kyoshiro
Yuya	→ Neechan*
Benitora	→ Airheaded Bonbon!
Yukimura	→ Yukimura
Sasuke	→ Me
Bontenmaru	→ Bon
Okuni	→ Izumo-no-Okuni

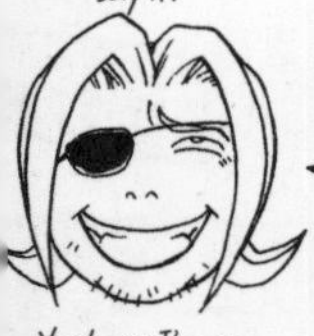

Yeah, so I'm an old fart.

Kyo	→ Kyo
Kyoshiro	→ Kyoshiro
Yuya	→ Yuya-chan
Benitora	→ Benitora-kun ♥
Yukimura	→ Yukimura ♥
Sasuke	→ Lil' guy
Bontenmaru	→ Me.
Okuni	→ Okuni-neechan
Akira	→ Spoiled Akira

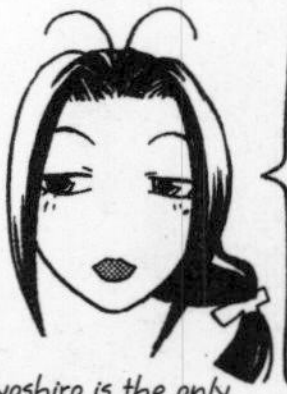

Kyoshiro is the only "-sama" for me!

Kyo	→ Kyo-san
Kyoshiro	→ Kyoshiro-sama
Yuya	→ Yuya-san
Benitora	→ Tora-san
Yukimura	→ Yukimura-san
Sasuke	→ Sasuke-kun
Bontenmaru	→ Bontenmaru-san
Okuni	→ Myself

There's some exceptions, but this is most of it...

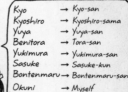

Well?! You learn anything--?!

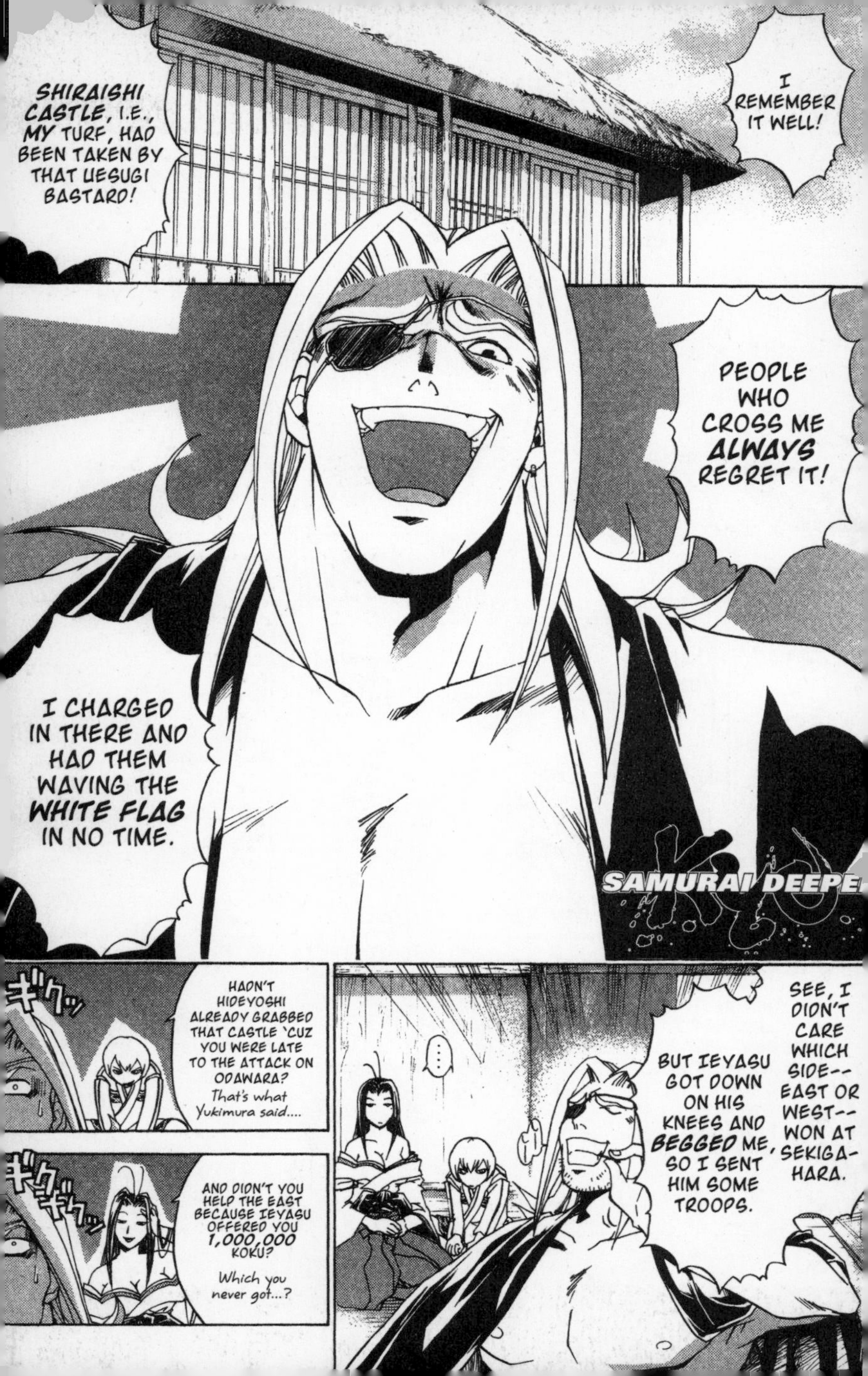
I REMEMBER IT WELL!
SHIRAISHI CASTLE, I.E., MY TURF, HAD BEEN TAKEN BY THAT UESUGI BASTARD!
PEOPLE WHO CROSS ME ALWAYS REGRET IT!
I CHARGED IN THERE AND HAD THEM WAVING THE WHITE FLAG IN NO TIME.
SAMURAI DEEPER
SEE, I DIDN'T CARE WHICH SIDE--EAST OR WEST--WON AT SEKIGAHARA.
BUT IEYASU GOT DOWN ON HIS KNEES AND BEGGED ME, SO I SENT HIM SOME TROOPS.
...
HADN'T HIDEYOSHI ALREADY GRABBED THAT CASTLE 'CUZ YOU WERE LATE TO THE ATTACK ON ODAWARA?
That's what Yukimura said....
ギクッ
AND DIDN'T YOU HELP THE EAST BECAUSE IEYASU OFFERED YOU 1,000,000 KOKU?
Which you never got...?
ギクギクッ

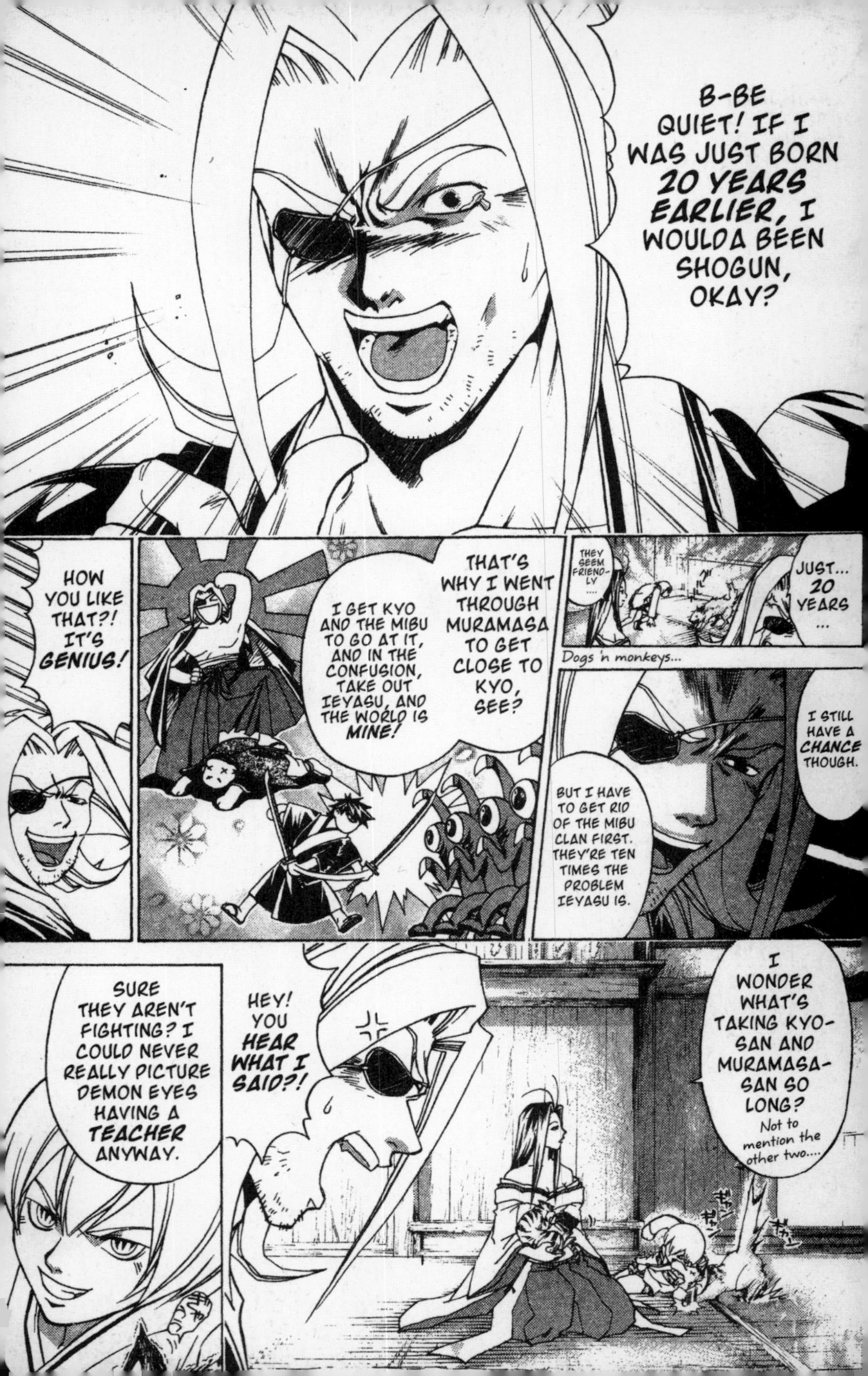
B-BE QUIET! IF I WAS JUST BORN 20 YEARS EARLIER, I WOULDA BEEN SHOGUN, OKAY?
JUST... 20 YEARS ...
THEY SEEM FRIENDLY....
Dogs 'n monkeys...
I STILL HAVE A CHANCE THOUGH.
BUT I HAVE TO GET RID OF THE MIBU CLAN FIRST. THEY'RE TEN TIMES THE PROBLEM IEYASU IS.
THAT'S WHY I WENT THROUGH MURAMASA TO GET CLOSE TO KYO, SEE?
I GET KYO AND THE MIBU TO GO AT IT, AND IN THE CONFUSION, TAKE OUT IEYASU, AND THE WORLD IS MINE!
HOW YOU LIKE THAT?! IT'S GENIUS!
I WONDER WHAT'S TAKING KYO-SAN AND MURAMASA-SAN SO LONG?
Not to mention the other two....
HEY! YOU HEAR WHAT I SAID?!
SURE THEY AREN'T FIGHTING? I COULD NEVER REALLY PICTURE DEMON EYES HAVING A TEACHER ANYWAY.

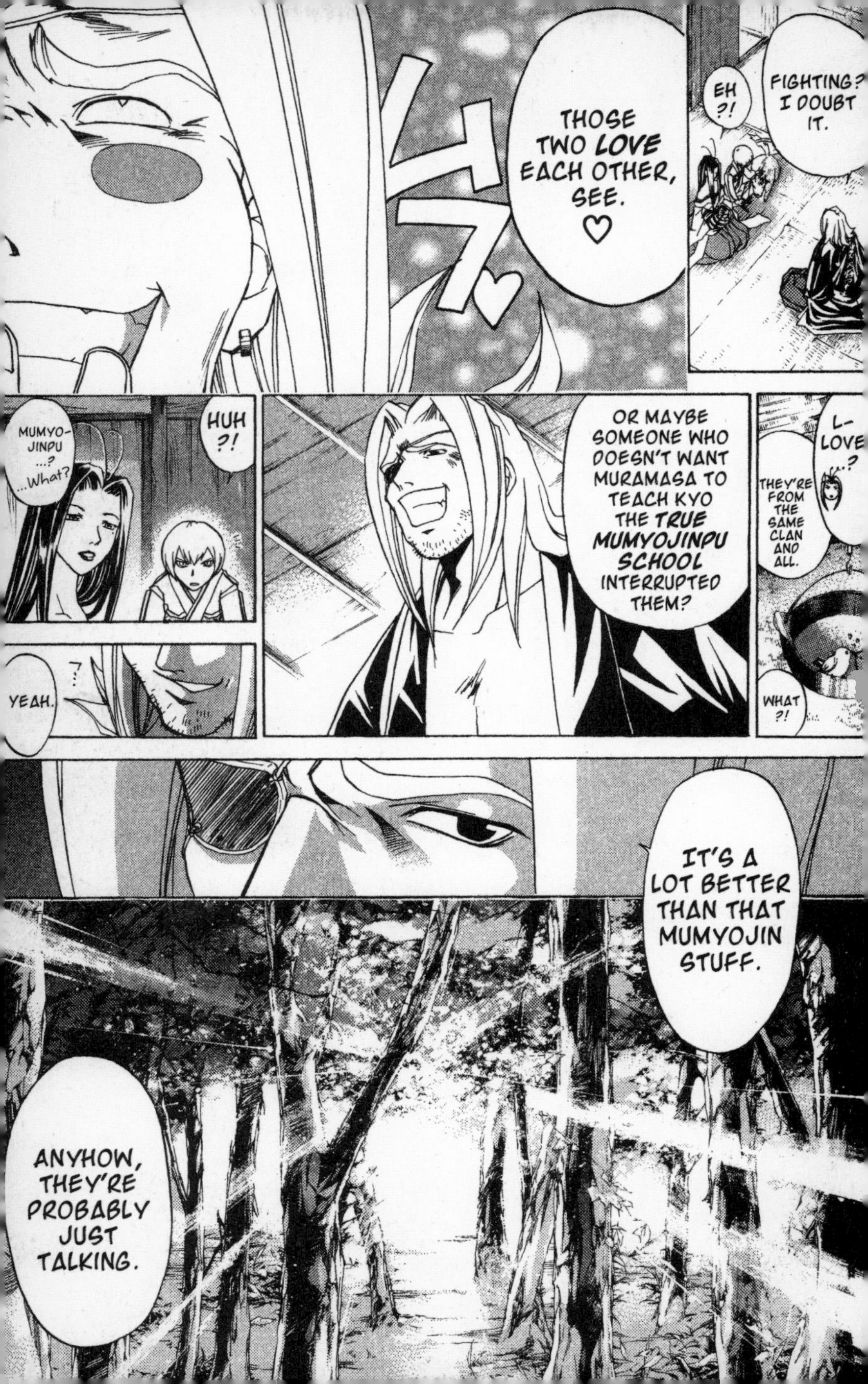

FIGHTING? I DOUBT IT.
EH ?!
THOSE TWO LOVE EACH OTHER, SEE. ♡
ムフ♡
L-LOVE ...?
THEY'RE FROM THE SAME CLAN AND ALL.
WHAT ?!
OR MAYBE SOMEONE WHO DOESN'T WANT MURAMASA TO TEACH KYO THE TRUE MUMYOJINPU SCHOOL INTERRUPTED THEM?
HUH ?!
MUMYO-JINPU ...? ...What?
?...
YEAH.
IT'S A LOT BETTER THAN THAT MUMYOJIN STUFF.
ANYHOW, THEY'RE PROBABLY JUST TALKING.

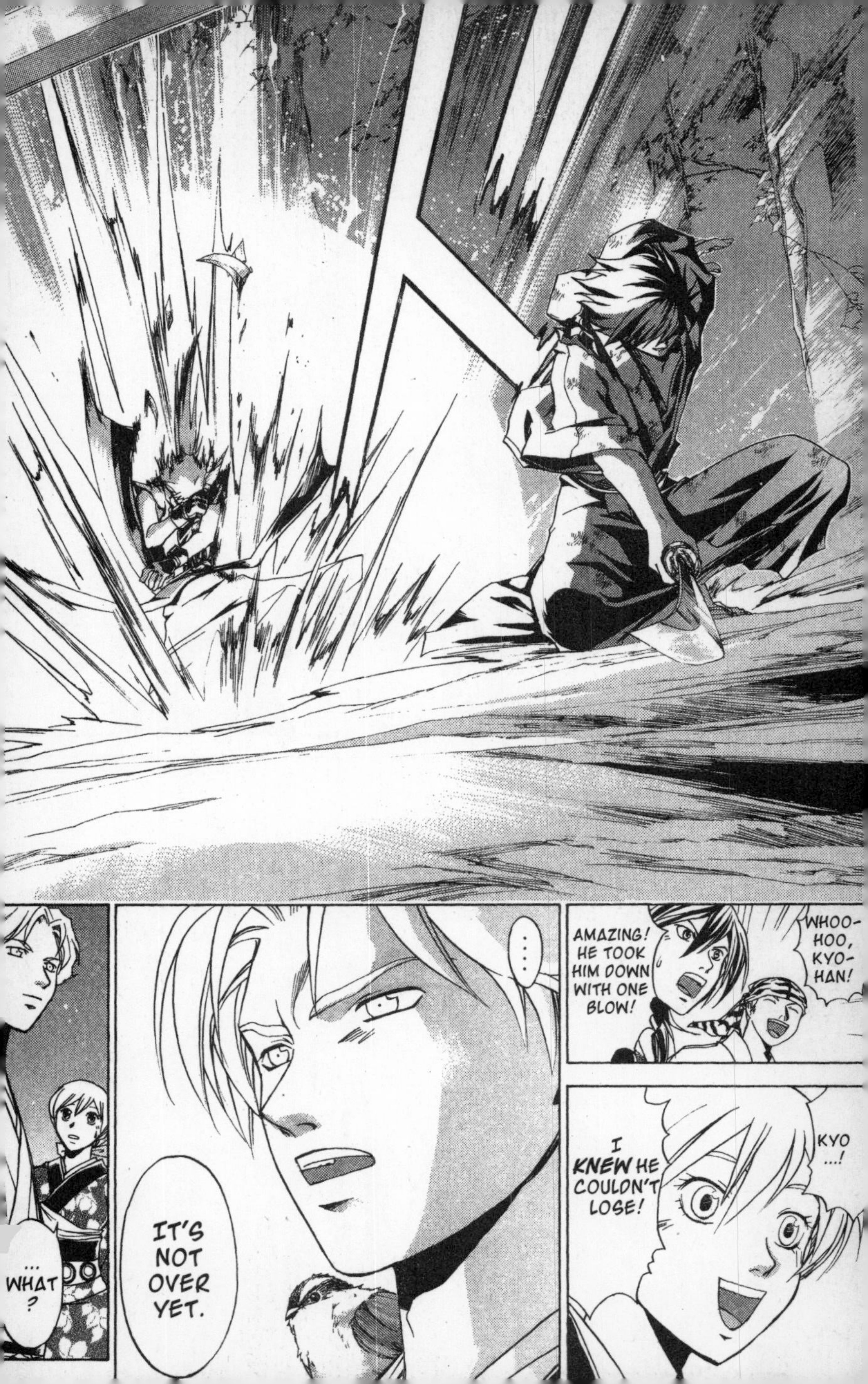
WHOO-HOO, KYO-HAN!
AMAZING! HE TOOK HIM DOWN WITH ONE BLOW!
KYO ...!
I **KNEW** HE COULDN'T LOSE!
....
IT'S NOT OVER YET.
... WHAT?

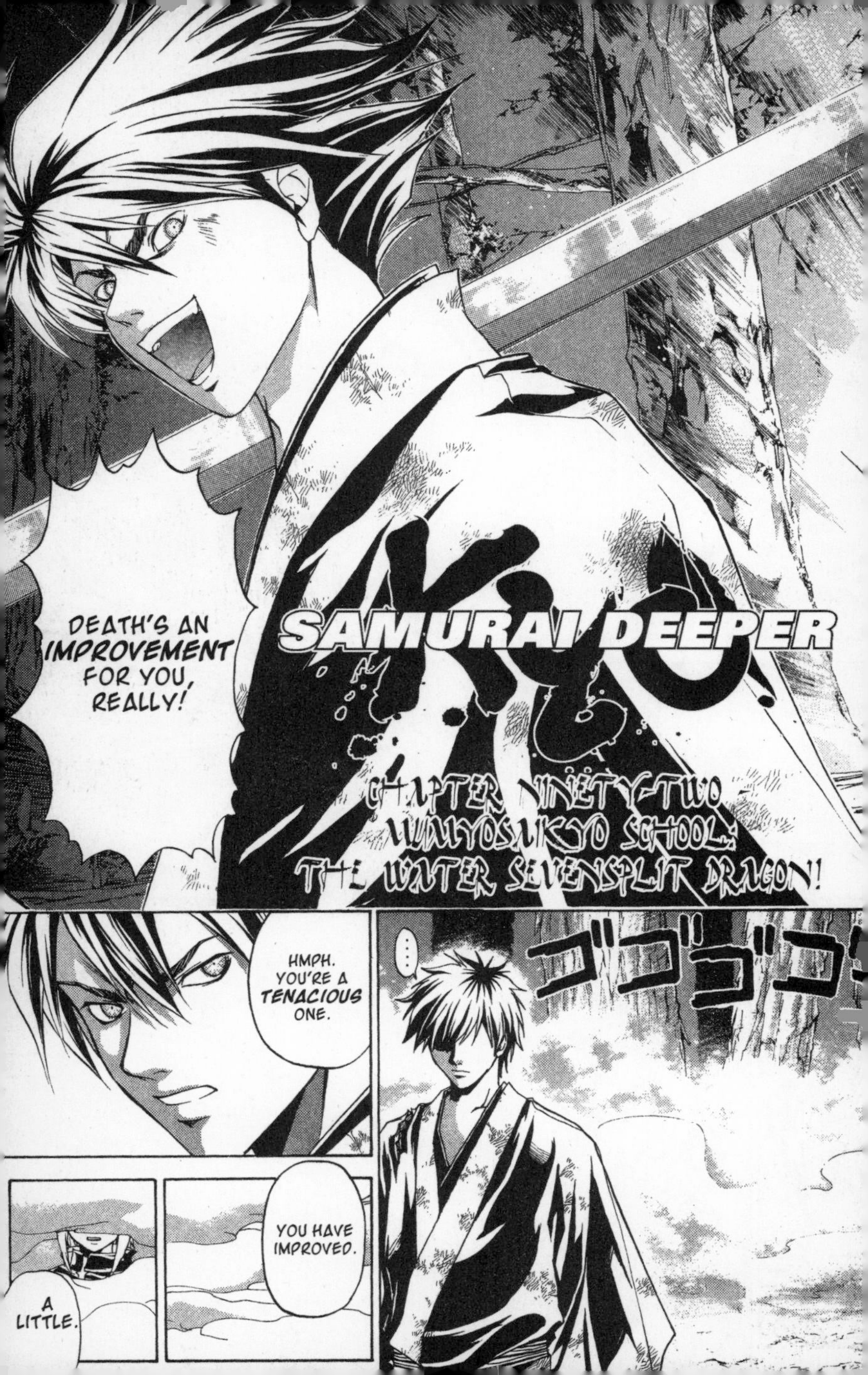
SAMURAI DEEPER KYO
CHAPTER NINETY-TWO
MUMYOSAKYO SCHOOL:
THE WATER SEVENSPLIT DRAGON!
DEATH'S AN IMPROVEMENT FOR YOU, REALLY!
...
ゴゴゴゴ
HMPH. YOU'RE A TENACIOUS ONE.
YOU HAVE IMPROVED.
A LITTLE.

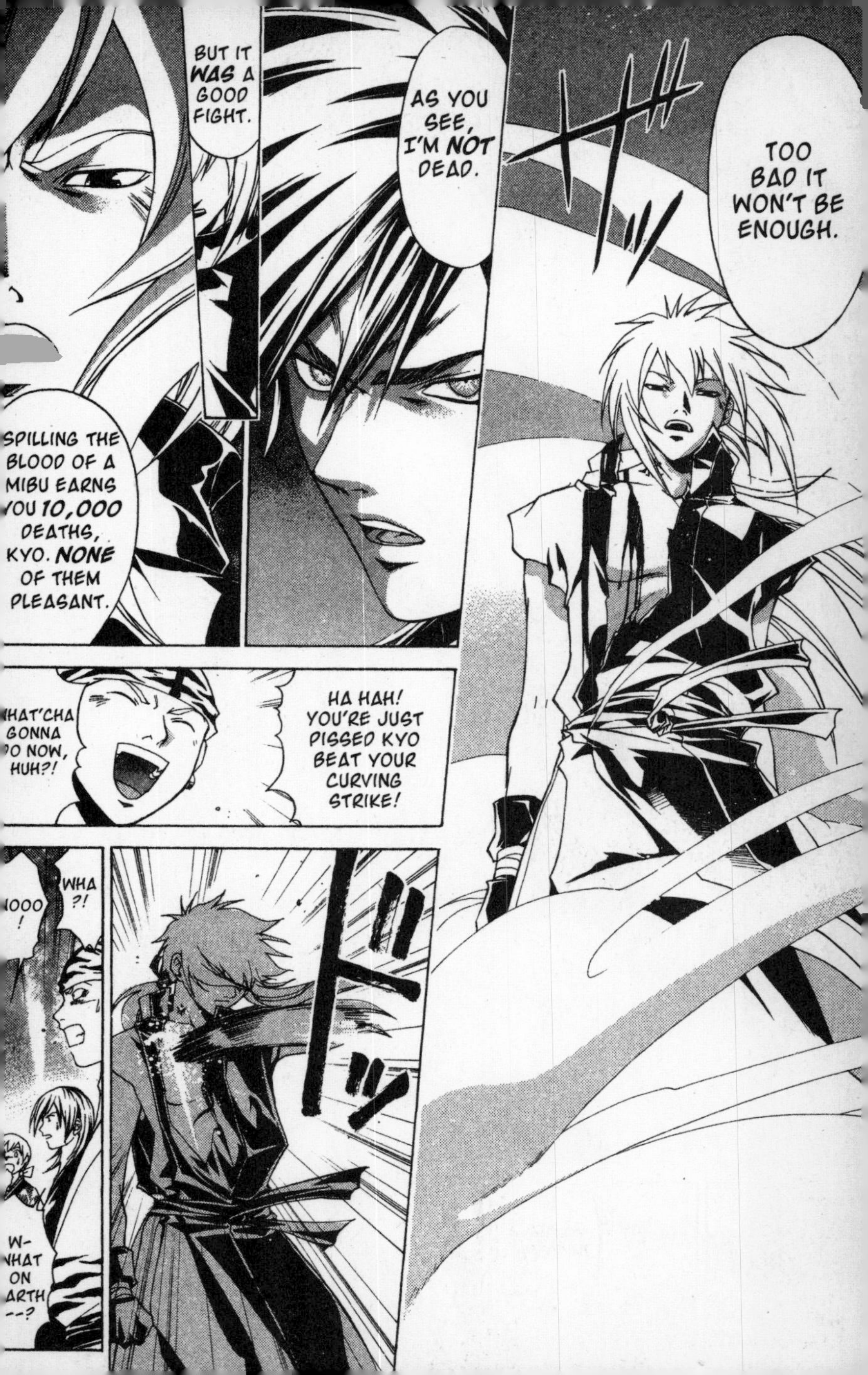
TOO BAD IT WON'T BE ENOUGH.
AS YOU SEE, I'M **NOT** DEAD.
BUT IT **WAS** A GOOD FIGHT.
SPILLING THE BLOOD OF A MIBU EARNS YOU **10,000** DEATHS, KYO. **NONE** OF THEM PLEASANT.
HA HAH! YOU'RE JUST PISSED KYO BEAT YOUR CURVING STRIKE!
WHAT'CHA GONNA DO NOW, HUH?!
WHA ?!
NOOO !
W-WHAT ON EARTH --?

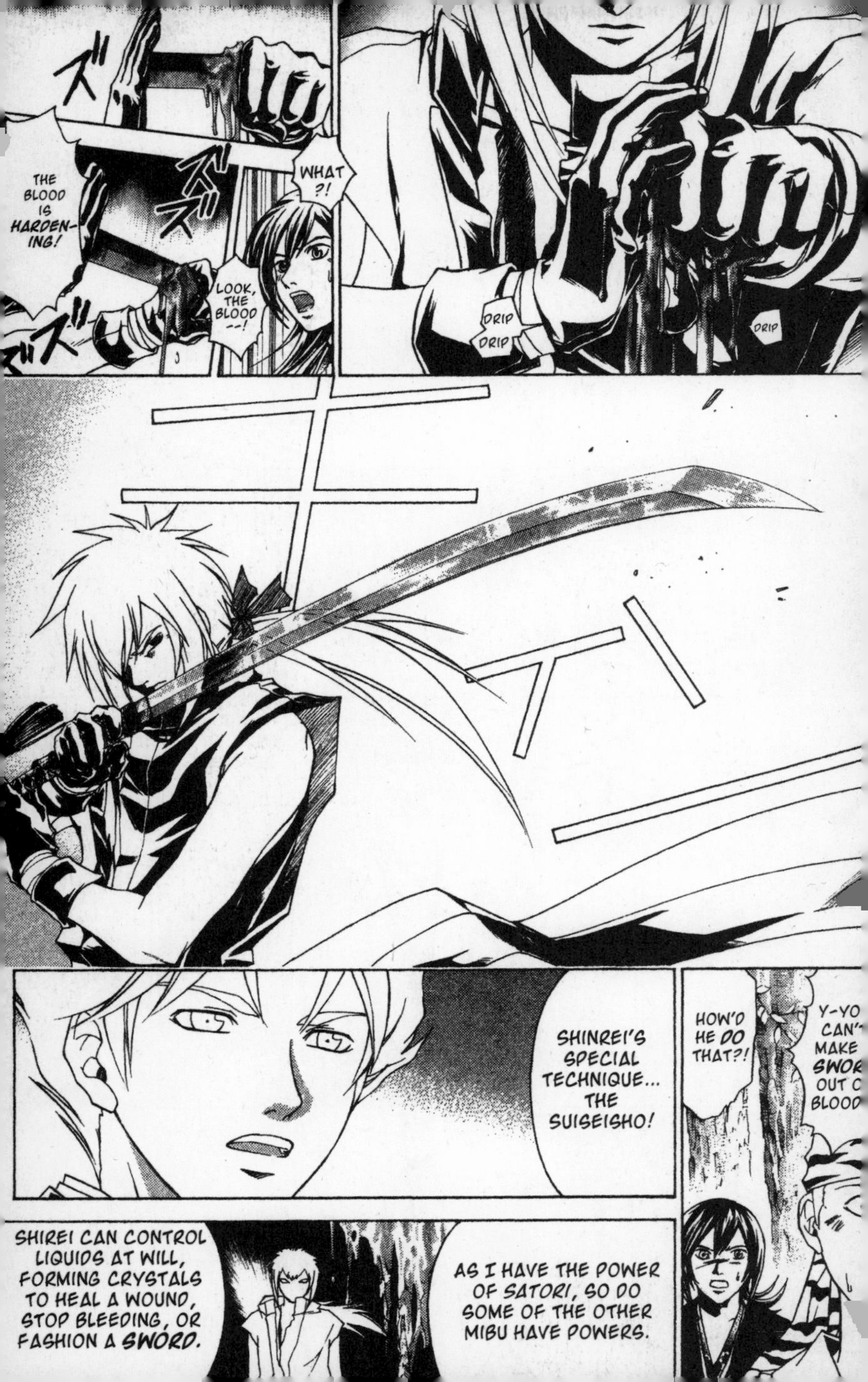
DRIP
DRIP
DRIP
WHAT ?!
LOOK, THE BLOOD --!
THE BLOOD IS HARDENING!
Y-YO CAN'- MAKE SWOR OUT O BLOOD
HOW'D HE DO THAT?!
SHINREI'S SPECIAL TECHNIQUE... THE SUISEISHO!
AS I HAVE THE POWER OF SATORI, SO DO SOME OF THE OTHER MIBU HAVE POWERS.
SHIREI CAN CONTROL LIQUIDS AT WILL, FORMING CRYSTALS TO HEAL A WOUND, STOP BLEEDING, OR FASHION A SWORD.

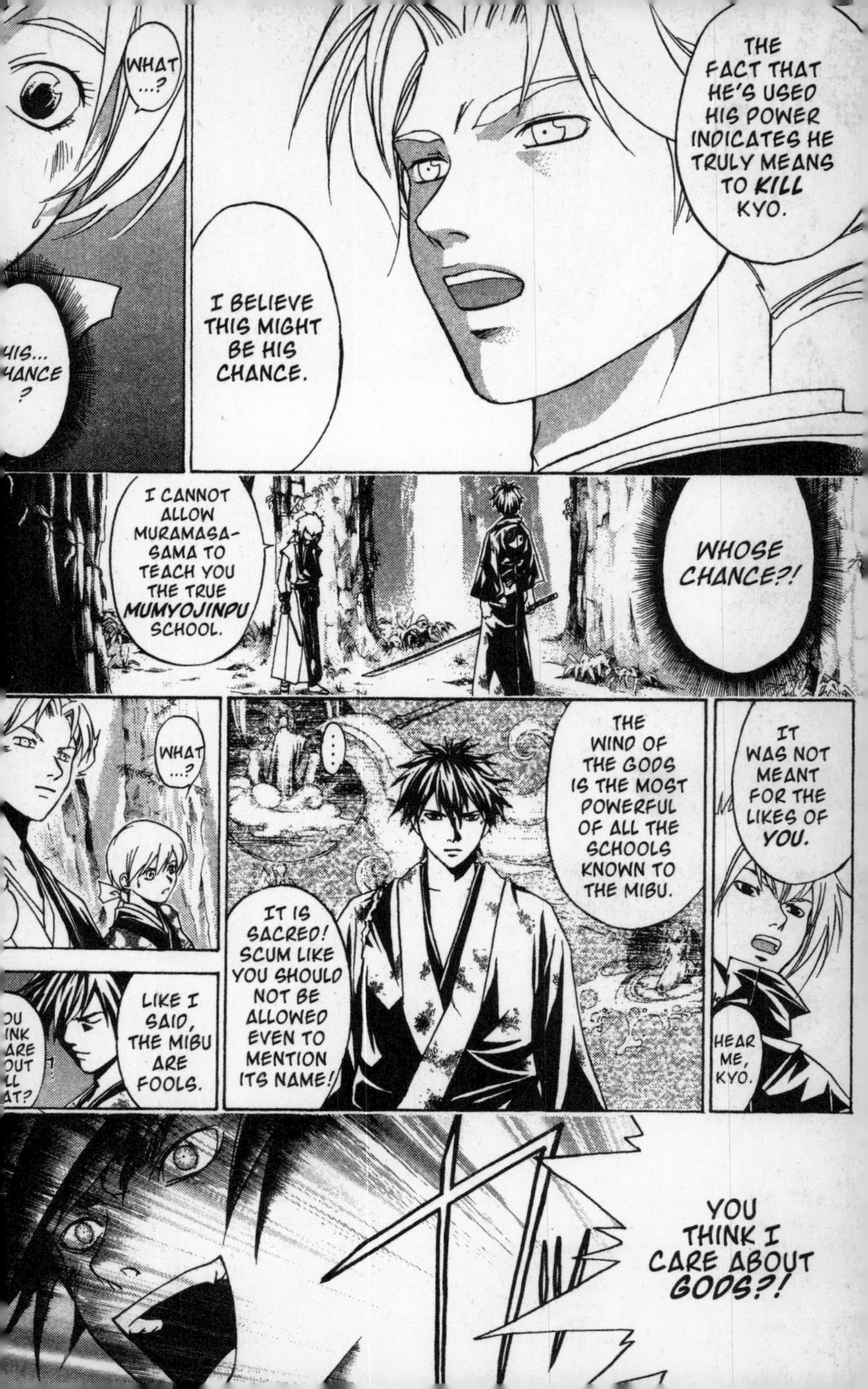
THE FACT THAT HE'S USED HIS POWER INDICATES HE TRULY MEANS TO **KILL** KYO.
I BELIEVE THIS MIGHT BE HIS CHANCE.
WHAT ...?
HIS... HANCE ?
WHOSE CHANCE?!
I CANNOT ALLOW MURAMASA-SAMA TO TEACH YOU THE TRUE **MUMYOJINPU** SCHOOL.
IT WAS NOT MEANT FOR THE LIKES OF **YOU.**
HEAR ME, KYO.
THE WIND OF THE GODS IS THE MOST POWERFUL OF ALL THE SCHOOLS KNOWN TO THE MIBU.
...
IT IS SACRED! SCUM LIKE YOU SHOULD NOT BE ALLOWED EVEN TO MENTION ITS NAME!
WHAT ...?
LIKE I SAID, THE MIBU ARE FOOLS.
OU INK ARE OUT LL AT?
YOU THINK I CARE ABOUT **GODS?!**

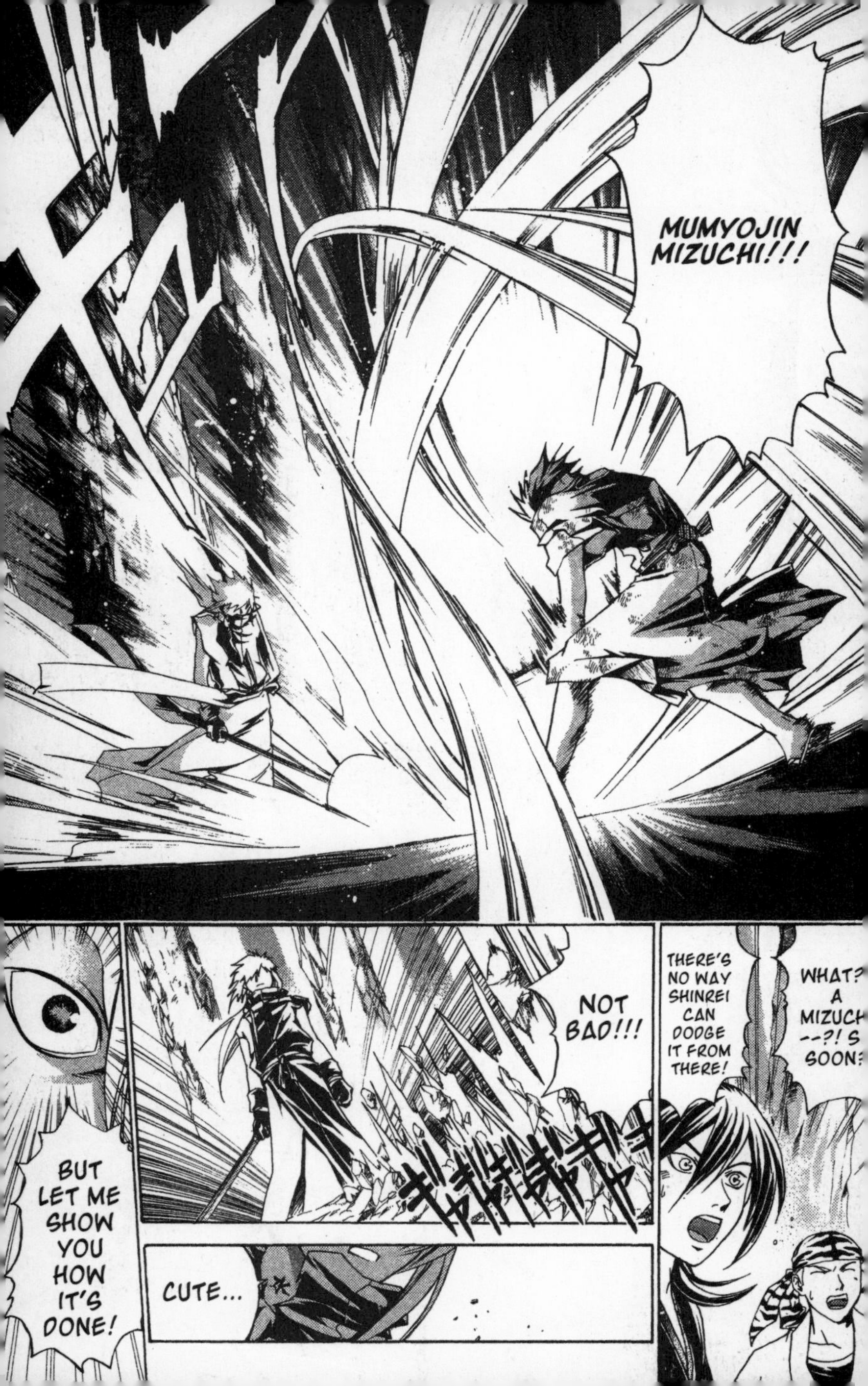
MUMYOJIN MIZUCHI!!!
WHAT? A MIZUCH --?! S SOON?
THERE'S NO WAY SHINREI CAN DODGE IT FROM THERE!
NOT BAD!!!
CUTE...
BUT LET ME SHOW YOU HOW IT'S DONE!

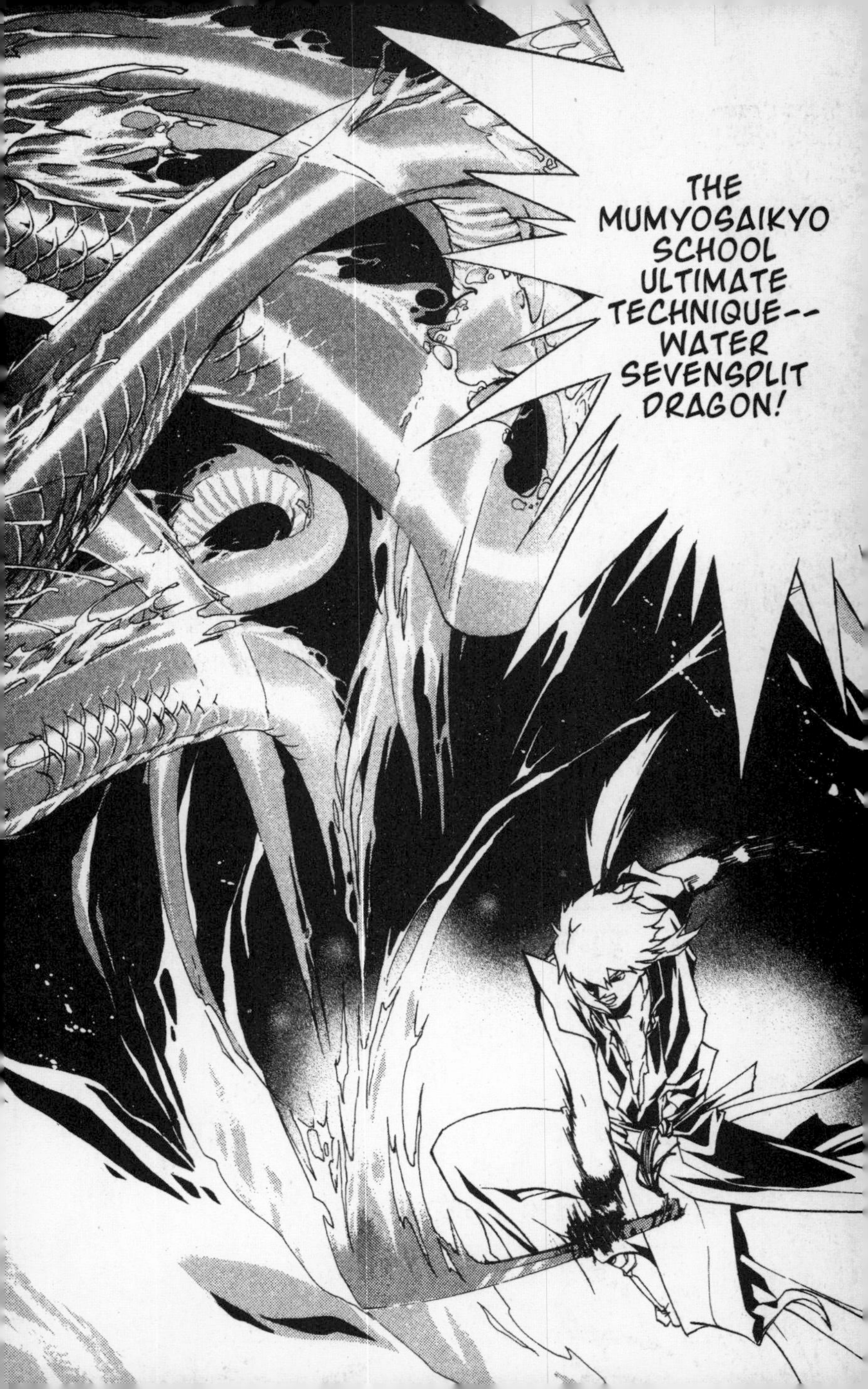
THE MUMYOSAIKYO SCHOOL ULTIMATE TECHNIQUE-- WATER SEVENSPLIT DRAGON!

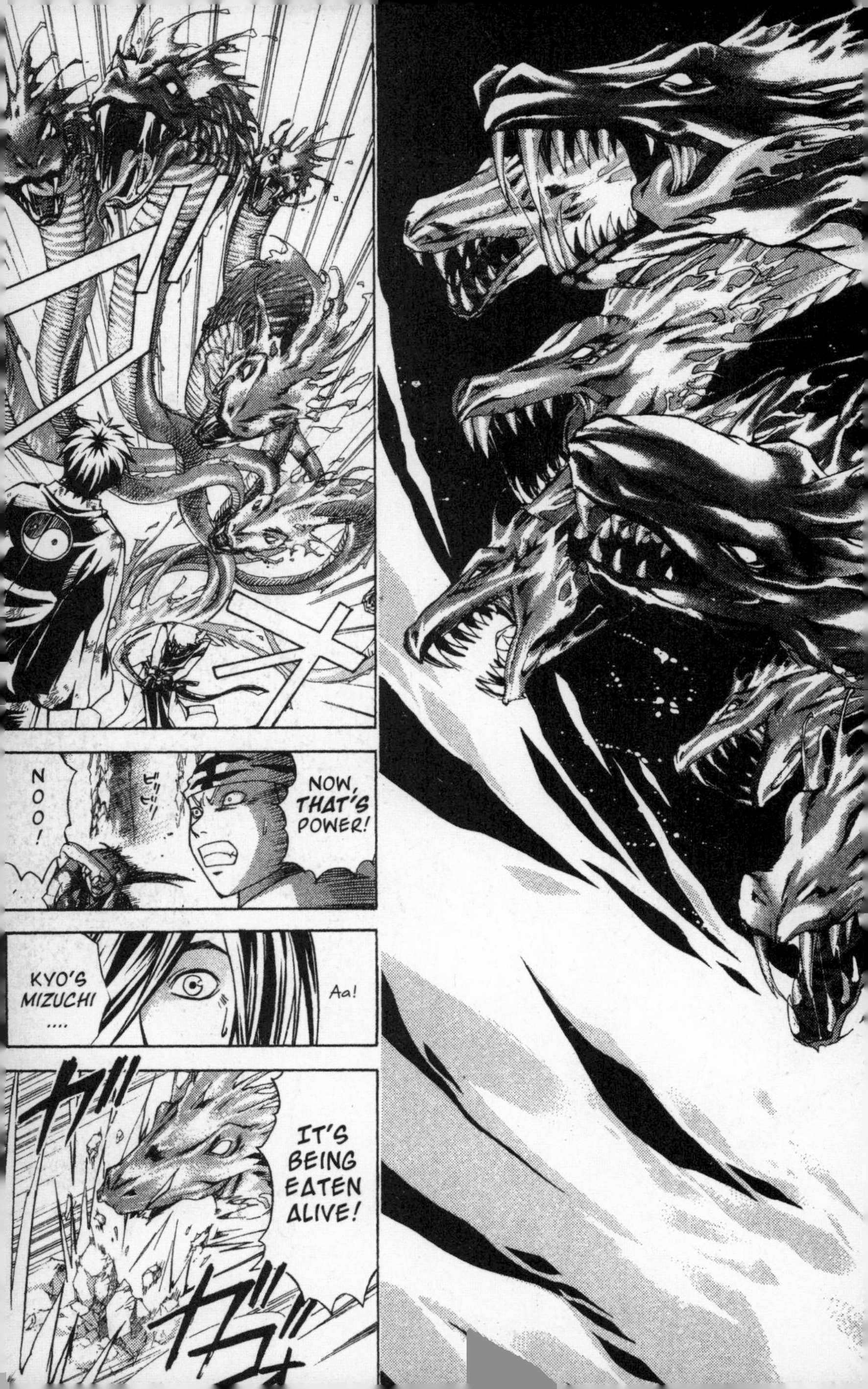
NOW, THAT'S POWER!
NOOO!
Aa!
KYO'S MIZUCHI ....
IT'S BEING EATEN ALIVE!

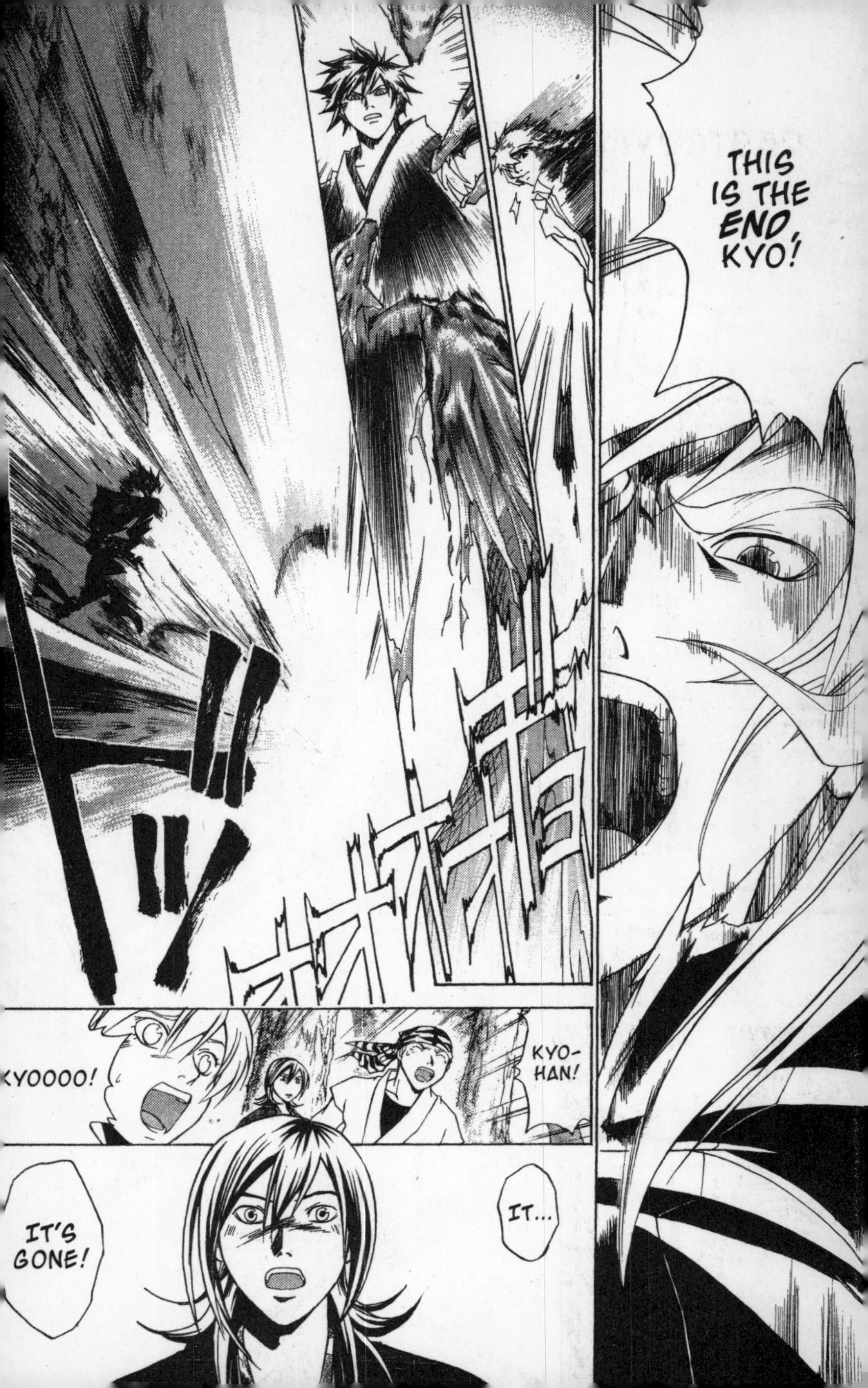
THIS IS THE END KYO!
KYO-HAN!
KYOOOO!
IT...
IT'S GONE!

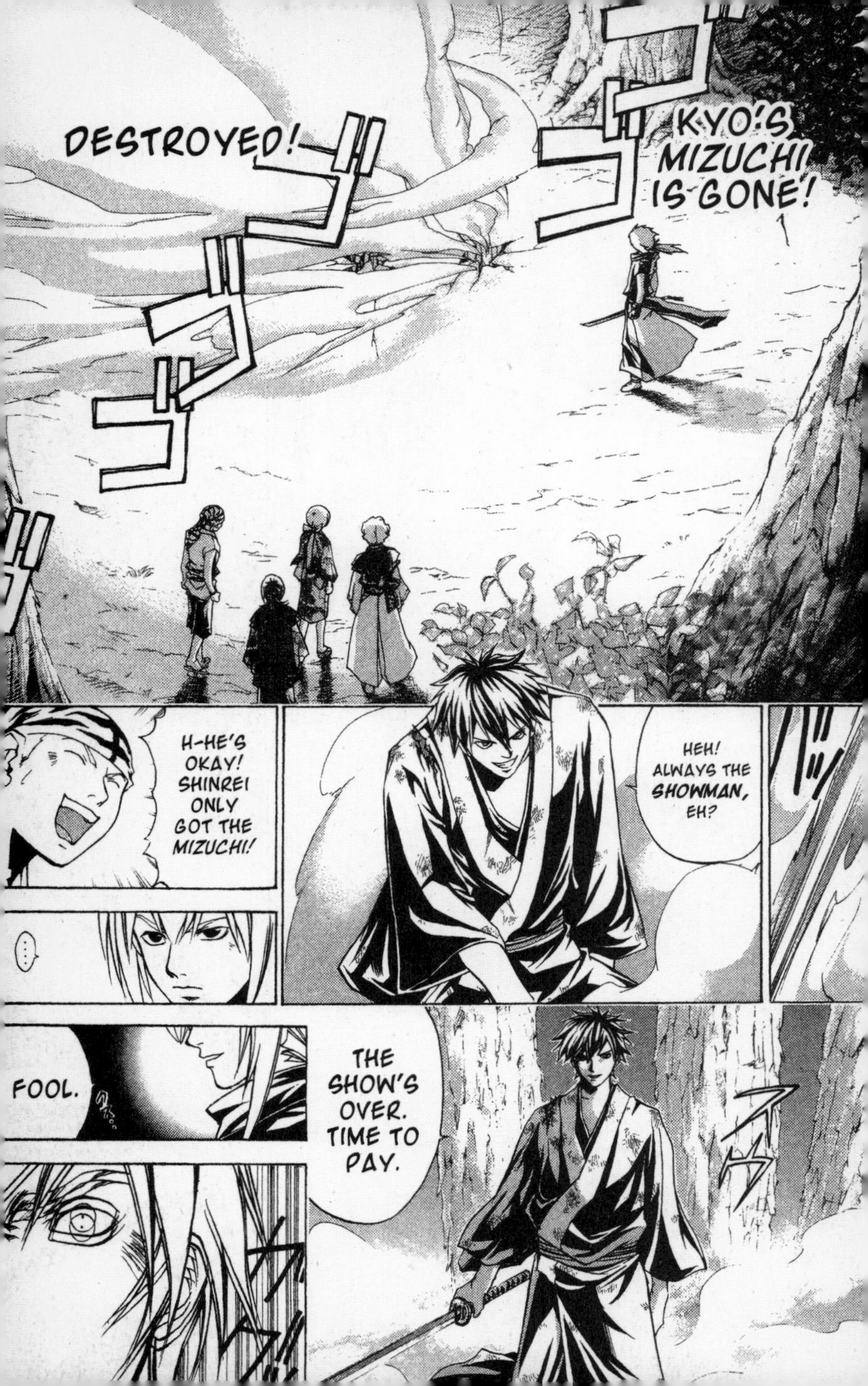
KYO'S MIZUCHI IS GONE!
DESTROYED!
HEH! ALWAYS THE SHOWMAN, EH?
H-HE'S OKAY! SHINREI ONLY GOT THE MIZUCHI!
...
THE SHOW'S OVER. TIME TO PAY.
FOOL.

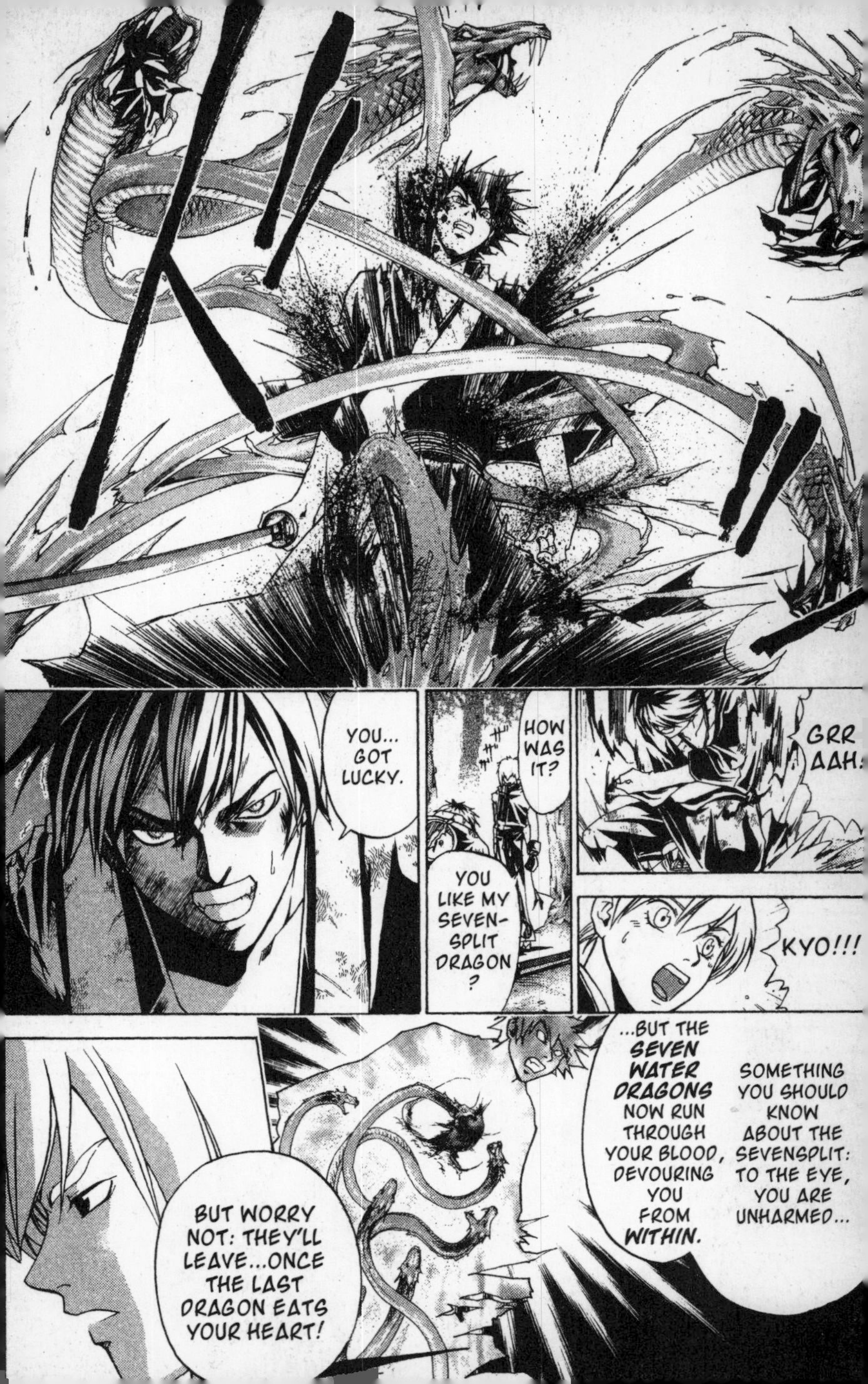
GRR AAH.
KYO!!!
HOW WAS IT?
YOU LIKE MY SEVEN-SPLIT DRAGON?
YOU... GOT LUCKY.
SOMETHING YOU SHOULD KNOW ABOUT THE SEVENSPLIT: TO THE EYE, YOU ARE UNHARMED...
...BUT THE **SEVEN WATER DRAGONS** NOW RUN THROUGH YOUR BLOOD, DEVOURING YOU FROM **WITHIN.**
BUT WORRY NOT: THEY'LL LEAVE...ONCE THE LAST DRAGON EATS YOUR HEART!

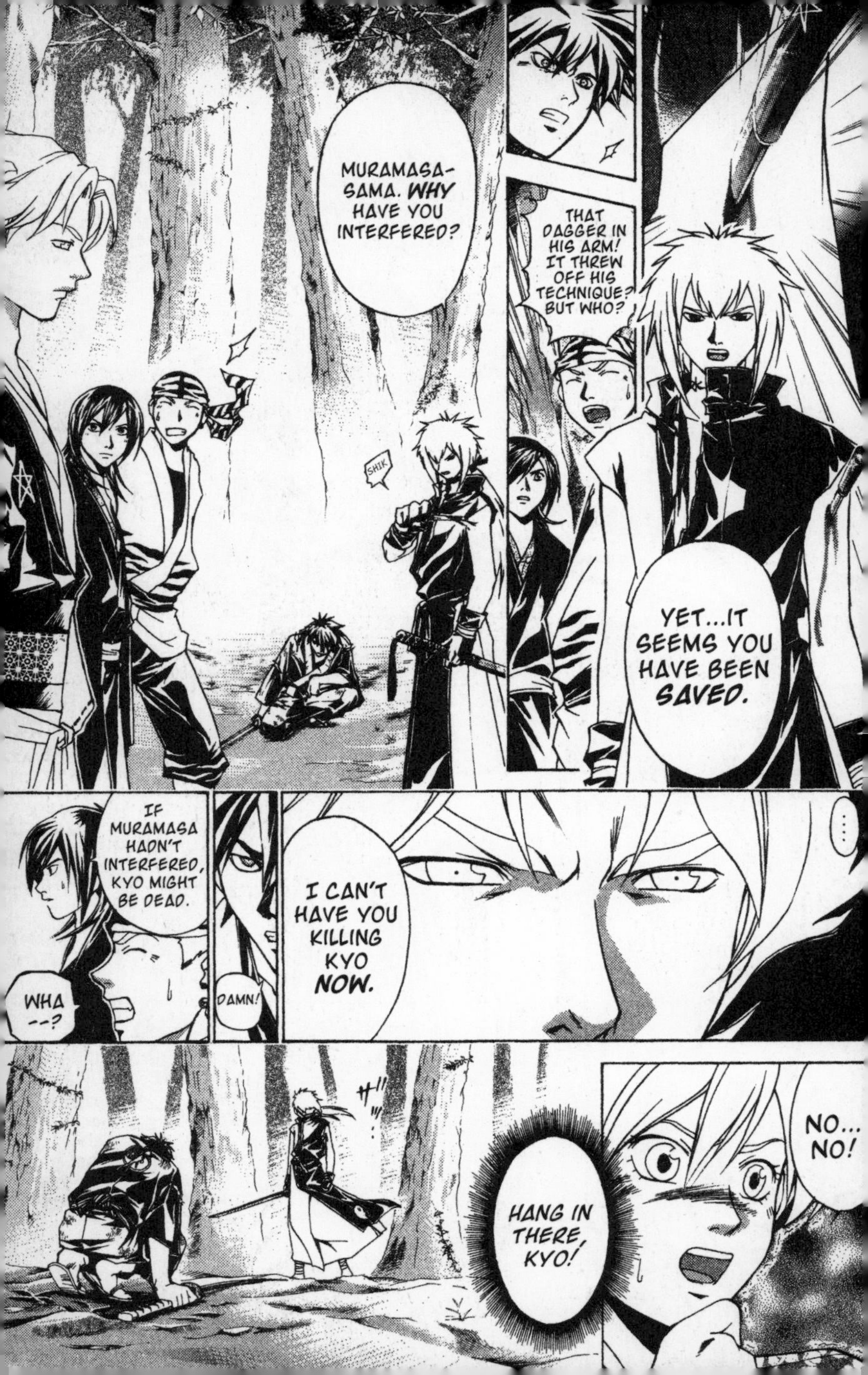
THAT DAGGER IN HIS ARM! IT THREW OFF HIS TECHNIQUE? BUT WHO?
YET...IT SEEMS YOU HAVE BEEN SAVED.
MURAMASA-SAMA. WHY HAVE YOU INTERFERED?
SHIK
...
I CAN'T HAVE YOU KILLING KYO NOW.
DAMN!
IF MURAMASA HADN'T INTERFERED, KYO MIGHT BE DEAD.
WHA--?
NO... NO!
HANG IN THERE, KYO!

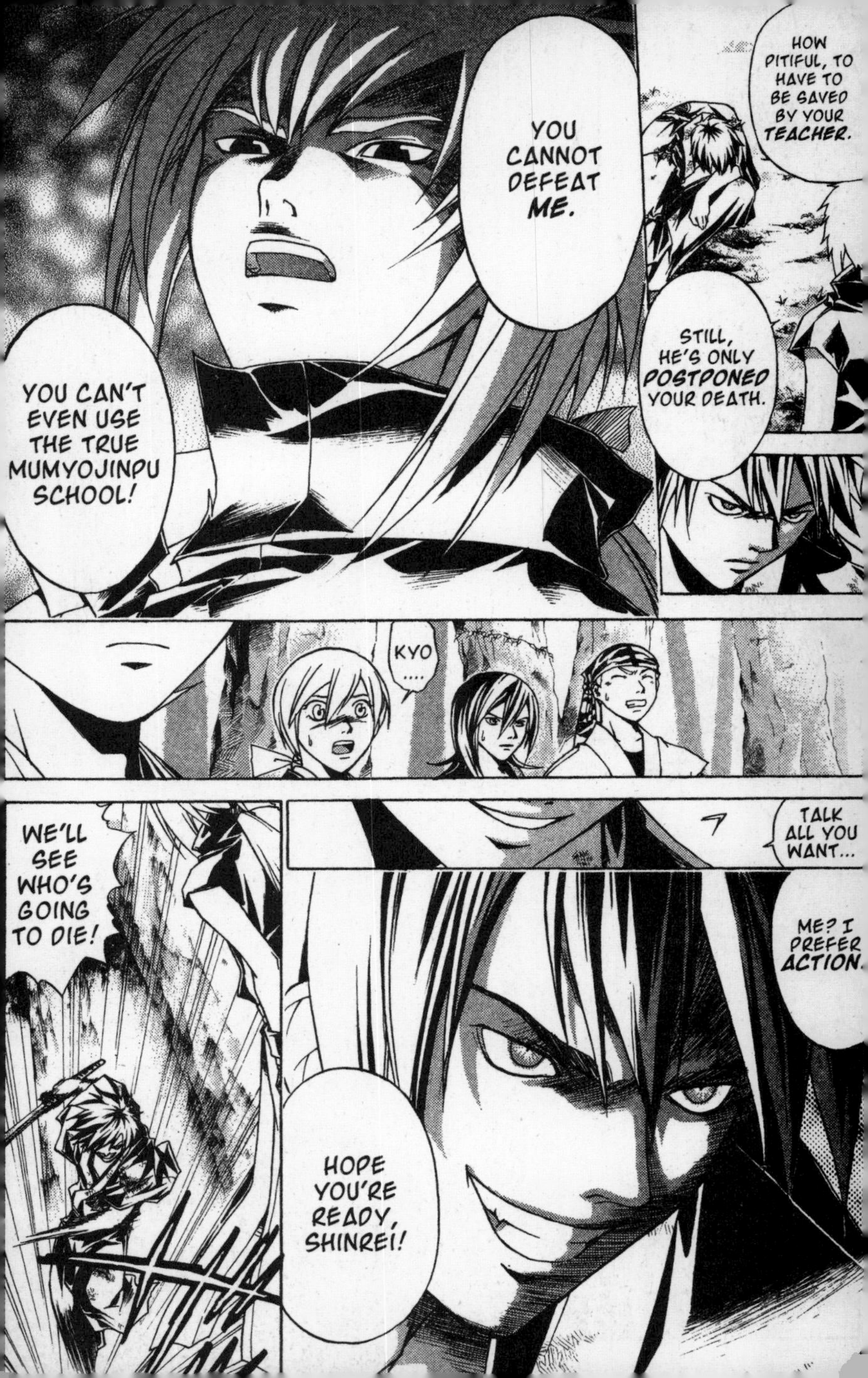
HOW PITIFUL, TO HAVE TO BE SAVED BY YOUR TEACHER.
STILL, HE'S ONLY POSTPONED YOUR DEATH.
YOU CANNOT DEFEAT ME.
YOU CAN'T EVEN USE THE TRUE MUMYOJINPU SCHOOL!
KYO .....
TALK ALL YOU WANT...
ME? I PREFER ACTION.
HOPE YOU'RE READY, SHINREI!
WE'LL SEE WHO'S GOING TO DIE!

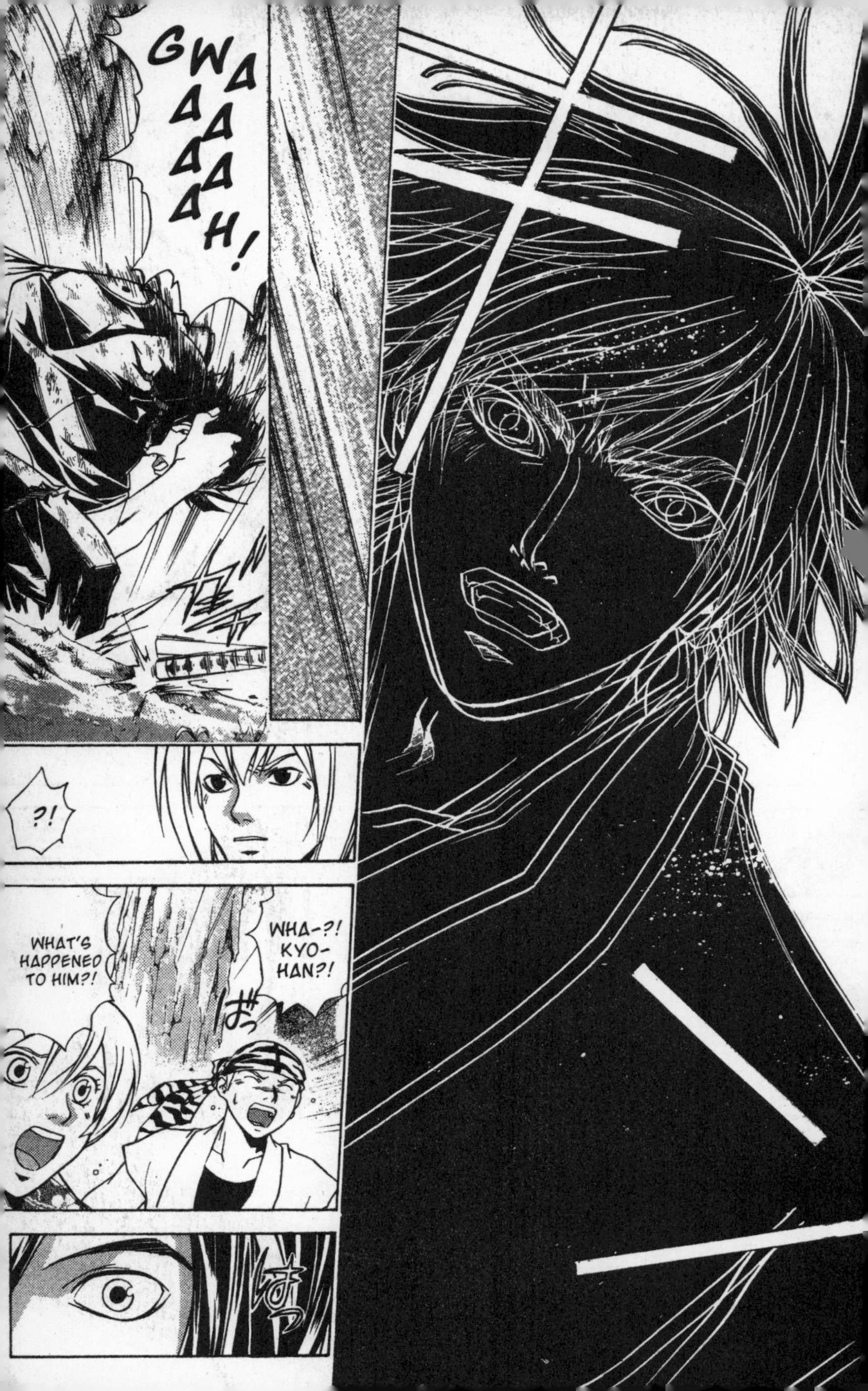
GWAAAAAAH!
?!
WHA-?! KYO-HAN?!
WHAT'S HAPPENED TO HIM?!

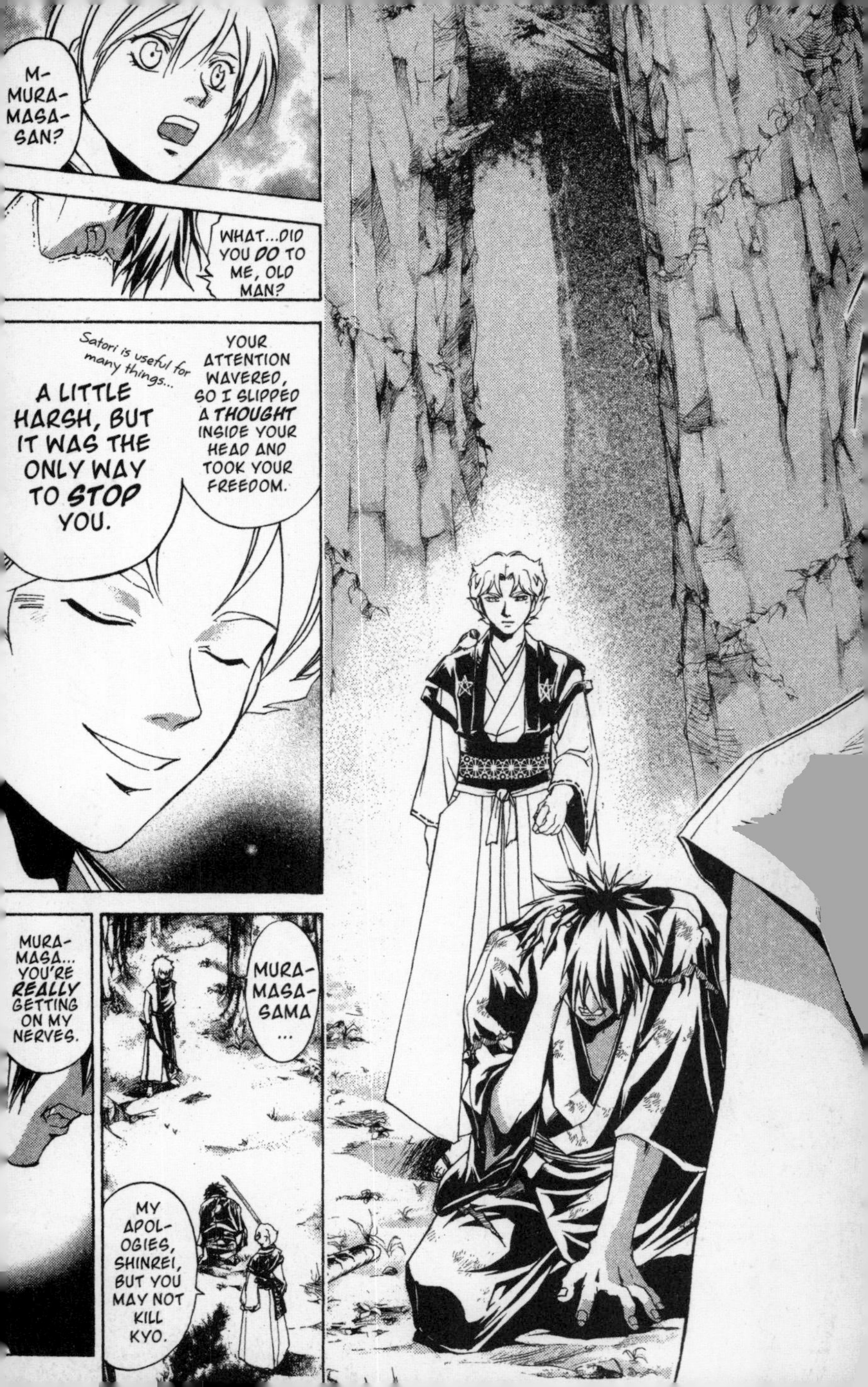
M-MURA-MASA-SAN?
WHAT...DID YOU DO TO ME, OLD MAN?
YOUR ATTENTION WAVERED, SO I SLIPPED A THOUGHT INSIDE YOUR HEAD AND TOOK YOUR FREEDOM.
Satori is useful for many things...
A LITTLE HARSH, BUT IT WAS THE ONLY WAY TO STOP YOU.
MURA-MASA-SAMA...
MY APOL-OGIES, SHINREI, BUT YOU MAY NOT KILL KYO.
MURA-MASA... YOU'RE REALLY GETTING ON MY NERVES.

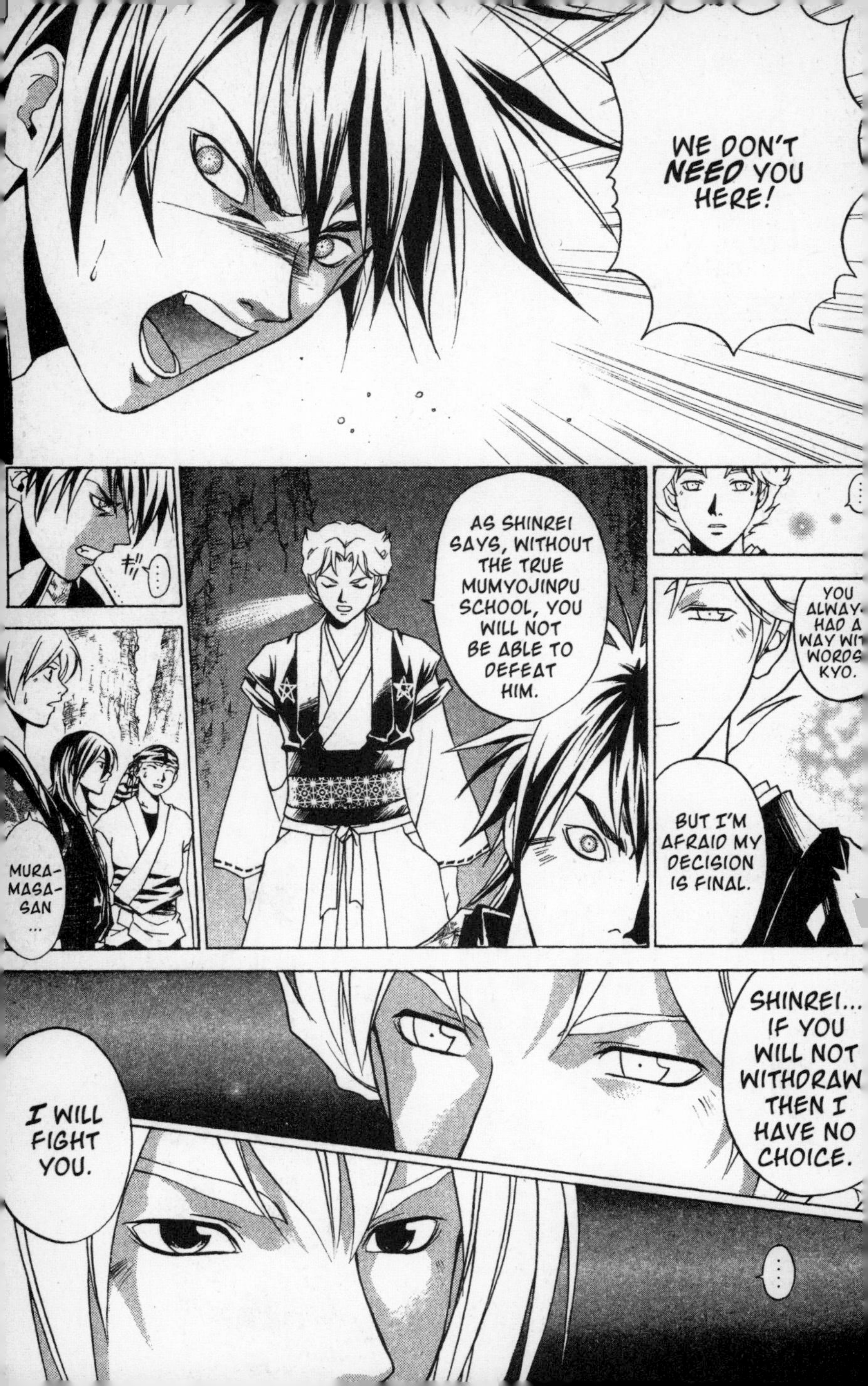
WE DON'T NEED YOU HERE!
…
YOU ALWAY HAD A WAY WI WORDS KYO.
BUT I'M AFRAID MY DECISION IS FINAL.
AS SHINREI SAYS, WITHOUT THE TRUE MUMYOJINPU SCHOOL, YOU WILL NOT BE ABLE TO DEFEAT HIM.
…
MURA-MASA-SAN …
SHINREI… IF YOU WILL NOT WITHDRAW THEN I HAVE NO CHOICE.
I WILL FIGHT YOU.
…

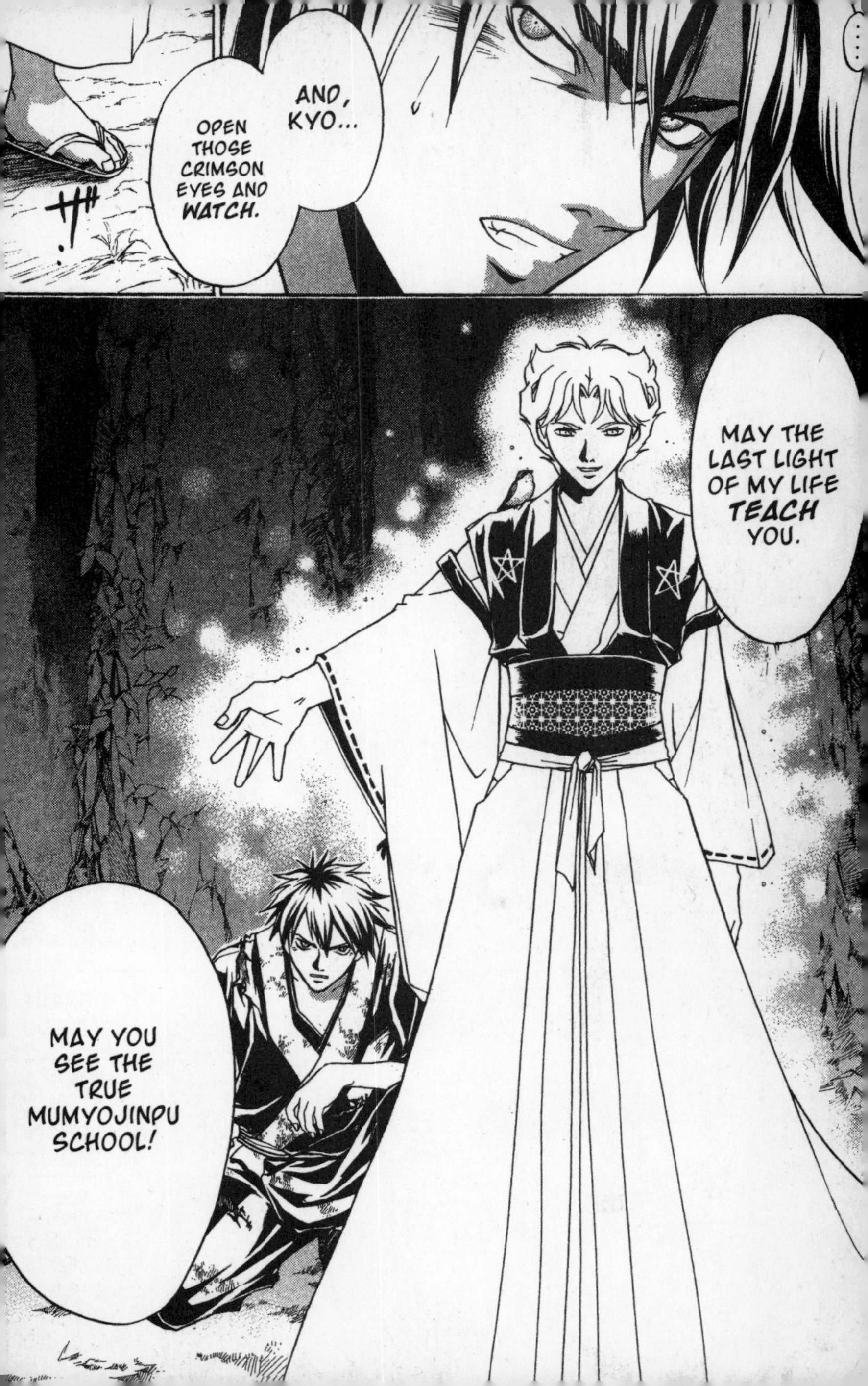
AND, KYO...
OPEN THOSE CRIMSON EYES AND WATCH.
MAY THE LAST LIGHT OF MY LIFE TEACH YOU.
MAY YOU SEE THE TRUE MUMYOJINPU SCHOOL!

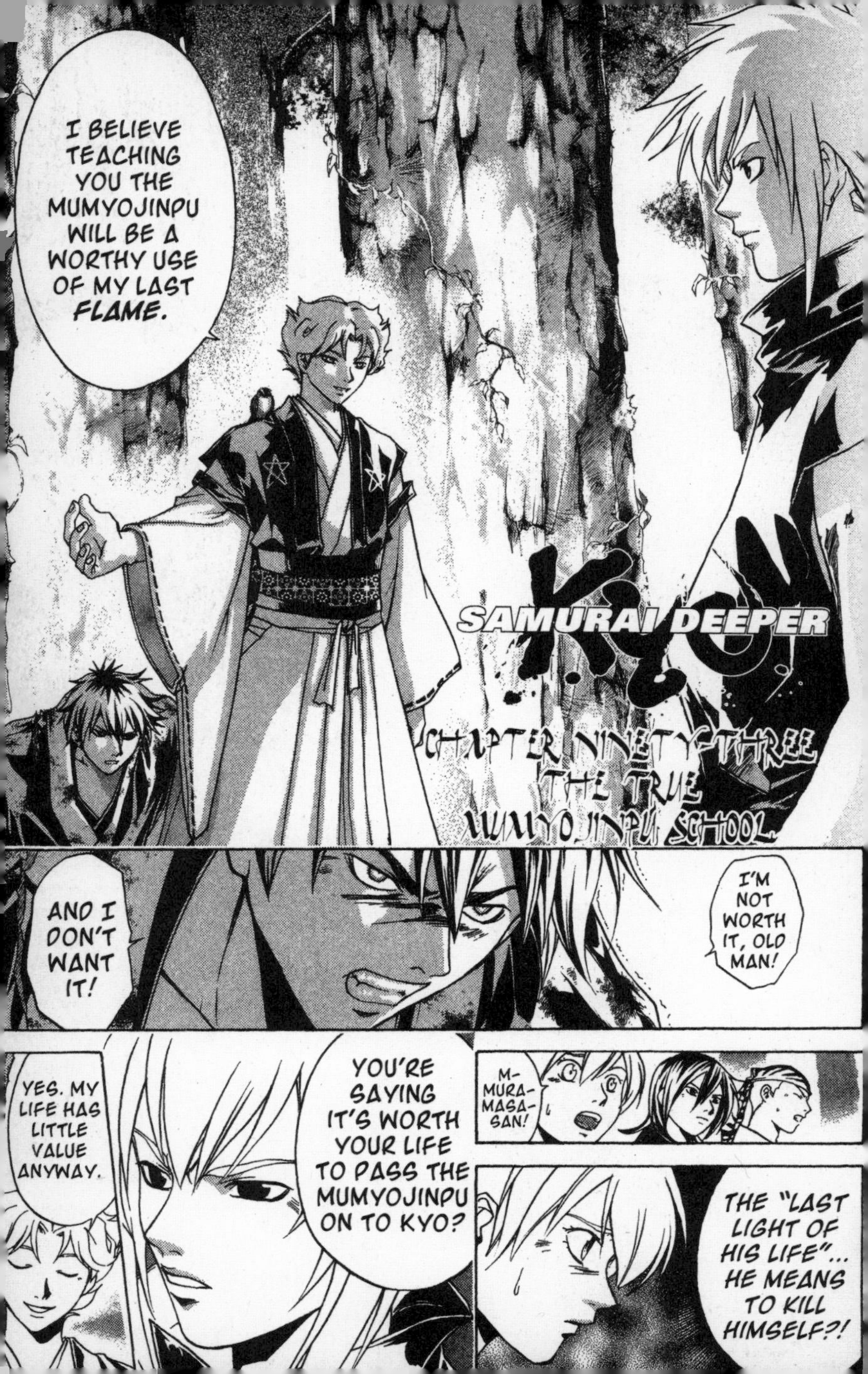
I BELIEVE TEACHING YOU THE MUMYOJINPU WILL BE A WORTHY USE OF MY LAST FLAME.
SAMURAI DEEPER KYO
CHAPTER NINETY-THREE THE TRUE MUMYOJINPU SCHOOL
I'M NOT WORTH IT, OLD MAN!
AND I DON'T WANT IT!
M-MURA-MASA-SAN!
THE "LAST LIGHT OF HIS LIFE"... HE MEANS TO KILL HIMSELF?!
YOU'RE SAYING IT'S WORTH YOUR LIFE TO PASS THE MUMYOJINPU ON TO KYO?
YES. MY LIFE HAS LITTLE VALUE ANYWAY.

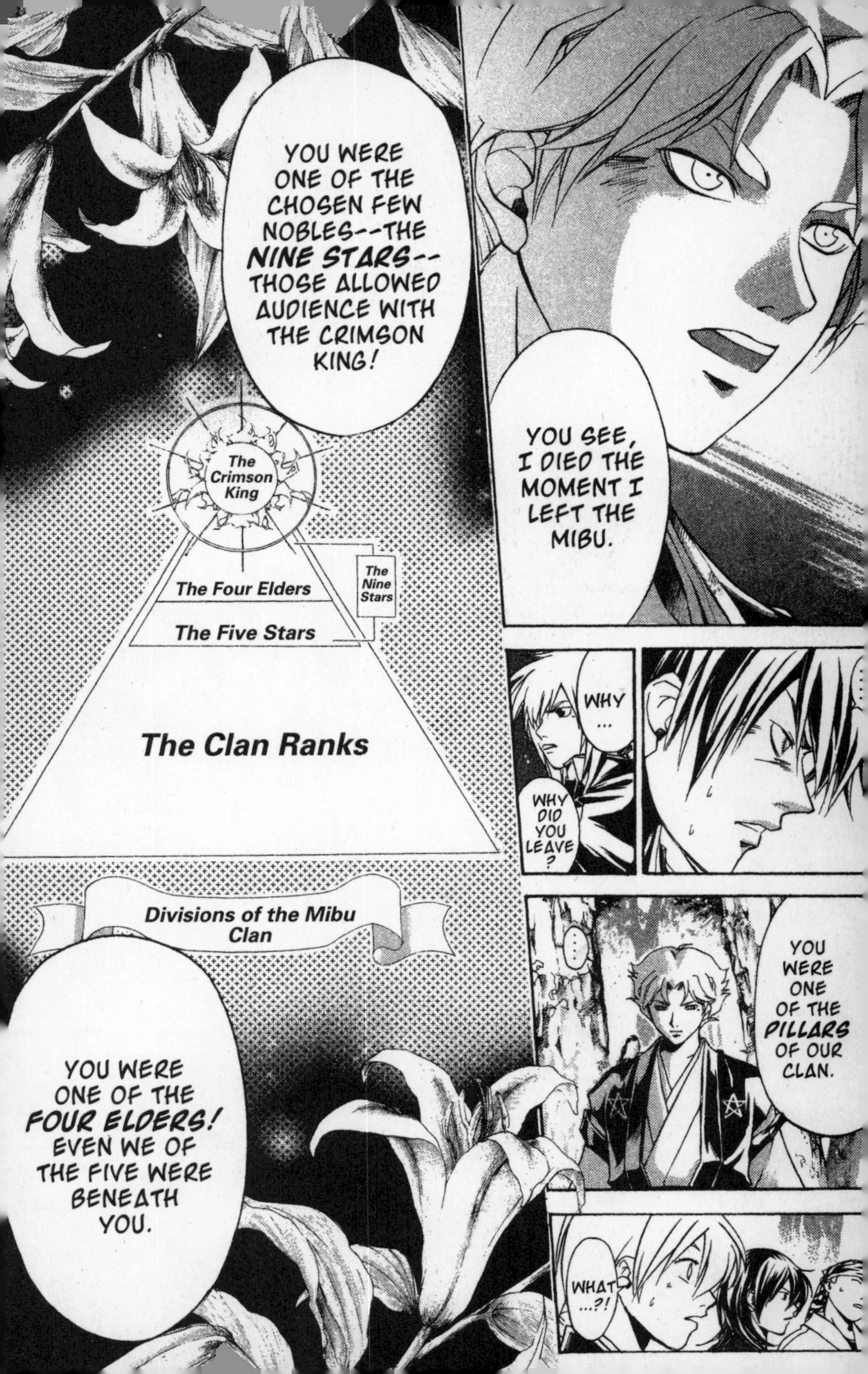
YOU SEE, I DIED THE MOMENT I LEFT THE MIBU.
...
WHY ...
WHY DID YOU LEAVE?
YOU WERE ONE OF THE PILLARS OF OUR CLAN.
...
WHAT ...?!
YOU WERE ONE OF THE CHOSEN FEW NOBLES--THE NINE STARS--THOSE ALLOWED AUDIENCE WITH THE CRIMSON KING!
The Crimson King
The Nine Stars
The Four Elders
The Five Stars
The Clan Ranks
Divisions of the Mibu Clan
YOU WERE ONE OF THE FOUR ELDERS! EVEN WE OF THE FIVE WERE BENEATH YOU.

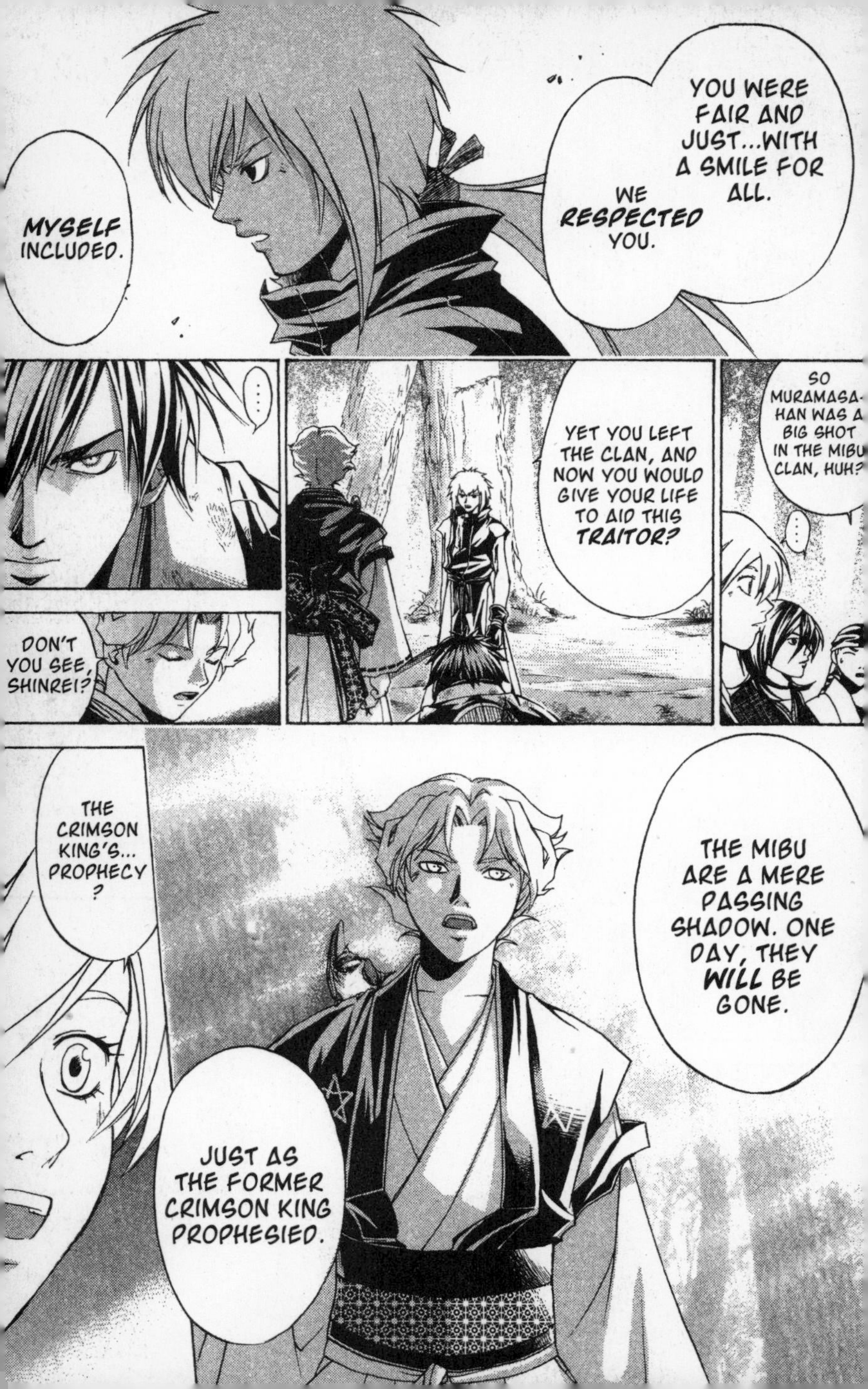
YOU WERE FAIR AND JUST...WITH A SMILE FOR ALL.
WE RESPECTED YOU.
MYSELF INCLUDED.
SO MURAMASA-HAN WAS A BIG SHOT IN THE MIBU CLAN, HUH?
....
YET YOU LEFT THE CLAN, AND NOW YOU WOULD GIVE YOUR LIFE TO AID THIS TRAITOR?
....
DON'T YOU SEE, SHINREI?
THE MIBU ARE A MERE PASSING SHADOW. ONE DAY, THEY WILL BE GONE.
JUST AS THE FORMER CRIMSON KING PROPHESIED.
THE CRIMSON KING'S... PROPHECY?

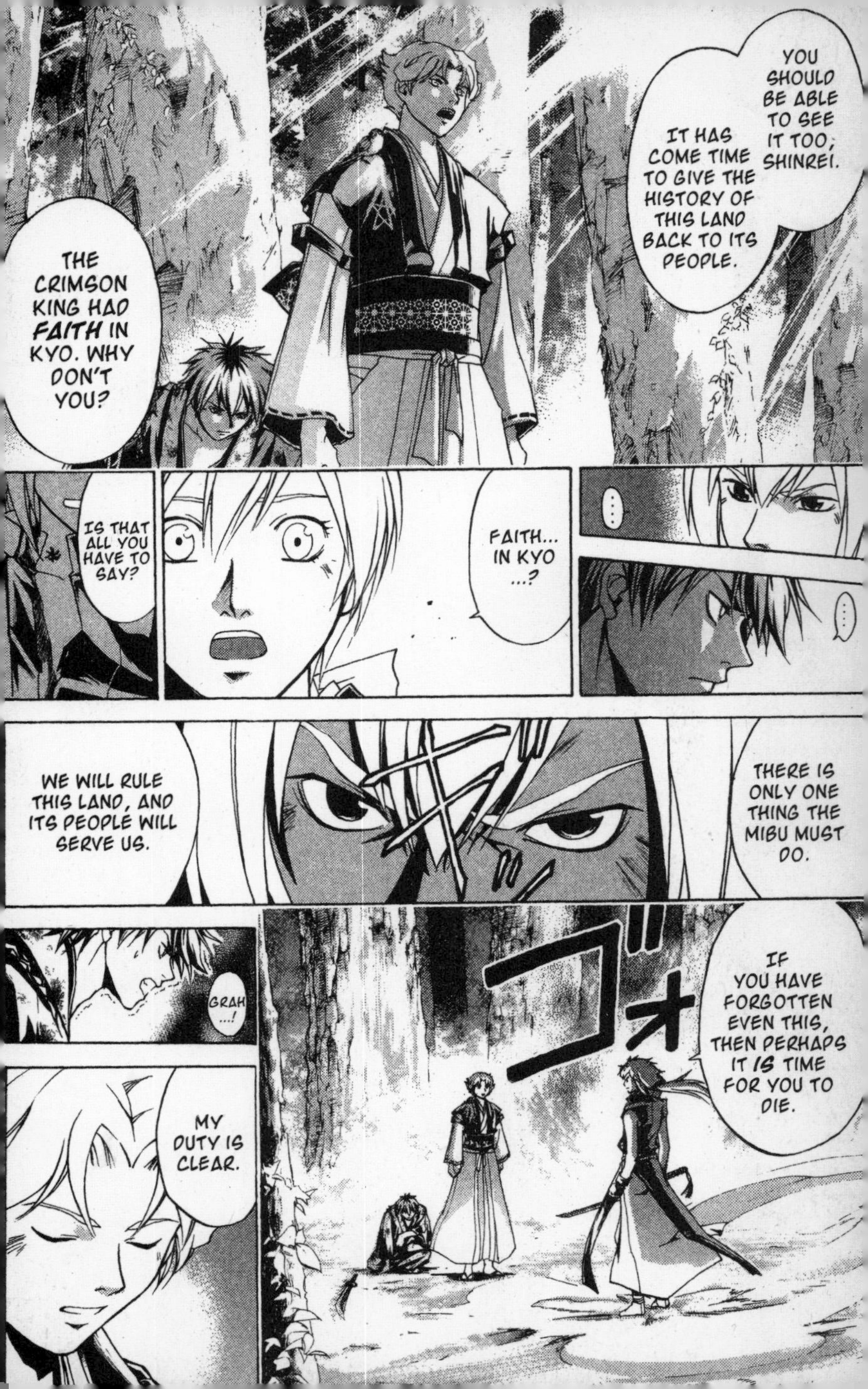
YOU SHOULD BE ABLE TO SEE IT TOO, SHINREI.
IT HAS COME TIME TO GIVE THE HISTORY OF THIS LAND BACK TO ITS PEOPLE.
THE CRIMSON KING HAD *FAITH* IN KYO. WHY DON'T YOU?
...
...
FAITH... IN KYO ...?
IS THAT ALL YOU HAVE TO SAY?
THERE IS ONLY ONE THING THE MIBU MUST DO.
WE WILL RULE THIS LAND, AND ITS PEOPLE WILL SERVE US.
ゴオ
IF YOU HAVE FORGOTTEN EVEN THIS, THEN PERHAPS IT *IS* TIME FOR YOU TO DIE.
GRAH ...!
MY DUTY IS CLEAR.

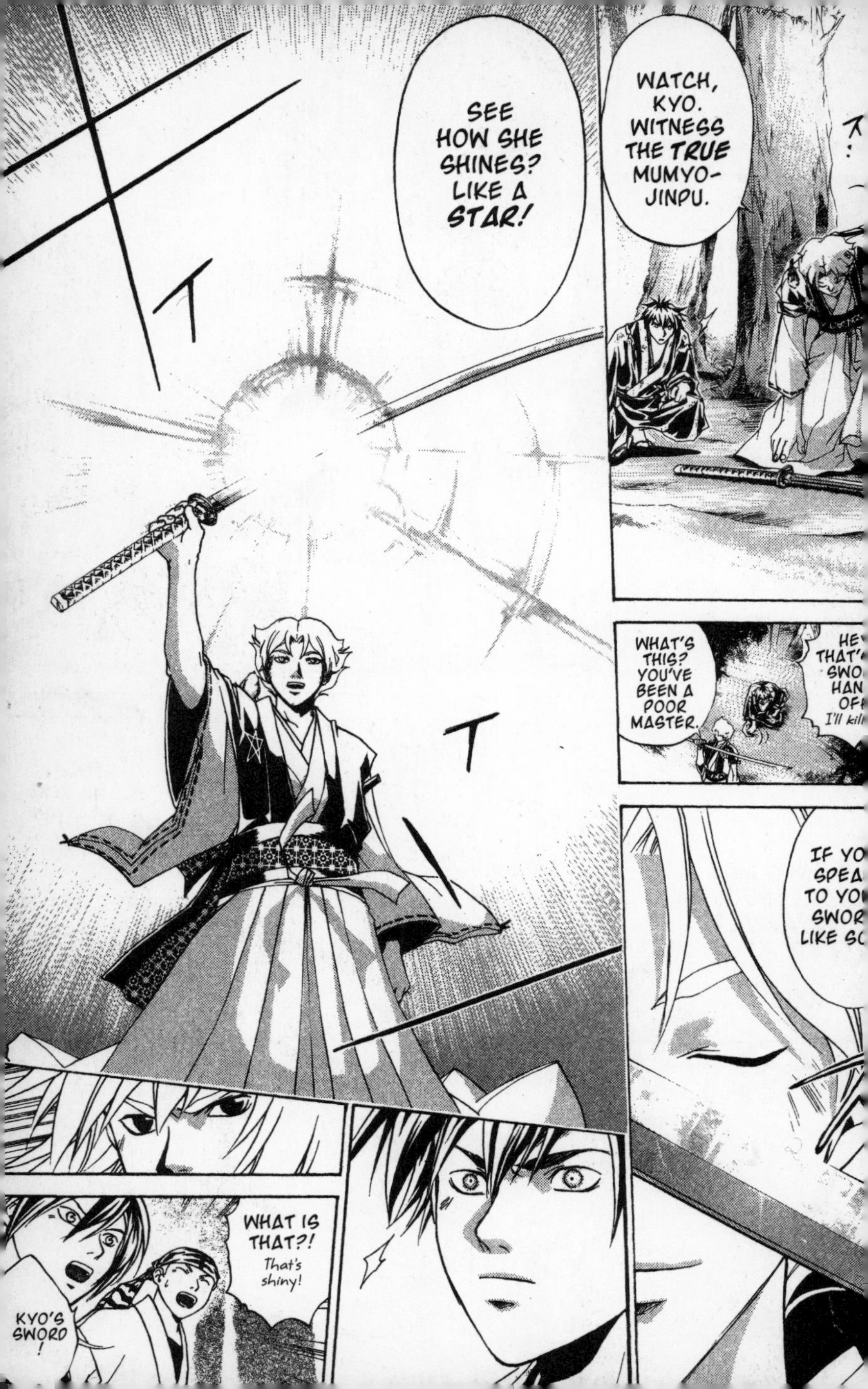

WATCH, KYO. WITNESS THE **TRUE** MUMYO-JINPU.
ス…
WHAT'S THIS? YOU'VE BEEN A POOR MASTER.
HE THAT' SWO HAN OF
I'll kil
IF YO SPEA TO YO SWOR LIKE S
SEE HOW SHE SHINES? LIKE A **STAR!**
WHAT IS THAT?!
That's shiny!
KYO'S SWORD!

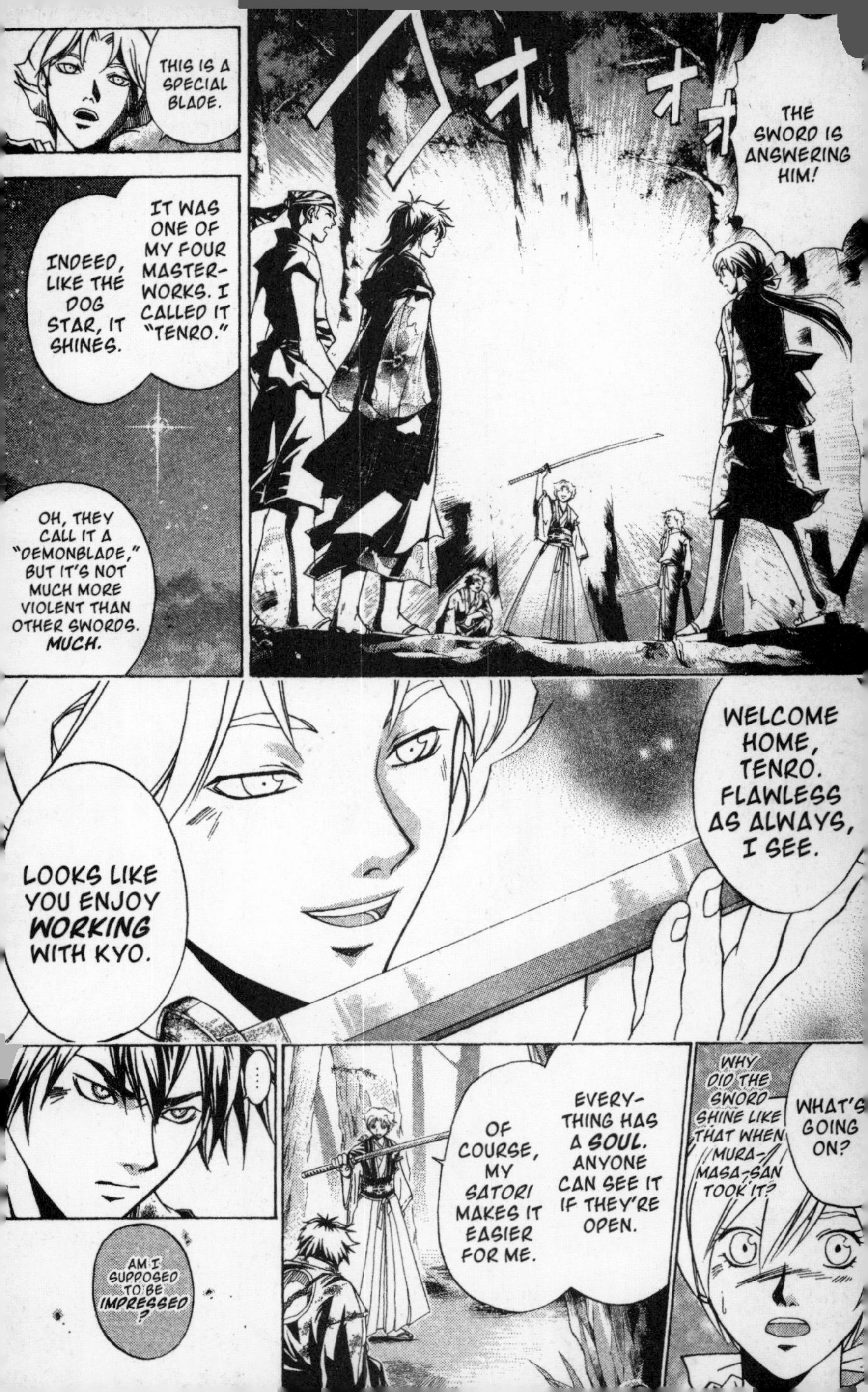
クオオオ
THE SWORD IS ANSWERING HIM!
THIS IS A SPECIAL BLADE.
IT WAS ONE OF MY FOUR MASTER-WORKS. I CALLED IT "TENRO."
INDEED, LIKE THE DOG STAR, IT SHINES.
OH, THEY CALL IT A "DEMONBLADE," BUT IT'S NOT MUCH MORE VIOLENT THAN OTHER SWORDS. *MUCH.*
WELCOME HOME, TENRO. FLAWLESS AS ALWAYS, I SEE.
LOOKS LIKE YOU ENJOY *WORKING* WITH KYO.
WHAT'S GOING ON?
WHY DID THE SWORD SHINE LIKE THAT WHEN MURA-MASA-SAN TOOK IT?
EVERY-THING HAS A **SOUL.** ANYONE CAN SEE IT IF THEY'RE OPEN.
OF COURSE, MY SATORI MAKES IT EASIER FOR ME.
...
AM I SUPPOSED TO BE *IMPRESSED*?

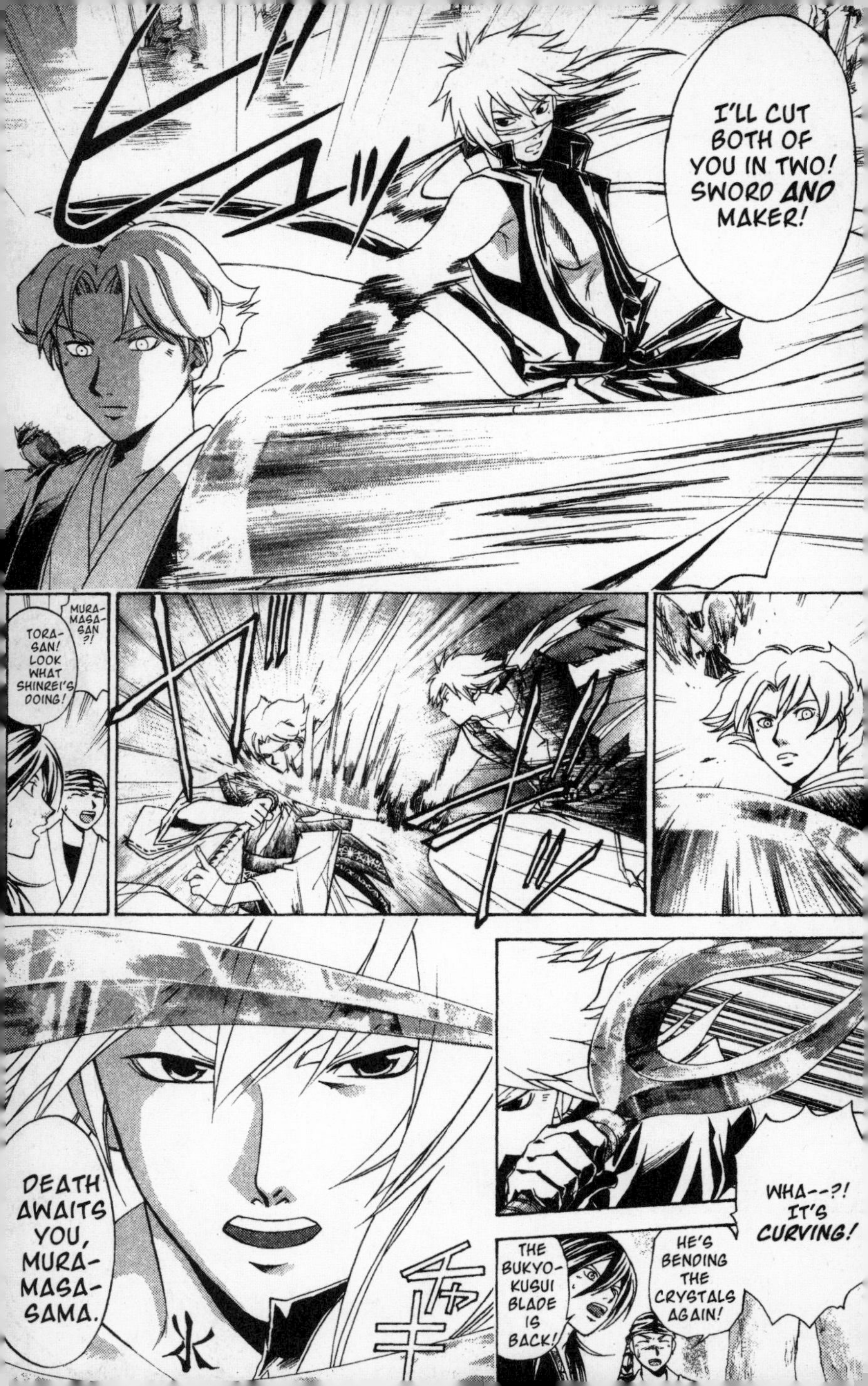
I'LL CUT BOTH OF YOU IN TWO! SWORD **AND** MAKER!
MURA-MASA-SAN?!
TORA-SAN! LOOK WHAT SHINREI'S DOING!
WHA--?! IT'S **CURVING!**
HE'S BENDING THE CRYSTALS AGAIN!
THE BUKYO-KUSUI BLADE IS BACK!
DEATH AWAITS YOU, MURA-MASA-SAMA.

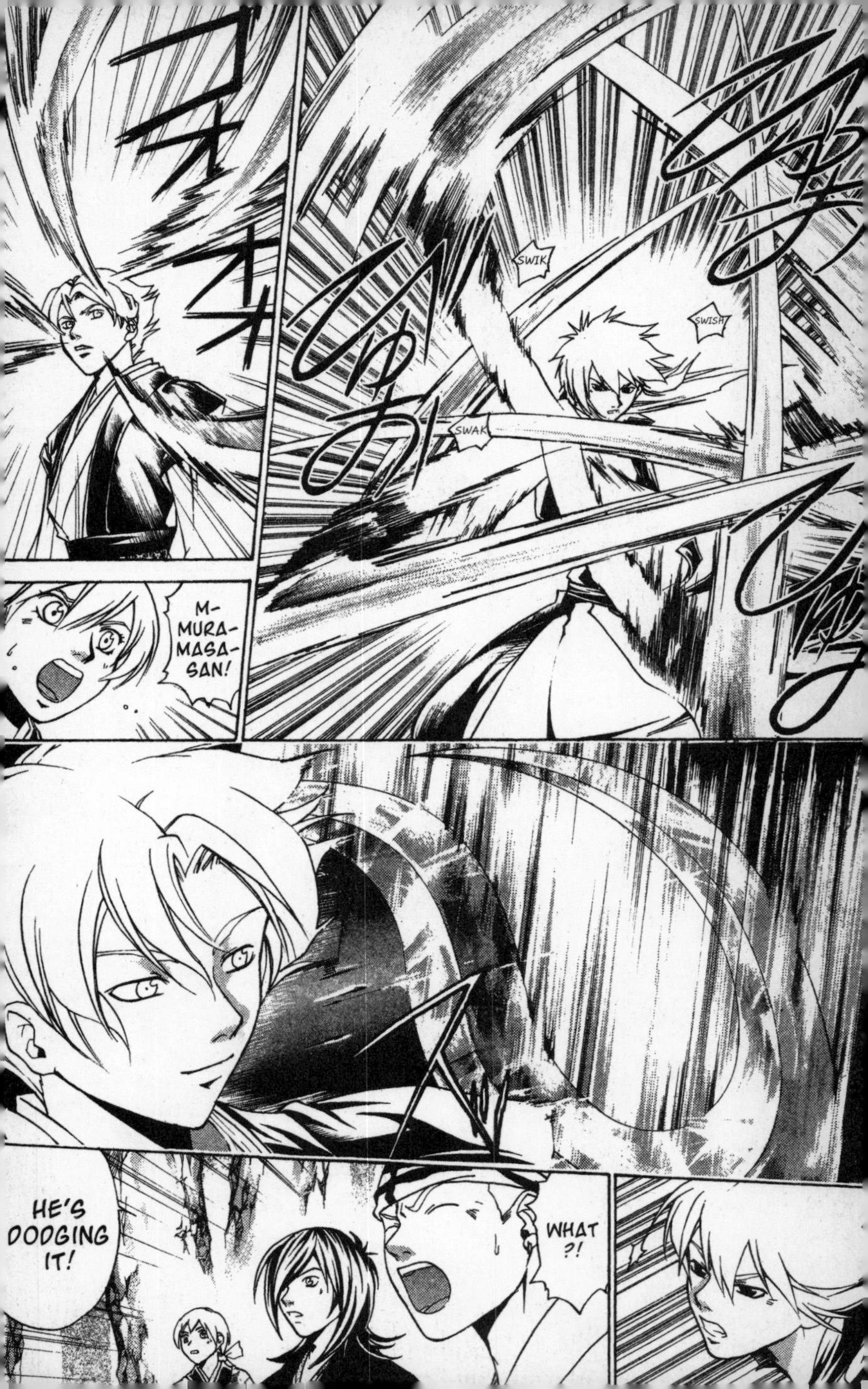
SWIK
SWISH
SWAK
M-MURA-MASA-SAN!
WHAT?!
HE'S DODGING IT!

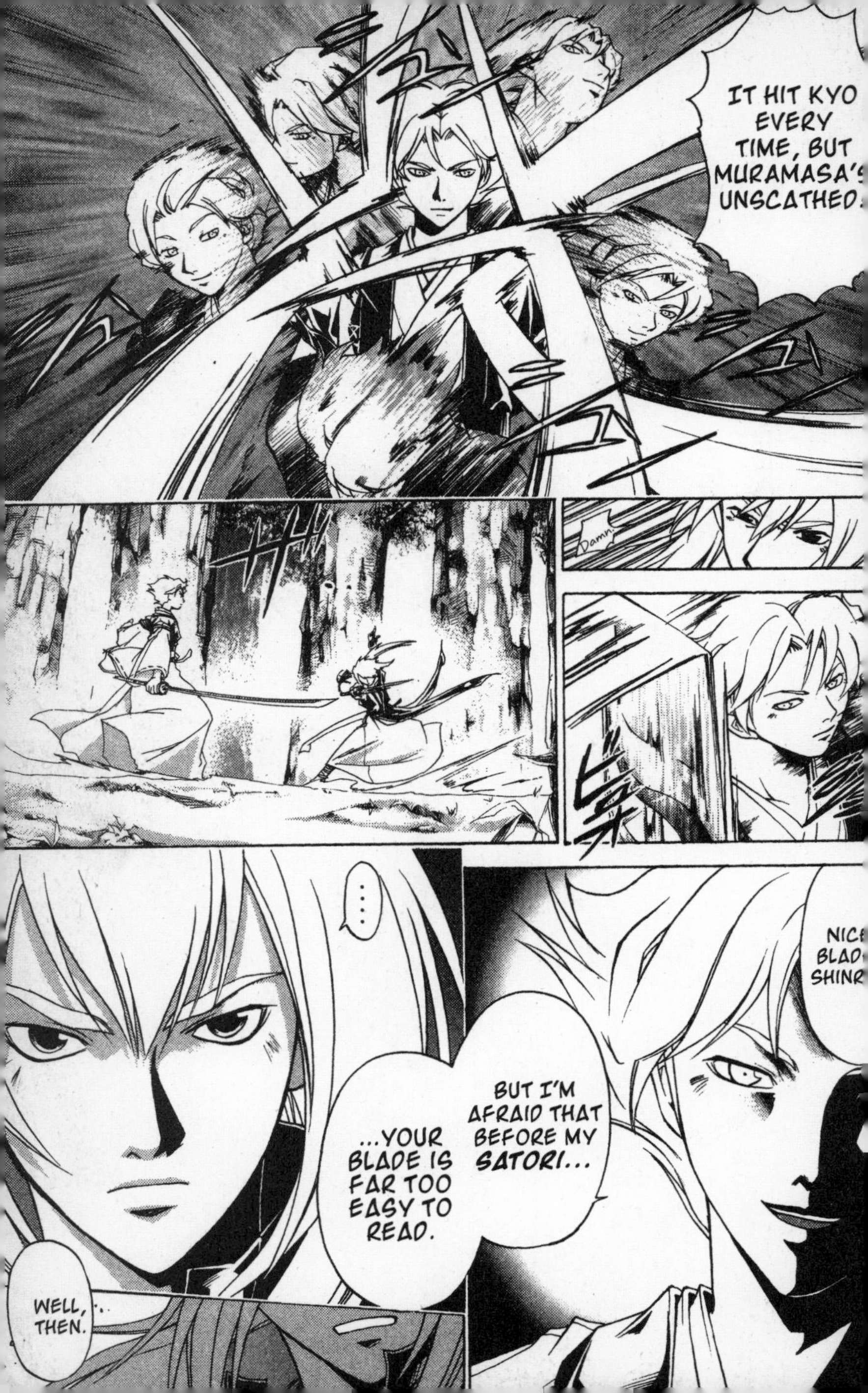
IT HIT KYO EVERY TIME, BUT MURAMASA'S UNSCATHED.
Damn.
NIC BLAD SHINR
BUT I'M AFRAID THAT BEFORE MY SATORI...
...YOUR BLADE IS FAR TOO EASY TO READ.
.....
WELL, THEN.

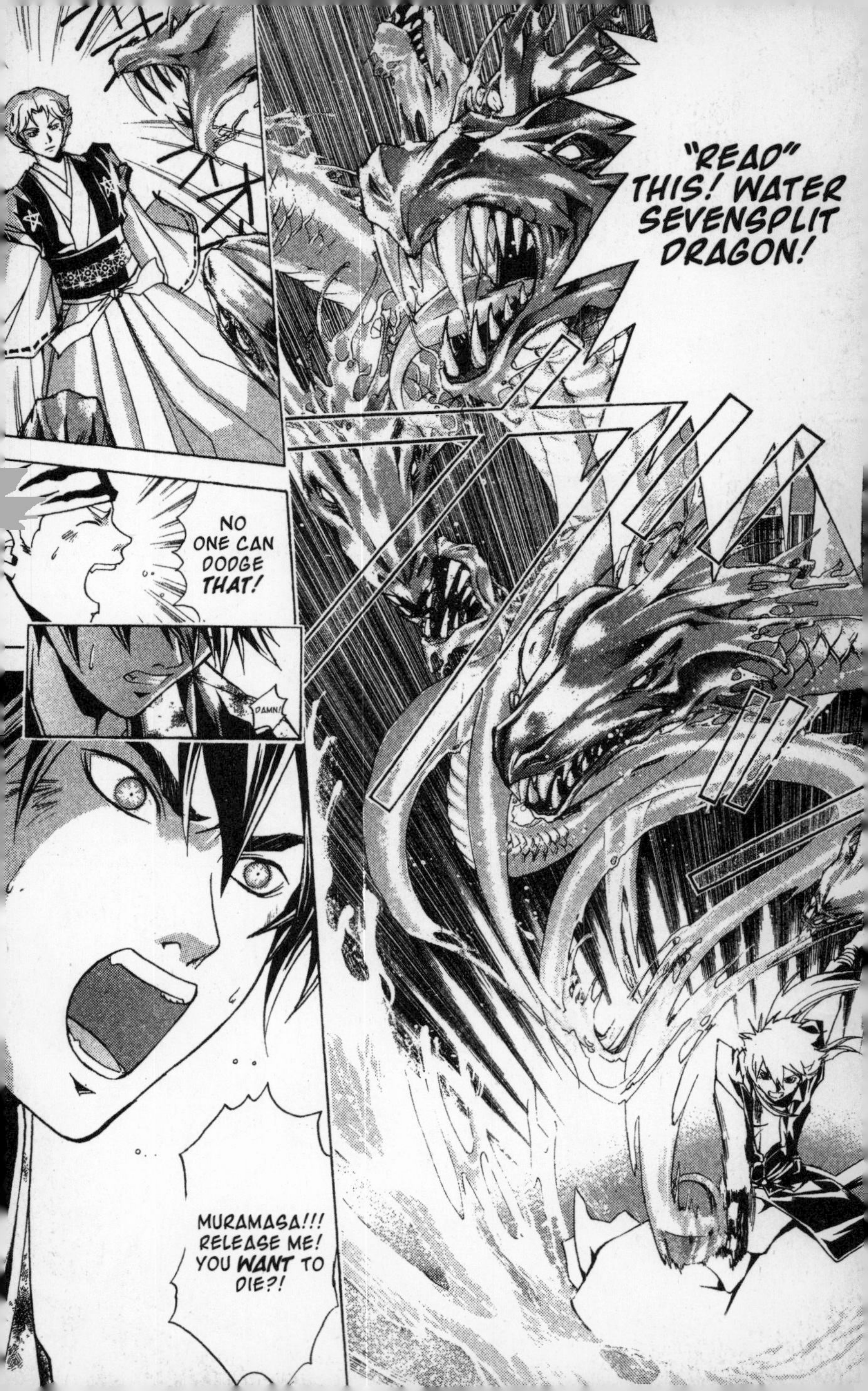
"READ" THIS! WATER SEVENSPLIT DRAGON!
NO ONE CAN DODGE THAT!
DAMN!
MURAMASA!!! RELEASE ME! YOU WANT TO DIE?!

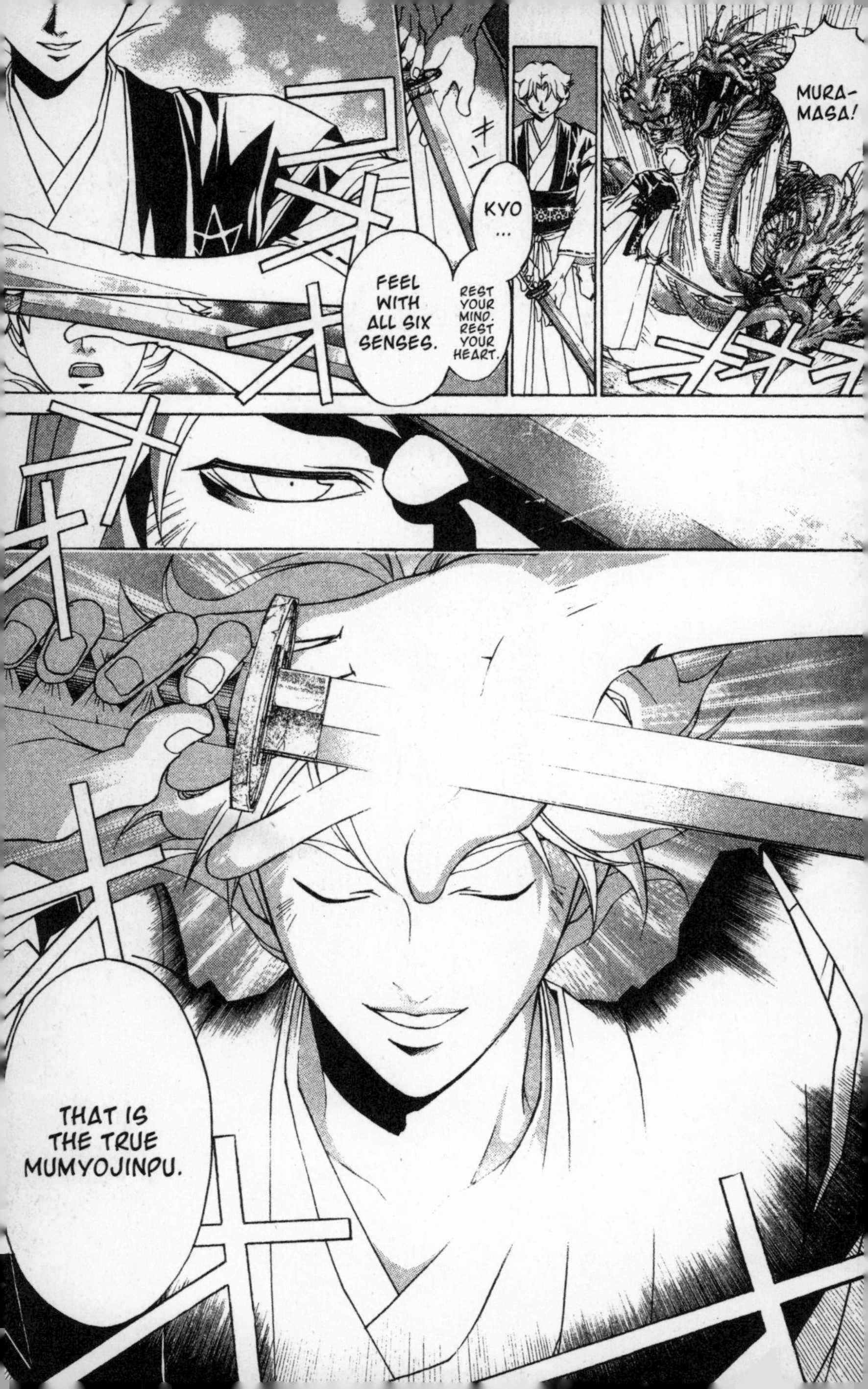
MURA-MASA!
KYO ...
REST YOUR MIND. REST YOUR HEART.
FEEL WITH ALL SIX SENSES.
THAT IS THE TRUE MUMYOJINPU.

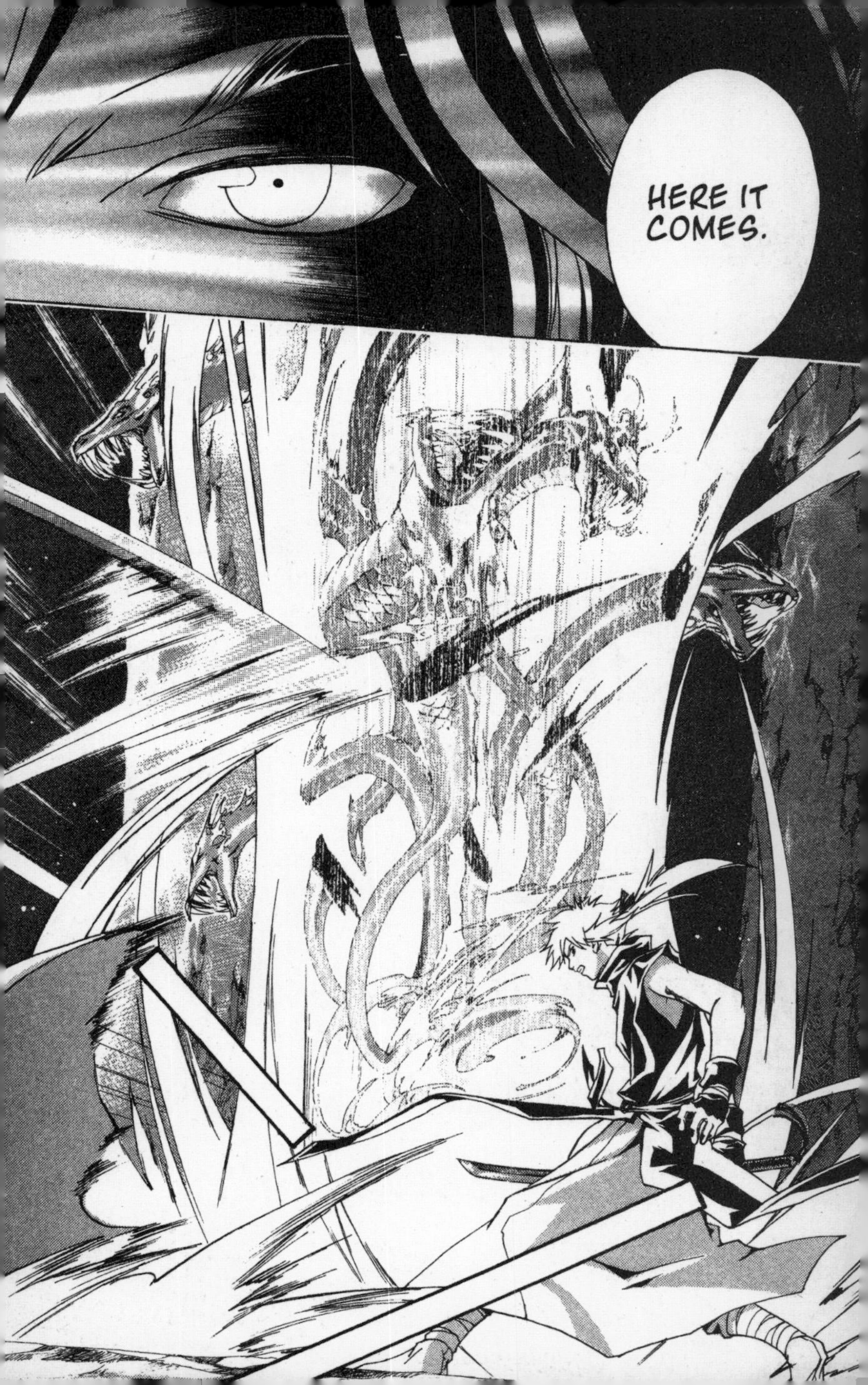
HERE IT COMES.

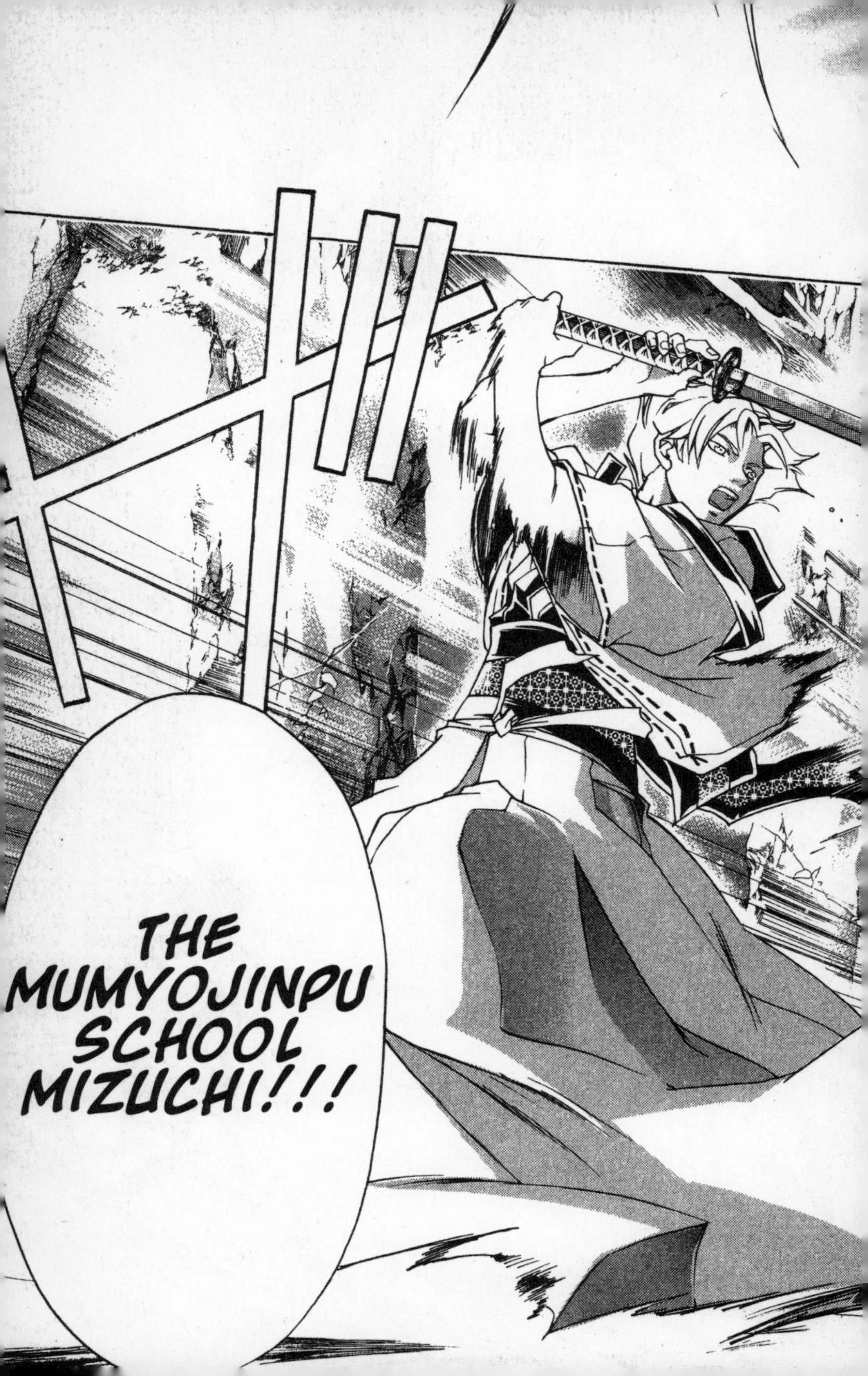
THE MUMYOJINPU SCHOOL MIZUCHI!!!

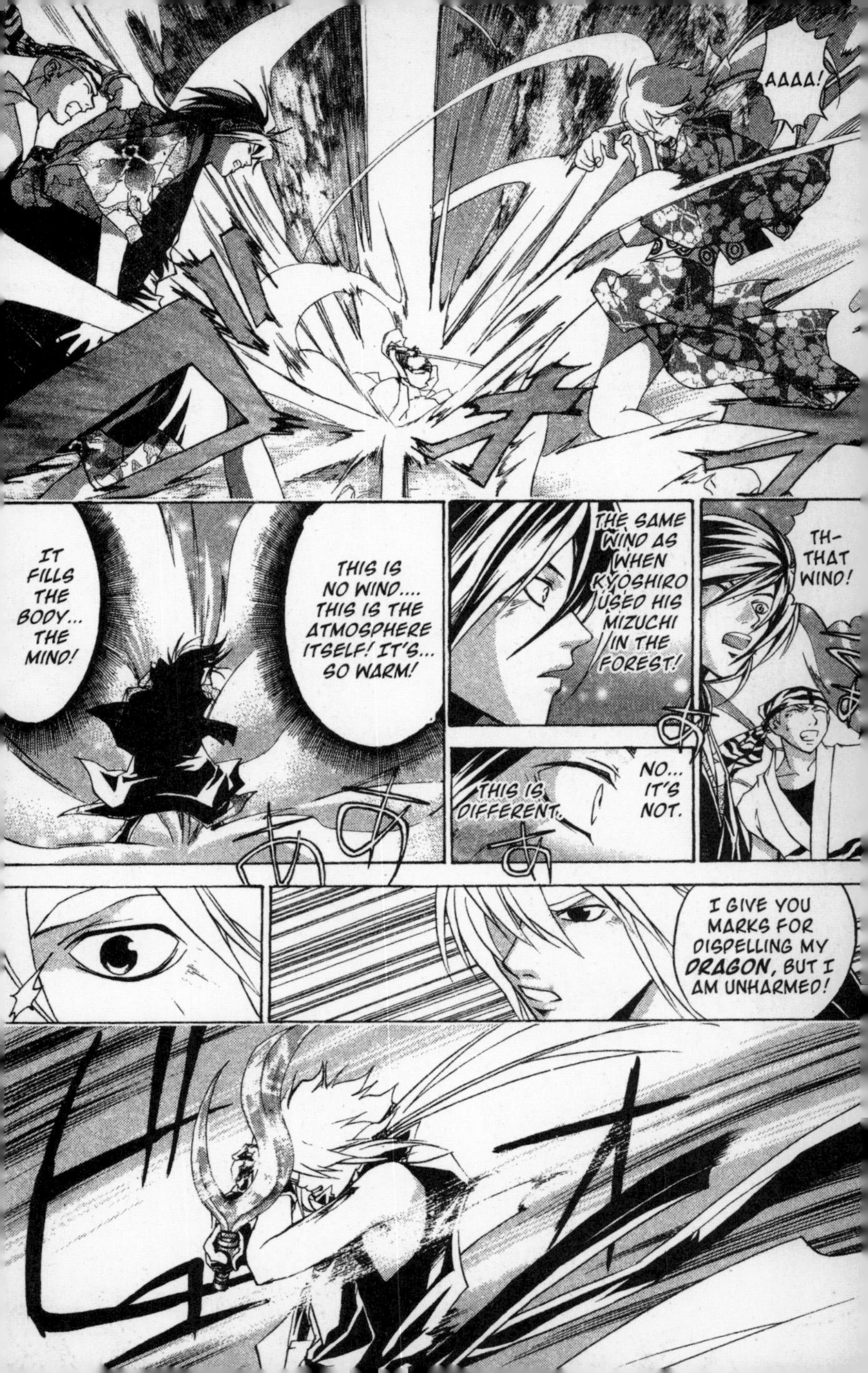
AAAA!
TH-THAT WIND!
THE SAME WIND AS WHEN KYOSHIRO USED HIS MIZUCHI IN THE FOREST!
NO... IT'S NOT.
THIS IS DIFFERENT.
THIS IS NO WIND.... THIS IS THE ATMOSPHERE ITSELF! IT'S... SO WARM!
IT FILLS THE BODY... THE MIND!
I GIVE YOU MARKS FOR DISPELLING MY DRAGON, BUT I AM UNHARMED!

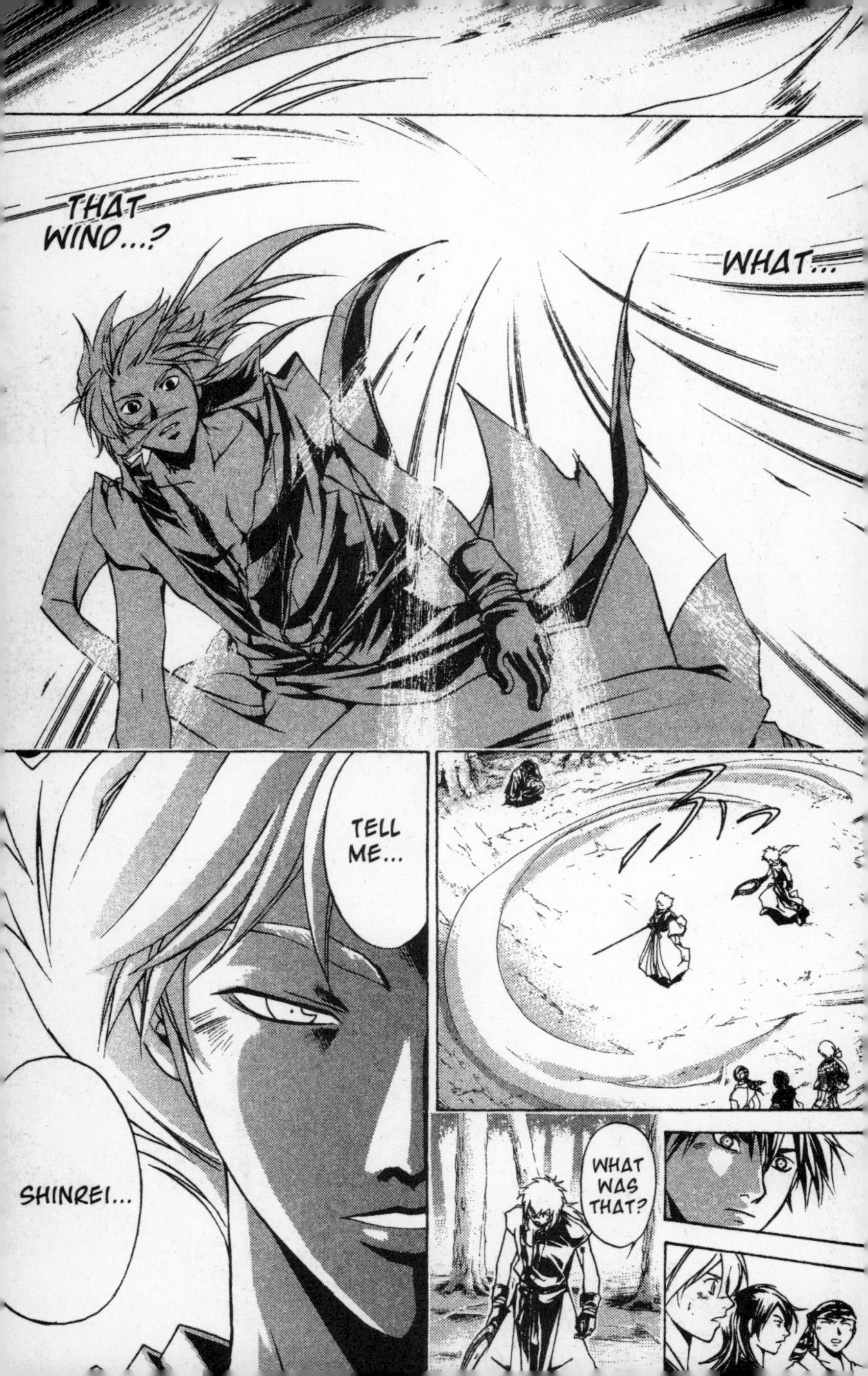
WHAT...
THAT WIND...?
WHAT WAS THAT?
TELL ME...
SHINREI...

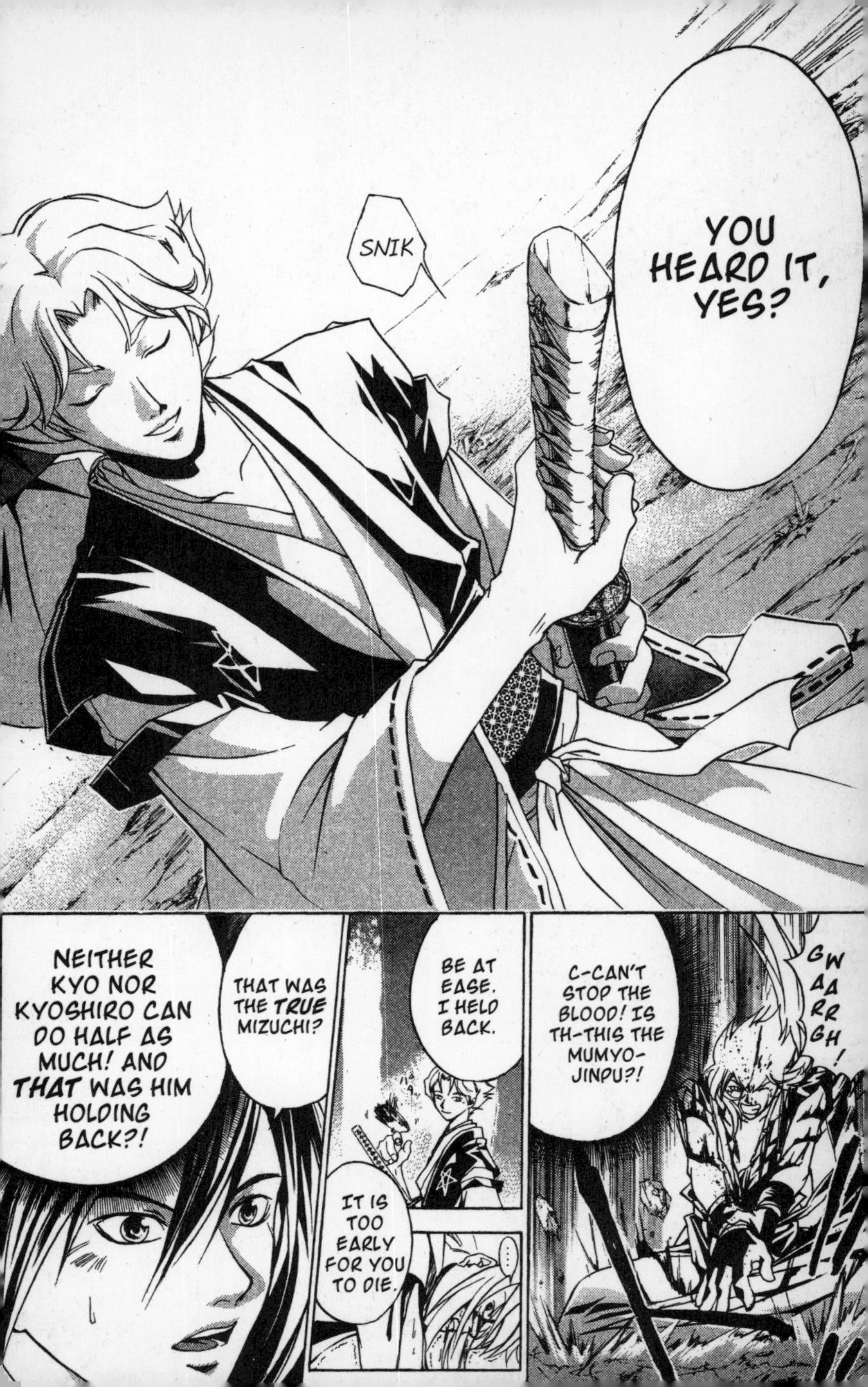
YOU HEARD IT, YES?
SNIK
GWAARRGH!
C-CAN'T STOP THE BLOOD! IS TH-THIS THE MUMYO-JINPU?!
BE AT EASE. I HELD BACK.
IT IS TOO EARLY FOR YOU TO DIE.
...
THAT WAS THE TRUE MIZUCHI?
NEITHER KYO NOR KYOSHIRO CAN DO HALF AS MUCH! AND THAT WAS HIM HOLDING BACK?!

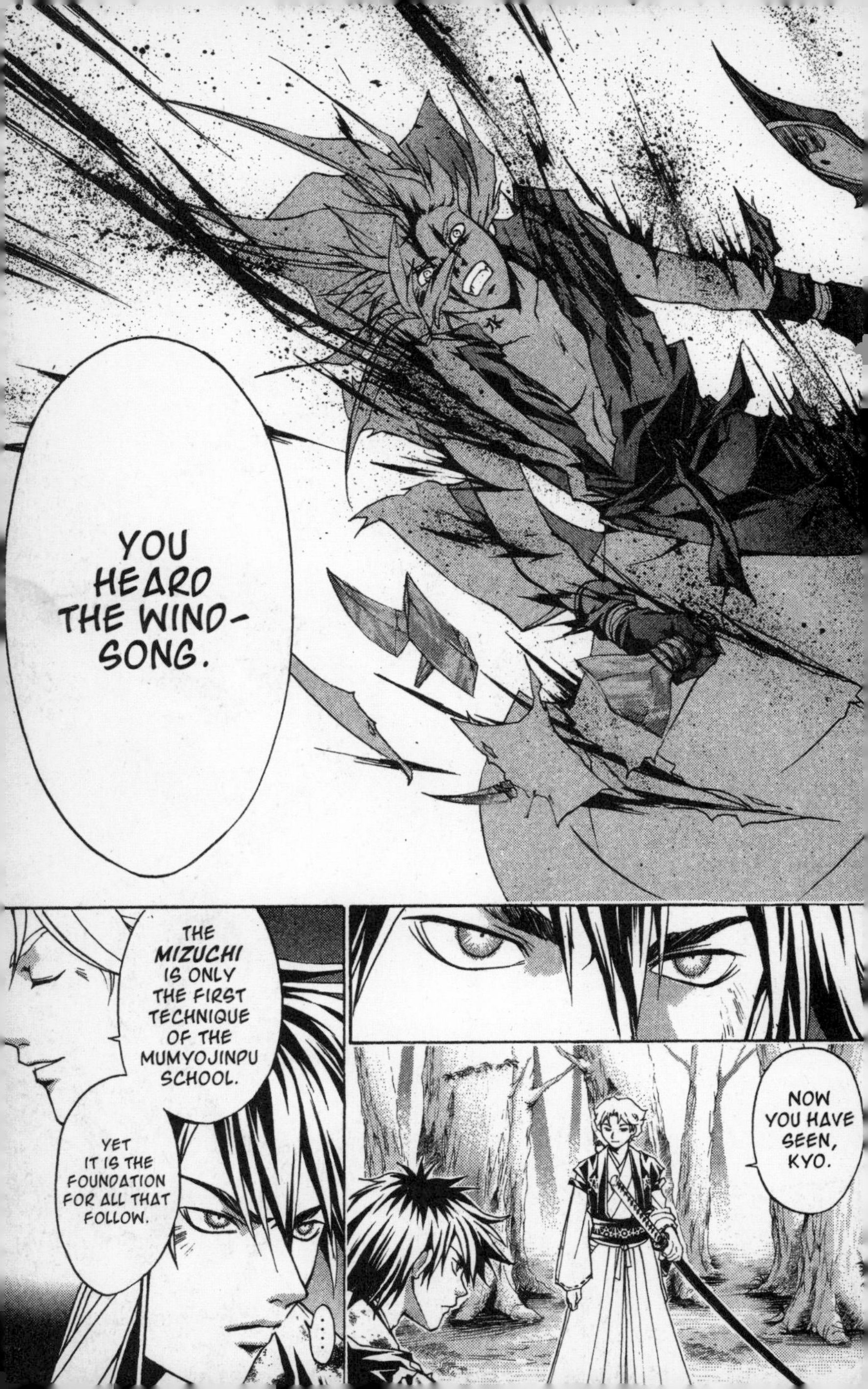
YOU HEARD THE WIND-SONG.
NOW YOU HAVE SEEN, KYO.
THE *MIZUCHI* IS ONLY THE FIRST TECHNIQUE OF THE MUMYOJINPU SCHOOL.
YET IT IS THE FOUNDATION FOR ALL THAT FOLLOW.
....

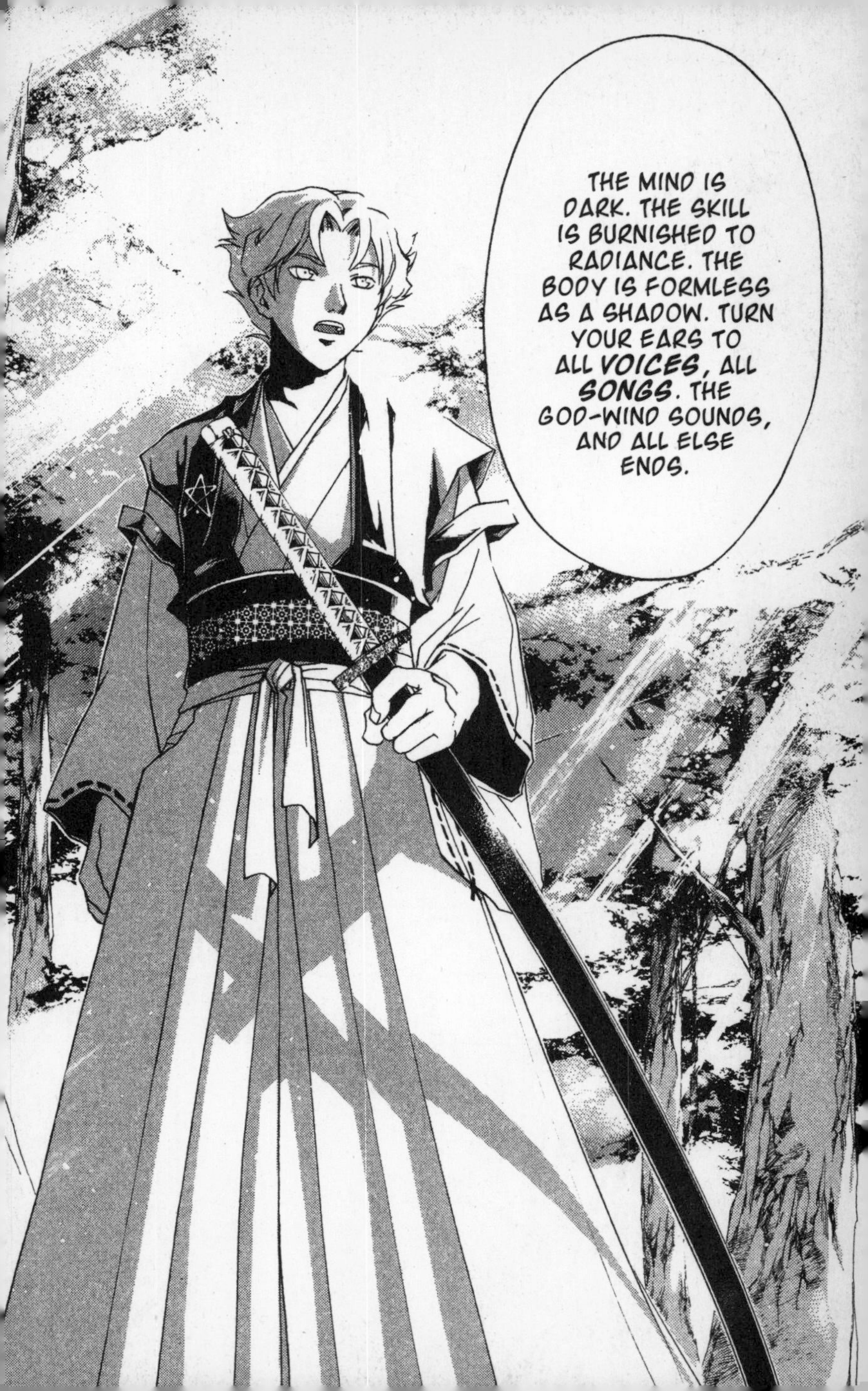
THE MIND IS DARK. THE SKILL IS BURNISHED TO RADIANCE. THE BODY IS FORMLESS AS A SHADOW. TURN YOUR EARS TO ALL VOICES, ALL SONGS. THE GOD-WIND SOUNDS, AND ALL ELSE ENDS.

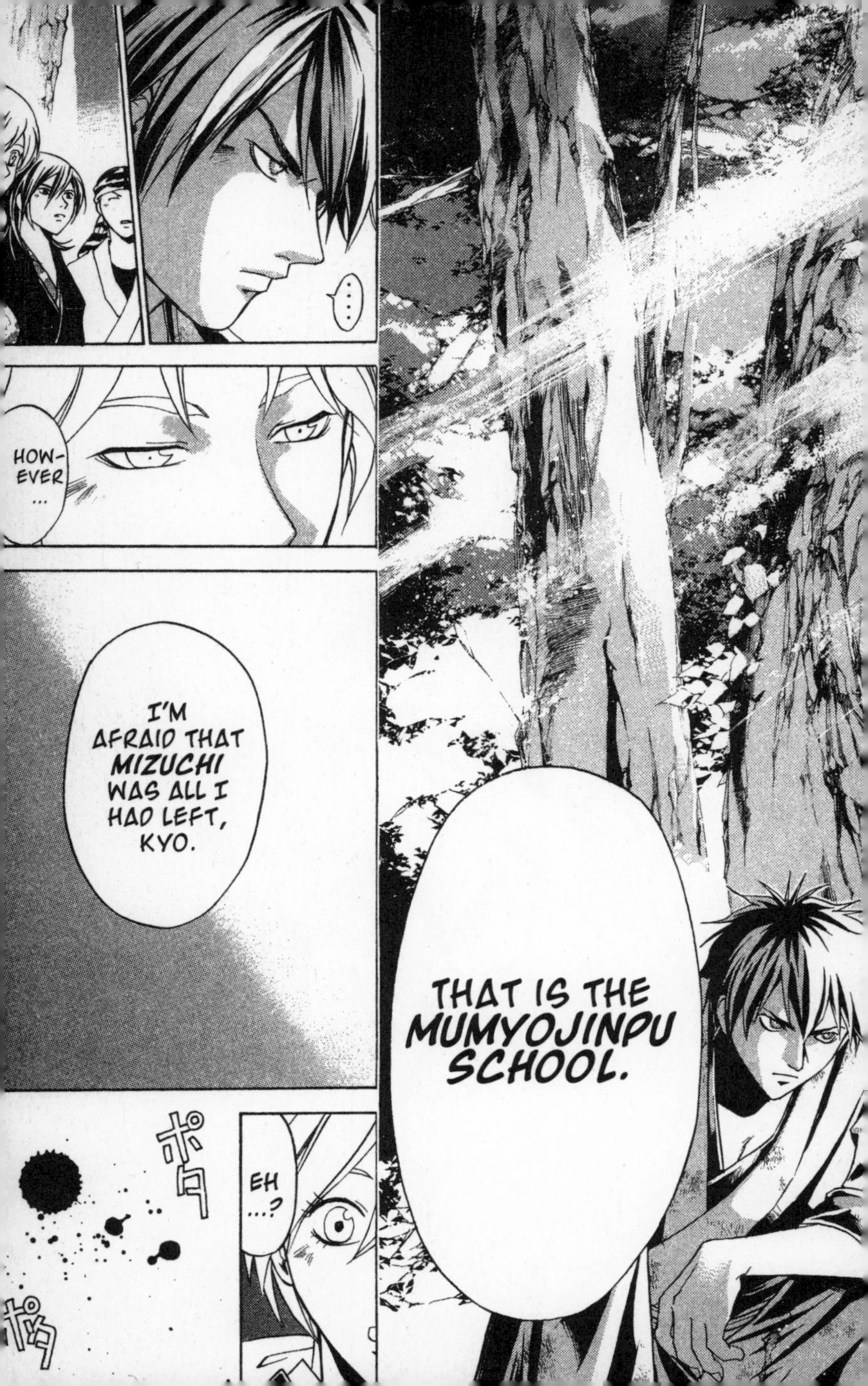
THAT IS THE MUMYOJINPU SCHOOL.
...
HOW-EVER ...
I'M AFRAID THAT MIZUCHI WAS ALL I HAD LEFT, KYO.
EH ...?
ポタ
ポタ

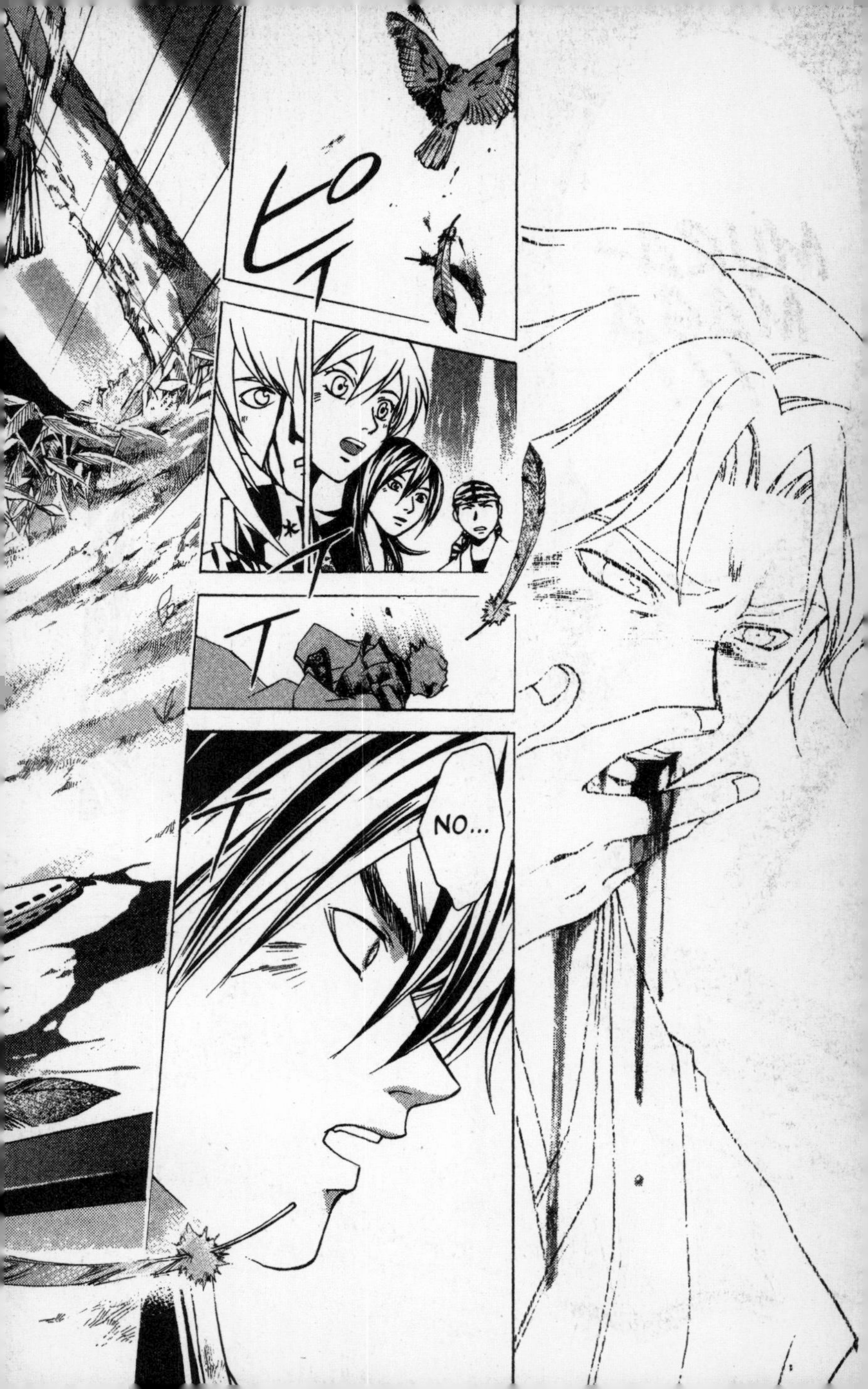
ピイ
NO...

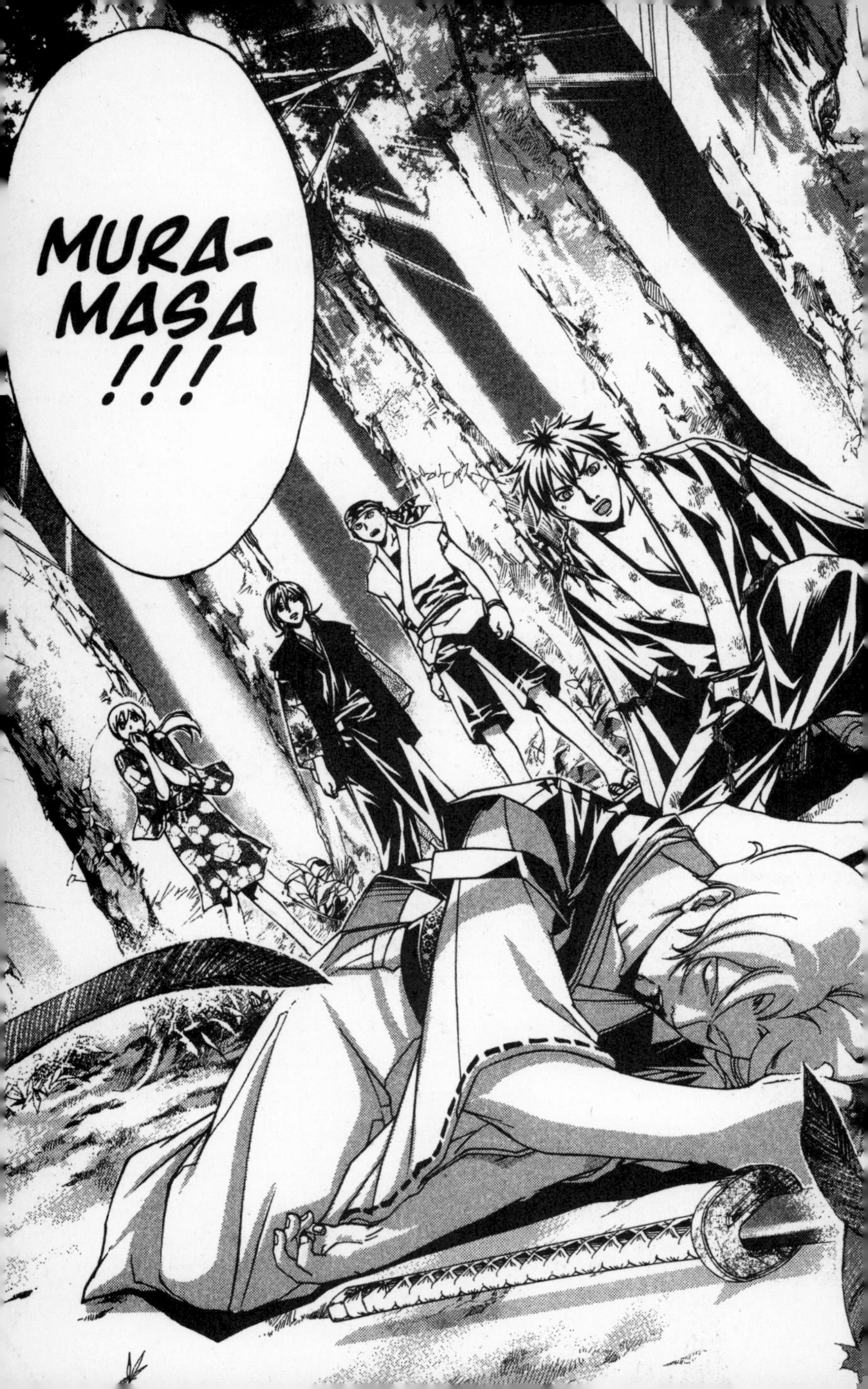
MURA-MASA !!!

THE CHARACTERS

ARE SOME CHARACTERS EASIER TO DO THAN OTHERS?
TORA, BON, AND SASUKE ARE ALL PRETTY EASY. KYO AND YUYA ARE HARD. GIRLS AND SILENT TYPES ARE TOUGH!

IS THAT A WAISTCLOTH AKIRA HAS AROUND HIS BELLY?
AKIRA'S KIMONO WAS THE HEIGHT OF FASHION IN ITS DAY. I TOOK THE SKIRTS DOWN A LITTLE SO HE WOULDN'T LOOK TOO FEMININE--THAT'S WHY HIS SASH LOOKS BIG. YEAH, I GUESS YOU COULD CALL IT A WAISTCLOTH.

HOW DID YUKIMURA GET TO THE FOREST IN VOL. 7?
HE WALKED.

ARE THOSE TWO HAIRS STICKING UP FROM OKUNI'S BANGS REALLY ANTENNAE?
IT'S A POWERFUL RADAR ARRAY FOR DETECTING STRONG MEN. (NOT)

IS YUYA-SAN'S PISTOL AN ORIGINAL DESIGN?
IT'S BASED ON A "THREE-SHOT REVOLVING MATCHLOCK" PISTOL, REDESIGNED FOR EASE OF USE. SINCE IT'S A MATCHLOCK, IT REALLY TAKES A WHILE TO FIRE, BUT I KIND OF SKIP THAT PART.

IS YUYA-SAN BENITORA'S FIRST LOVE?
TORA'S THE TYPE TO FALL PRETTY EASILY, BUT I THINK YUYA IS THE FIRST GIRL HE'S REALLY BEEN DETERMINED TO PROTECT AT ALL COSTS.

IS YUYA-SAN THE ONE WHO TAKES CARE OF KYO'S WOUNDS?
CHECK OUT THE SECOND FRAME ON PAGE 110, VOL. 10. THE ANSWER IS WHOEVER IS AVAILABLE.

DO THE CHARACTERS EVER, UM, RELIEVE THEMSELVES?
YES. THOUGH YUYA-SAN HAS BEEN CONSTIPATED OF LATE.

IS BASARA A GUY OR A GIRL?
HE'S A GUY. SPECIFICALLY, HE'S THE REBORN NOBUNAGA'S SERVANT. JUST THINK ABOUT HOW YUKIMURA KILLED HIM--HE WOULDN'T DO THAT TO A GIRL!

IN VOL. 10, DIDN'T YUKIMURA CALL ANAYAMA KOSUKE HIS "DEAR LITTLE KOSUKE"? WHAT'S UP WITH THAT?
SEE, YUKIMURA LOVES HIM LIKE A DAUGHTER! SAIZO IS LIKE THE YOUNGER BROTHER, AND SASUKE IS THE SON. ONE HAPPY FAMILY!

WHY IS KYO FICTIONAL, WHEN YUKIMURA AND IEYASU ARE BASED ON HISTORICAL FIGURES?
I THOUGHT A CHARACTER LIKE KYO FIT IN THE WARRING STATES PERIOD--BACK WHEN YOUR BELIEFS COULD MEAN LIFE OR DEATH. THEN I STARTED TO WONDER WHAT IT WOULD BE LIKE IF HE INTERACTED WITH REAL HISTORICAL FIGURES.... ONLY IN SDK CAN YOU ENJOY BOTH! I HOPE YOU ALL FIND A CHARACTER YOU LIKE!

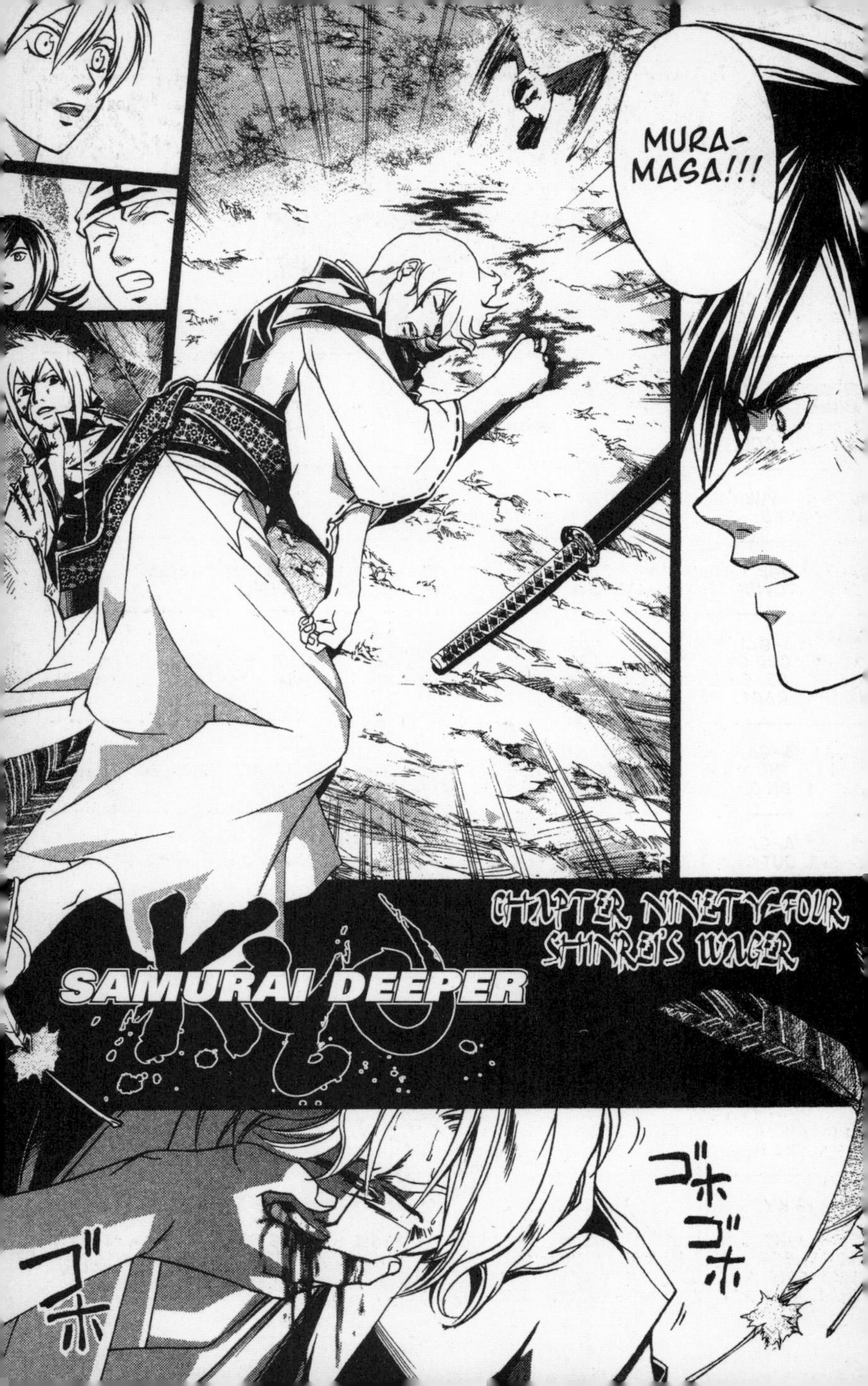
MURA-MASA!!!
CHAPTER NINETY-FOUR
SHINREI'S WAGER
SAMURAI DEEPER
ゴホゴホ
ゴホ

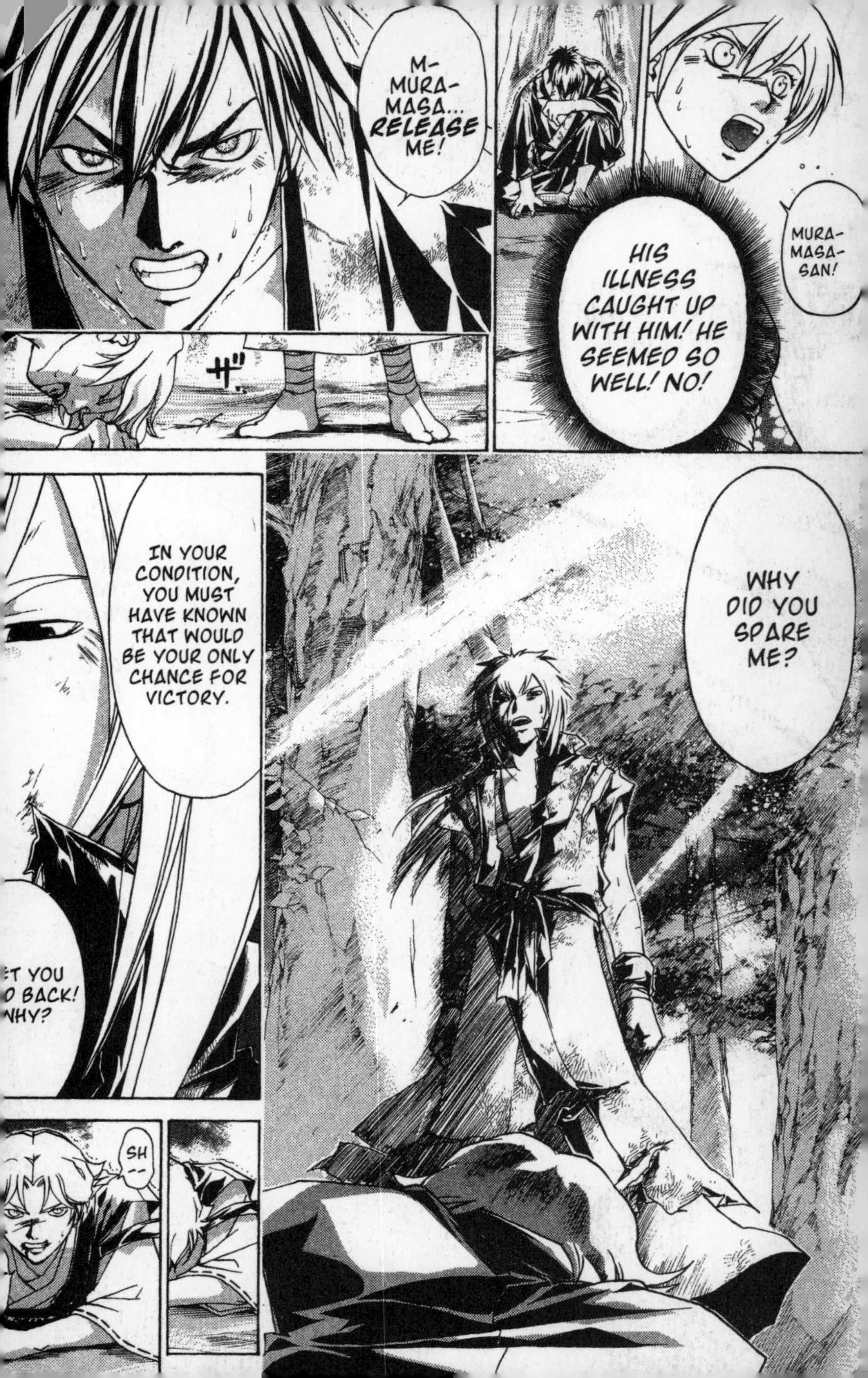
. .
MURA-MASA-SAN!
HIS ILLNESS CAUGHT UP WITH HIM! HE SEEMED SO WELL! NO!
M-MURA-MASA... RELEASE ME!
ザッ
WHY DID YOU SPARE ME?
IN YOUR CONDITION, YOU MUST HAVE KNOWN THAT WOULD BE YOUR ONLY CHANCE FOR VICTORY.
SH--

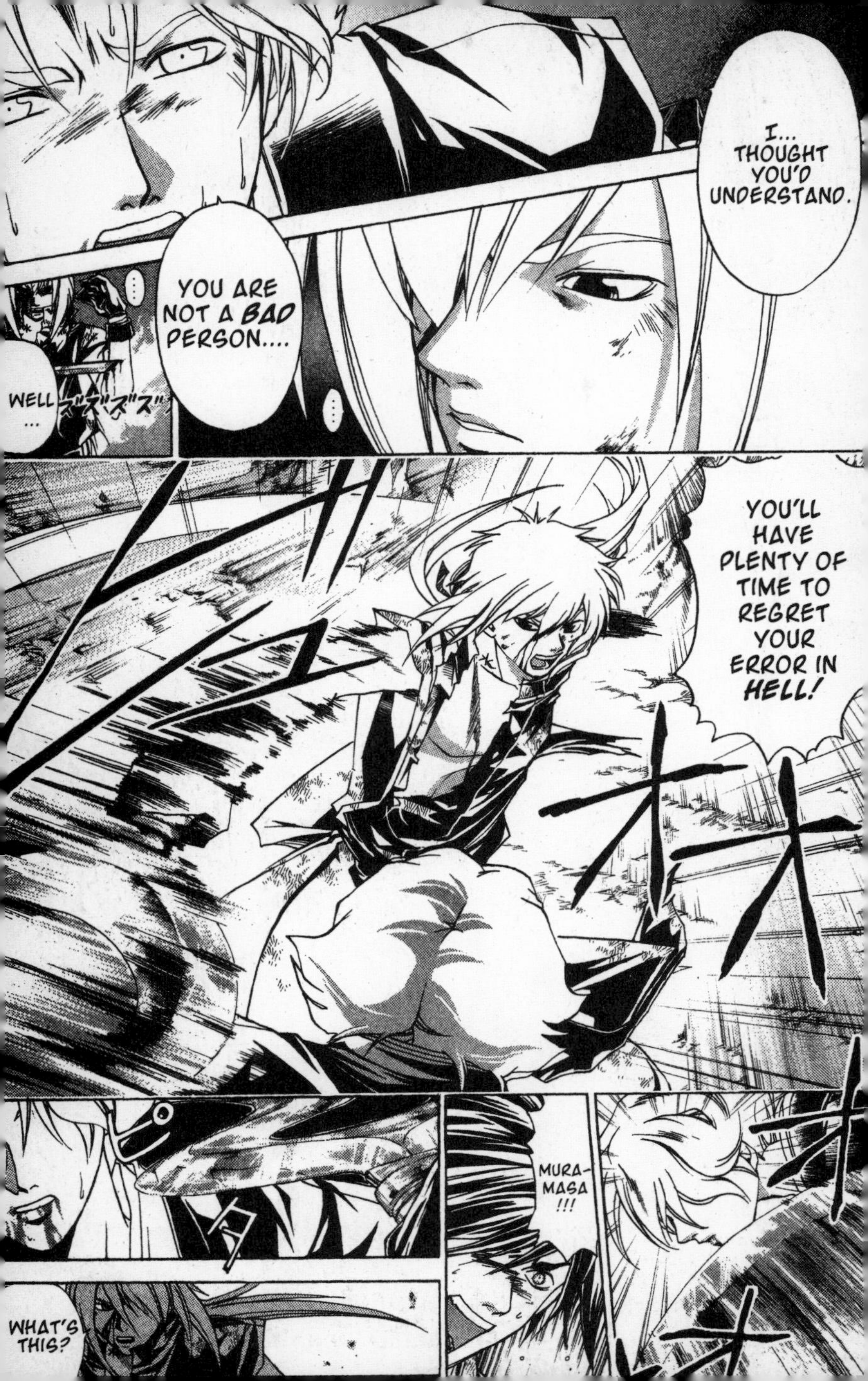
I... THOUGHT YOU'D UNDERSTAND.
...
YOU ARE NOT A ***BAD*** PERSON....
...
WELL ...
ズズズズ
YOU'LL HAVE PLENTY OF TIME TO REGRET YOUR ERROR IN ***HELL!***
MURA-MASA !!!
WHAT'S THIS?

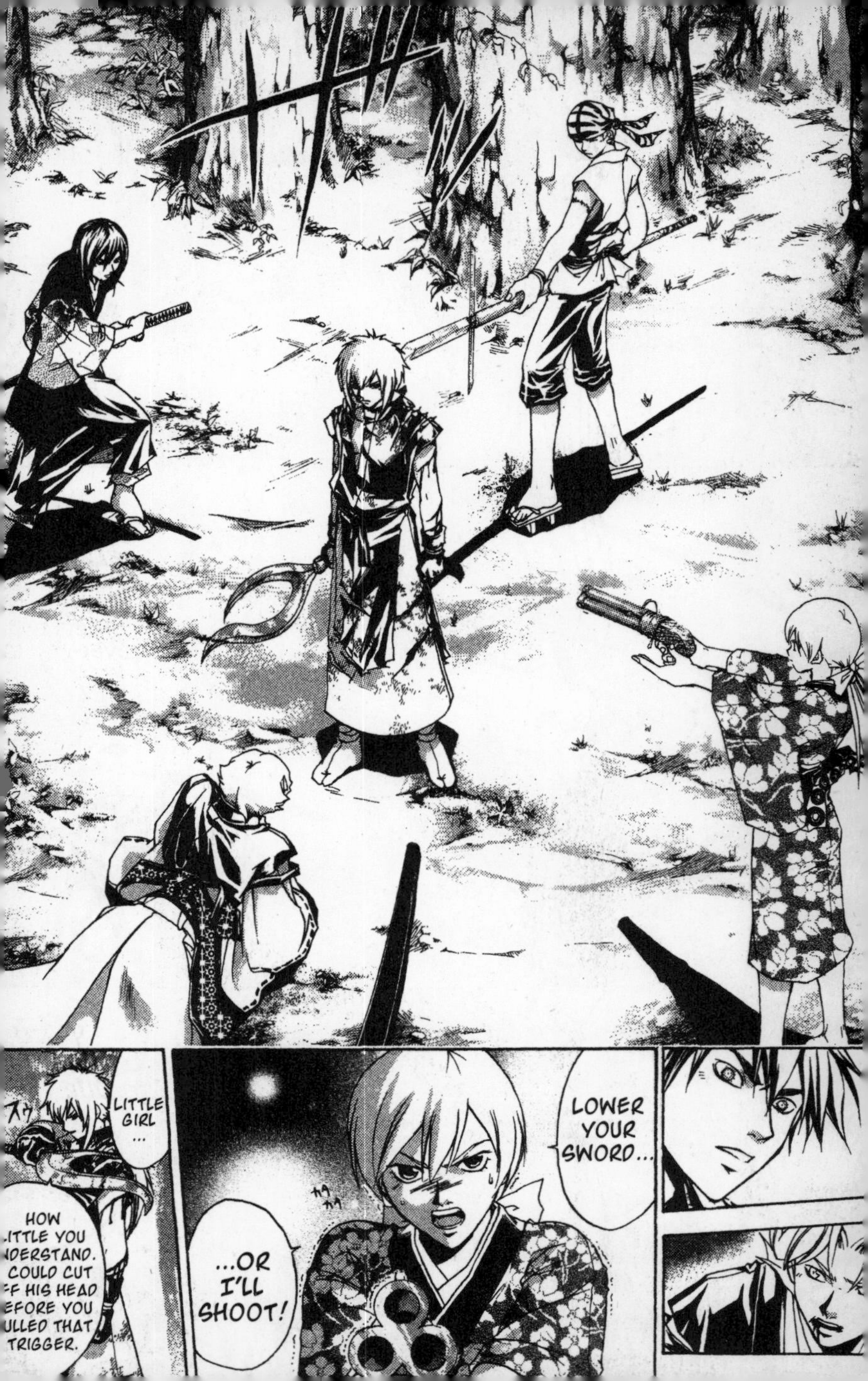
LOWER YOUR SWORD...
...OR I'LL SHOOT!
LITTLE GIRL ...
HOW LITTLE YOU NDERSTAND. COULD CUT F HIS HEAD EFORE YOU ULLED THAT TRIGGER.

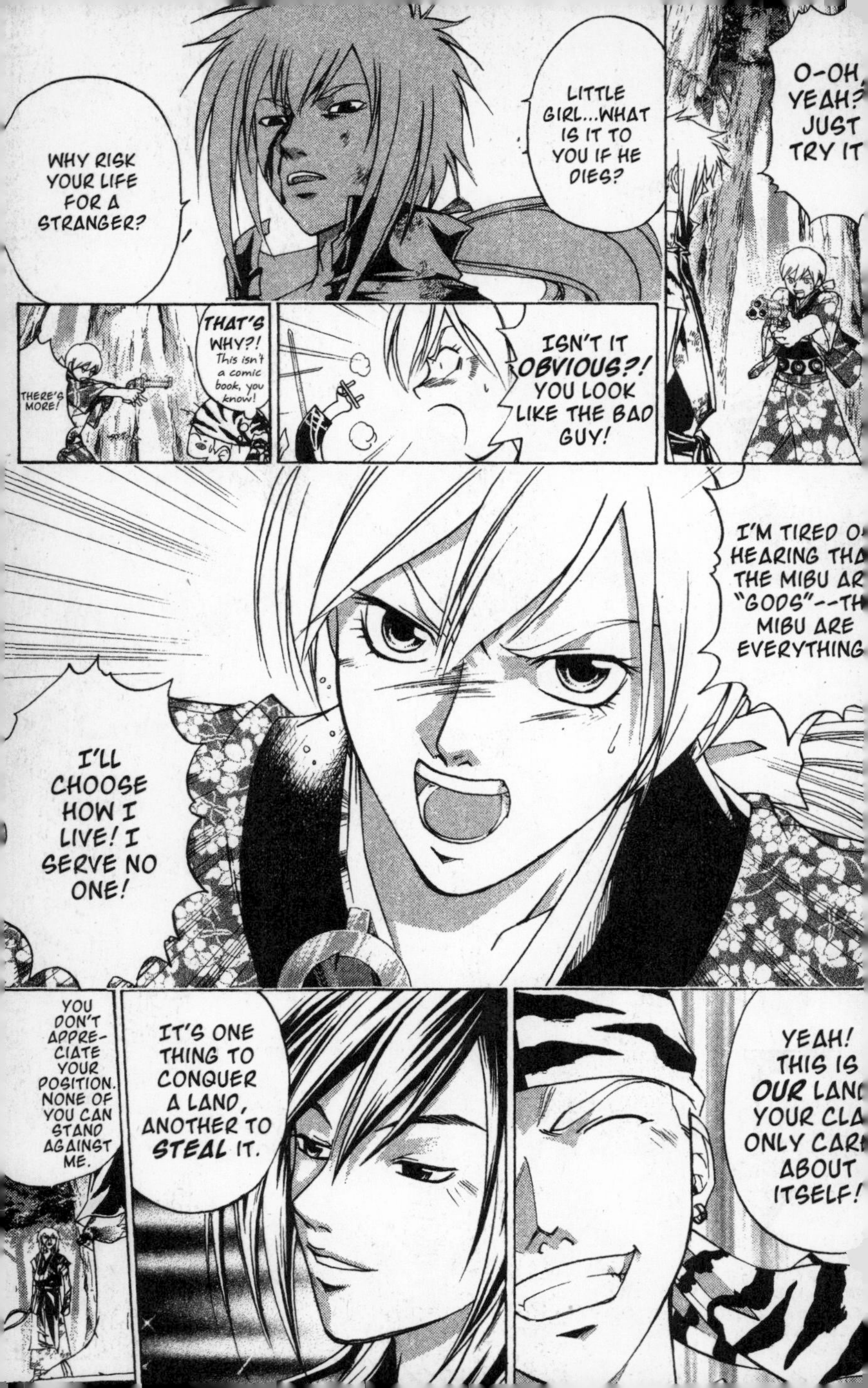

O-OH, YEAH? JUST TRY IT
LITTLE GIRL...WHAT IS IT TO YOU IF HE DIES?
WHY RISK YOUR LIFE FOR A STRANGER?
ISN'T IT *OBVIOUS?!* YOU LOOK LIKE THE BAD GUY!
THAT'S WHY?!
This isn't a comic book, you know!
THERE'S MORE!
I'M TIRED O HEARING THA THE MIBU AR "GODS"--TH MIBU ARE EVERYTHING
I'LL CHOOSE HOW I LIVE! I SERVE NO ONE!
YEAH! THIS IS *OUR* LAN YOUR CLA ONLY CAR ABOUT ITSELF!
IT'S ONE THING TO CONQUER A LAND, ANOTHER TO *STEAL* IT.
YOU DON'T APPRECIATE YOUR POSITION. NONE OF YOU CAN STAND AGAINST ME.

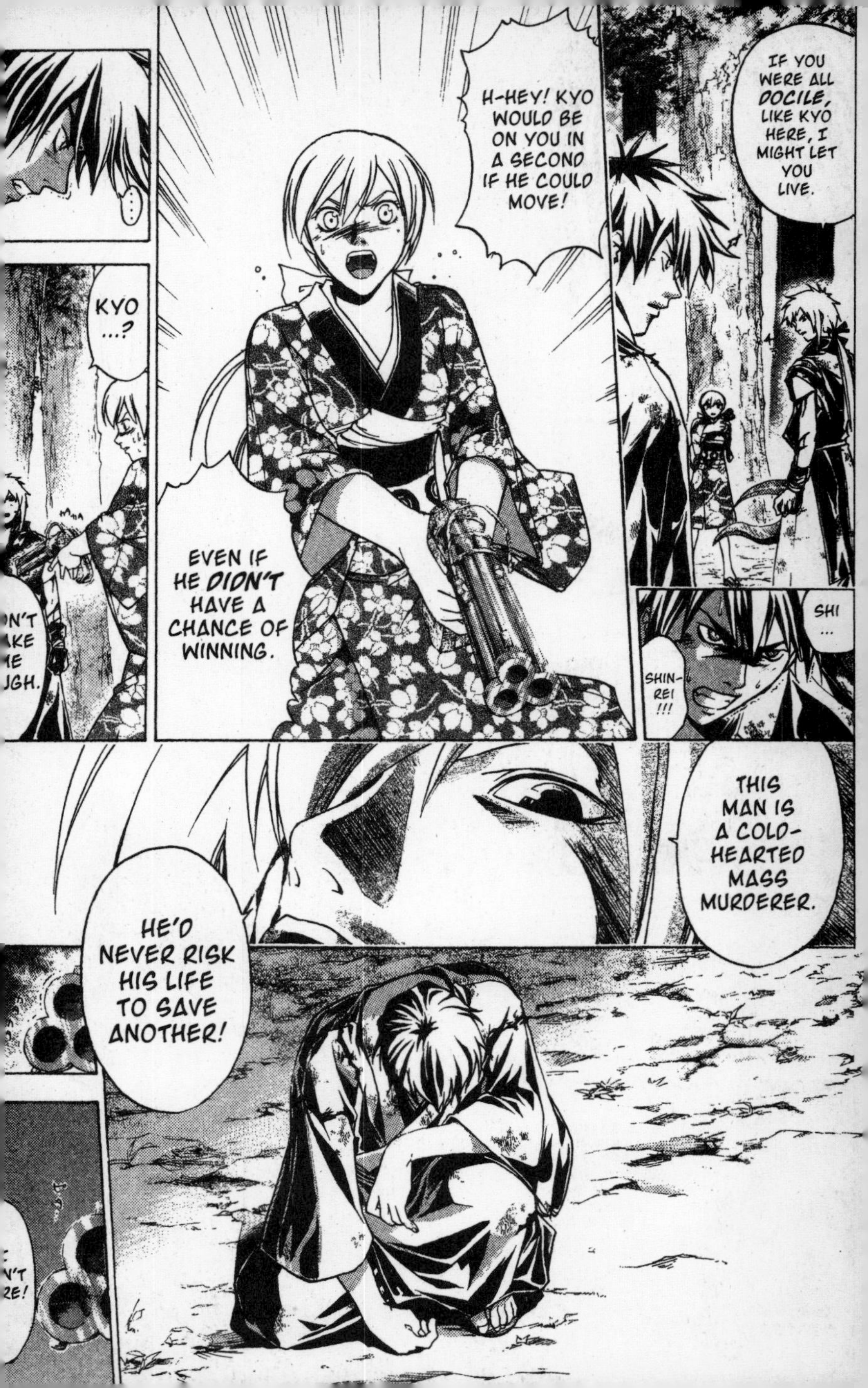

IF YOU WERE ALL DOCILE, LIKE KYO HERE, I MIGHT LET YOU LIVE.
SHI ...
SHIN-REI !!!
H-HEY! KYO WOULD BE ON YOU IN A SECOND IF HE COULD MOVE!
EVEN IF HE DIDN'T HAVE A CHANCE OF WINNING.
...
KYO ...?
THIS MAN IS A COLD-HEARTED MASS MURDERER.
HE'D NEVER RISK HIS LIFE TO SAVE ANOTHER!

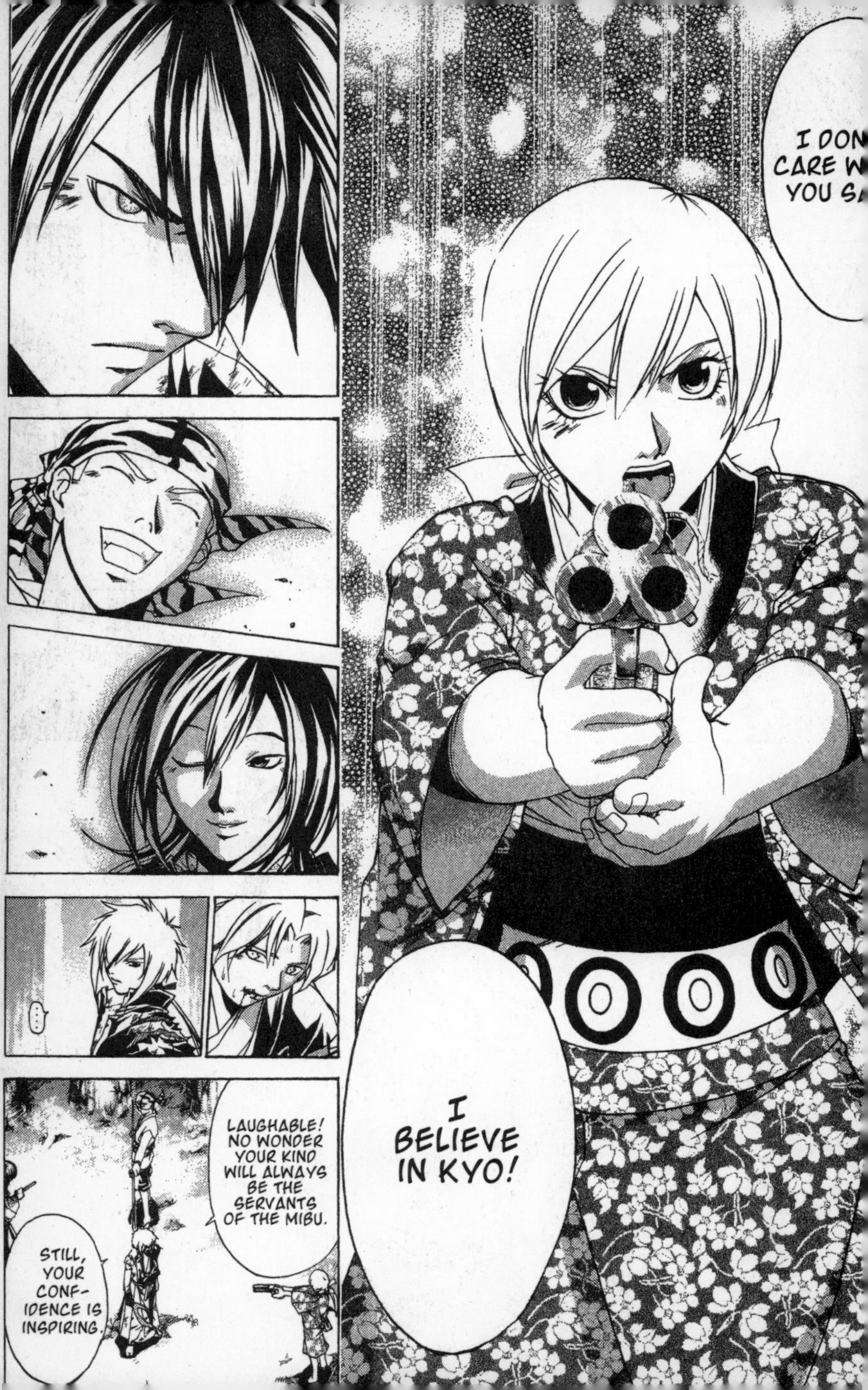
I DON CARE W YOU SA
I BELIEVE IN KYO!
...
LAUGHABLE! NO WONDER YOUR KIND WILL ALWAYS BE THE SERVANTS OF THE MIBU.
STILL, YOUR CONF-IDENCE IS INSPIRING.

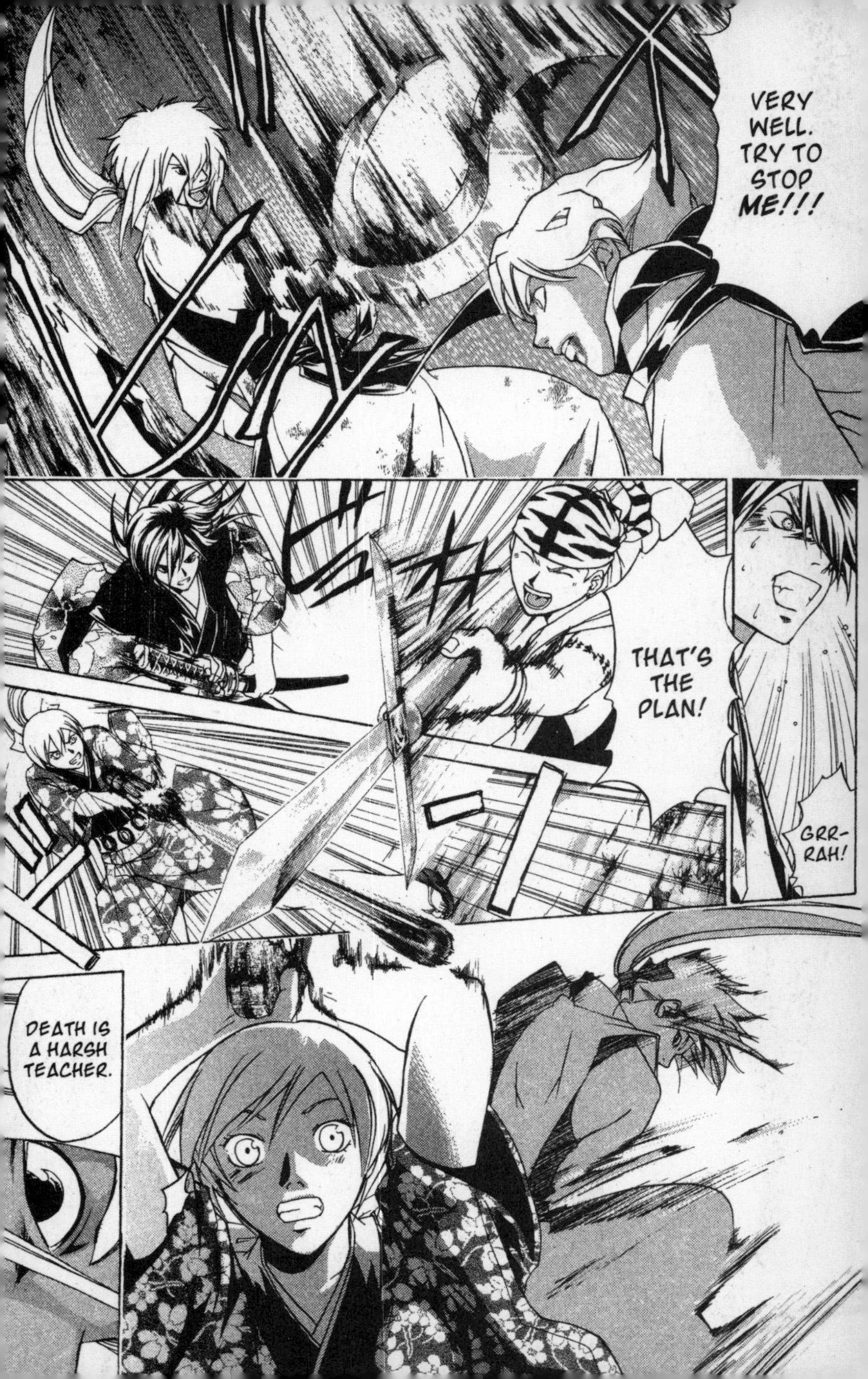
VERY WELL. TRY TO STOP ME!!!
GRR-RAH!
THAT'S THE PLAN!
DEATH IS A HARSH TEACHER.

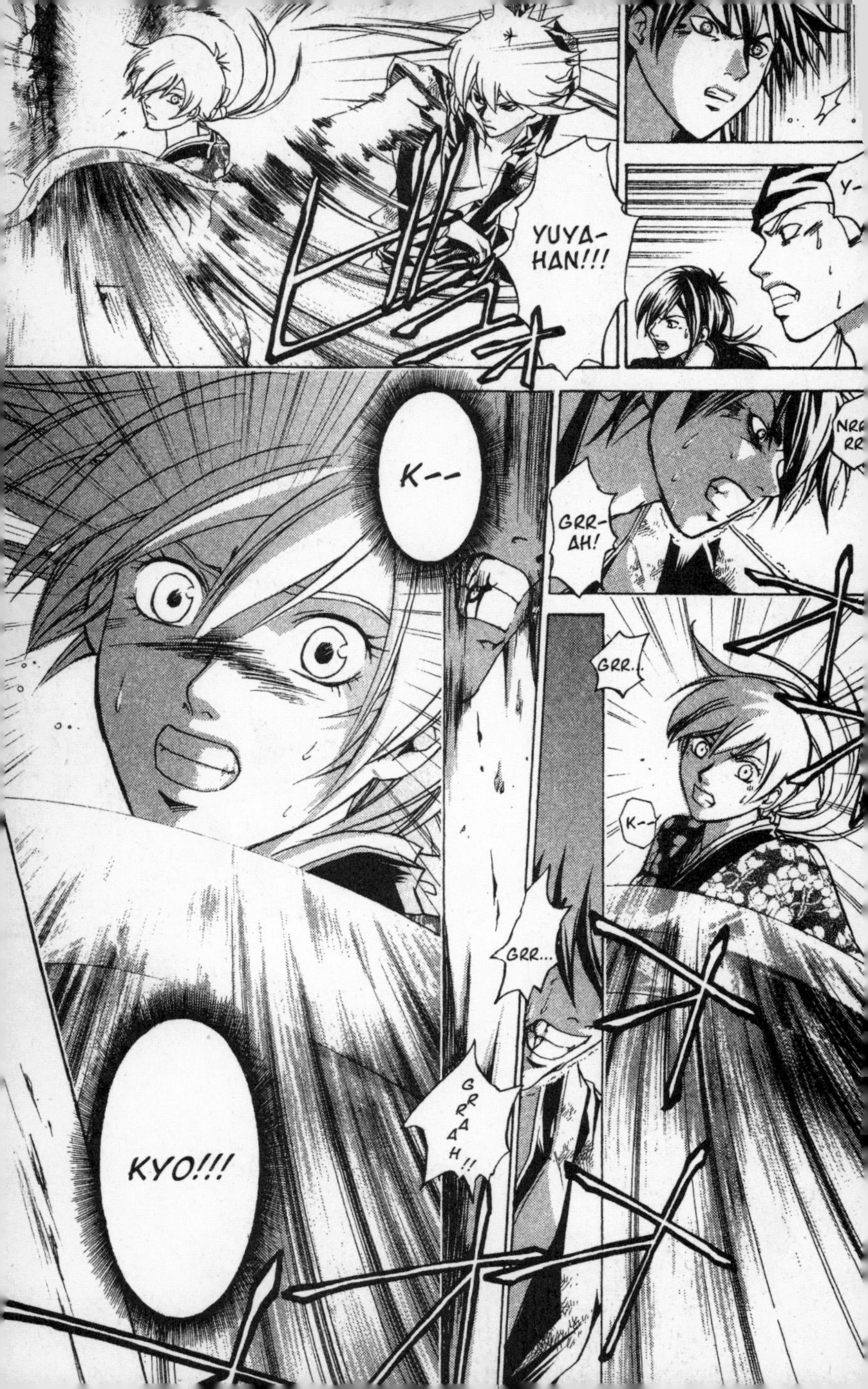
Y-
YUYA-HAN!!!
NRR RR
GRR-AH!
GRR...
K--
K--
GRR...
GRRAH!!
KYO!!!

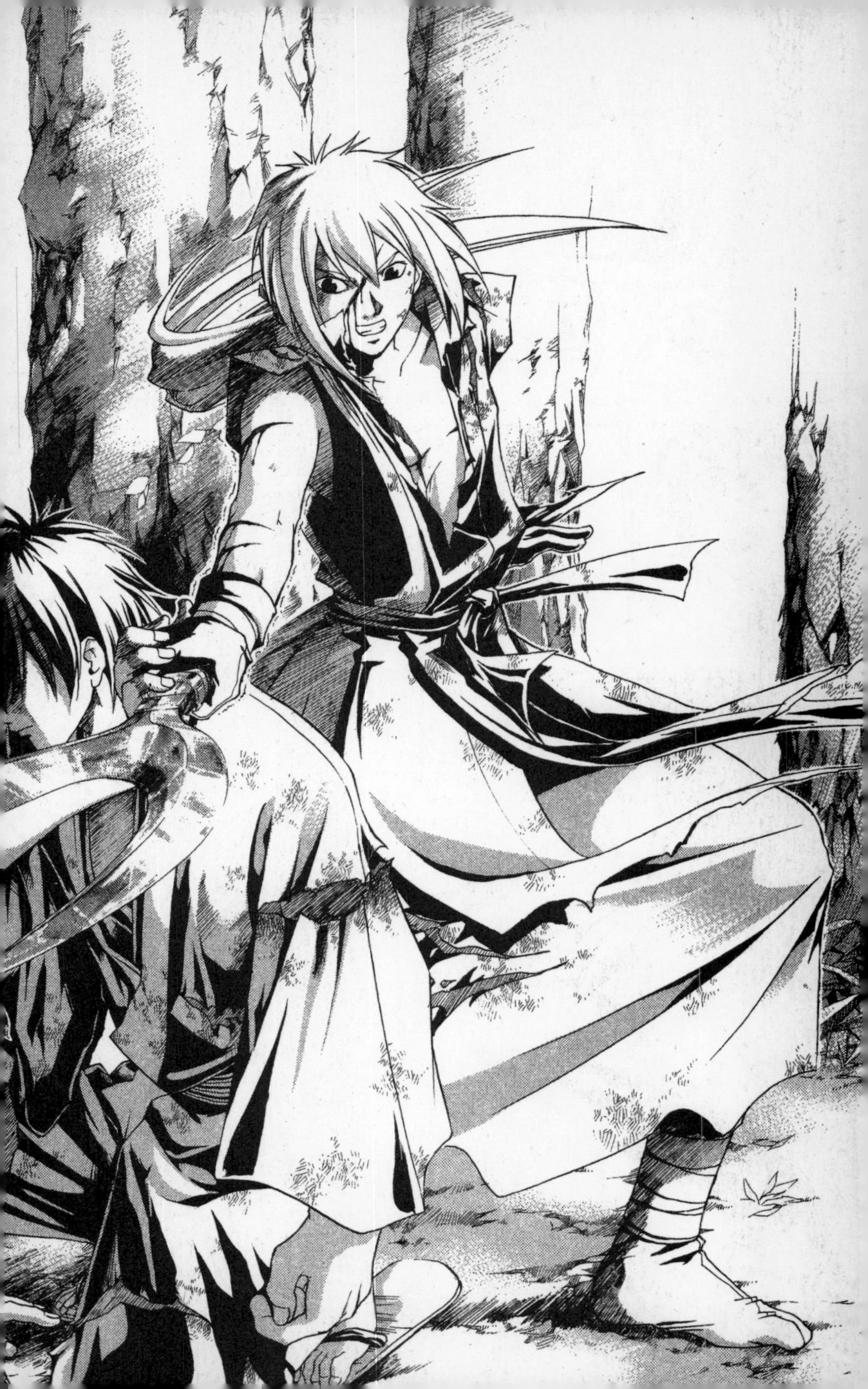

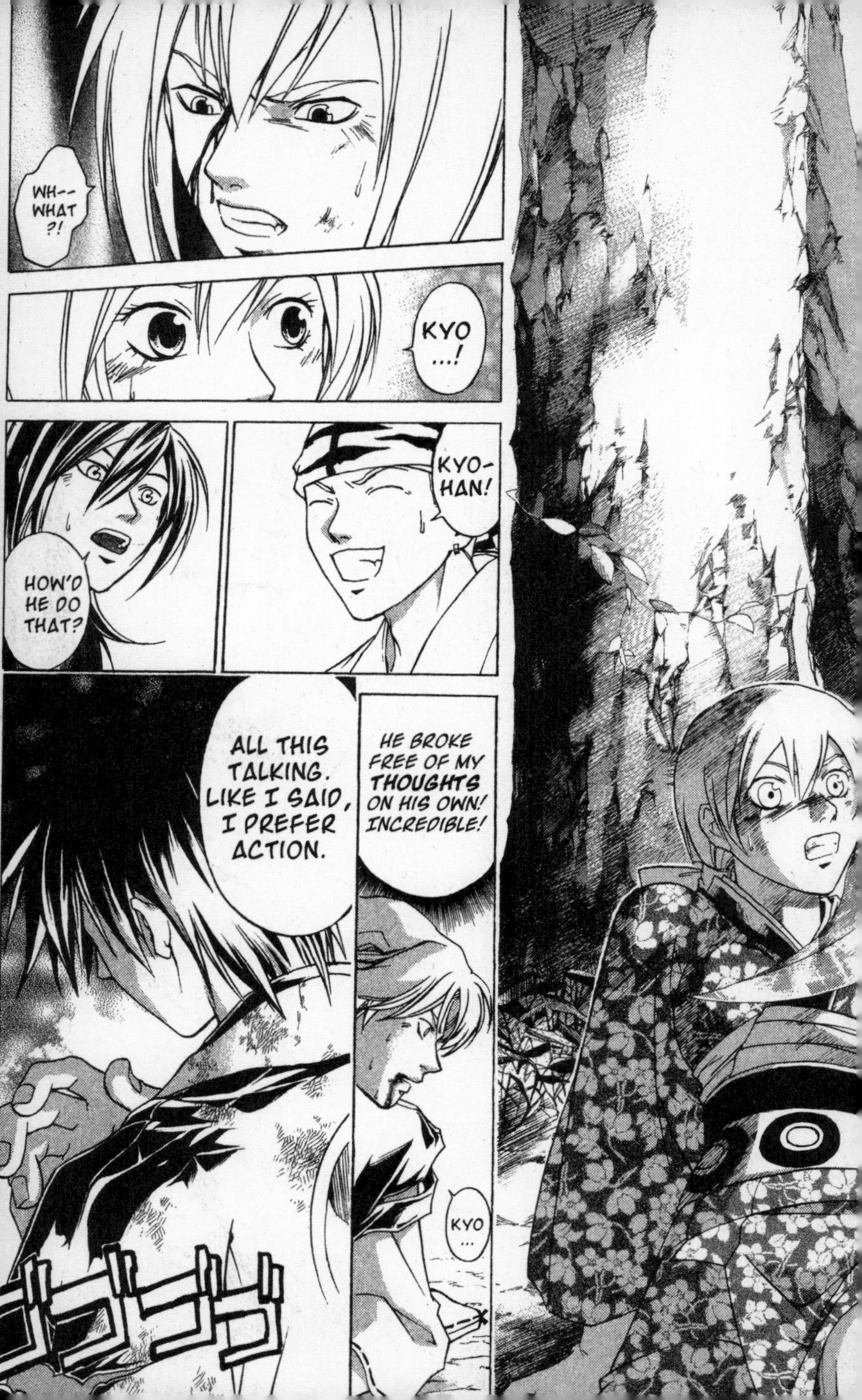
WH-- WHAT?!
KYO...!
KYO-HAN!
HOW'D HE DO THAT?
HE BROKE FREE OF MY **THOUGHTS** ON HIS OWN! INCREDIBLE!
KYO...
ALL THIS TALKING. LIKE I SAID, I PREFER ACTION.

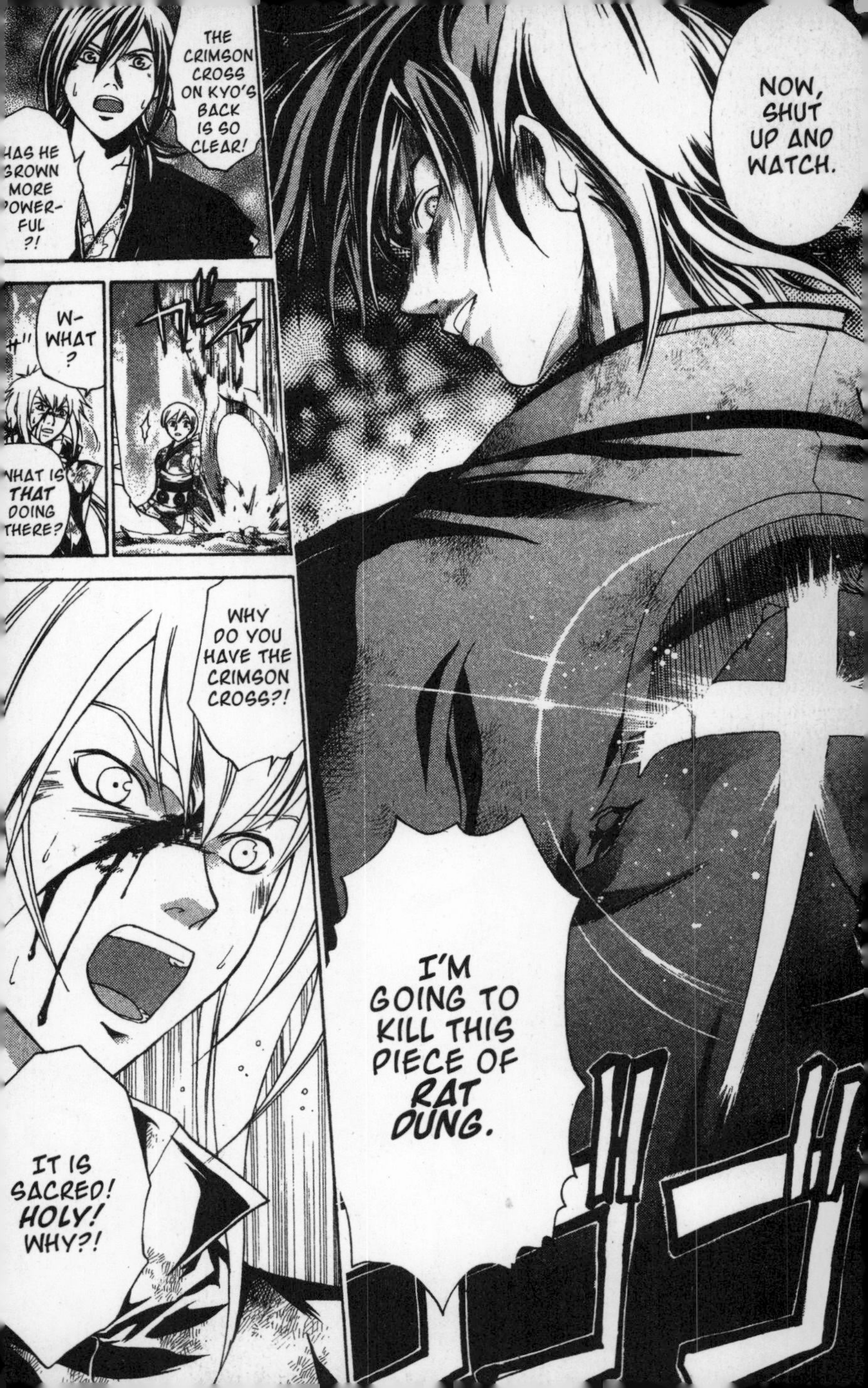
NOW, SHUT UP AND WATCH.
I'M GOING TO KILL THIS PIECE OF RAT DUNG.
THE CRIMSON CROSS ON KYO'S BACK IS SO CLEAR!
HAS HE GROWN MORE POWERFUL?!
W-WHAT?
WHAT IS THAT DOING THERE?
WHY DO YOU HAVE THE CRIMSON CROSS?!
IT IS SACRED! HOLY! WHY?!

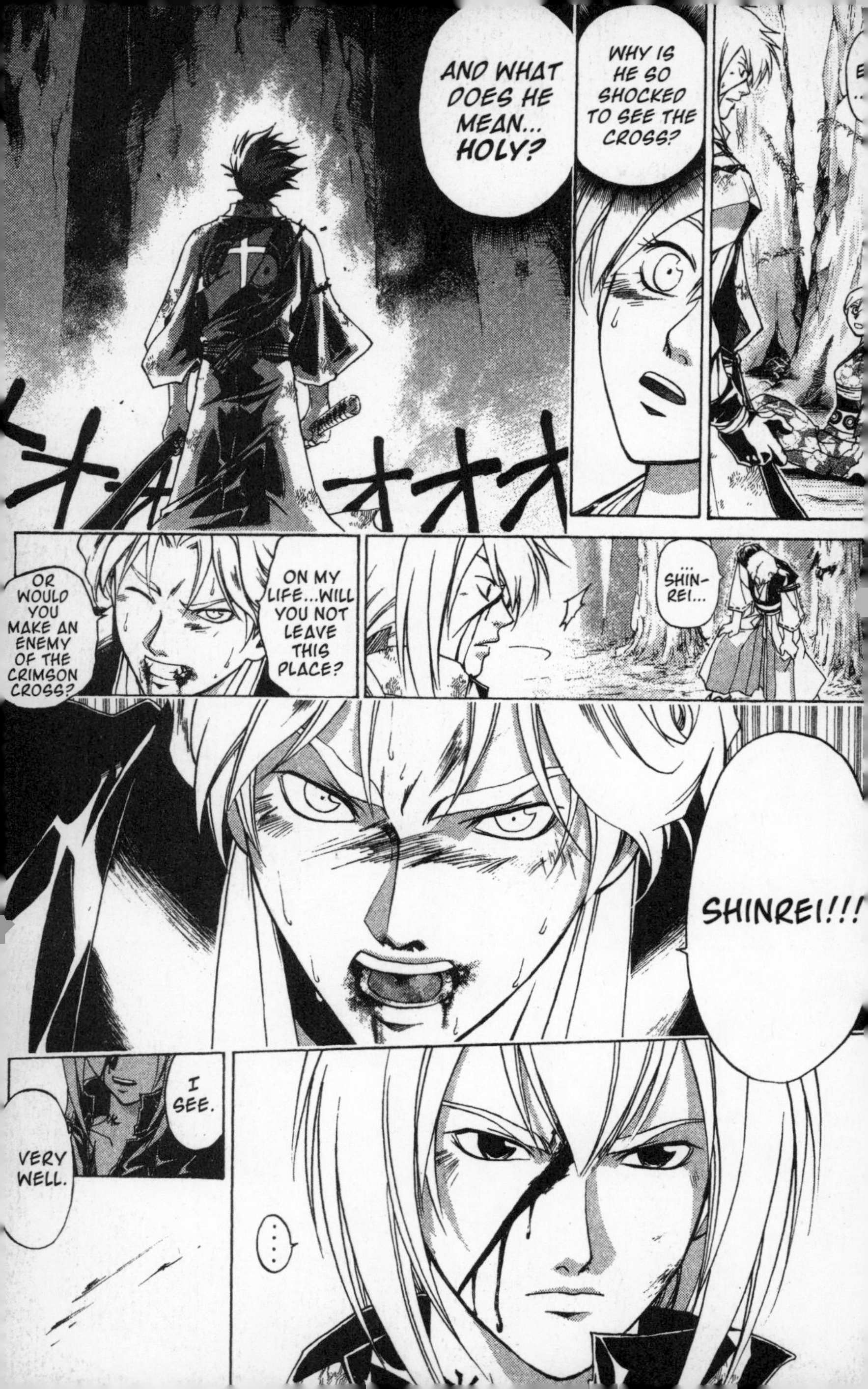
WHY IS HE SO SHOCKED TO SEE THE CROSS?
AND WHAT DOES HE MEAN... HOLY?
オオオ
...SHIN-REI...
ON MY LIFE...WILL YOU NOT LEAVE THIS PLACE?
OR WOULD YOU MAKE AN ENEMY OF THE CRIMSON CROSS?
SHINREI!!!
....
I SEE.
VERY WELL.

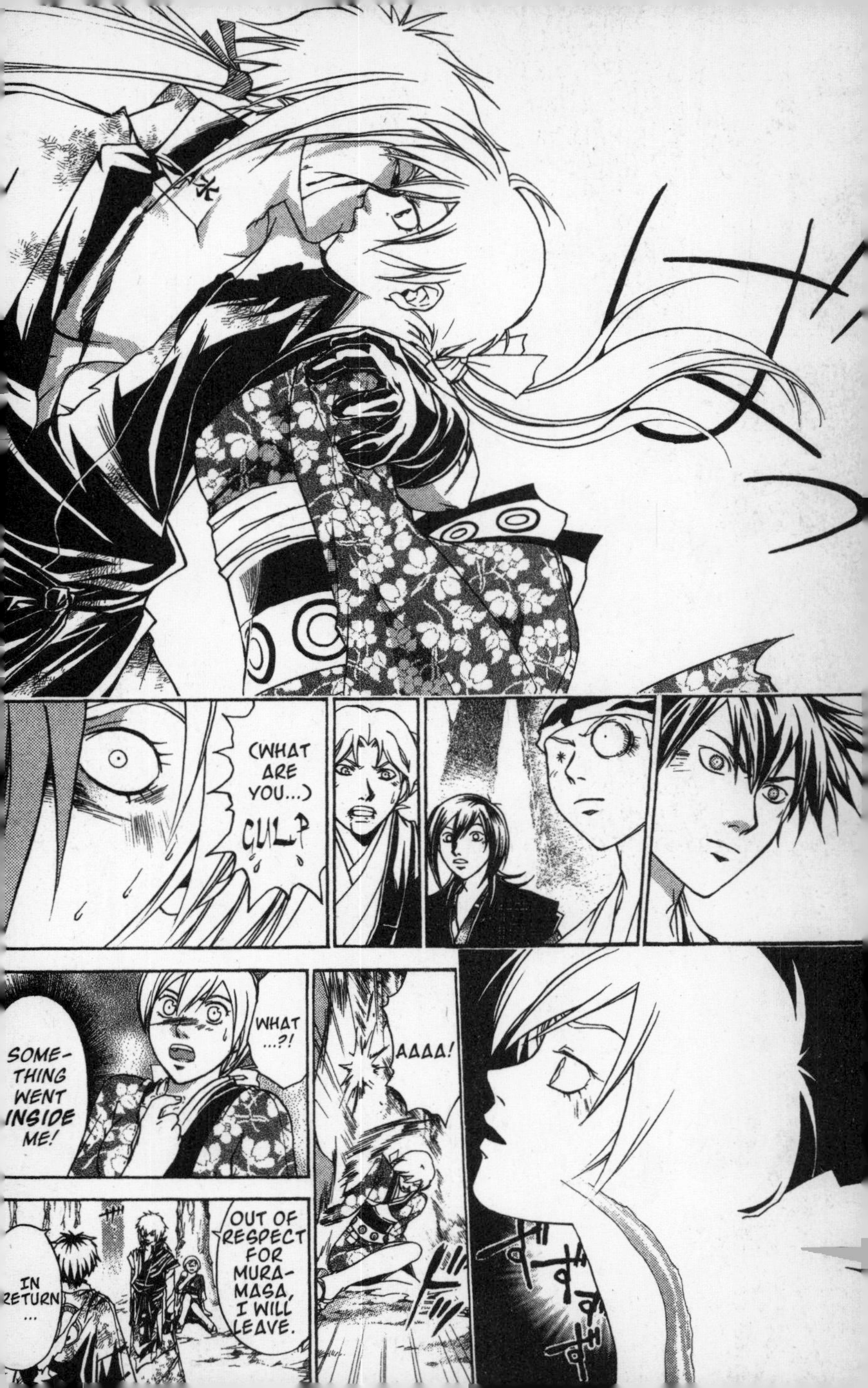
(WHAT ARE YOU...)
GULP
AAAA!
WHAT ...?!
SOME-THING WENT INSIDE ME!
OUT OF RESPECT FOR MURA-MASA, I WILL LEAVE.
IN RETURN ...

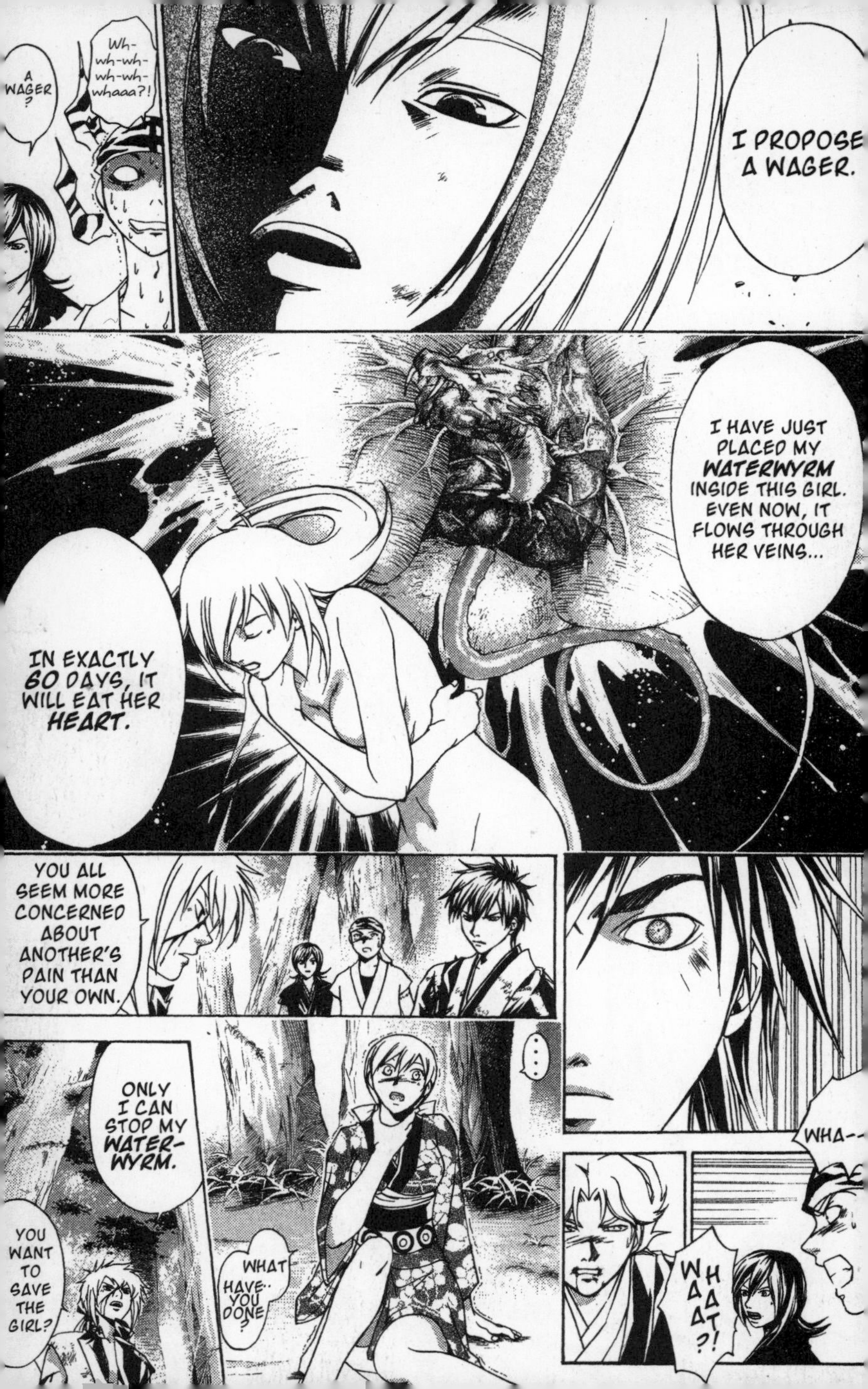
I PROPOSE A WAGER.
Wh-wh-wh-wh-wh-whaaa?!
A WAGER?
I HAVE JUST PLACED MY **WATERWYRM** INSIDE THIS GIRL. EVEN NOW, IT FLOWS THROUGH HER VEINS...
IN EXACTLY **60** DAYS, IT WILL EAT HER **HEART**.
WHA--
WHAAT?!
YOU ALL SEEM MORE CONCERNED ABOUT ANOTHER'S PAIN THAN YOUR OWN.
...
ONLY I CAN STOP MY **WATER-WYRM**.
WHAT HAVE.. YOU DONE?
YOU WANT TO SAVE THE GIRL?

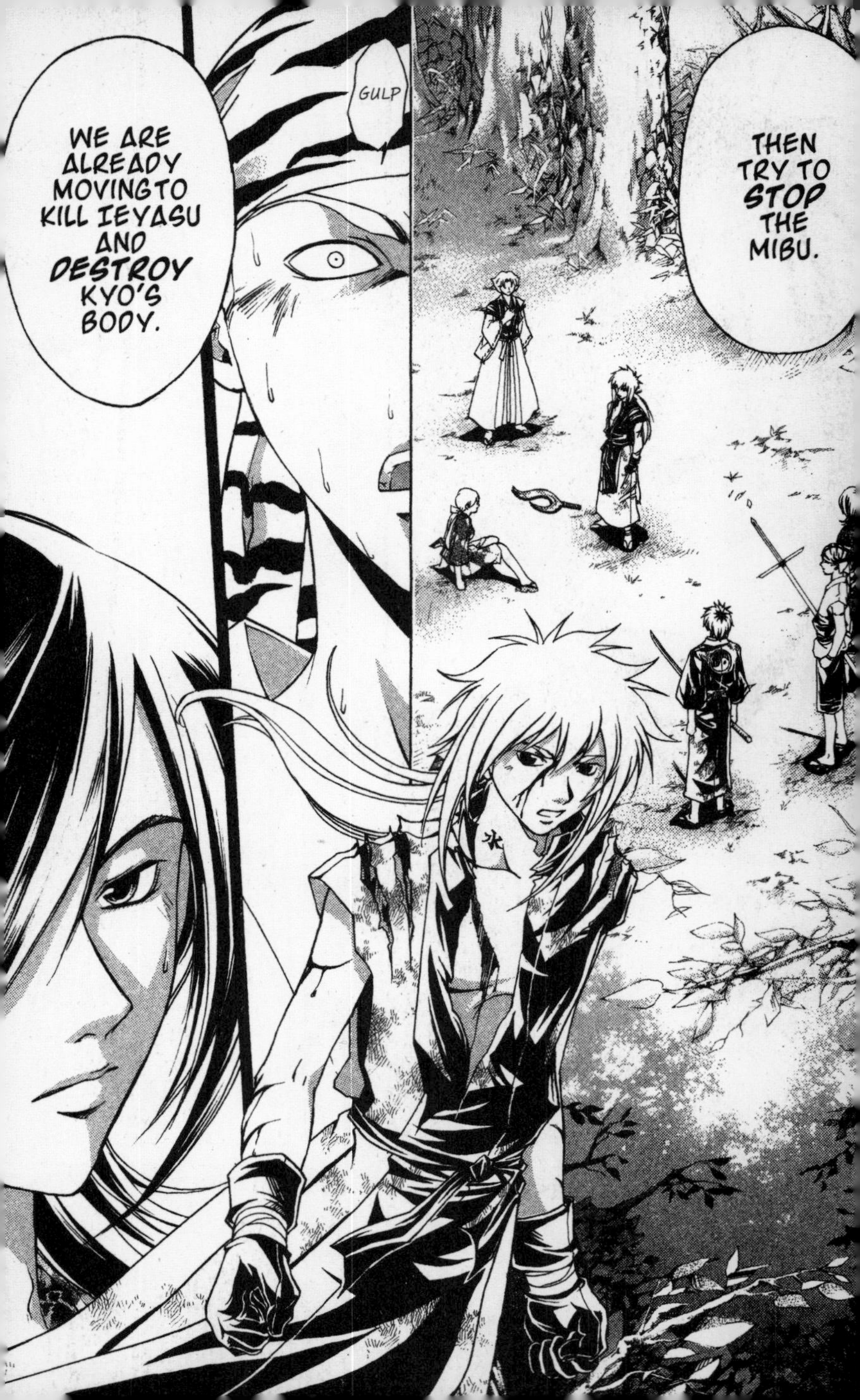
THEN TRY TO STOP THE MIBU.
GULP
WE ARE ALREADY MOVING TO KILL IEYASU AND DESTROY KYO'S BODY.

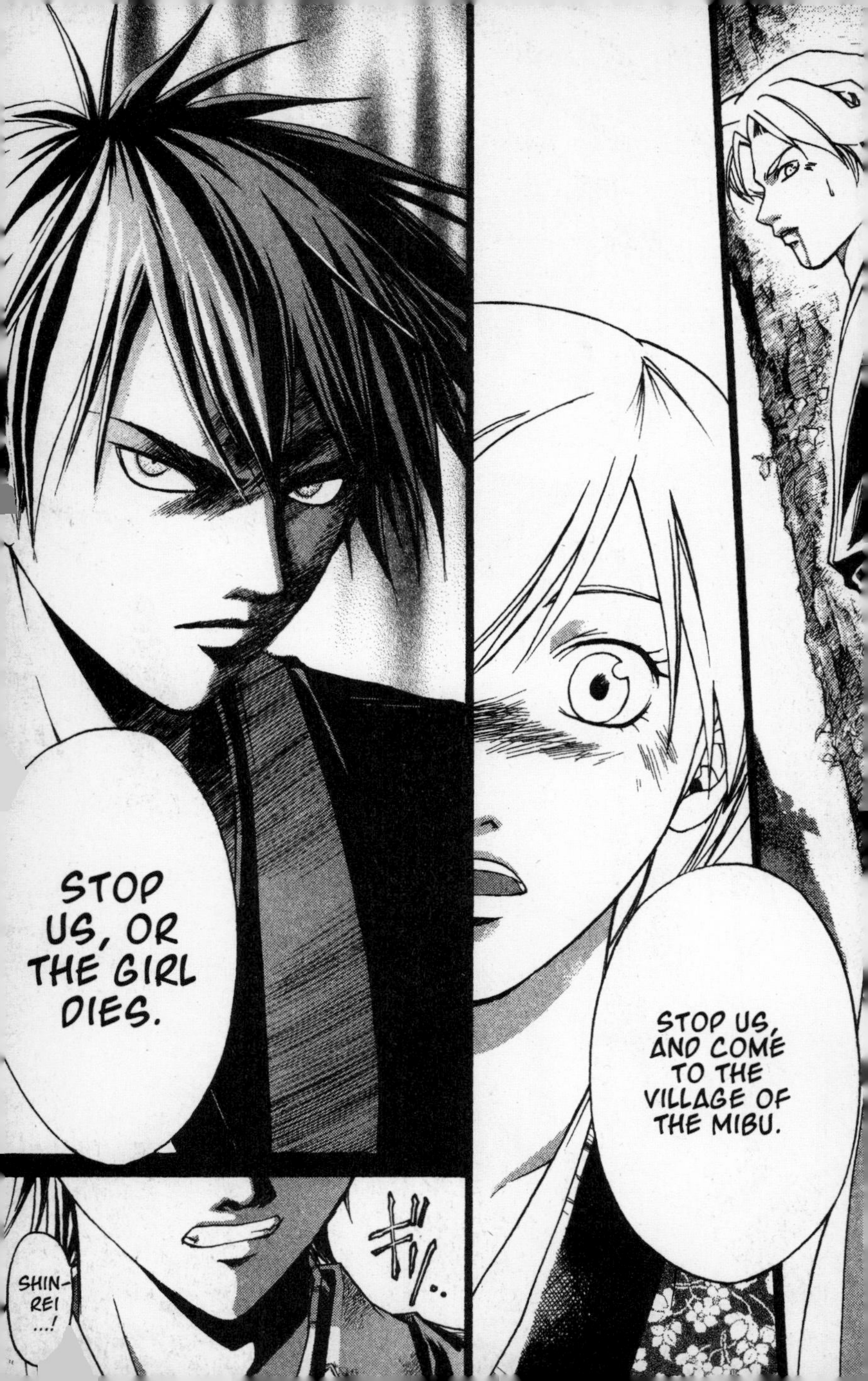
STOP US, AND COME TO THE VILLAGE OF THE MIBU.
STOP US, OR THE GIRL DIES.
ギリ..
SHIN-REI ...!

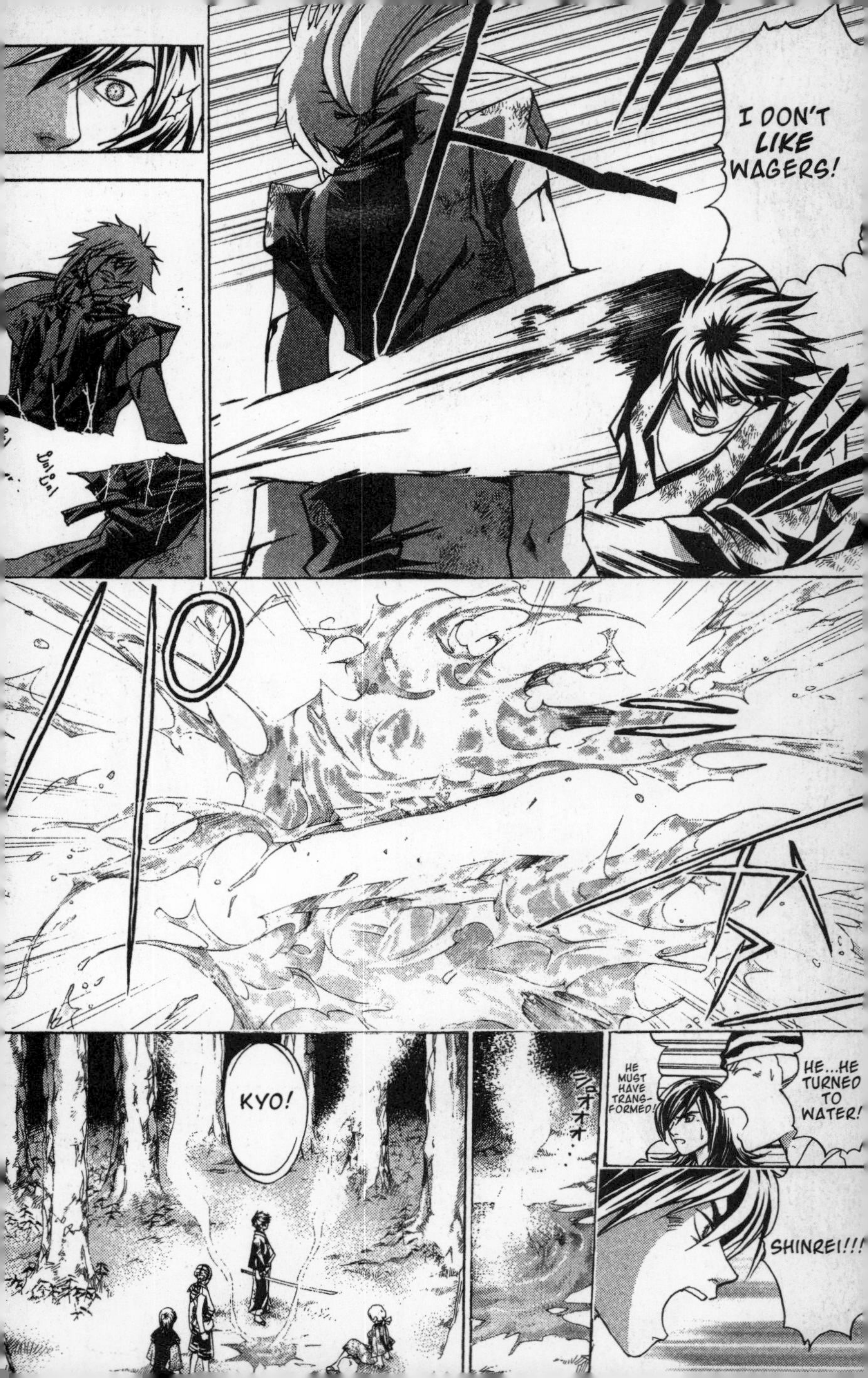
I DON'T LIKE WAGERS!
HE...HE TURNED TO WATER!
HE MUST HAVE TRANS-FORMED!
SHINREI!!!
KYO!

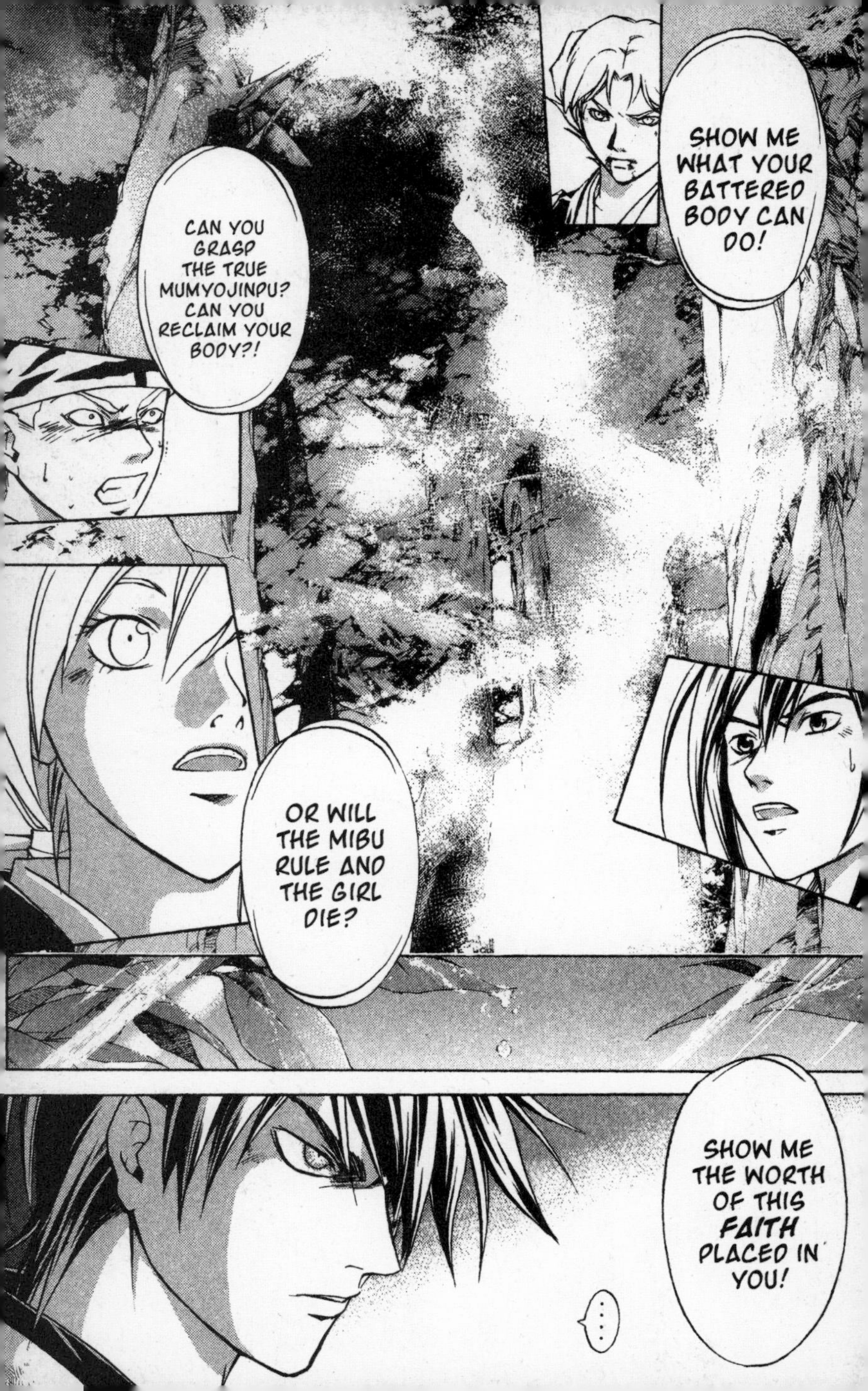
SHOW ME WHAT YOUR BATTERED BODY CAN DO!
CAN YOU GRASP THE TRUE MUMYOJINPU? CAN YOU RECLAIM YOUR BODY?!
OR WILL THE MIBU RULE AND THE GIRL DIE?
SHOW ME THE WORTH OF THIS **FAITH** PLACED IN YOU!
...

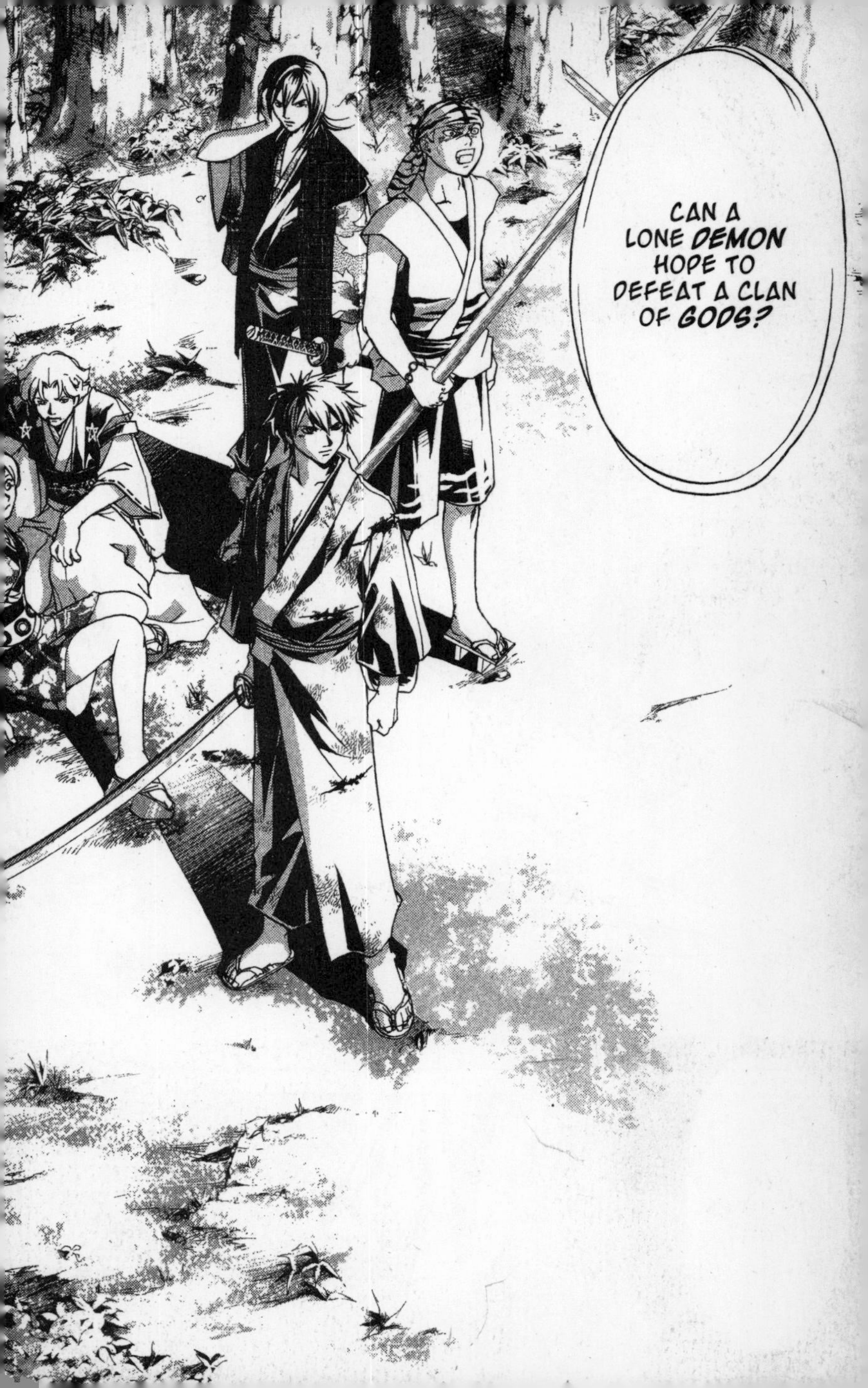
CAN A LONE DEMON HOPE TO DEFEAT A CLAN OF GODS?

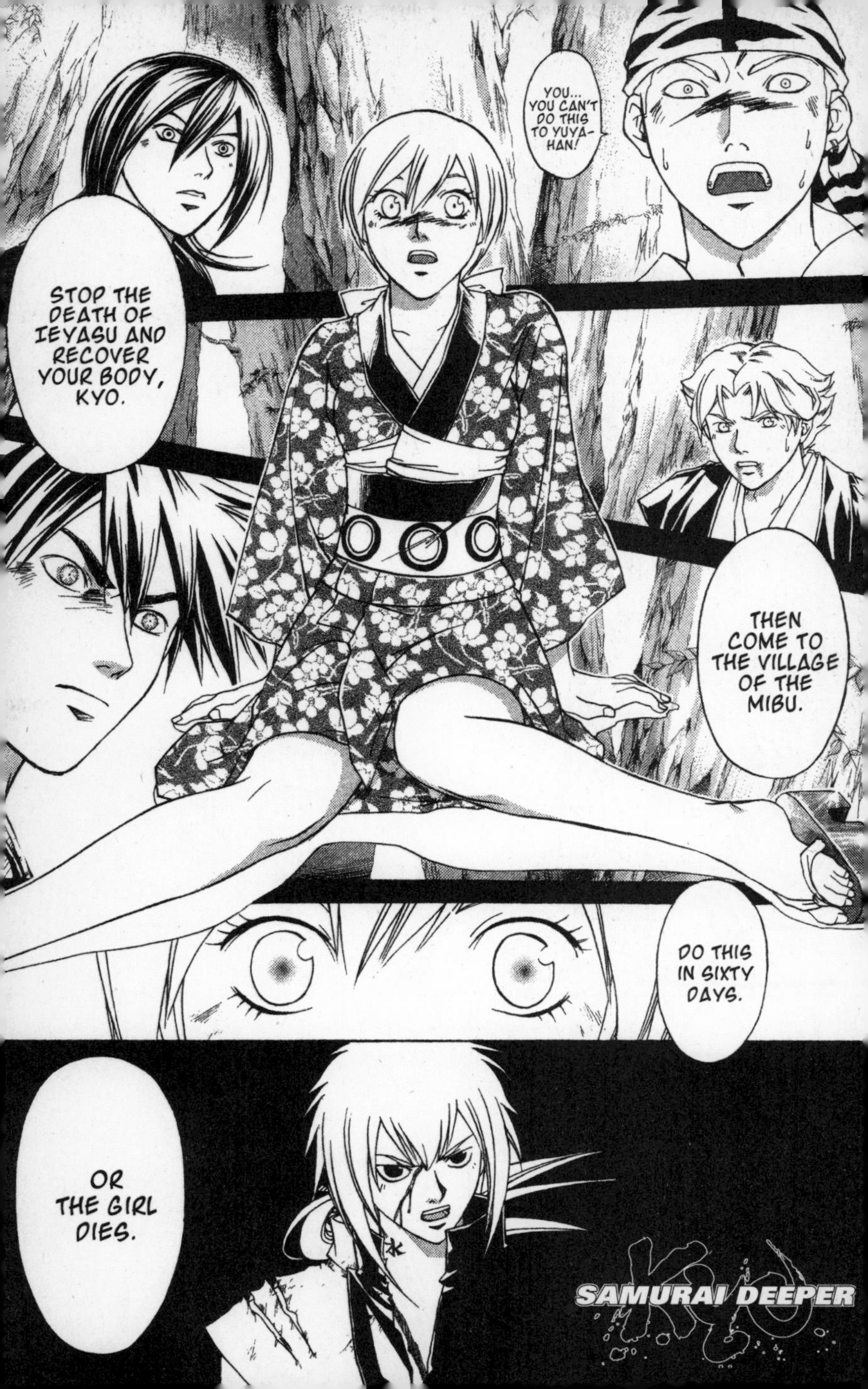
YOU... YOU CAN'T DO THIS TO YUYA-HAN!
STOP THE DEATH OF IEYASU AND RECOVER YOUR BODY, KYO.
THEN COME TO THE VILLAGE OF THE MIBU.
DO THIS IN SIXTY DAYS.
OR THE GIRL DIES.
SAMURAI DEEPER KYO

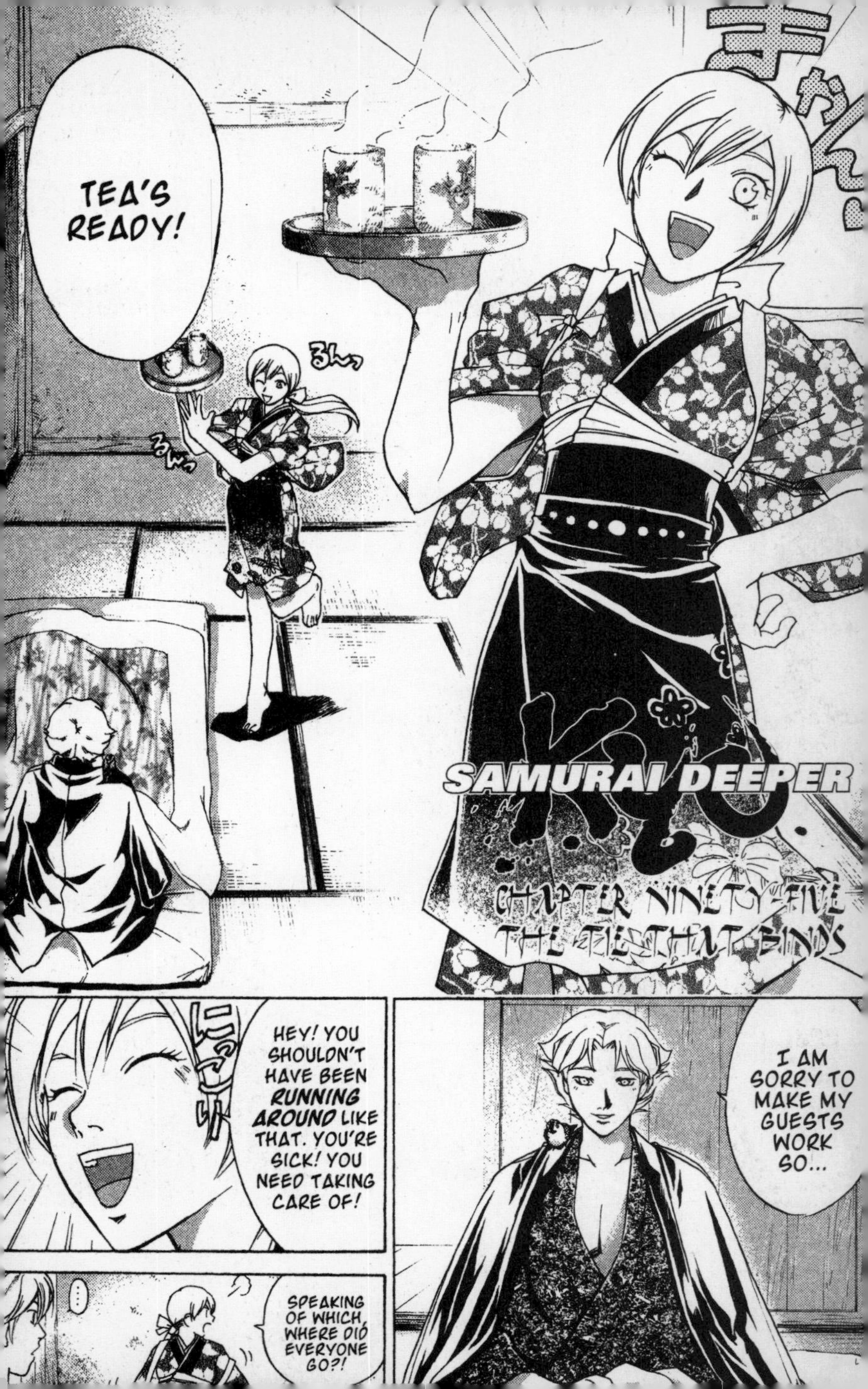
TEA'S READY!
SAMURAI DEEPER
CHAPTER NINETY-FIVE
THE TIE THAT BINDS
I AM SORRY TO MAKE MY GUESTS WORK SO...
HEY! YOU SHOULDN'T HAVE BEEN RUNNING AROUND LIKE THAT. YOU'RE SICK! YOU NEED TAKING CARE OF!
SPEAKING OF WHICH, WHERE DID EVERYONE GO?!
...

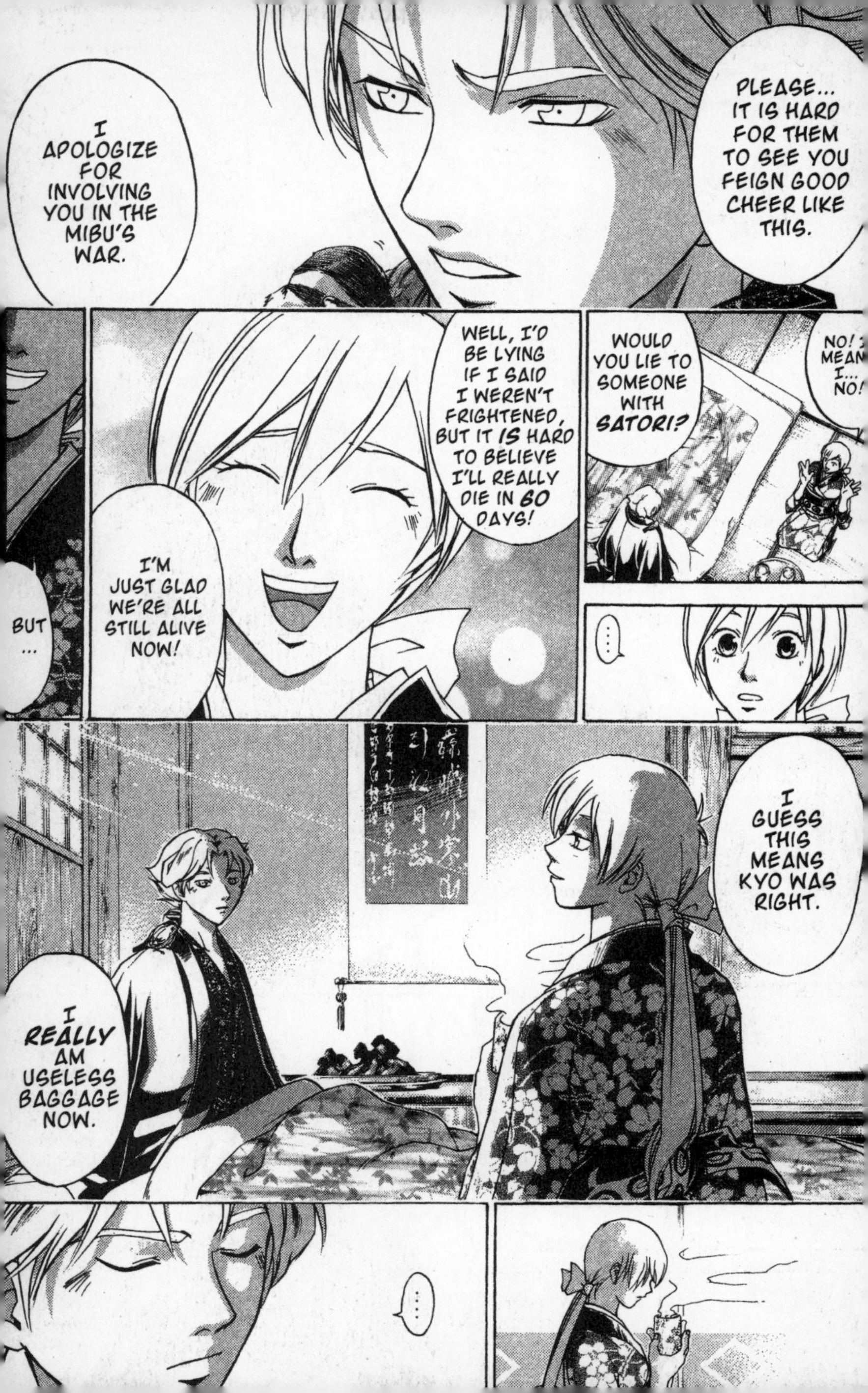
PLEASE... IT IS HARD FOR THEM TO SEE YOU FEIGN GOOD CHEER LIKE THIS.
I APOLOGIZE FOR INVOLVING YOU IN THE MIBU'S WAR.
NO! MEAN I... NO!
WOULD YOU LIE TO SOMEONE WITH SATORI?
...
WELL, I'D BE LYING IF I SAID I WEREN'T FRIGHTENED, BUT IT IS HARD TO BELIEVE I'LL REALLY DIE IN 60 DAYS!
I'M JUST GLAD WE'RE ALL STILL ALIVE NOW!
BUT ...
I GUESS THIS MEANS KYO WAS RIGHT.
I REALLY AM USELESS BAGGAGE NOW.
.....

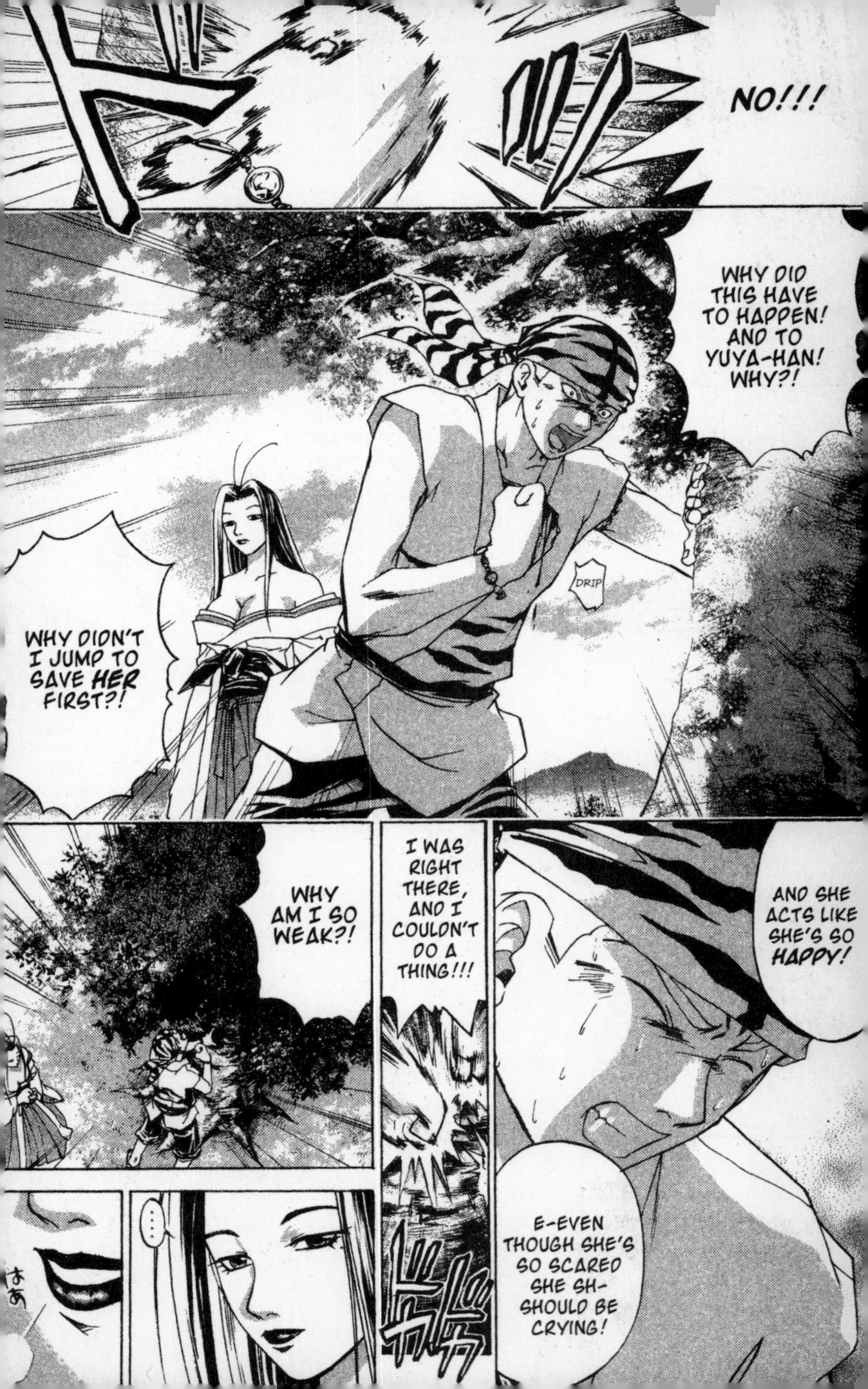

NO!!!
WHY DID THIS HAVE TO HAPPEN! AND TO YUYA-HAN! WHY?!
DRIP
WHY DIDN'T I JUMP TO SAVE HER FIRST?!
AND SHE ACTS LIKE SHE'S SO HAPPY!
E-EVEN THOUGH SHE'S SO SCARED SHE SH-SHOULD BE CRYING!
I WAS RIGHT THERE, AND I COULDN'T DO A THING!!!
WHY AM I SO WEAK?!
....
まあ

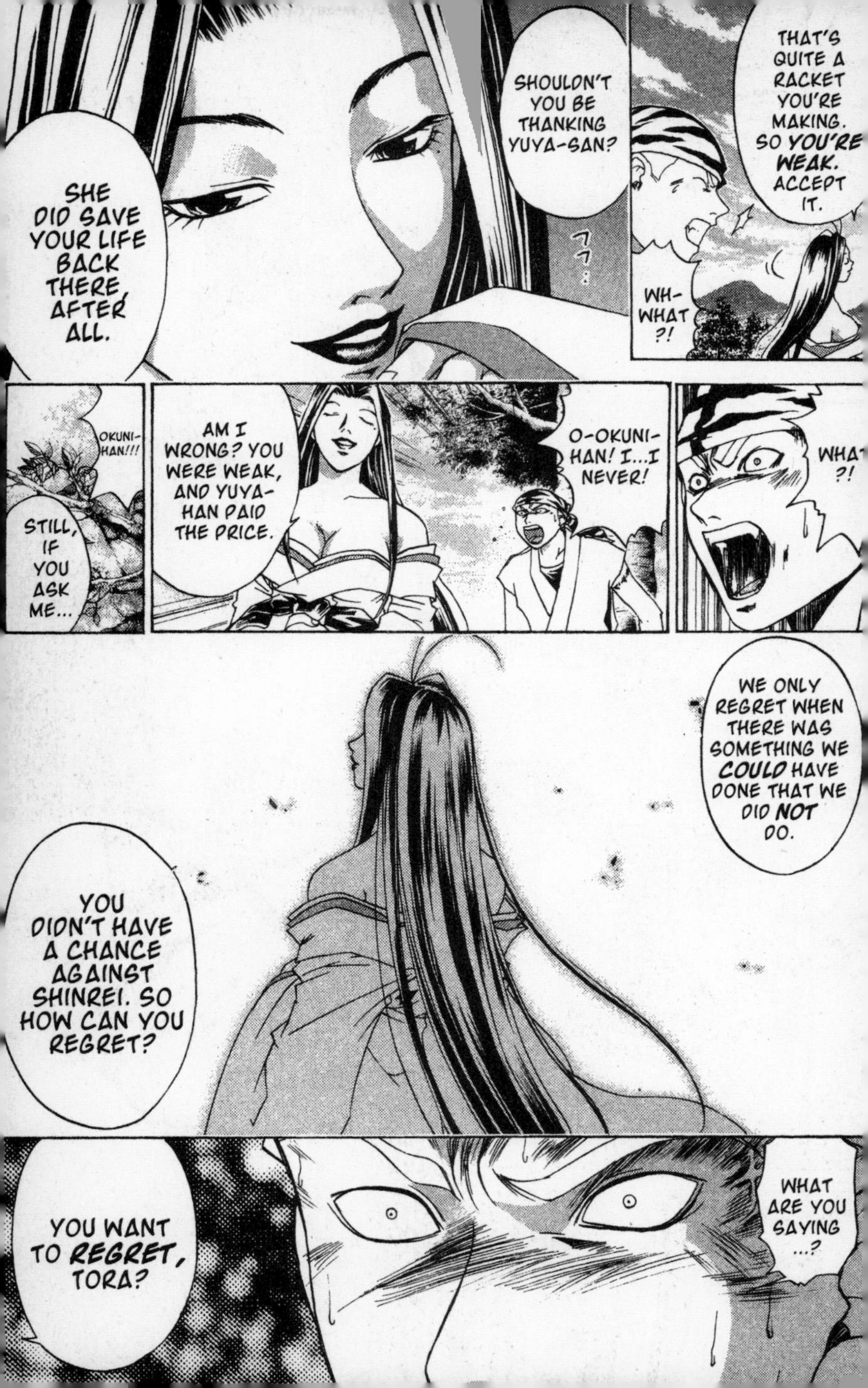
THAT'S QUITE A RACKET YOU'RE MAKING. SO *YOU'RE WEAK.* ACCEPT IT.
WH- WHAT ?!
SHOULDN'T YOU BE THANKING YUYA-SAN?
フフ…
SHE DID SAVE YOUR LIFE BACK THERE, AFTER ALL.
WHA ?!
O-OKUNI-HAN! I...I NEVER!
AM I WRONG? YOU WERE WEAK, AND YUYA-HAN PAID THE PRICE.
OKUNI-HAN!!!
STILL, IF YOU ASK ME...
WE ONLY REGRET WHEN THERE WAS SOMETHING WE *COULD* HAVE DONE THAT WE DID *NOT* DO.
YOU DIDN'T HAVE A CHANCE AGAINST SHINREI. SO HOW CAN YOU REGRET?
WHAT ARE YOU SAYING ...?
YOU WANT TO *REGRET*, TORA?

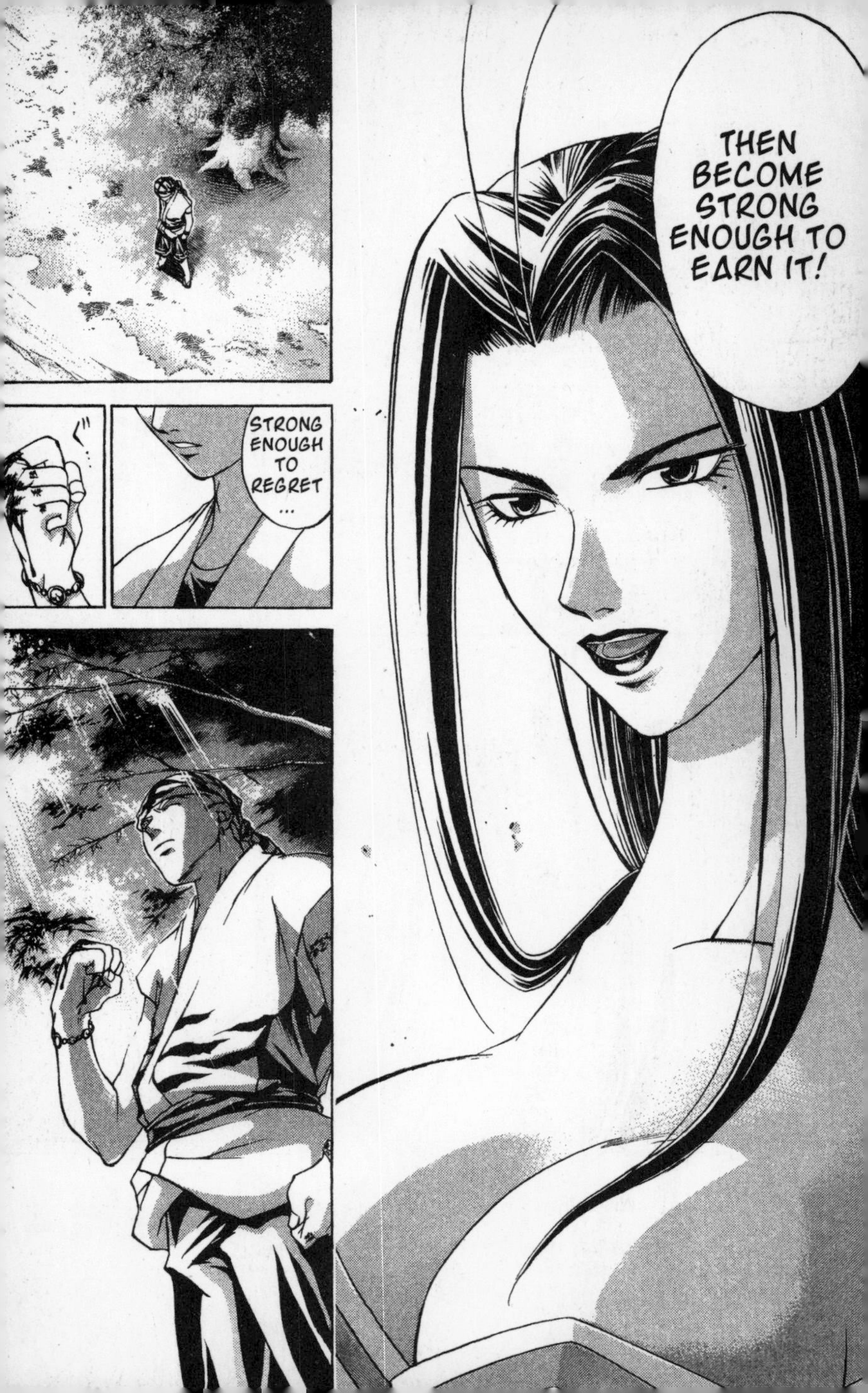
THEN BECOME STRONG ENOUGH TO EARN IT!
STRONG ENOUGH TO REGRET ...

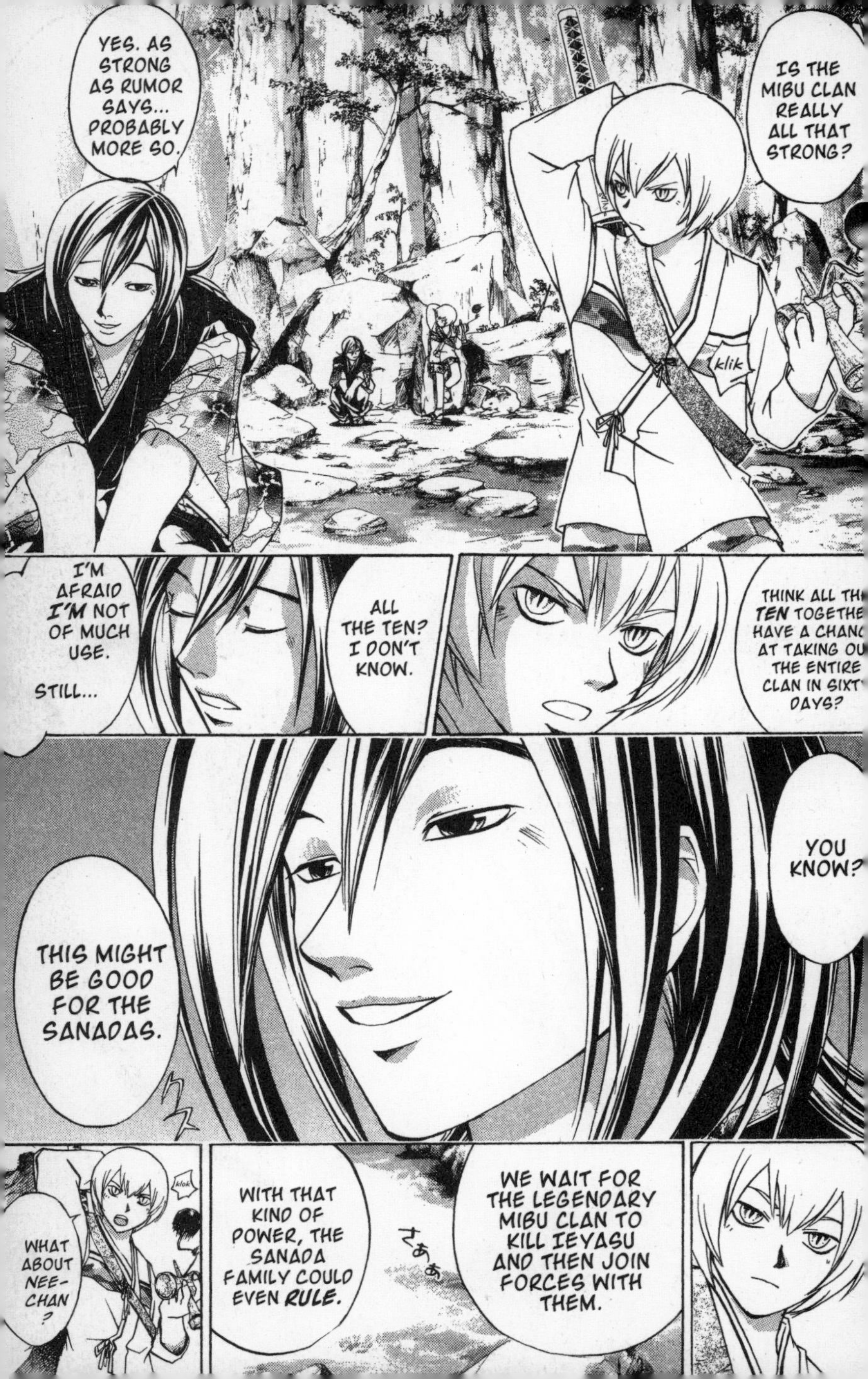
IS THE MIBU CLAN REALLY ALL THAT STRONG?
klik
YES. AS STRONG AS RUMOR SAYS... PROBABLY MORE SO.
THINK ALL TH TEN TOGETHE HAVE A CHANC AT TAKING OU THE ENTIRE CLAN IN SIXT DAYS?
ALL THE TEN? I DON'T KNOW.
I'M AFRAID *I'M* NOT OF MUCH USE.
STILL...
YOU KNOW?
THIS MIGHT BE GOOD FOR THE SANADAS.
WE WAIT FOR THE LEGENDARY MIBU CLAN TO KILL IEYASU AND THEN JOIN FORCES WITH THEM.
さああ
WITH THAT KIND OF POWER, THE SANADA FAMILY COULD EVEN **RULE**.
klok
WHAT ABOUT NEE-CHAN?

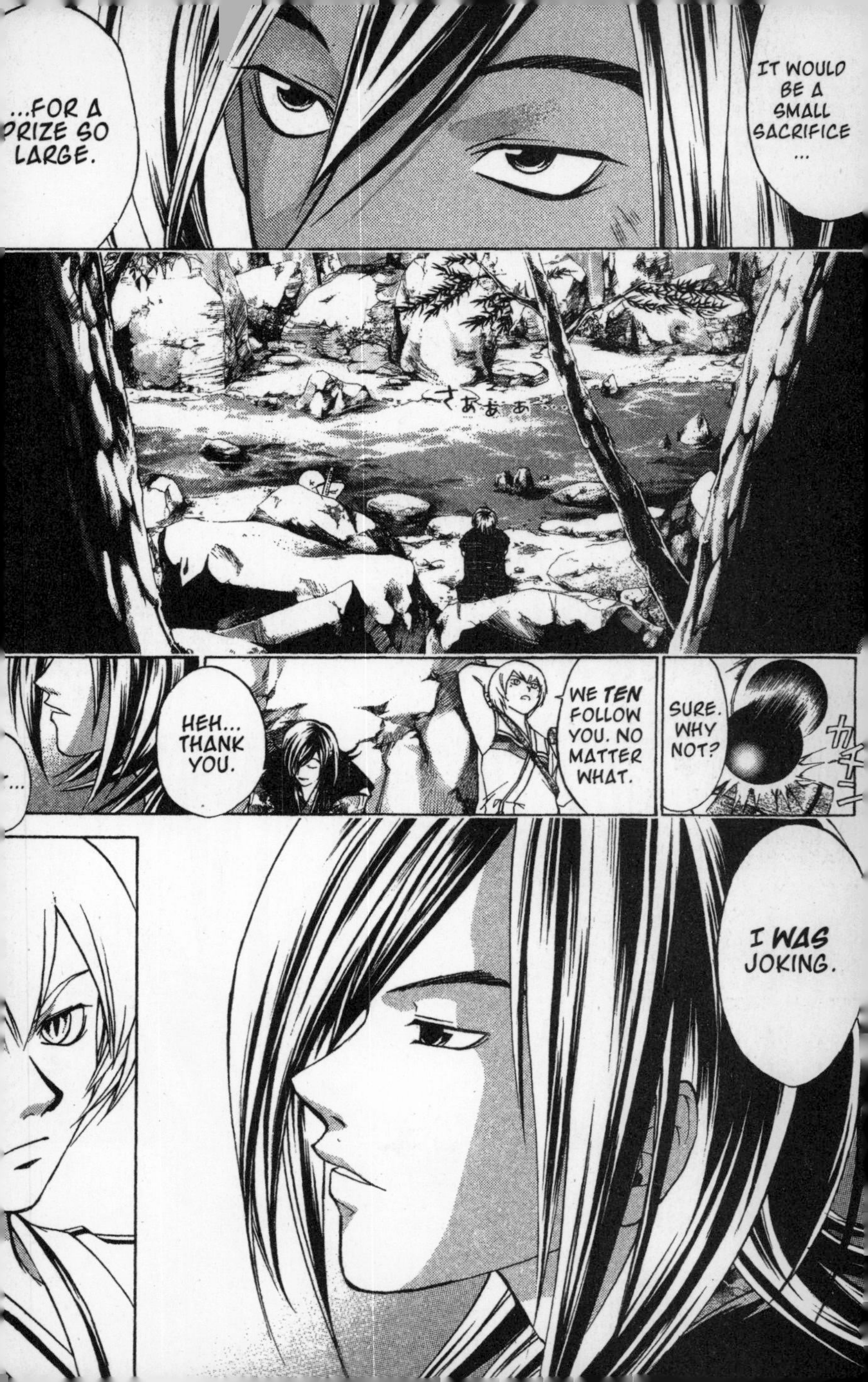
IT WOULD BE A SMALL SACRIFICE ...
...FOR A PRIZE SO LARGE.
さあぁあ
...
SURE. WHY NOT?
WE TEN FOLLOW YOU. NO MATTER WHAT.
HEH... THANK YOU.
...
I WAS JOKING.

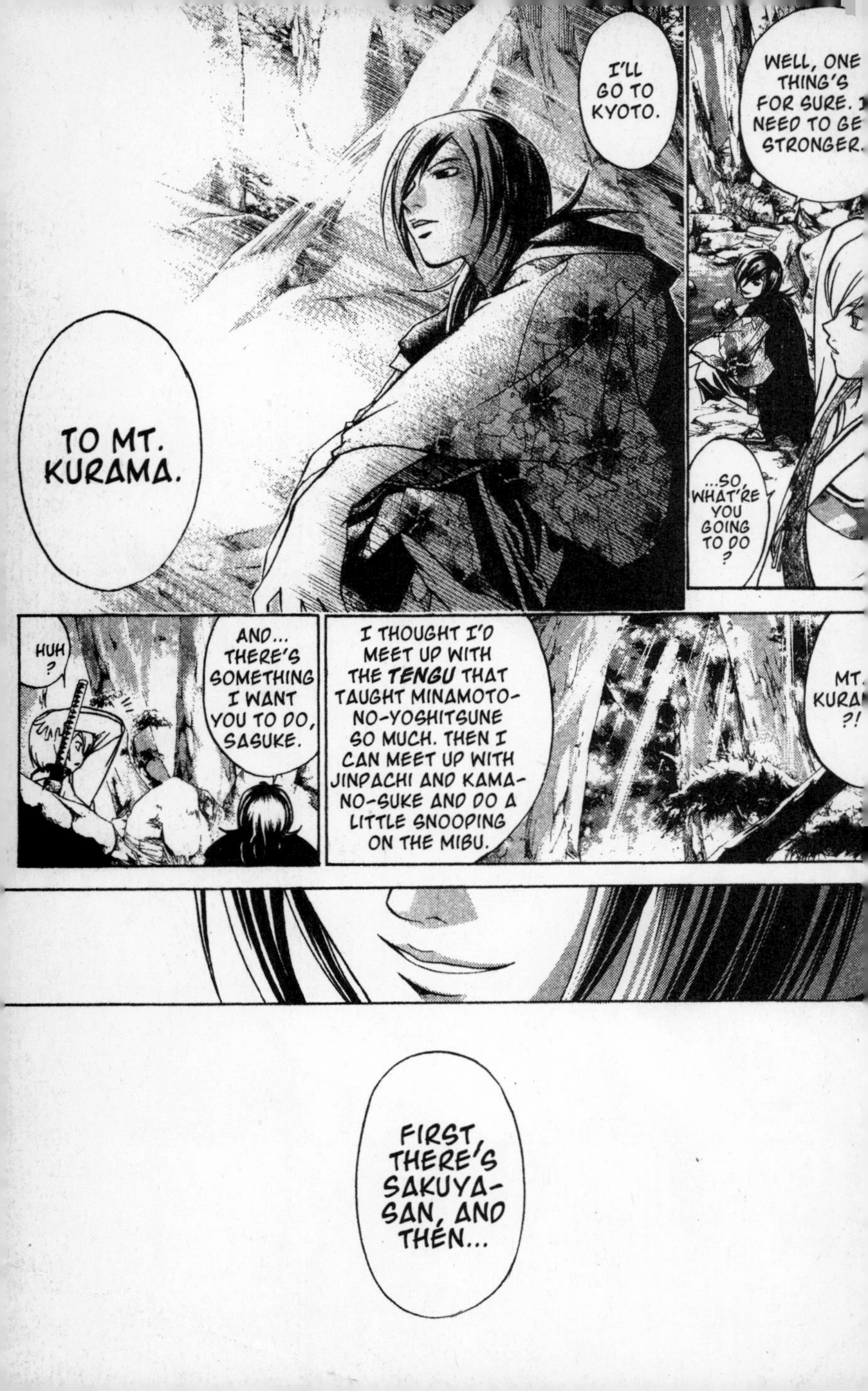
WELL, ONE THING'S FOR SURE. I NEED TO GE STRONGER.
...SO, WHAT'RE YOU GOING TO DO?
I'LL GO TO KYOTO.
TO MT. KURAMA.
MT. KURA ?!
I THOUGHT I'D MEET UP WITH THE *TENGU* THAT TAUGHT MINAMOTO-NO-YOSHITSUNE SO MUCH. THEN I CAN MEET UP WITH JINPACHI AND KAMA-NO-SUKE AND DO A LITTLE SNOOPING ON THE MIBU.
AND... THERE'S SOMETHING I WANT YOU TO DO, SASUKE.
HUH?
FIRST THERE'S SAKUYA-SAN, AND THEN...

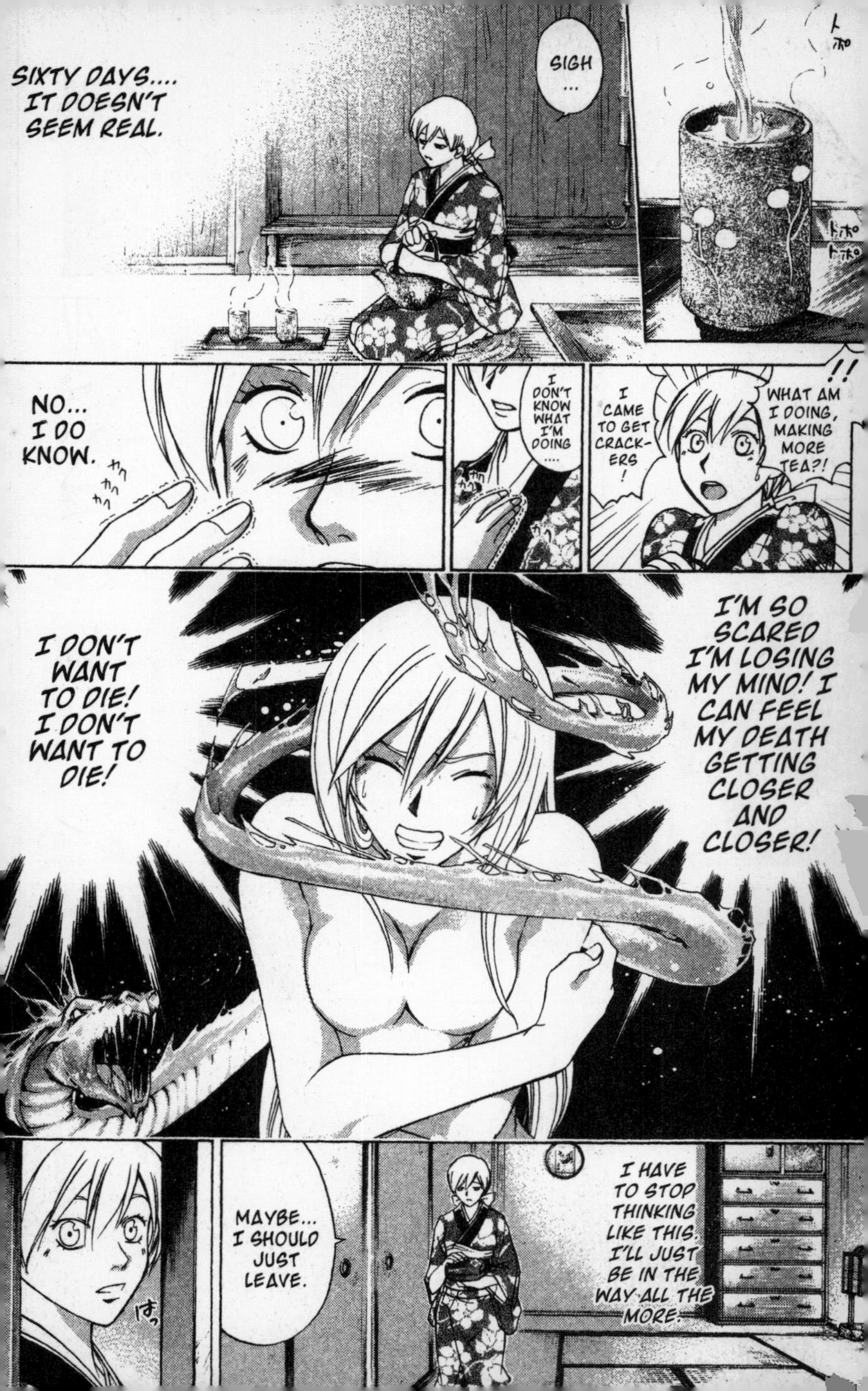

トポ
トポ
トポ
SIGH ...
SIXTY DAYS.... IT DOESN'T SEEM REAL.
!!
WHAT AM I DOING, MAKING MORE TEA?!
I CAME TO GET CRACKERS!
I DON'T KNOW WHAT I'M DOING ....
NO... I DO KNOW.
I'M SO SCARED I'M LOSING MY MIND! I CAN FEEL MY DEATH GETTING CLOSER AND CLOSER!
I DON'T WANT TO DIE! I DON'T WANT TO DIE!
I HAVE TO STOP THINKING LIKE THIS. I'LL JUST BE IN THE WAY ALL THE MORE.
MAYBE... I SHOULD JUST LEAVE.
はっ

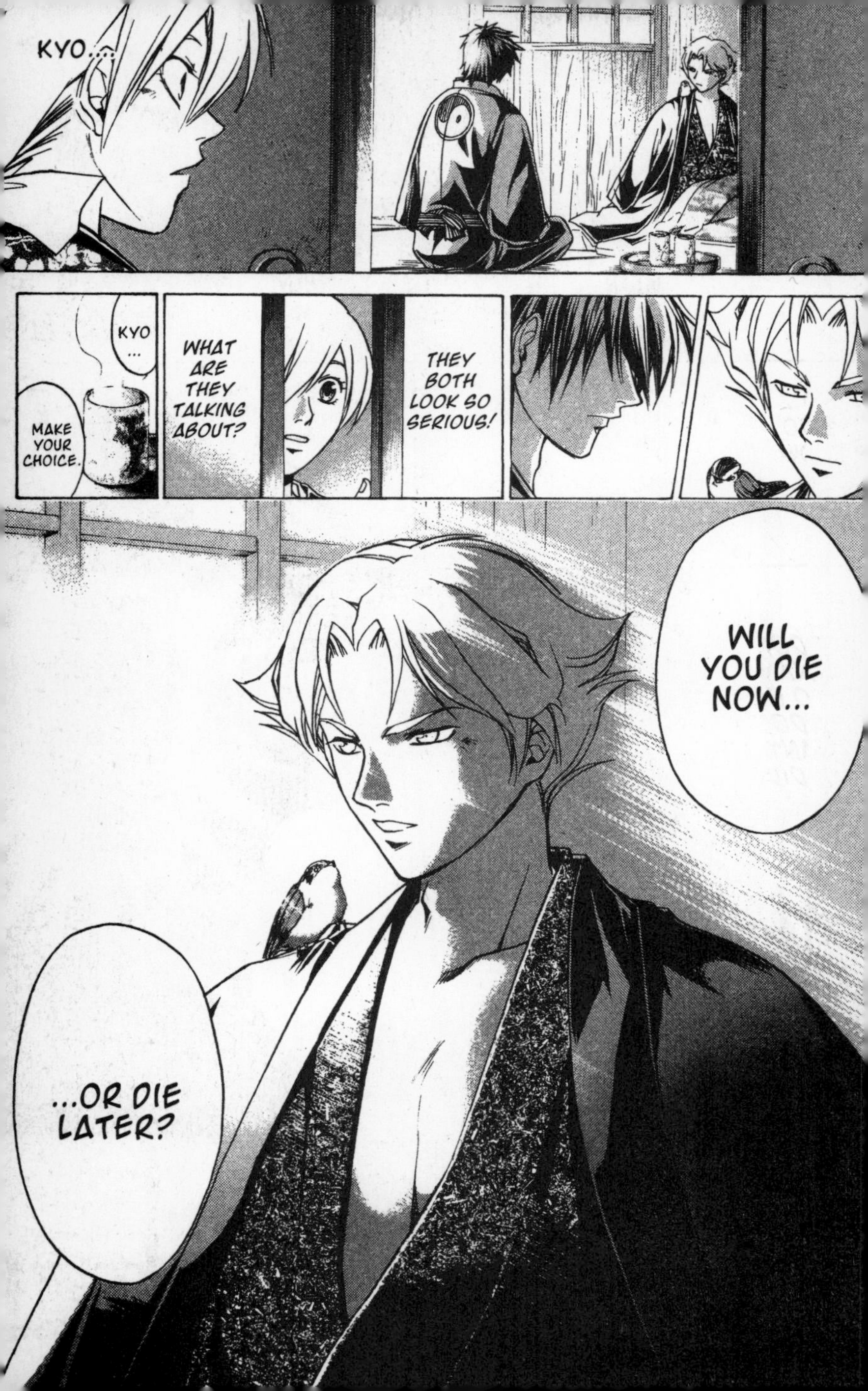
KYO...
THEY BOTH LOOK SO SERIOUS!
WHAT ARE THEY TALKING ABOUT?
KYO...
MAKE YOUR CHOICE.
WILL YOU DIE NOW...
...OR DIE LATER?

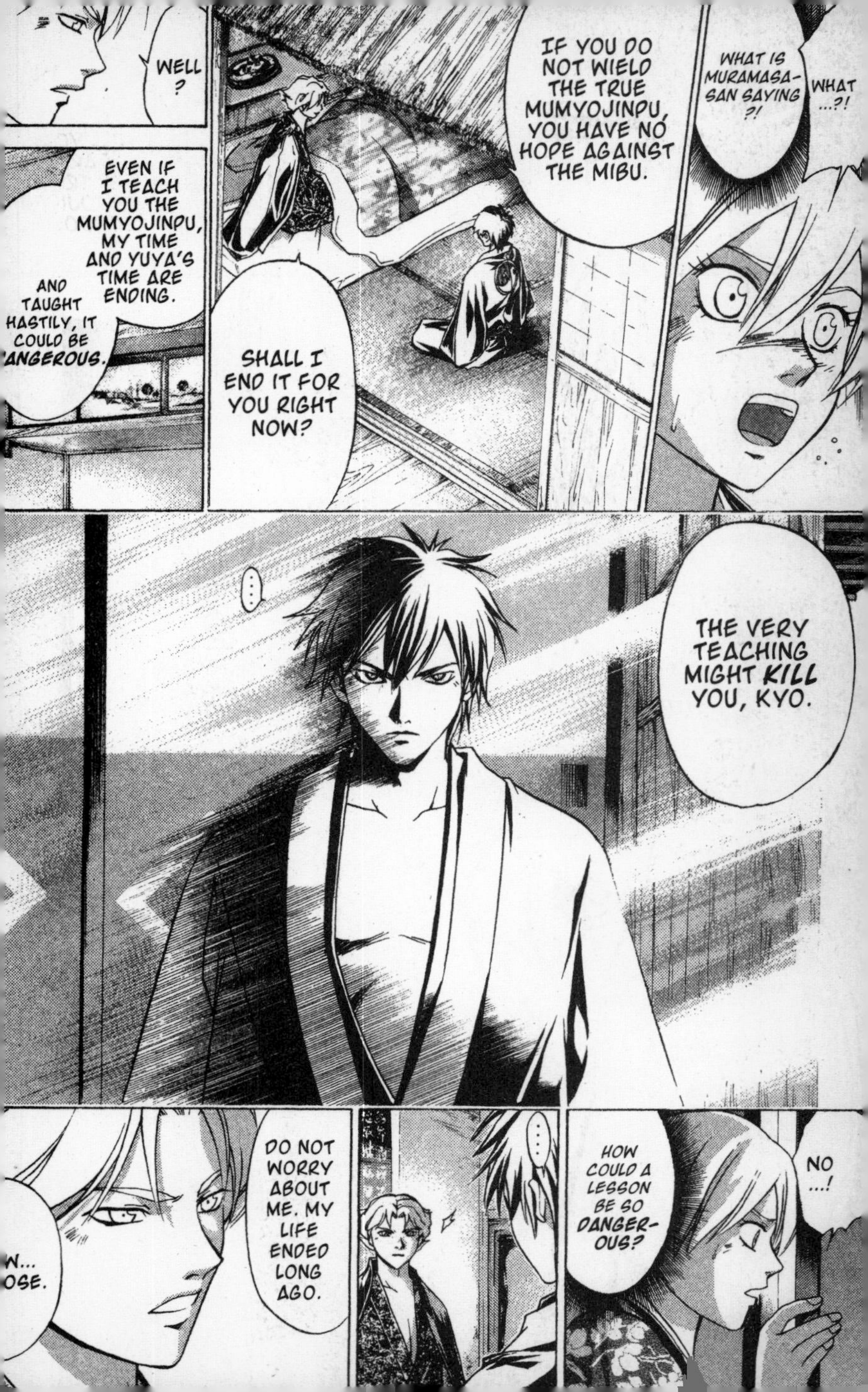
WHAT ...?!
WHAT IS MURAMASA-SAN SAYING ?!
IF YOU DO NOT WIELD THE TRUE MUMYOJINPU, YOU HAVE NO HOPE AGAINST THE MIBU.
SHALL I END IT FOR YOU RIGHT NOW?
WELL ?
EVEN IF I TEACH YOU THE MUMYOJINPU, MY TIME AND YUYA'S TIME ARE ENDING.
AND TAUGHT HASTILY, IT COULD BE ANGEROUS.
THE VERY TEACHING MIGHT KILL YOU, KYO.
...
NO ...!
HOW COULD A LESSON BE SO DANGER-OUS?
...
DO NOT WORRY ABOUT ME. MY LIFE ENDED LONG AGO.
N... OSE.

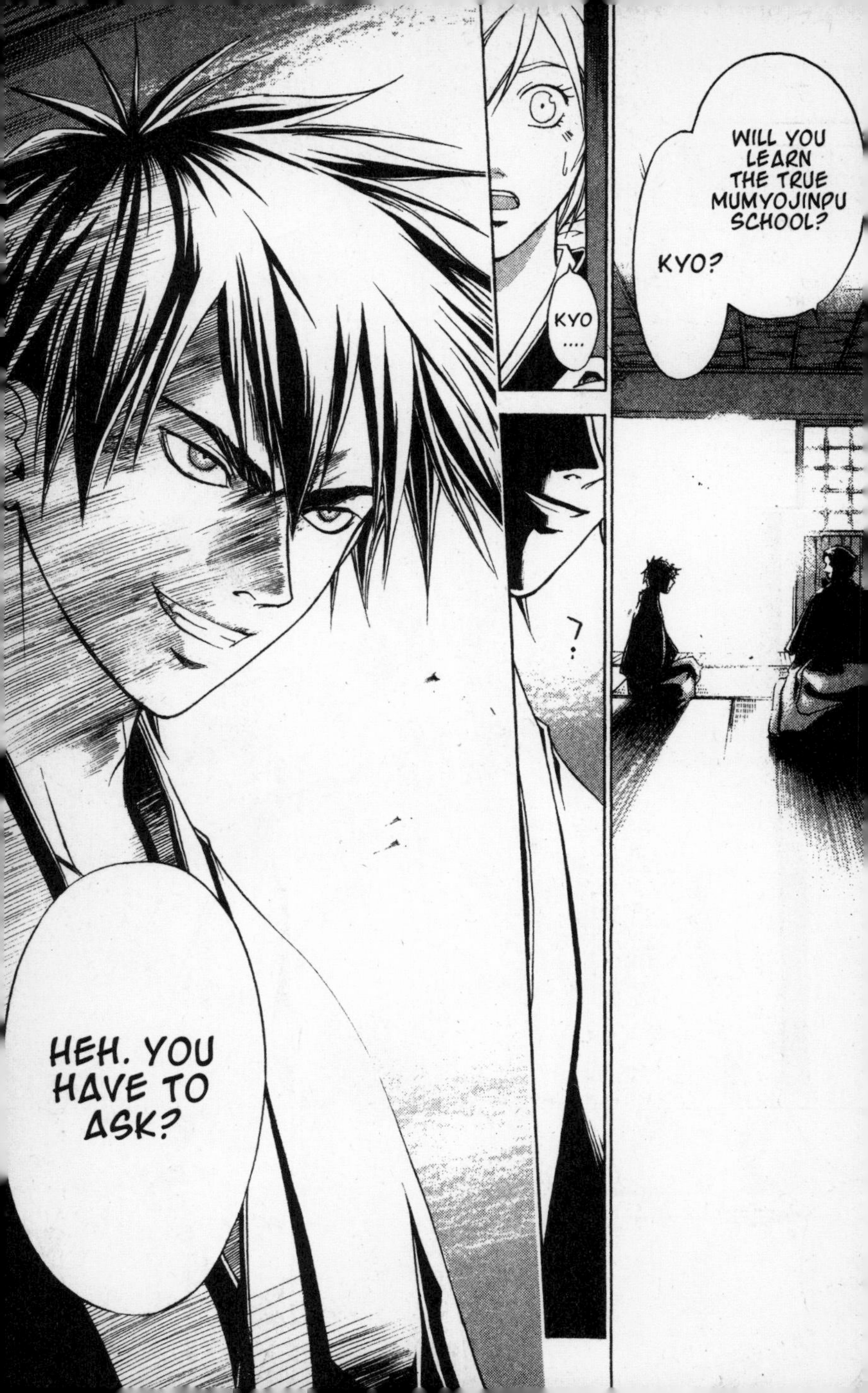
WILL YOU LEARN THE TRUE MUMYOJINPU SCHOOL?
KYO?
KYO .....
HEH. YOU HAVE TO ASK?

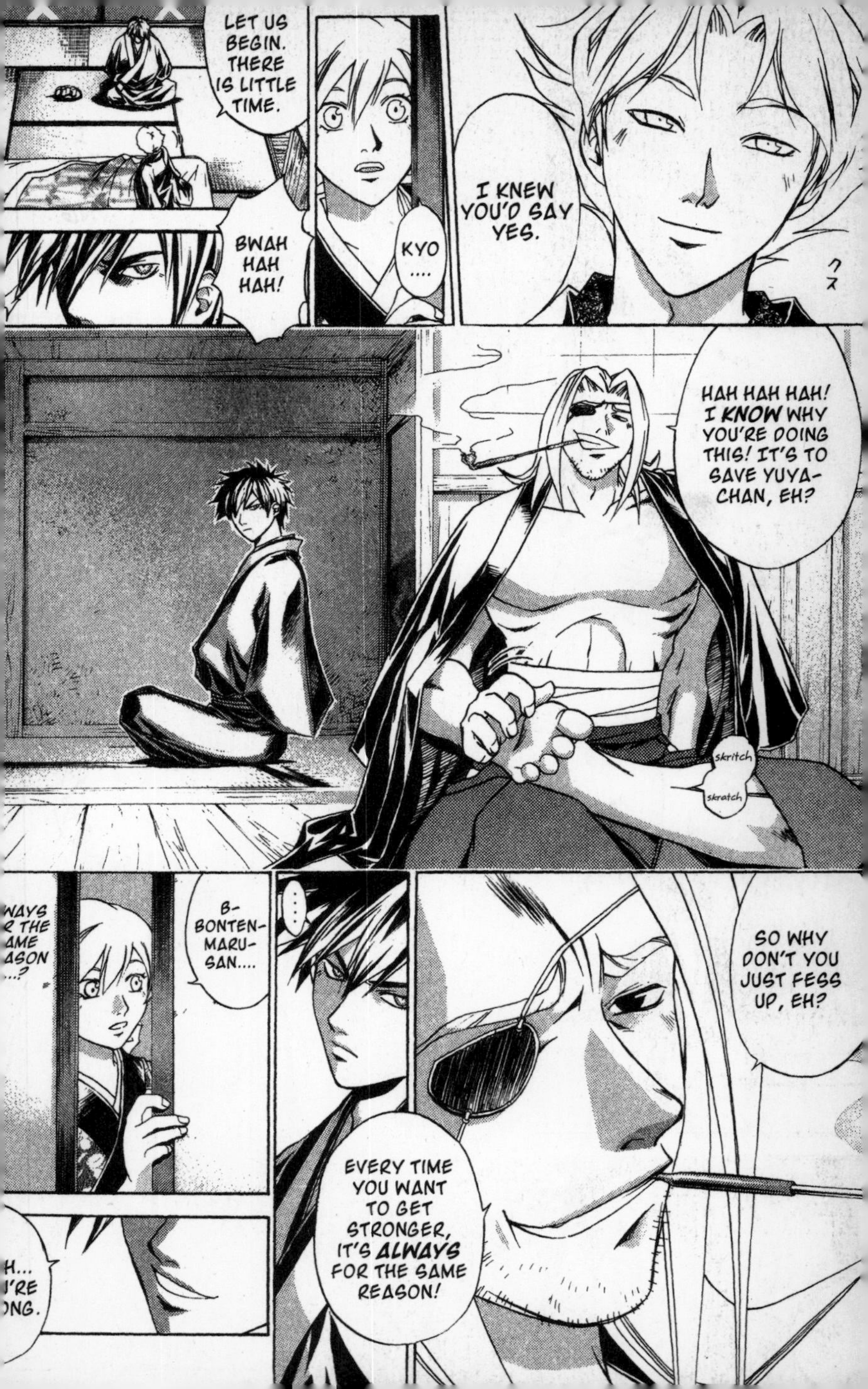
I KNEW YOU'D SAY YES.
KYO ....
LET US BEGIN. THERE IS LITTLE TIME.
BWAH HAH HAH!
HAH HAH HAH! I **KNOW** WHY YOU'RE DOING THIS! IT'S TO SAVE YUYA-CHAN, EH?
skritch
skratch
SO WHY DON'T YOU JUST FESS UP, EH?
...
EVERY TIME YOU WANT TO GET STRONGER, IT'S **ALWAYS** FOR THE SAME REASON!
B-BONTEN-MARU-SAN....

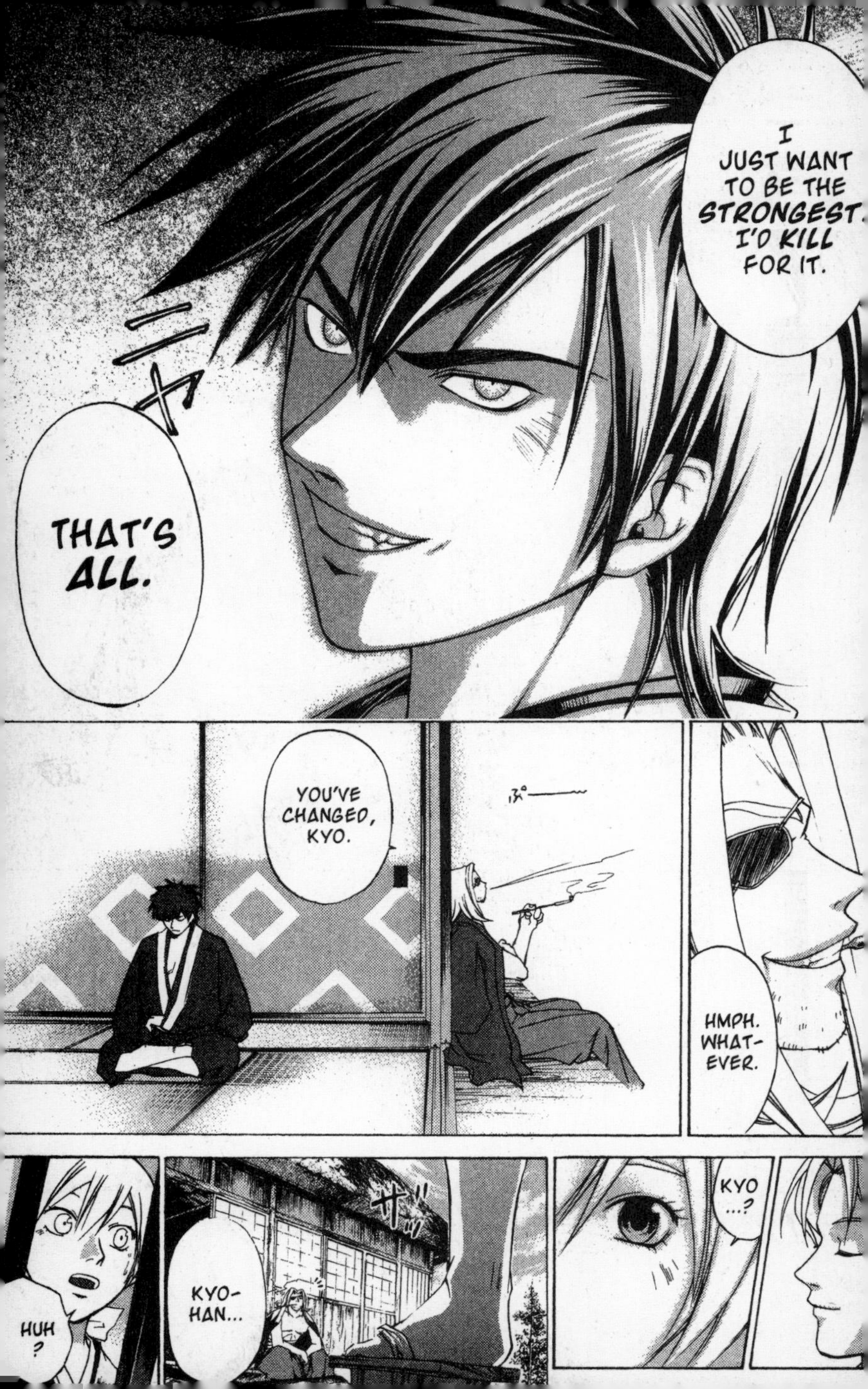
I JUST WANT TO BE THE STRONGEST. I'D KILL FOR IT.
THAT'S ALL.
HMPH. WHATEVER.
YOU'VE CHANGED, KYO.
KYO ...?
KYO-HAN...
HUH ?

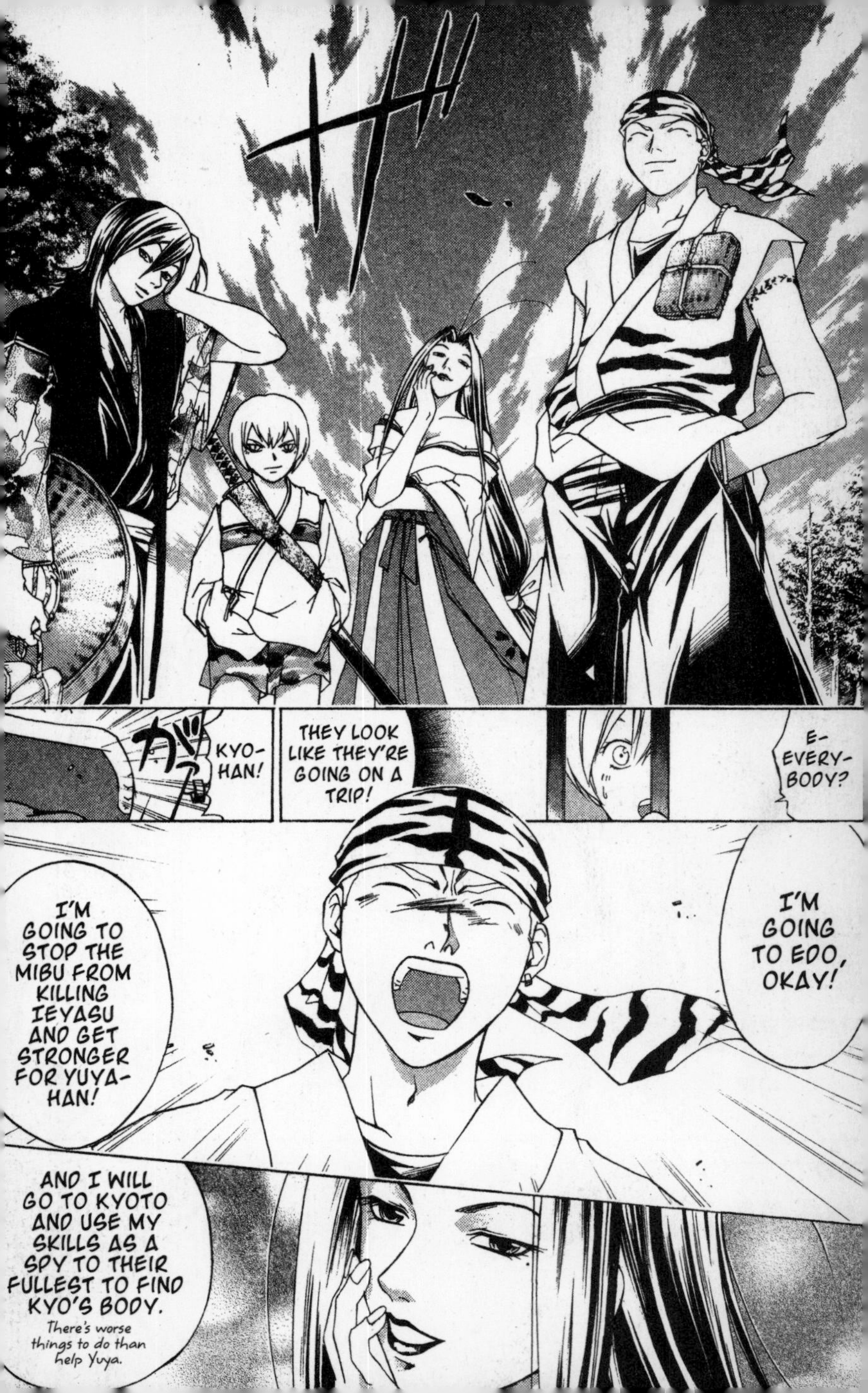
E- EVERY- BODY?
THEY LOOK LIKE THEY'RE GOING ON A TRIP!
KYO- HAN!
I'M GOING TO EDO, OKAY!
I'M GOING TO STOP THE MIBU FROM KILLING IEYASU AND GET STRONGER FOR YUYA- HAN!
AND I WILL GO TO KYOTO AND USE MY SKILLS AS A SPY TO THEIR FULLEST TO FIND KYO'S BODY.
There's worse things to do than help Yuya.

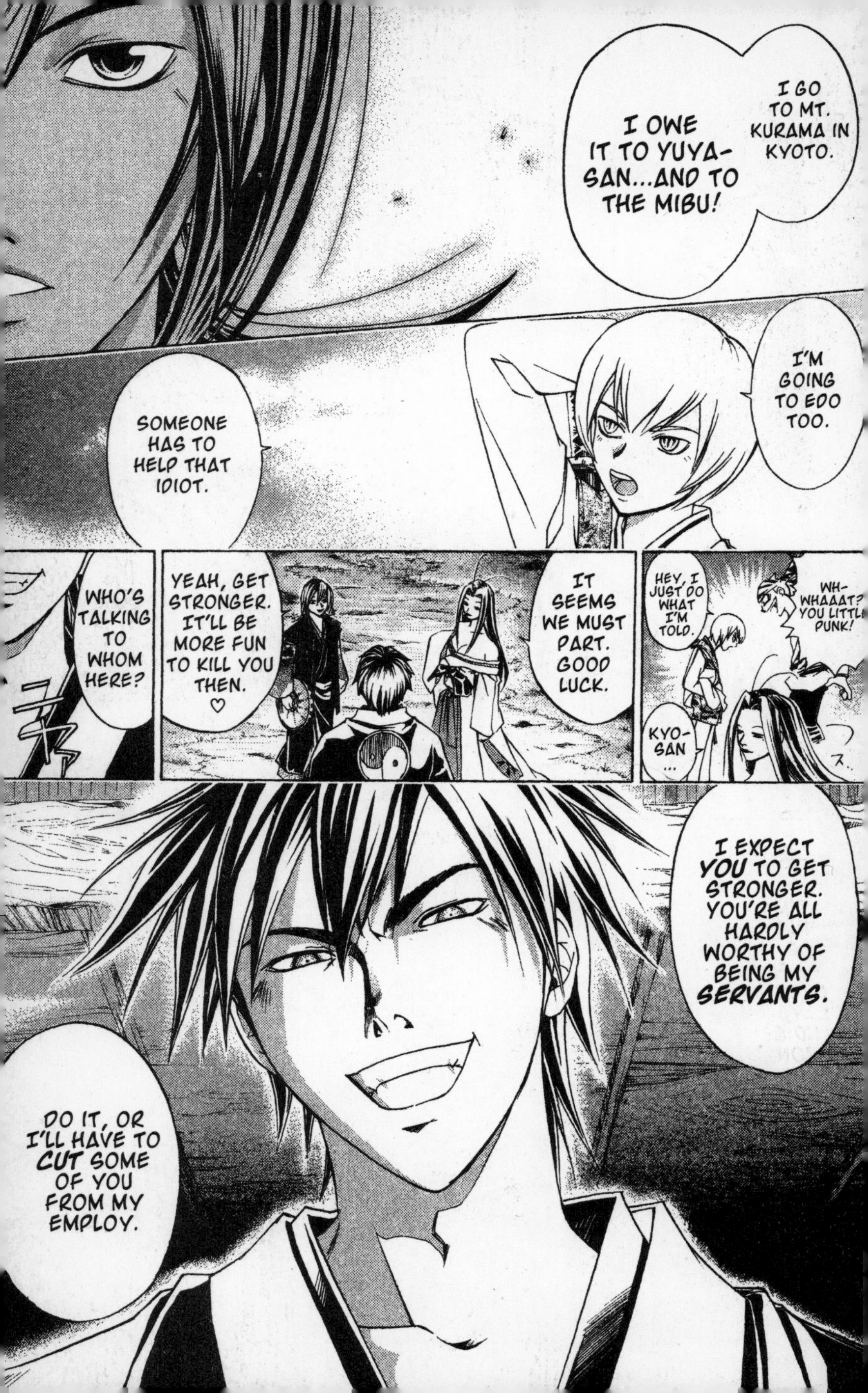
I GO TO MT. KURAMA IN KYOTO.
I OWE IT TO YUYA-SAN...AND TO THE MIBU!
I'M GOING TO EDO TOO.
SOMEONE HAS TO HELP THAT IDIOT.
HEY, I JUST DO WHAT I'M TOLD.
WH-WHAAAT? YOU LITTLE PUNK!
KYO-SAN ...
IT SEEMS WE MUST PART. GOOD LUCK.
YEAH, GET STRONGER. IT'LL BE MORE FUN TO KILL YOU THEN. ♡
WHO'S TALKING TO WHOM HERE?
I EXPECT YOU TO GET STRONGER. YOU'RE ALL HARDLY WORTHY OF BEING MY SERVANTS.
DO IT, OR I'LL HAVE TO CUT SOME OF YOU FROM MY EMPLOY.

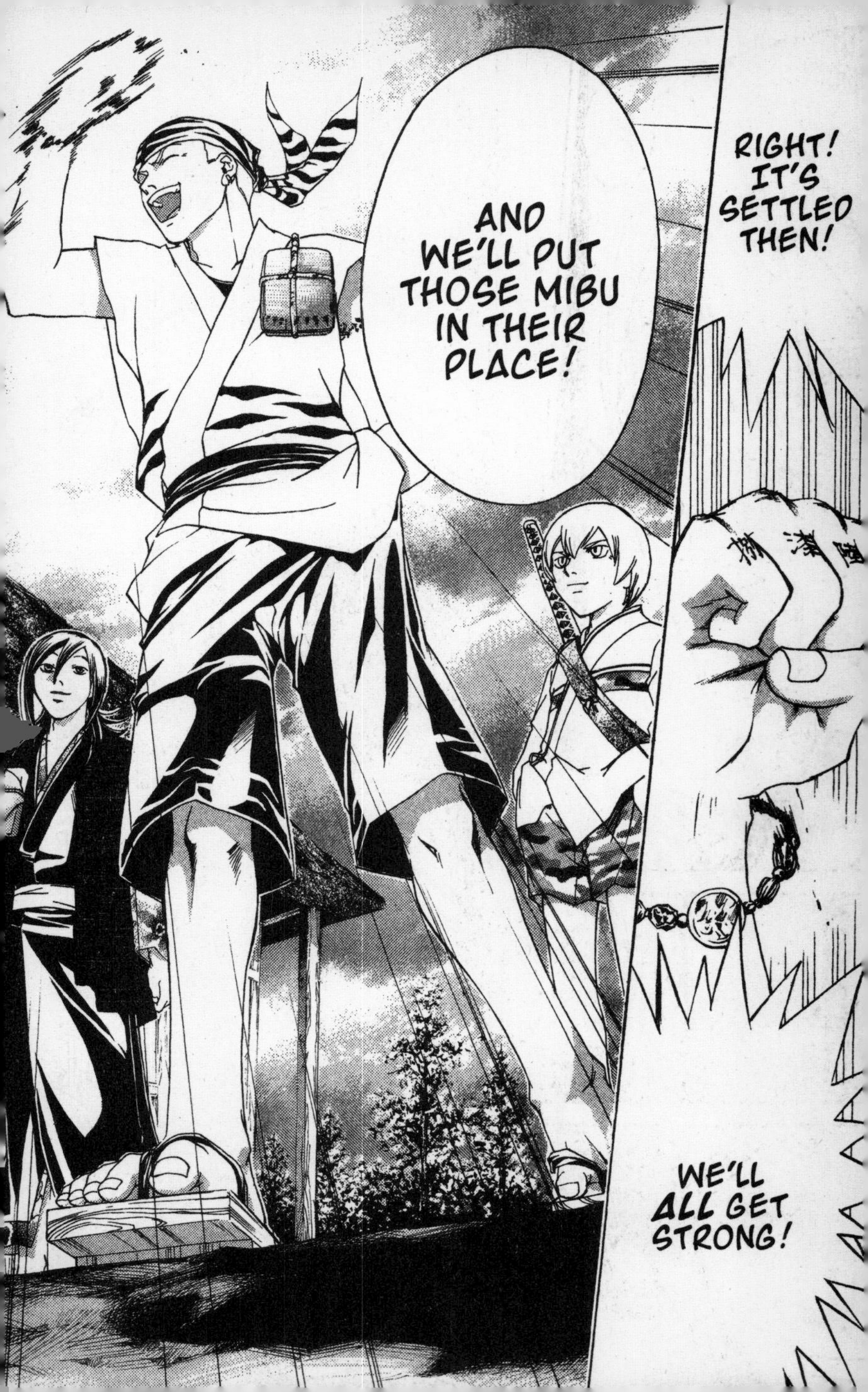
RIGHT! IT'S SETTLED THEN!
AND WE'LL PUT THOSE MIBU IN THEIR PLACE!
WE'LL ALL GET STRONG!

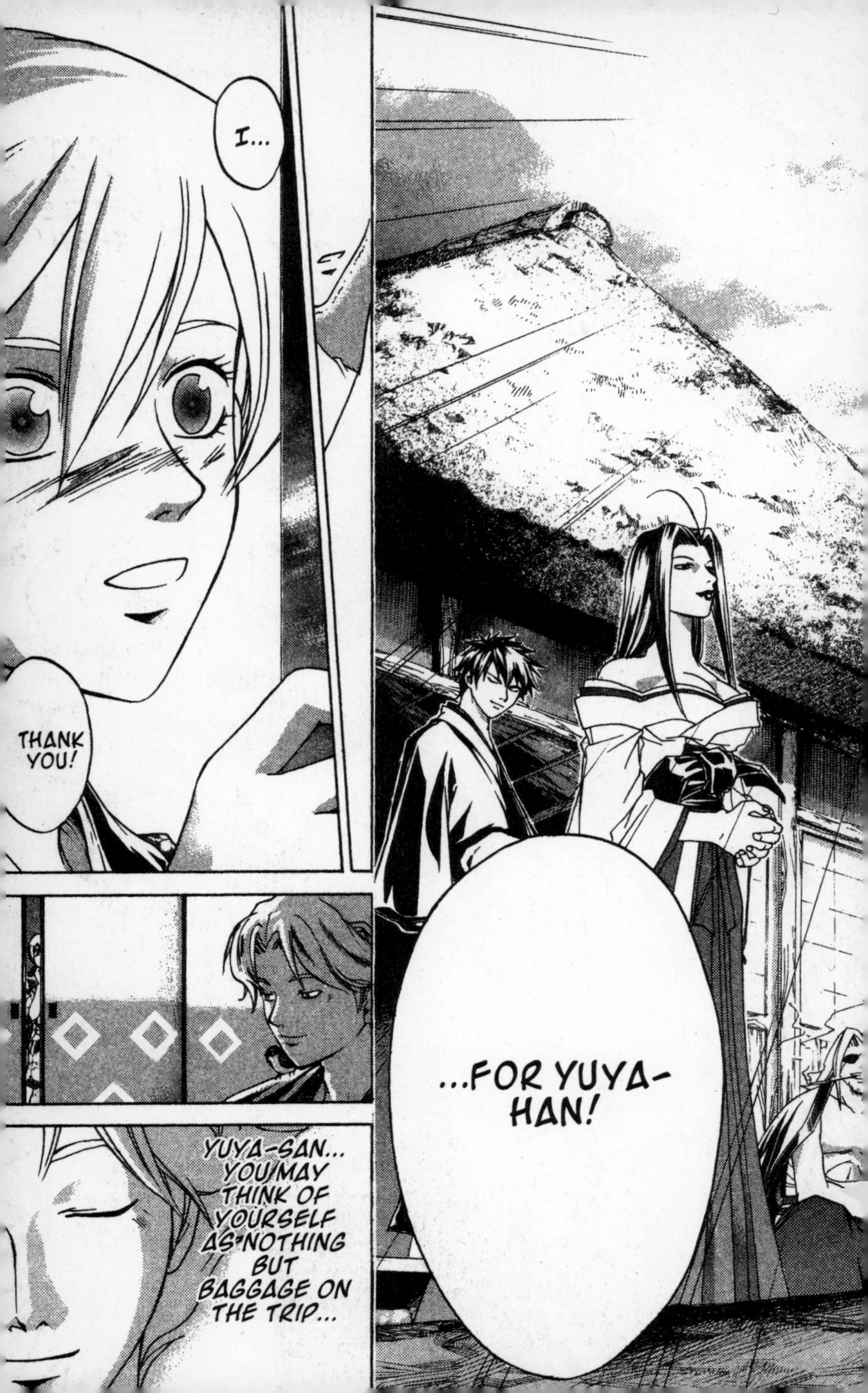
I...
THANK YOU!
YUYA-SAN... YOU MAY THINK OF YOURSELF AS NOTHING BUT BAGGAGE ON THE TRIP...
...FOR YUYA-HAN!

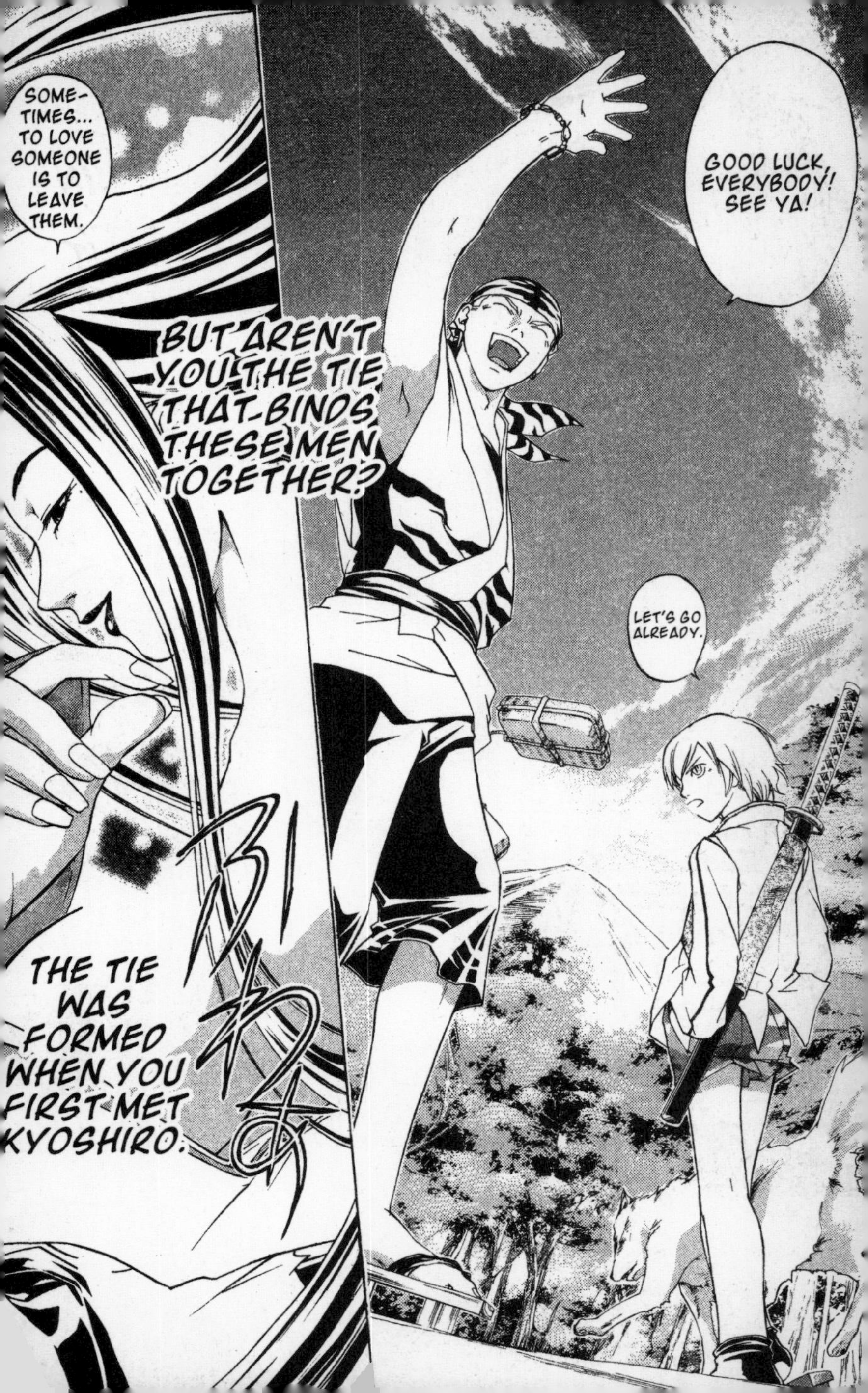
GOOD LUCK, EVERYBODY! SEE YA!
LET'S GO ALREADY.
SOME-TIMES... TO LOVE SOMEONE IS TO LEAVE THEM.
BUT AREN'T YOU THE TIE THAT BINDS THESE MEN TOGETHER?
THE TIE WAS FORMED WHEN YOU FIRST MET KYOSHIRO.

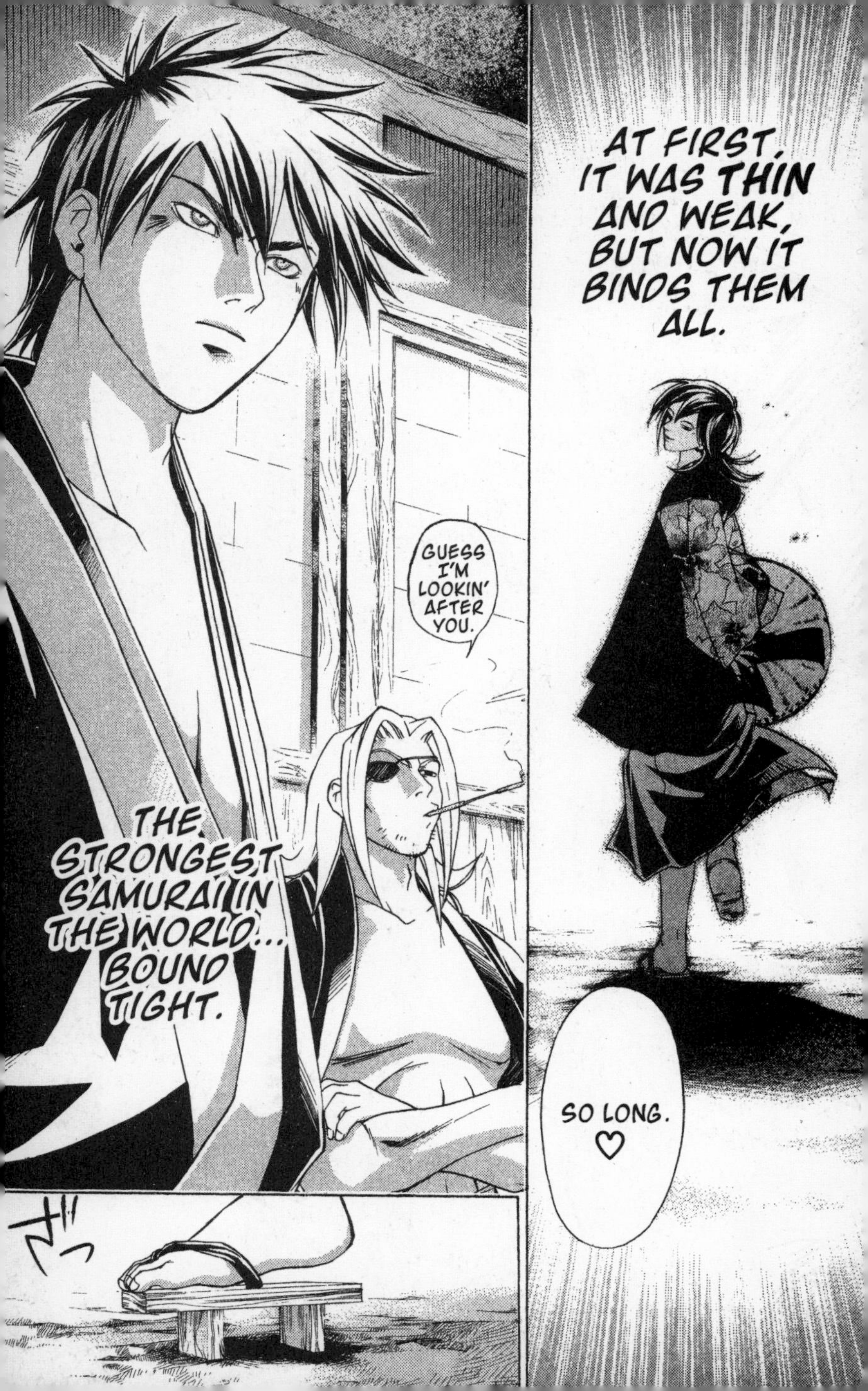
AT FIRST IT WAS THIN AND WEAK, BUT NOW IT BINDS THEM ALL.
SO LONG. ♡
GUESS I'M LOOKIN' AFTER YOU.
THE STRONGEST SAMURAI IN THE WORLD... BOUND TIGHT.
ざっ

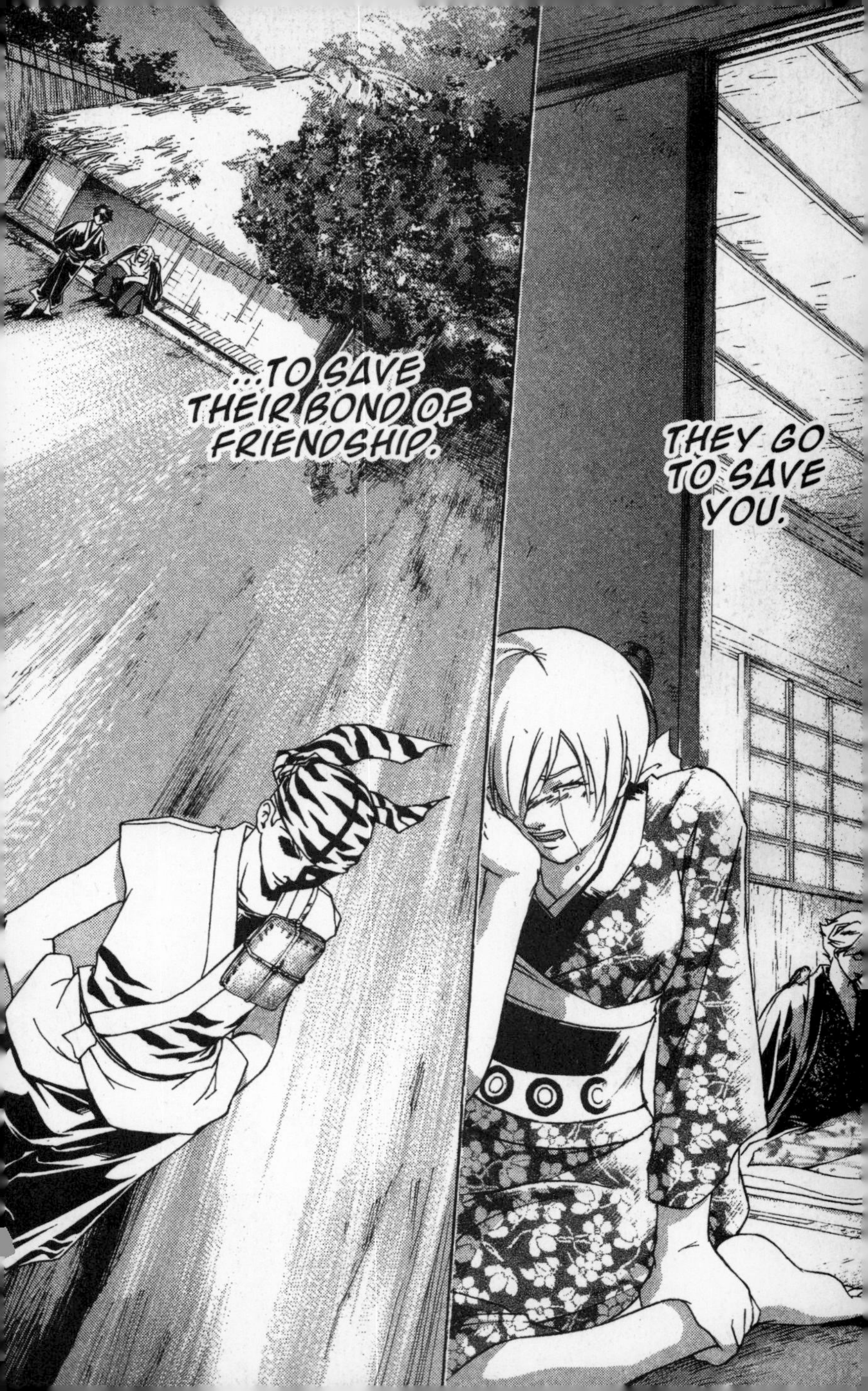
THEY GO TO SAVE YOU.
...TO SAVE THEIR BOND OF FRIENDSHIP.

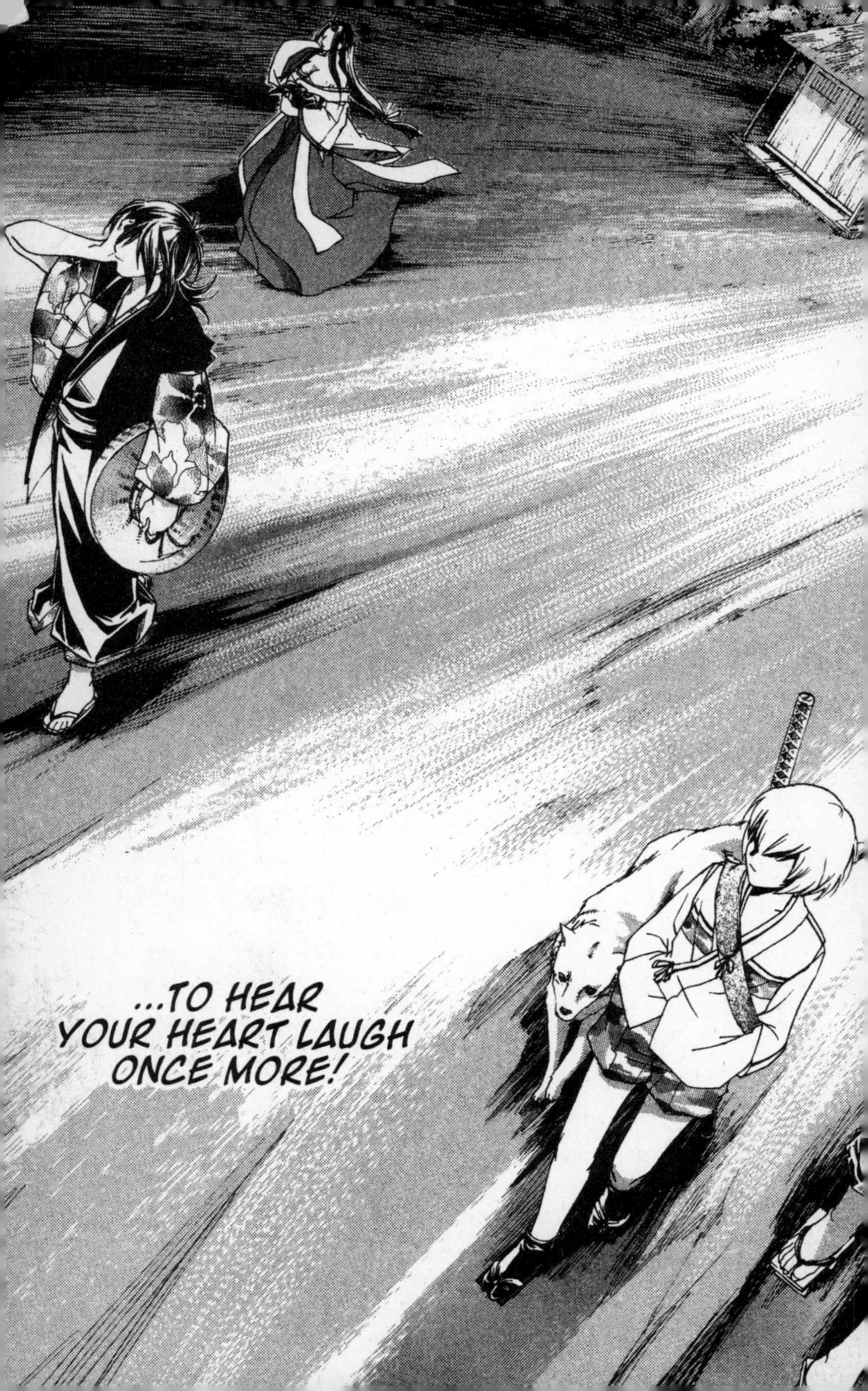
...TO HEAR YOUR HEART LAUGH ONCE MORE!

Akimine-kun's Q&A CORNER

ALL ABOUT SDK

Q: DO YOU HAVE MODELS FOR YOUR CHARACTERS? HOW DO YOU CREATE THEM?
A: I TRY NOT TO THINK OF ANYTHING WHEN I'M FIRST DESIGNING CHARACTERS--SO I'M PROBABLY REMEMBERING THINGS FROM MY CHILDHOOD. WELL, MORE LIKE IMPRESSIONS.

Q: HOW DO YOU COME UP WITH THE STORY?
A: BASICALLY, I LET THE CHARACTERS MOVE IN WAYS THAT SEEM NATURAL FOR THEM. SOMETIMES, EVEN I'M SURPRISED BY WHAT THEY DO. I FIND MYSELF SAYING THINGS LIKE "AH, SO THAT'S WHAT YOU WERE THINKING, TORA." STILL, WITH SUCH A FREE-SPIRITED GROUP, IT'S EASY TO GET SIDETRACKED. IT'S ALWAYS A BALANCE BETWEEN KEEPING THE CHARACTER'S PERSONALITIES INTACT AND KEEPING THE STORY ON TRACK.

Q: YOU SEEM TO HAVE A LOT OF "SUGGESTIVE" CONTENT. YOU LIKE THAT KIND OF STUFF?
A: YES! ...IS THERE REALLY THAT MUCH?

Q: THE TITLE IS TOO LONG. HOW SHOULD I SHORTEN IT?
A: WELL, SOME PEOPLE CALL IT "KYO" AND SOME PEOPLE CALL IT "DEEPER KYO." WHICHEVER WORKS!

Q: A LOT OF MANGA LOOKS DIFFERENT AFTER THE FIRST FEW ISSUES, BUT YOURS STAYS PRETTY MUCH THE SAME. DO YOU PRACTICE AT THAT?
A: ACTUALLY, I THINK THE STYLE HAS CHANGED (WHOOPS). I ALWAYS THINK I SHOULD BE PRACTICING EVEN MORE.

Q: HEY, I NOTICED THAT YOU CHANGED FROM "POSTCARDS" TO "FAN LETTERS" IN THE "DRAW LIKE KAMIJO AKIMINE!" CORNER!
A: HUH? IS THAT SO WRONG? SOME PEOPLE THOUGHT THAT THEY COULD ONLY SEND IN POSTCARDS....

Q: HAVE YOU EVER THOUGHT OF DOING AN SDK ANIME, GAME, OR MOVIE?
A: THAT'S NOT SOMETHING THAT I GET TO DECIDE...AND I'M A MANGA ARTIST, SO I'LL KEEP DOING MY MANGA!

Q: HOW MANY VOLUMES WILL THERE BE IN SDK?
A: I WANT TO WRITE TO THE BITTER END! OF COURSE, IF PEOPLE STOP READING, IT WILL END...SO I'VE JUST GOT TO KEEP IT INTERESTING!

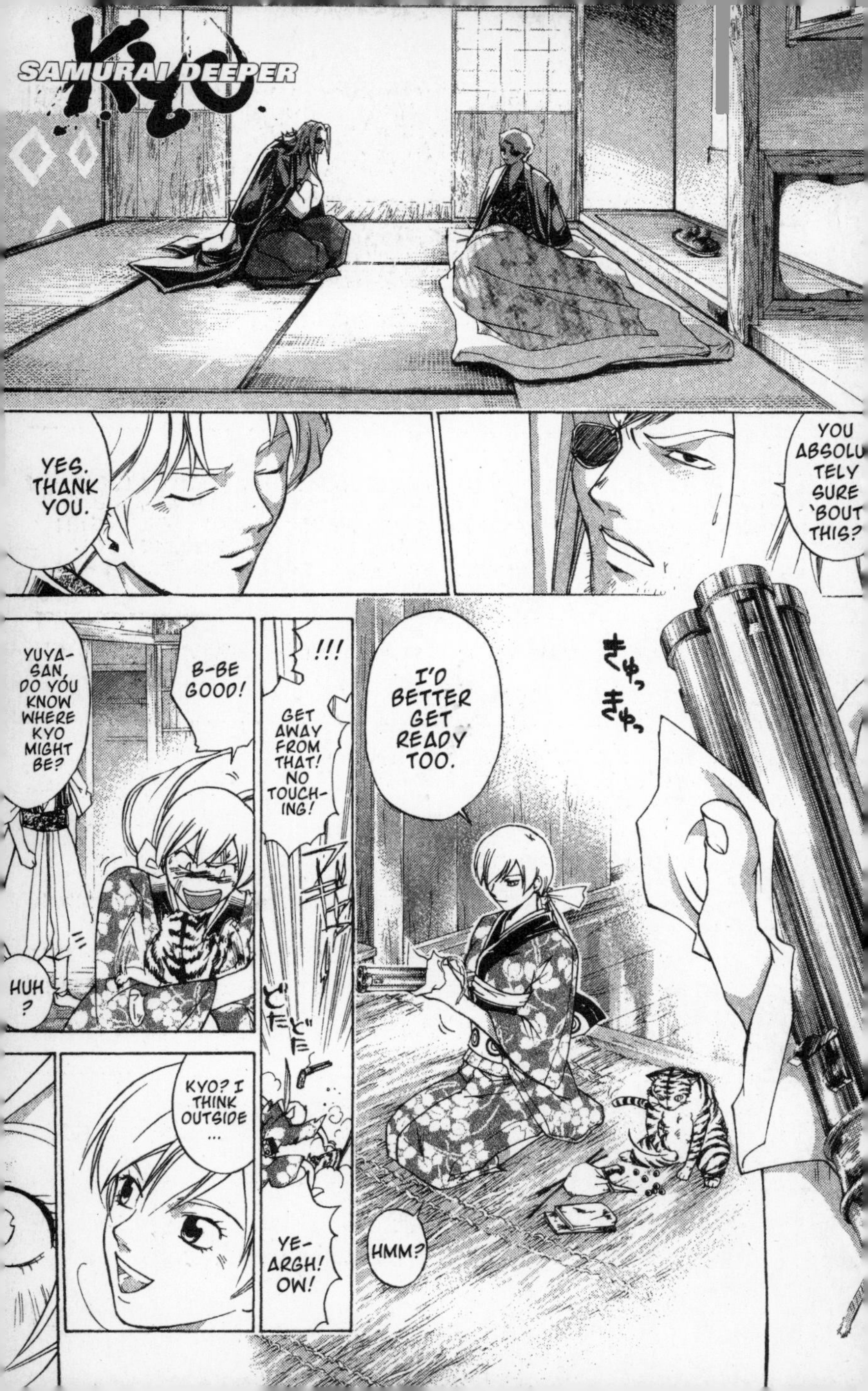
SAMURAI DEEPER KYO
YOU ABSOLUTELY SURE 'BOUT THIS?
YES. THANK YOU.
きゅっ きゅっ
I'D BETTER GET READY TOO.
HMM?
!!!
GET AWAY FROM THAT! NO TOUCHING!
どた どた
YE-ARGH! OW!
B-BE GOOD!
YUYA-SAN, DO YOU KNOW WHERE KYO MIGHT BE?
HUH?
KYO? I THINK OUTSIDE ...

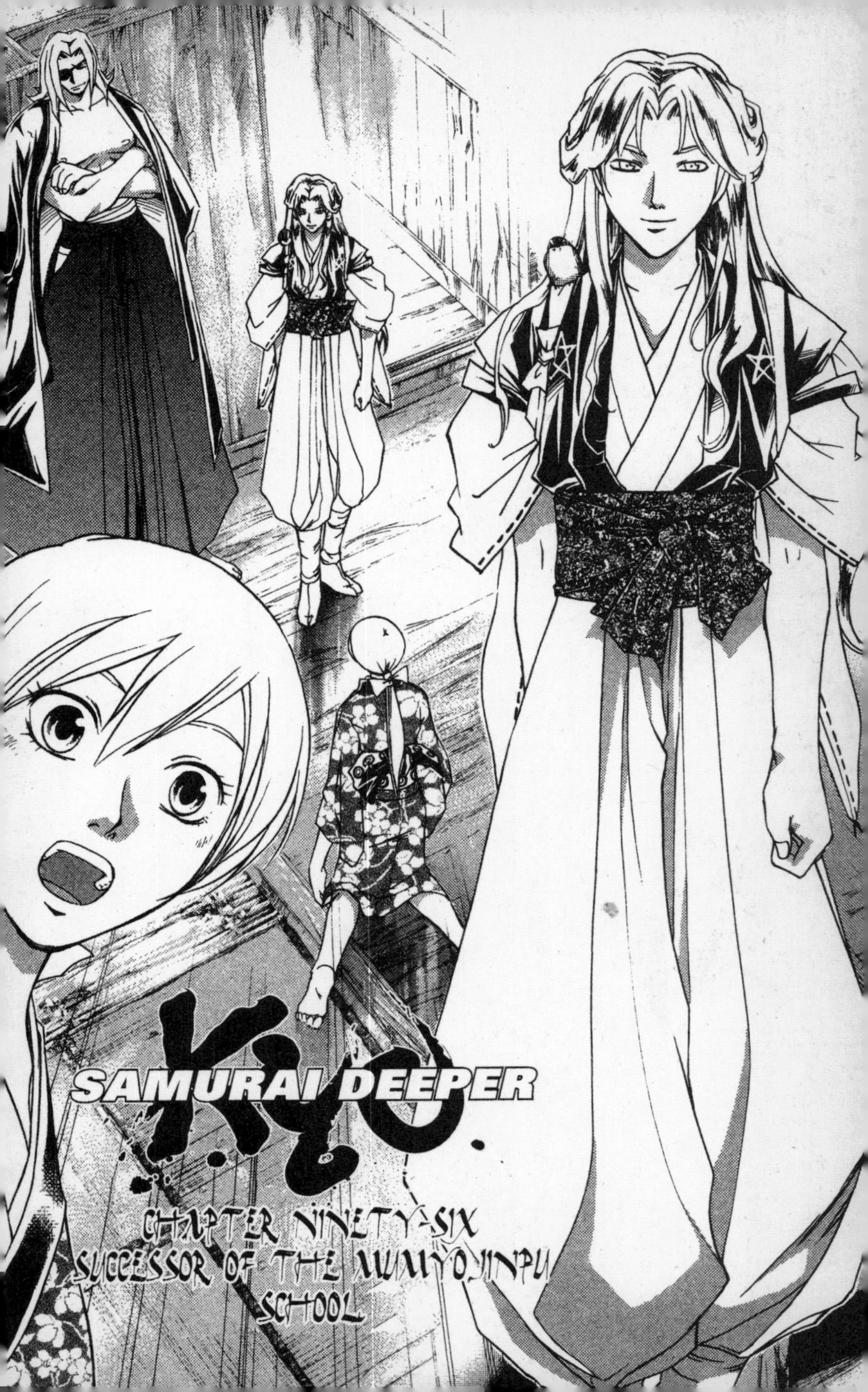

SAMURAI DEEPER
KYO
CHAPTER NINETY-SIX
SUCCESSOR OF THE MUMYOJINPU
SCHOOL

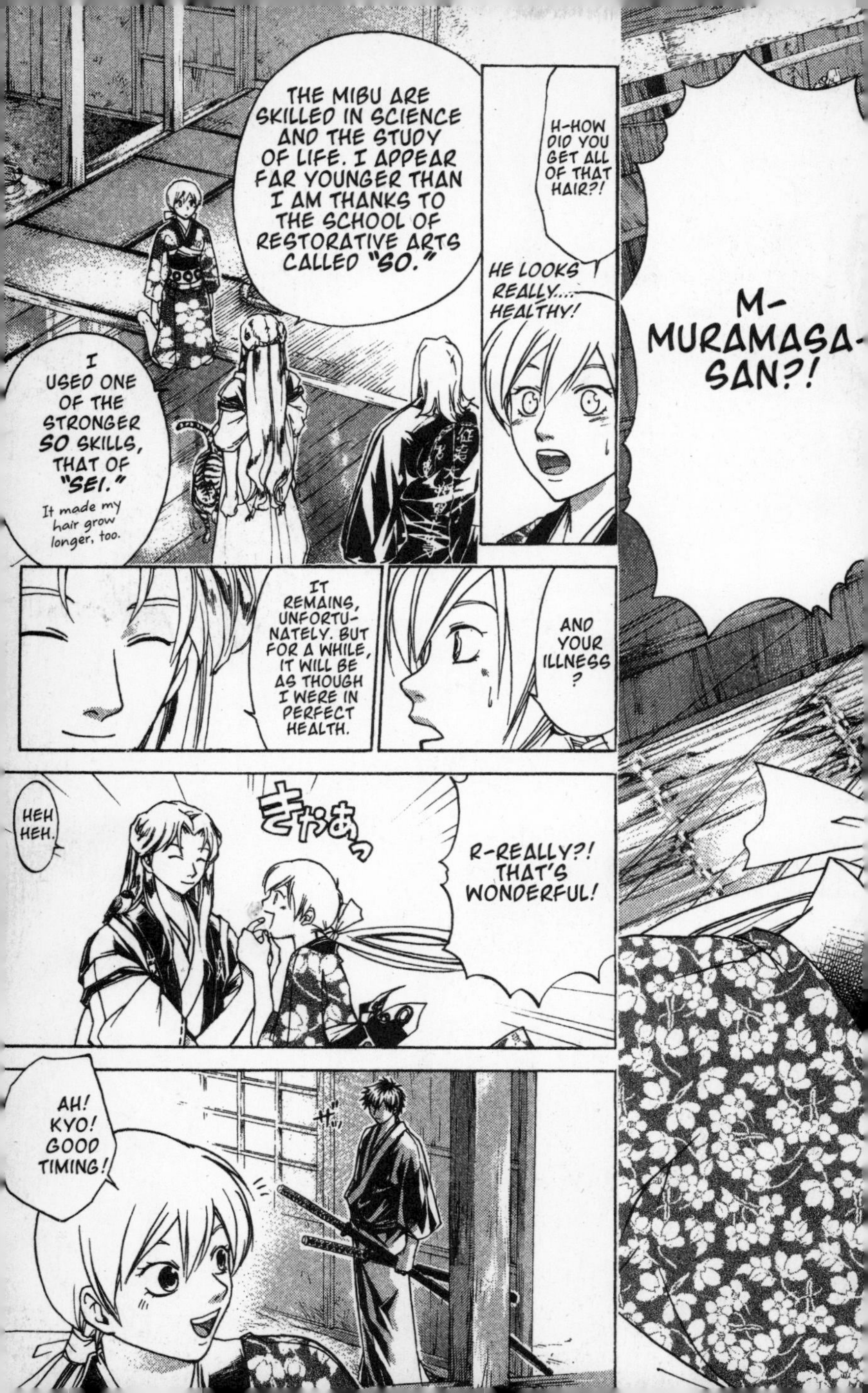
M-MURAMASA-SAN?!
H-HOW DID YOU GET ALL OF THAT HAIR?!
HE LOOKS REALLY... HEALTHY!
THE MIBU ARE SKILLED IN SCIENCE AND THE STUDY OF LIFE. I APPEAR FAR YOUNGER THAN I AM THANKS TO THE SCHOOL OF RESTORATIVE ARTS CALLED "SO."
I USED ONE OF THE STRONGER SO SKILLS, THAT OF "SEI."
It made my hair grow longer, too.
AND YOUR ILLNESS?
IT REMAINING, UNFORTU-NATELY. BUT FOR A WHILE, IT WILL BE AS THOUGH I WERE IN PERFECT HEALTH.
R-REALLY?! THAT'S WONDERFUL!
きゃあっ
HEH HEH.
AH! KYO! GOOD TIMING!
ザッ

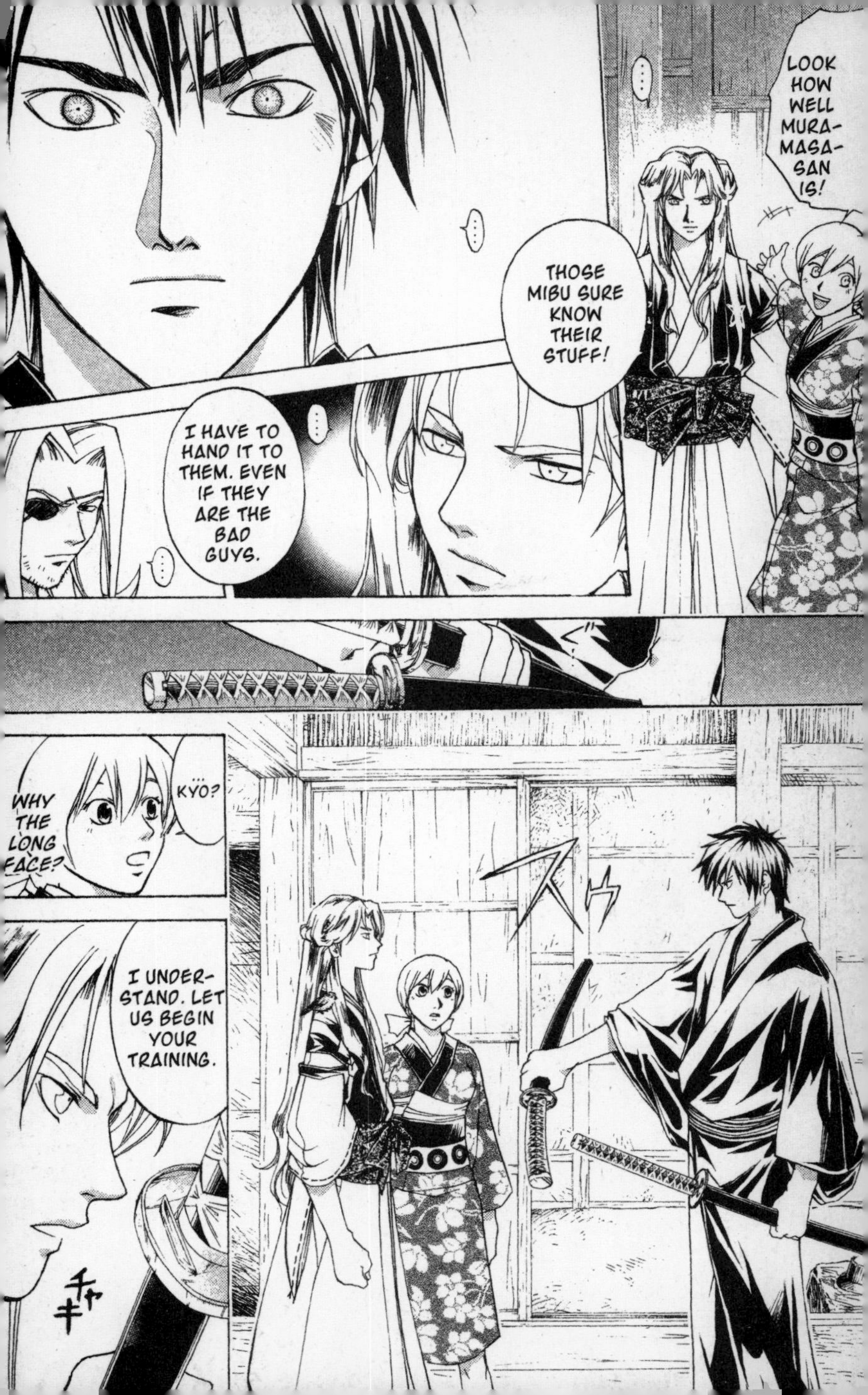
LOOK HOW WELL MURAMASA-SAN IS!
...
...
THOSE MIBU SURE KNOW THEIR STUFF!
...
I HAVE TO HAND IT TO THEM. EVEN IF THEY ARE THE BAD GUYS.
...
...KYŌ?
WHY THE LONG FACE?
I UNDERSTAND. LET US BEGIN YOUR TRAINING.
チャキ

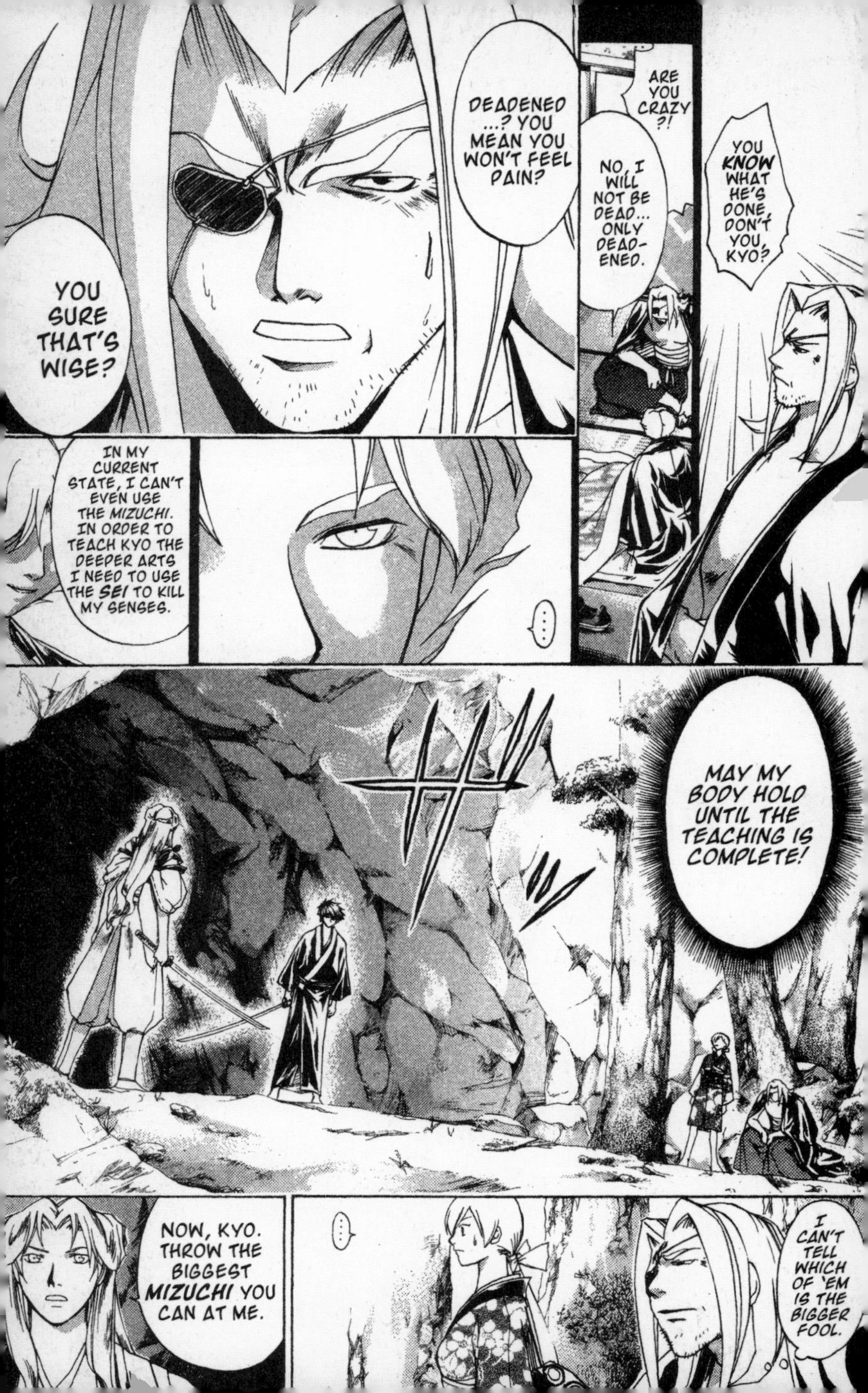
ARE YOU CRAZY?!
YOU **KNOW** WHAT HE'S DONE, DON'T YOU, KYO?
NO, I WILL NOT BE DEAD... ONLY DEAD-ENED.
DEADENED ...? YOU MEAN YOU WON'T FEEL PAIN?
YOU SURE THAT'S WISE?
...
IN MY CURRENT STATE, I CAN'T EVEN USE THE *MIZUCHI*. IN ORDER TO TEACH KYO THE DEEPER ARTS I NEED TO USE THE ***SEI*** TO KILL MY SENSES.
MAY MY BODY HOLD UNTIL THE TEACHING IS COMPLETE!
I CAN'T TELL WHICH OF 'EM IS THE BIGGER FOOL.
...
NOW, KYO. THROW THE BIGGEST ***MIZUCHI*** YOU CAN AT ME.

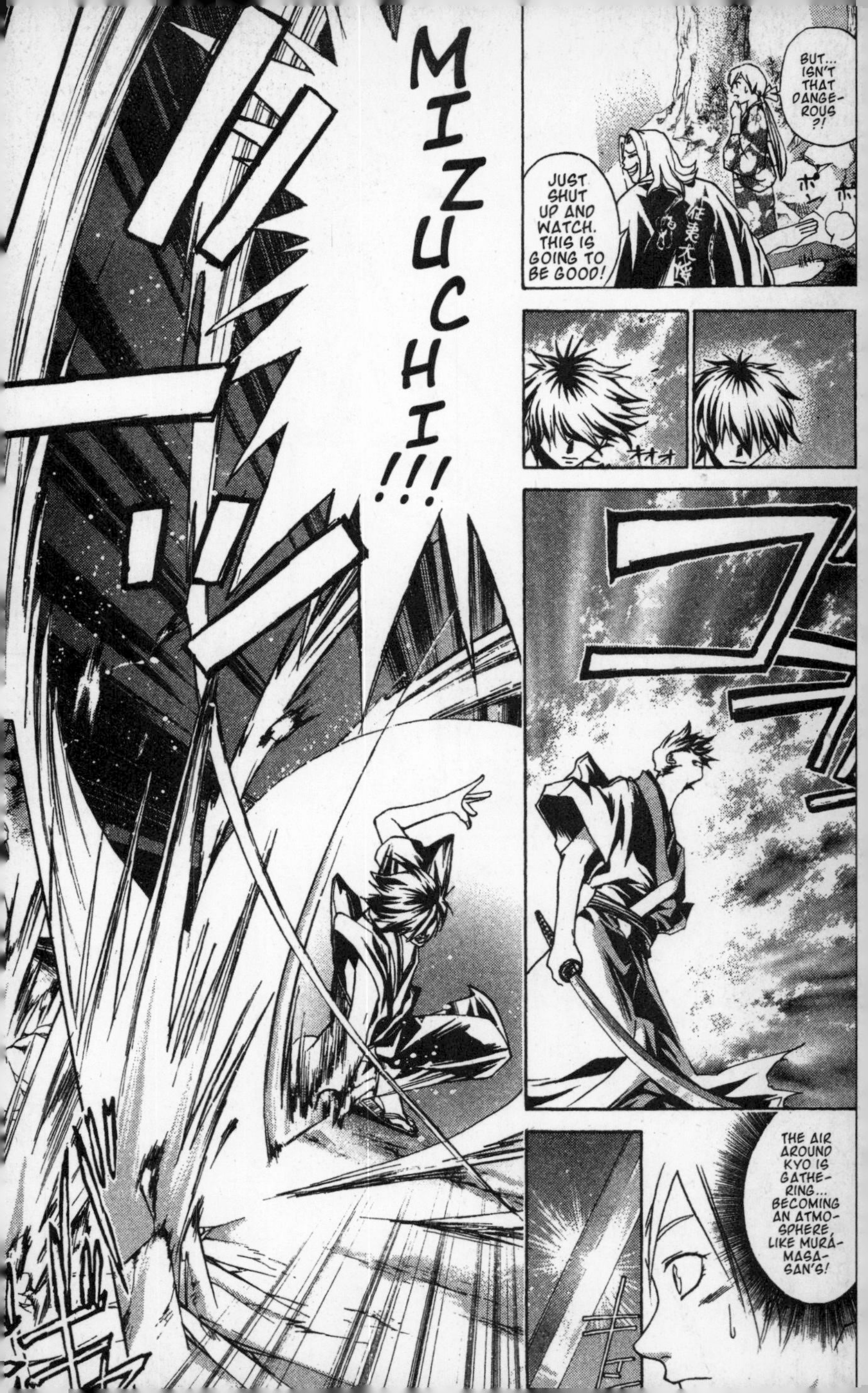
BUT... ISN'T THAT DANGEROUS?!
JUST SHUT UP AND WATCH. THIS IS GOING TO BE GOOD!
THE AIR AROUND KYO IS GATHERING... BECOMING AN ATMOSPHERE LIKE MURAMASA-SAN'S!
MIZUCHI!!!

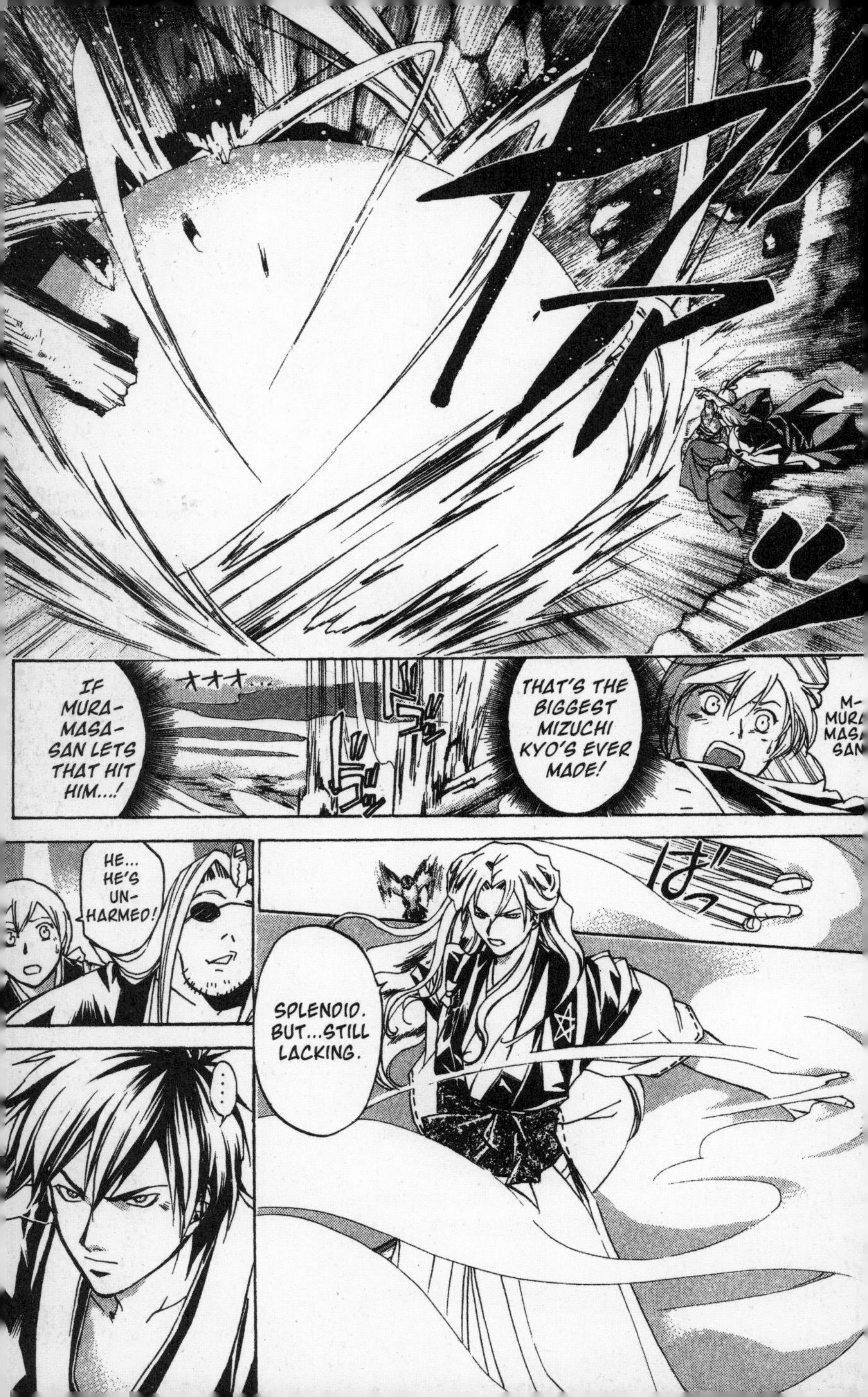
M-MURA-MASA-SAN
THAT'S THE BIGGEST MIZUCHI KYO'S EVER MADE!
オオオ...
IF MURA-MASA-SAN LETS THAT HIT HIM...!
ばっ
SPLENDID. BUT...STILL LACKING.
HE... HE'S UN-HARMED!
...

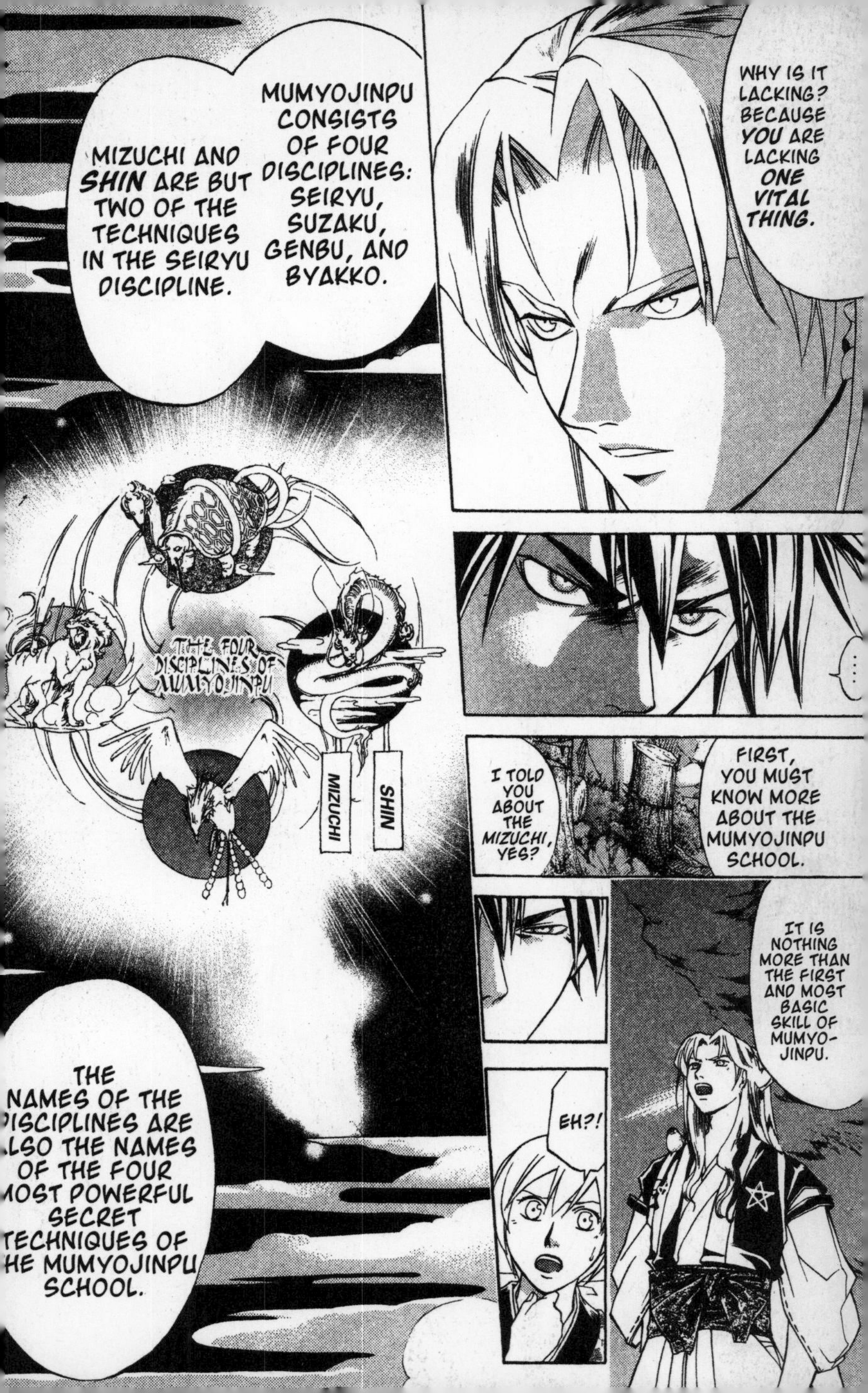
WHY IS IT LACKING? BECAUSE YOU ARE LACKING ONE VITAL THING.
...
FIRST, YOU MUST KNOW MORE ABOUT THE MUMYOJINPU SCHOOL.
I TOLD YOU ABOUT THE MIZUCHI, YES?
IT IS NOTHING MORE THAN THE FIRST AND MOST BASIC SKILL OF MUMYO-JINPU.
EH?!
MUMYOJINPU CONSISTS OF FOUR DISCIPLINES: SEIRYU, SUZAKU, GENBU, AND BYAKKO.
MIZUCHI AND SHIN ARE BUT TWO OF THE TECHNIQUES IN THE SEIRYU DISCIPLINE.
THE FOUR DISCIPLINES OF MUMYOJINPU
SHIN
MIZUCHI
THE NAMES OF THE ISCIPLINES ARE LSO THE NAMES OF THE FOUR OST POWERFUL SECRET ECHNIQUES OF HE MUMYOJINPU SCHOOL.

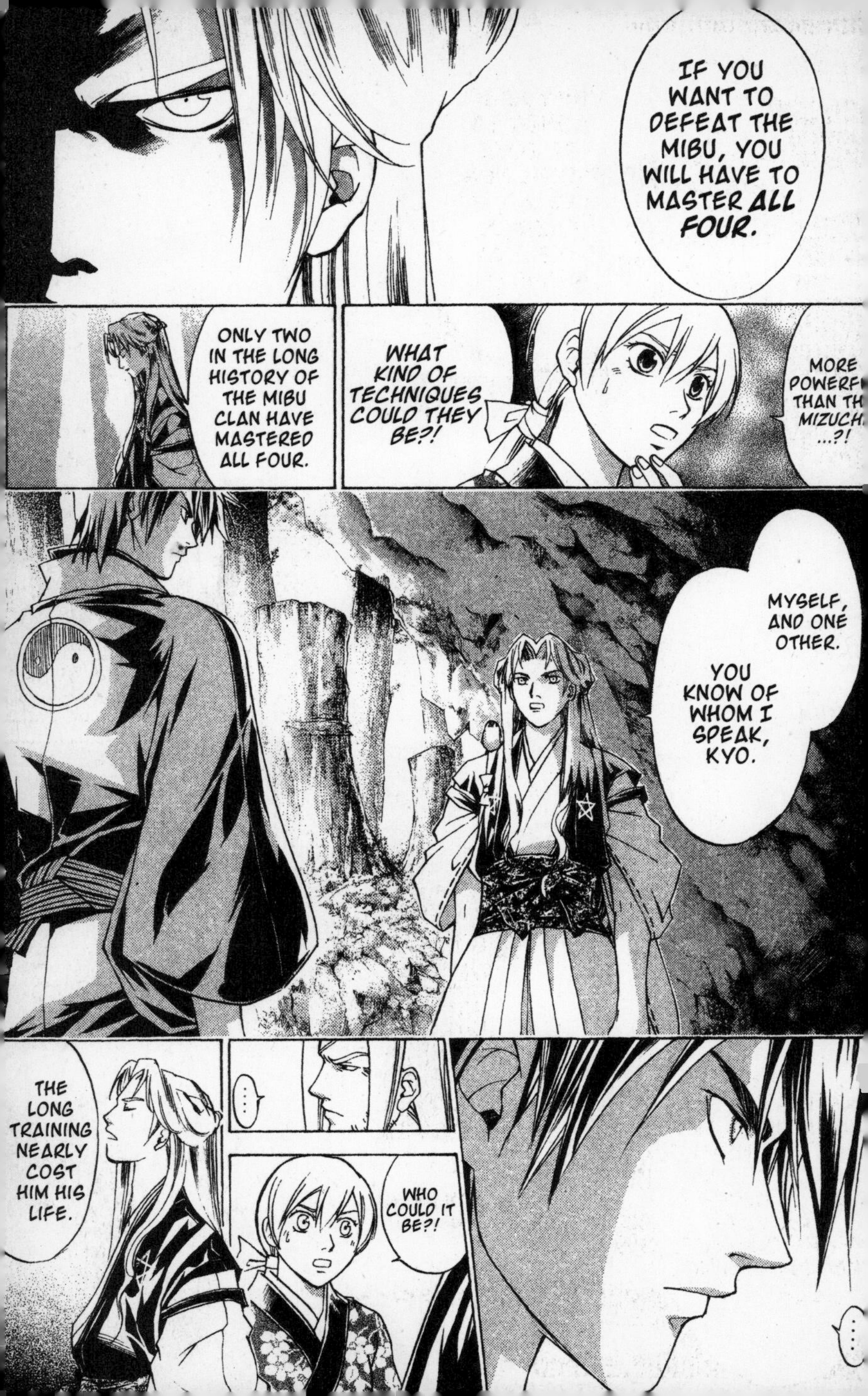
IF YOU WANT TO DEFEAT THE MIBU, YOU WILL HAVE TO MASTER ALL FOUR.
MORE POWERF THAN TH MIZUCH ...?!
WHAT KIND OF TECHNIQUES COULD THEY BE?!
ONLY TWO IN THE LONG HISTORY OF THE MIBU CLAN HAVE MASTERED ALL FOUR.
MYSELF, AND ONE OTHER.
YOU KNOW OF WHOM I SPEAK, KYO.
...
...
WHO COULD IT BE?!
THE LONG TRAINING NEARLY COST HIM HIS LIFE.

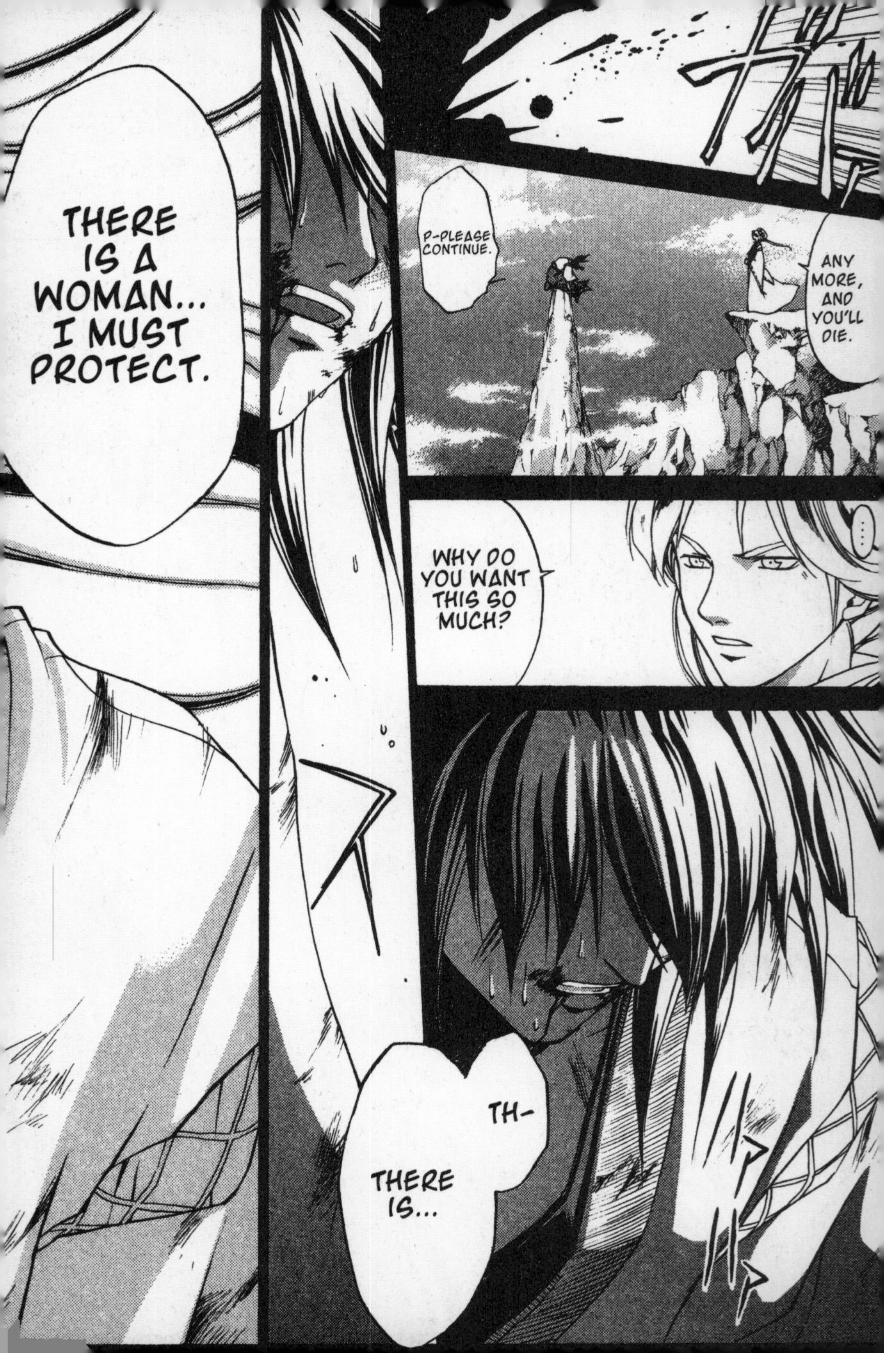
ANY MORE, AND YOU'LL DIE.
P-PLEASE CONTINUE.
...
WHY DO YOU WANT THIS SO MUCH?
TH-
THERE IS...
THERE IS A WOMAN... I MUST PROTECT.

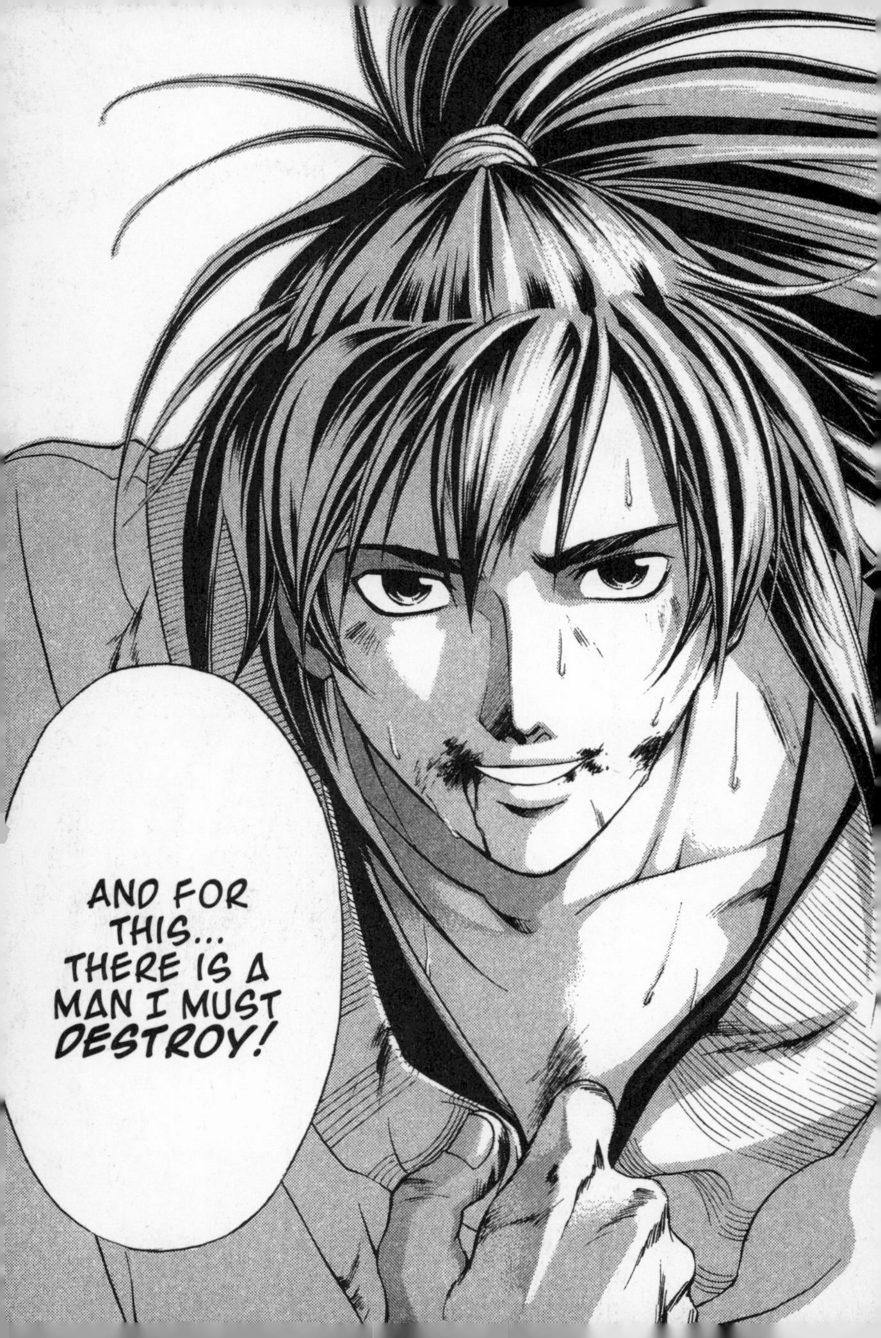
AND FOR THIS... THERE IS A MAN I MUST DESTROY!

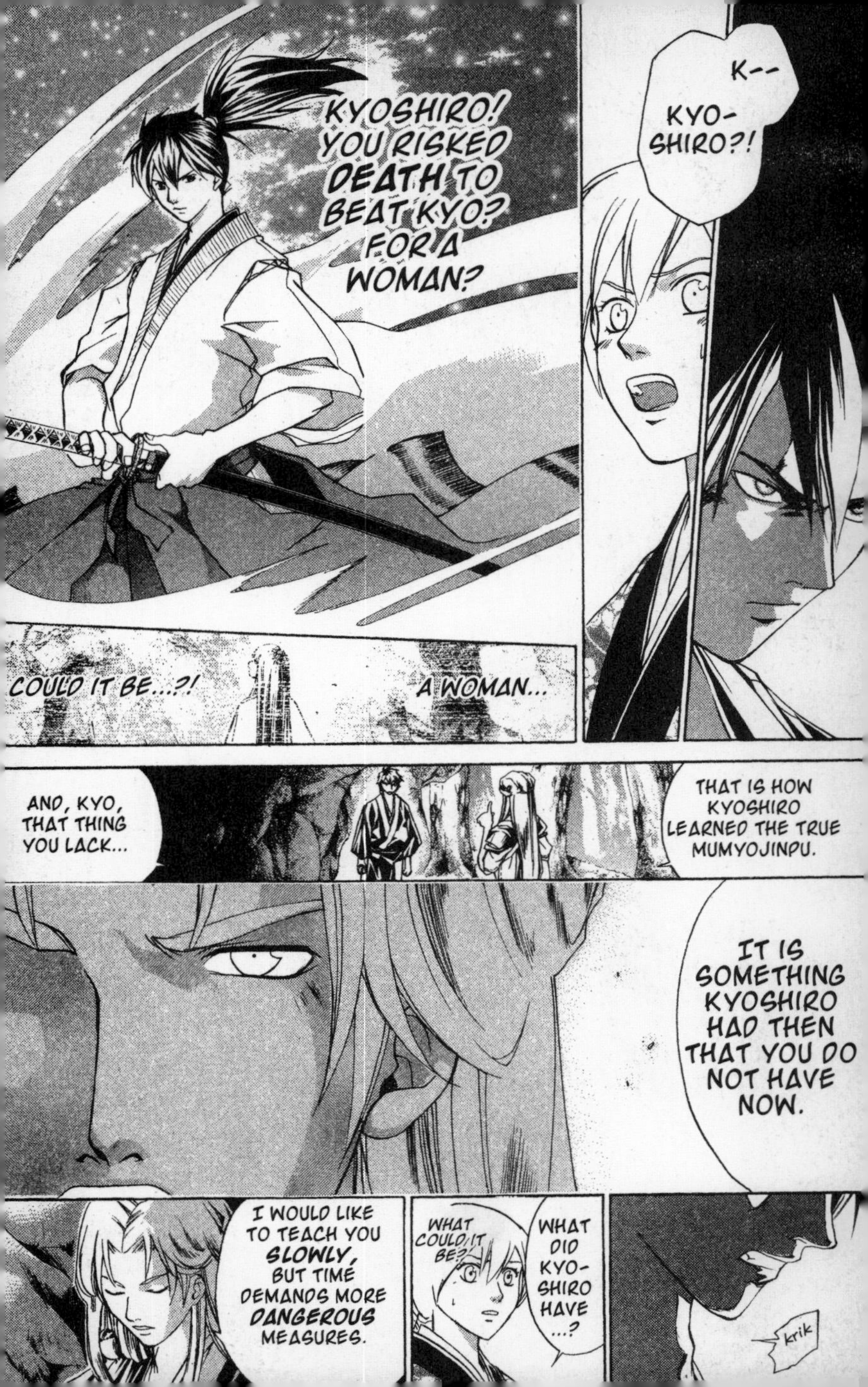
K-- KYO-SHIRO?!
KYOSHIRO! YOU RISKED DEATH TO BEAT KYO? FOR A WOMAN?
A WOMAN...
COULD IT BE...?!
THAT IS HOW KYOSHIRO LEARNED THE TRUE MUMYOJINPU.
AND, KYO, THAT THING YOU LACK...
IT IS SOMETHING KYOSHIRO HAD THEN THAT YOU DO NOT HAVE NOW.
krik
WHAT DID KYO-SHIRO HAVE ...?
WHAT COULD IT BE?
I WOULD LIKE TO TEACH YOU SLOWLY, BUT TIME DEMANDS MORE DANGEROUS MEASURES.

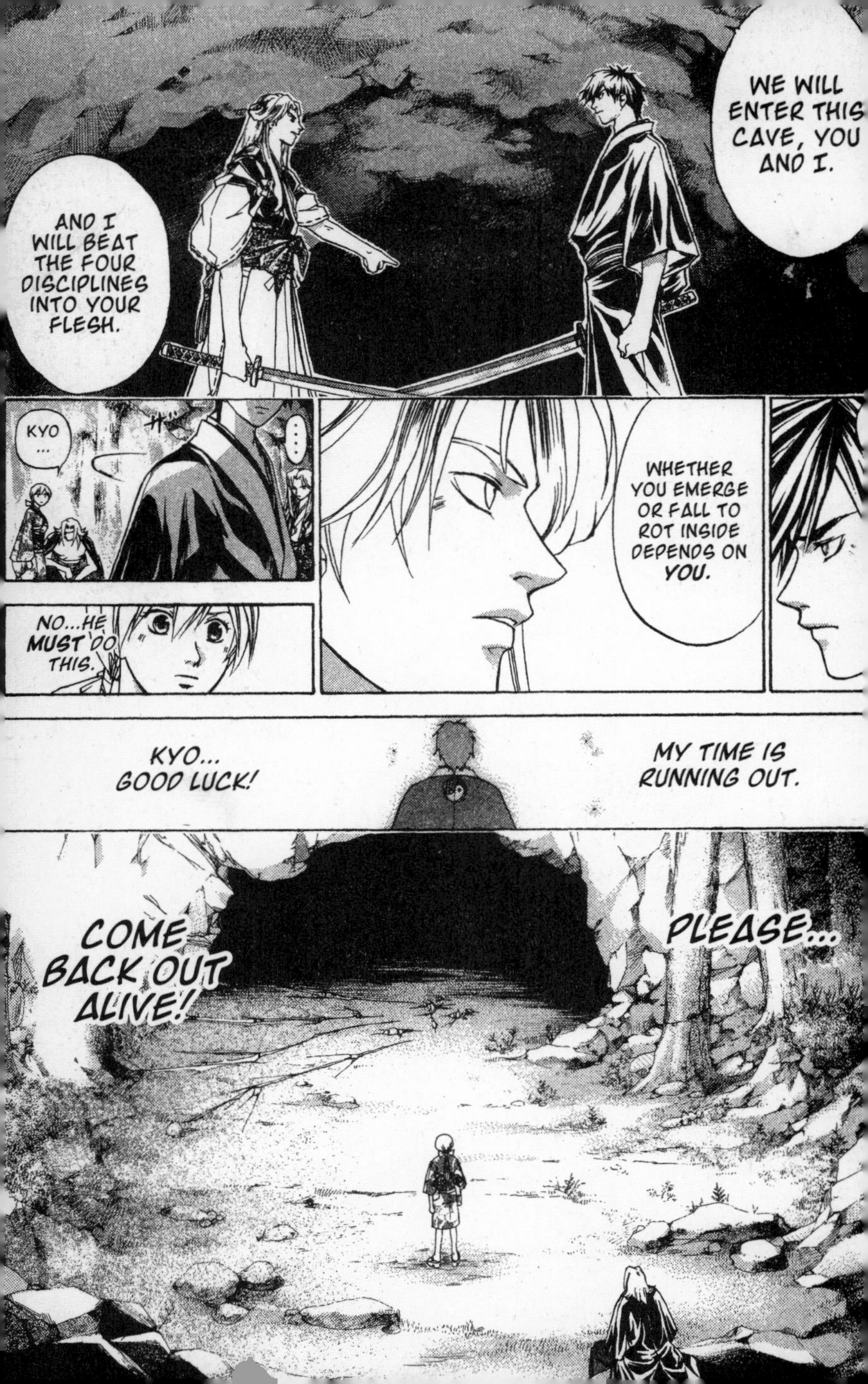
WE WILL ENTER THIS CAVE, YOU AND I.
AND I WILL BEAT THE FOUR DISCIPLINES INTO YOUR FLESH.
WHETHER YOU EMERGE OR FALL TO ROT INSIDE DEPENDS ON YOU.
KYO ...
....
NO...HE MUST DO THIS.
MY TIME IS RUNNING OUT.
KYO... GOOD LUCK!
PLEASE...
COME BACK OUT ALIVE!

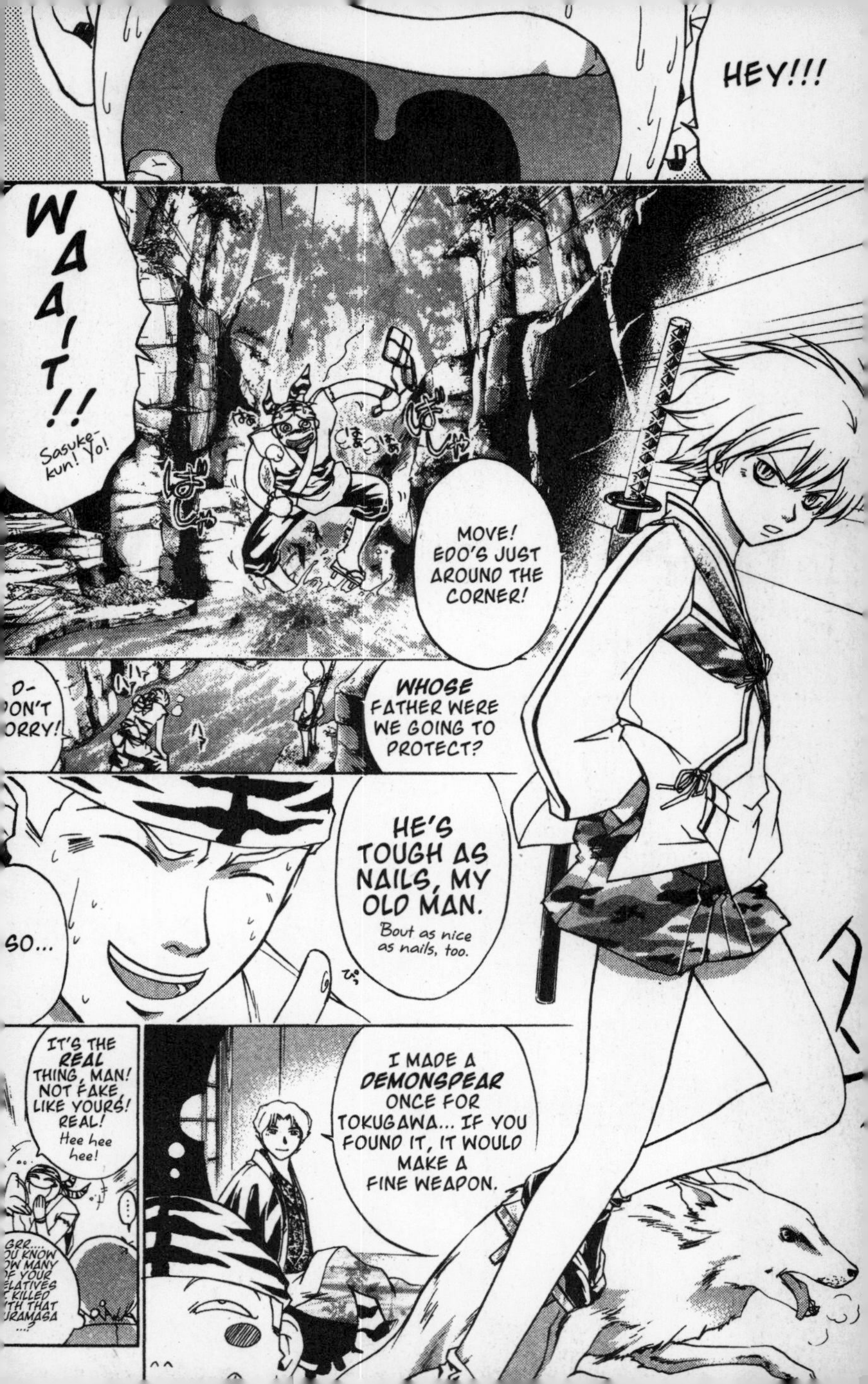
HEY!!!
WAAIT!!
Sasuke-kun! Yo!
MOVE! EDO'S JUST AROUND THE CORNER!
WHOSE FATHER WERE WE GOING TO PROTECT?
D- ON'T ORRY!
HE'S TOUGH AS NAILS, MY OLD MAN.
'Bout as nice as nails, too.
SO...
I MADE A DEMONSPEAR ONCE FOR TOKUGAWA... IF YOU FOUND IT, IT WOULD MAKE A FINE WEAPON.
IT'S THE REAL THING, MAN! NOT FAKE LIKE YOURS! REAL!
Hee hee hee!
GRR... OU KNOW OW MANY OF YOUR ELATIVES KILLED ITH THAT URAMASA ...?

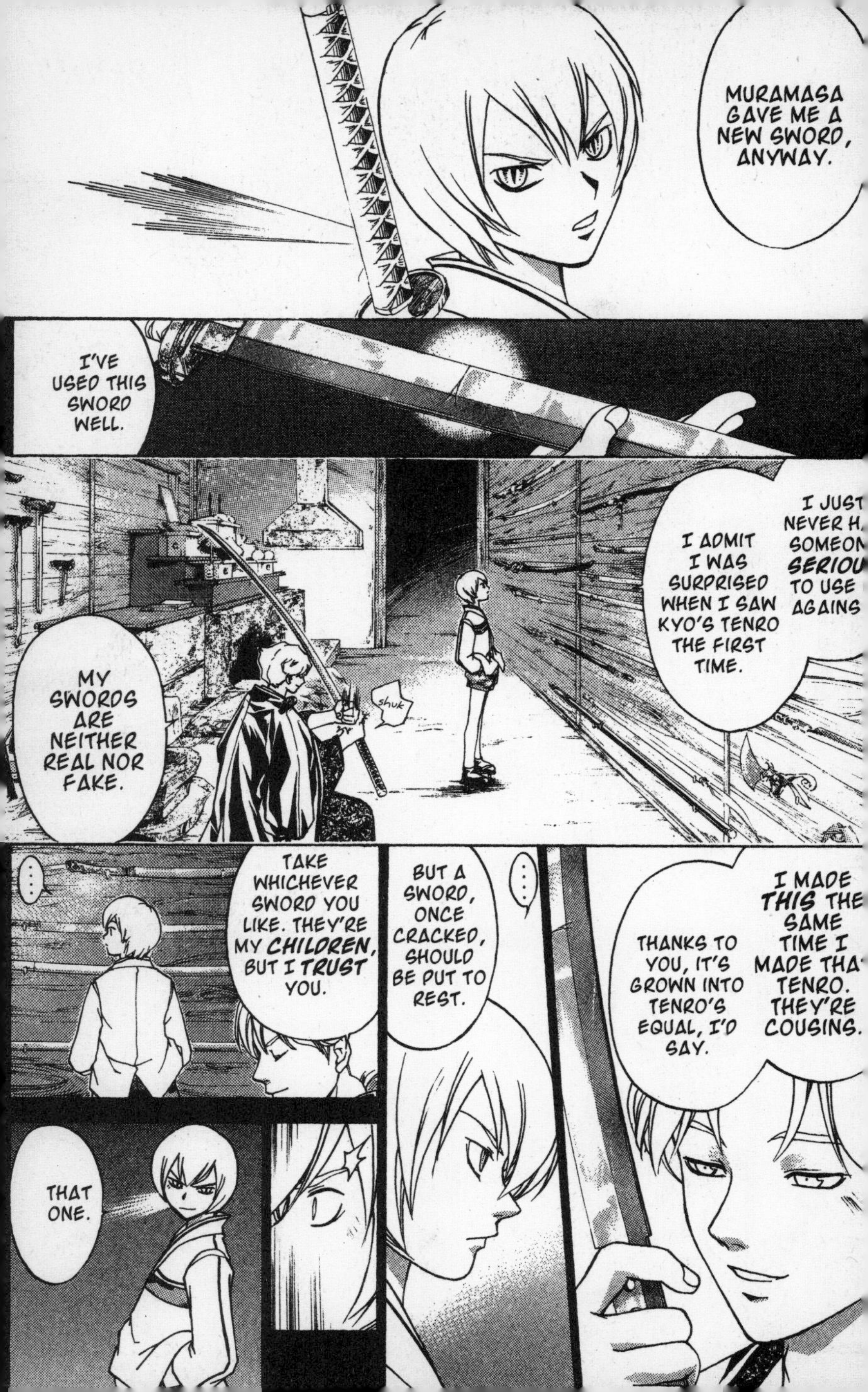
MURAMASA GAVE ME A NEW SWORD, ANYWAY.
I'VE USED THIS SWORD WELL.
I JUST NEVER H SOMEON SERIOU TO USE AGAINS
I ADMIT I WAS SURPRISED WHEN I SAW KYO'S TENRO THE FIRST TIME.
shuk
MY SWORDS ARE NEITHER REAL NOR FAKE.
I MADE THIS THE SAME TIME I MADE THA TENRO. THEY'RE COUSINS.
THANKS TO YOU, IT'S GROWN INTO TENRO'S EQUAL, I'D SAY.
...
BUT A SWORD, ONCE CRACKED, SHOULD BE PUT TO REST.
TAKE WHICHEVER SWORD YOU LIKE. THEY'RE MY CHILDREN, BUT I TRUST YOU.
...
THAT ONE.

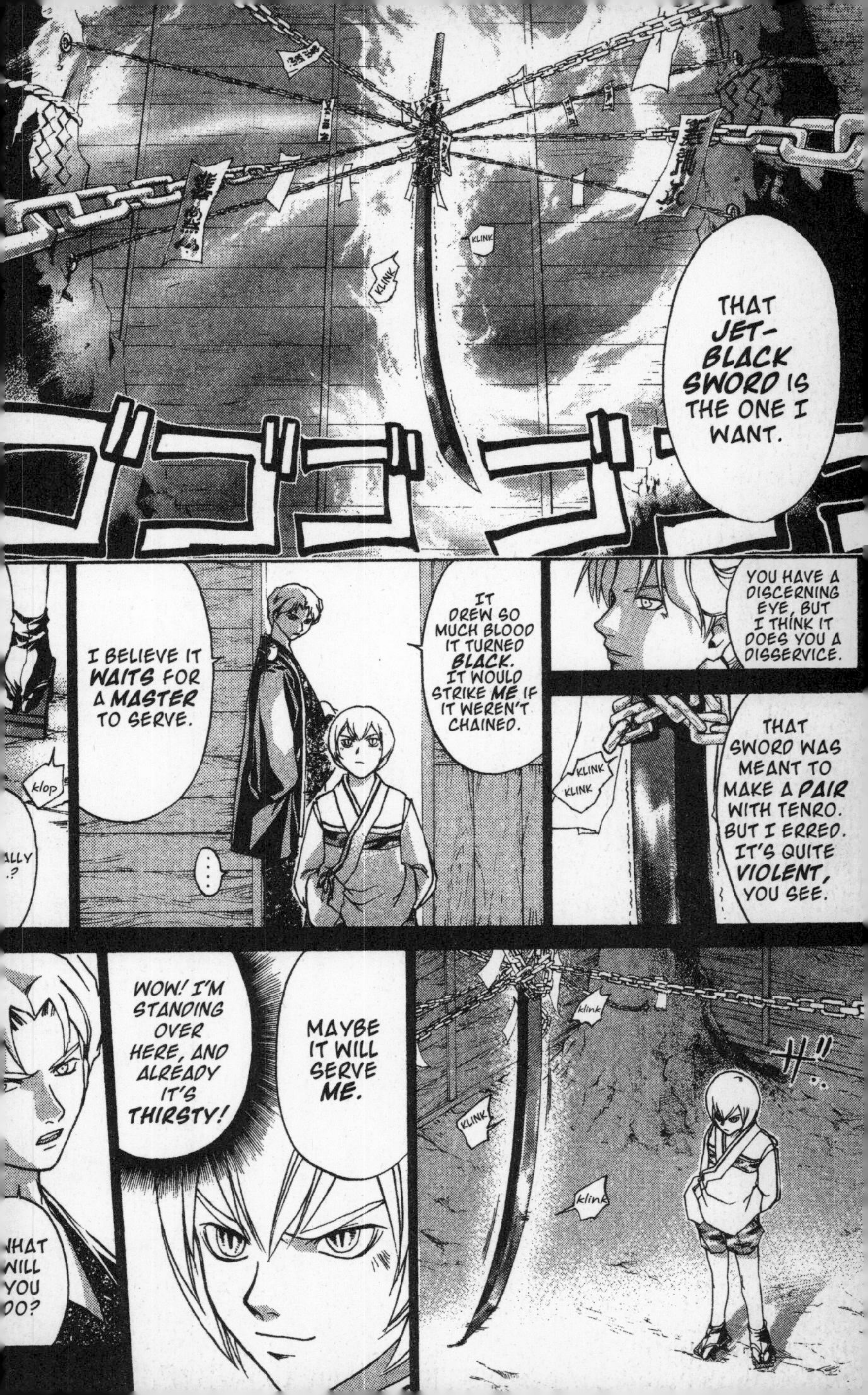
KLINK
KLINK
THAT JET-BLACK SWORD IS THE ONE I WANT.
YOU HAVE A DISCERNING EYE, BUT I THINK IT DOES YOU A DISSERVICE.
KLINK
KLINK
THAT SWORD WAS MEANT TO MAKE A PAIR WITH TENRO. BUT I ERRED. IT'S QUITE VIOLENT, YOU SEE.
IT DREW SO MUCH BLOOD IT TURNED BLACK. IT WOULD STRIKE ME IF IT WEREN'T CHAINED.
I BELIEVE IT WAITS FOR A MASTER TO SERVE.
...
klop
klink
KLINK
klink
MAYBE IT WILL SERVE ME.
WOW! I'M STANDING OVER HERE, AND ALREADY IT'S THIRSTY!

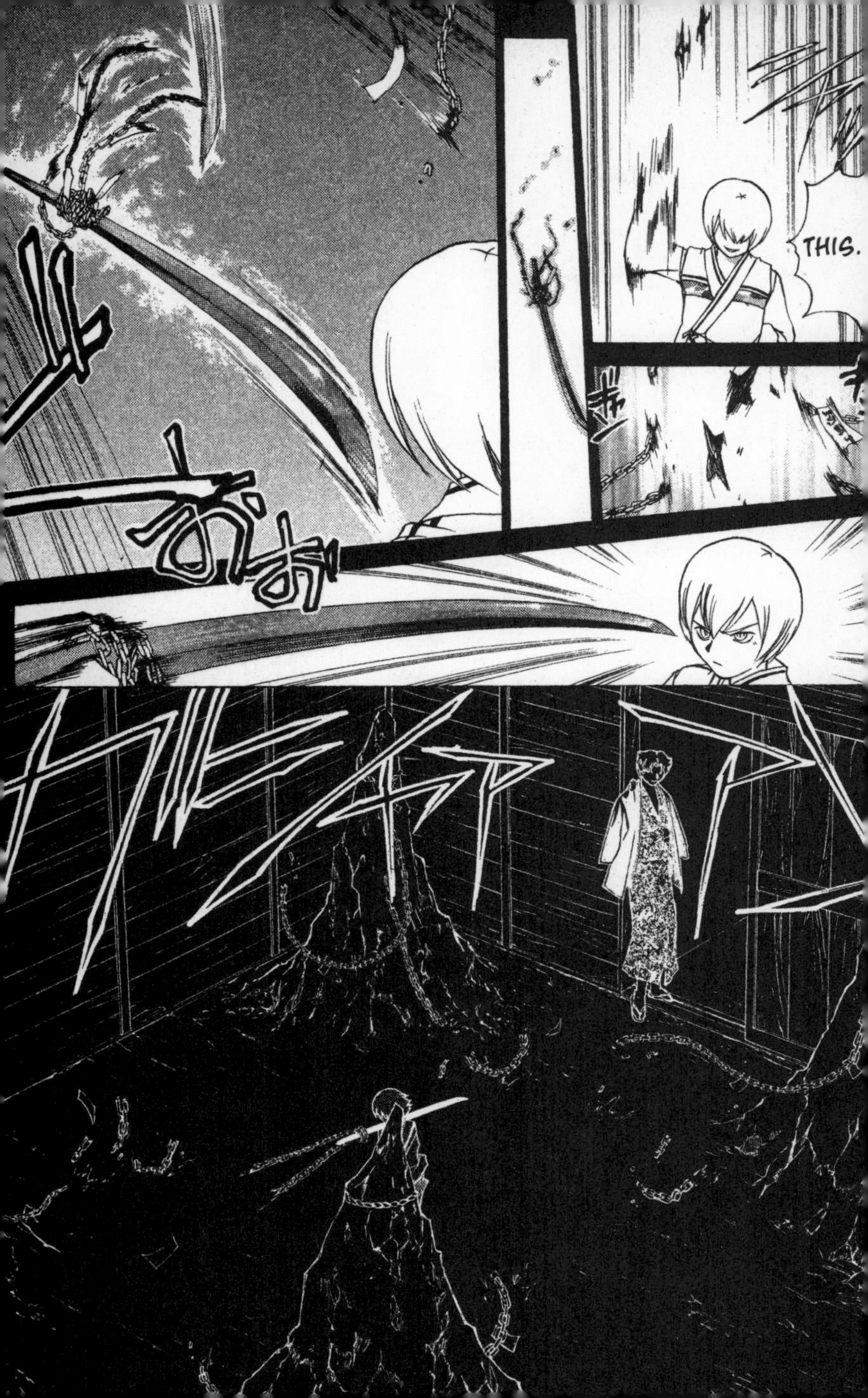
THIS.

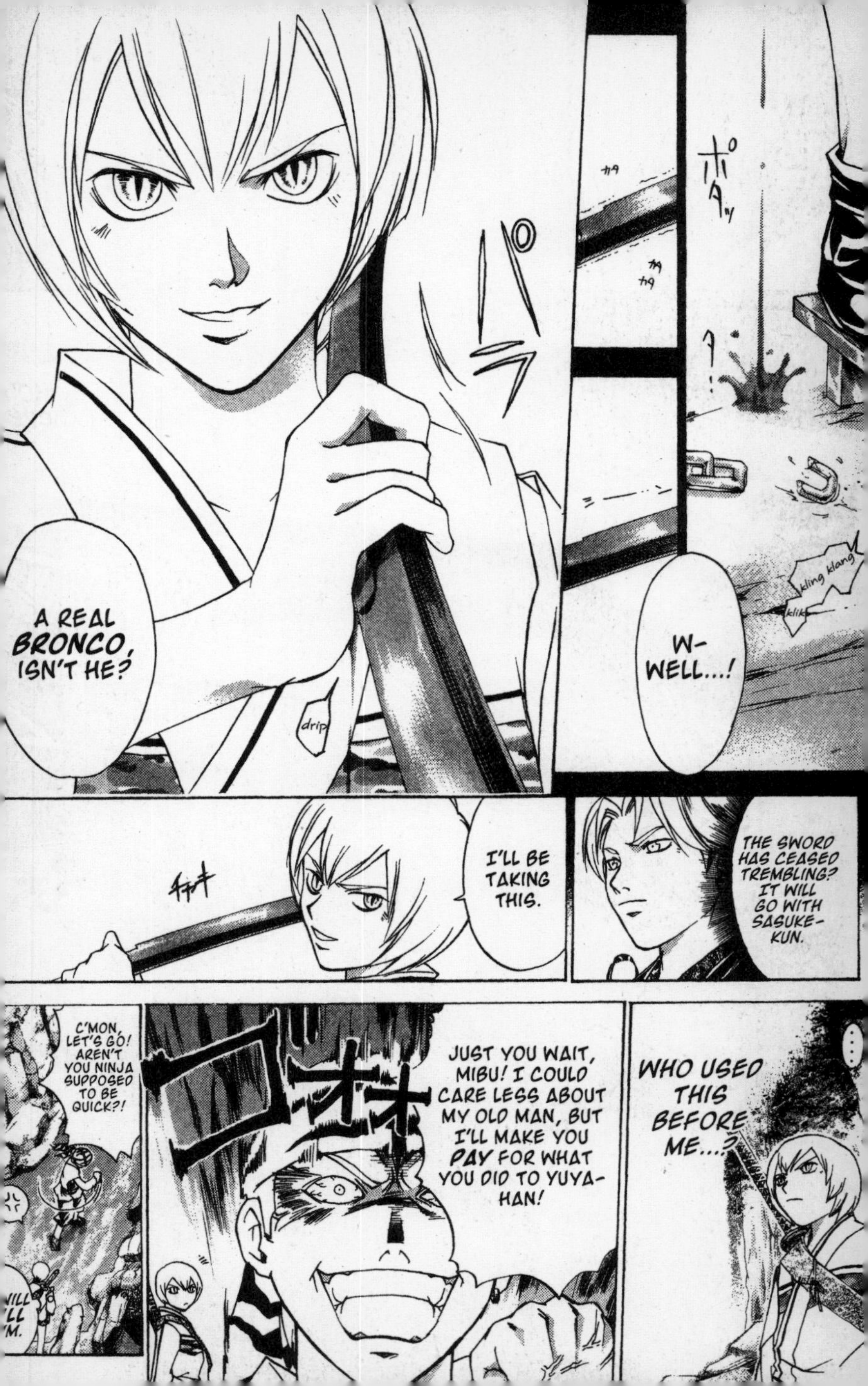

kling klang
klik
W-WELL...!
A REAL BRONCO, ISN'T HE?
drip
THE SWORD HAS CEASED TREMBLING? IT WILL GO WITH SASUKE-KUN.
I'LL BE TAKING THIS.
...
WHO USED THIS BEFORE ME...?
JUST YOU WAIT, MIBU! I COULD CARE LESS ABOUT MY OLD MAN, BUT I'LL MAKE YOU PAY FOR WHAT YOU DID TO YUYA-HAN!
C'MON, LET'S GO! AREN'T YOU NINJA SUPPOSED TO BE QUICK?!

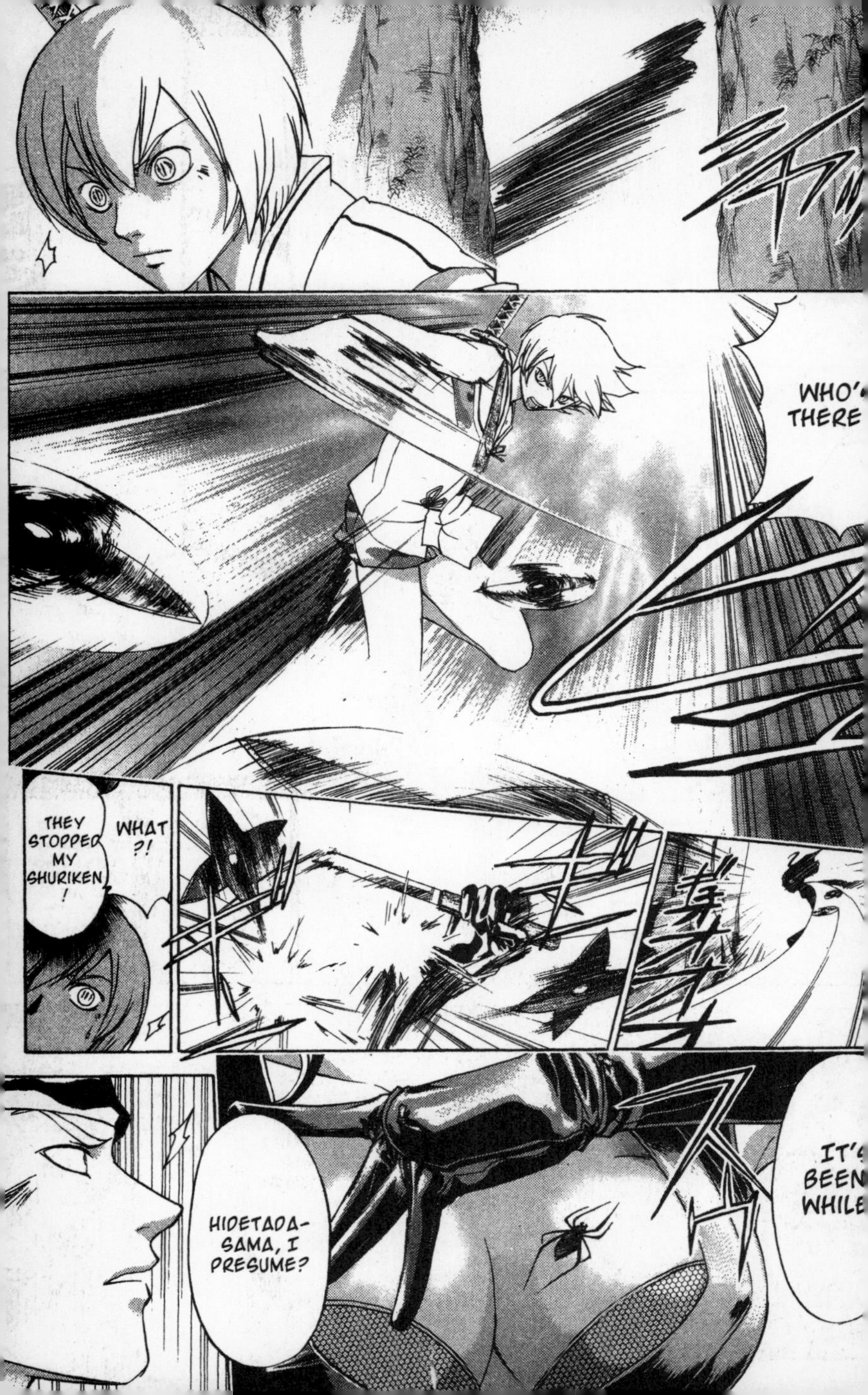
WHO' THERE
WHAT ?!
THEY STOPPED MY SHURIKEN !
IT' BEEN WHILE
HIDETADA-SAMA, I PRESUME?

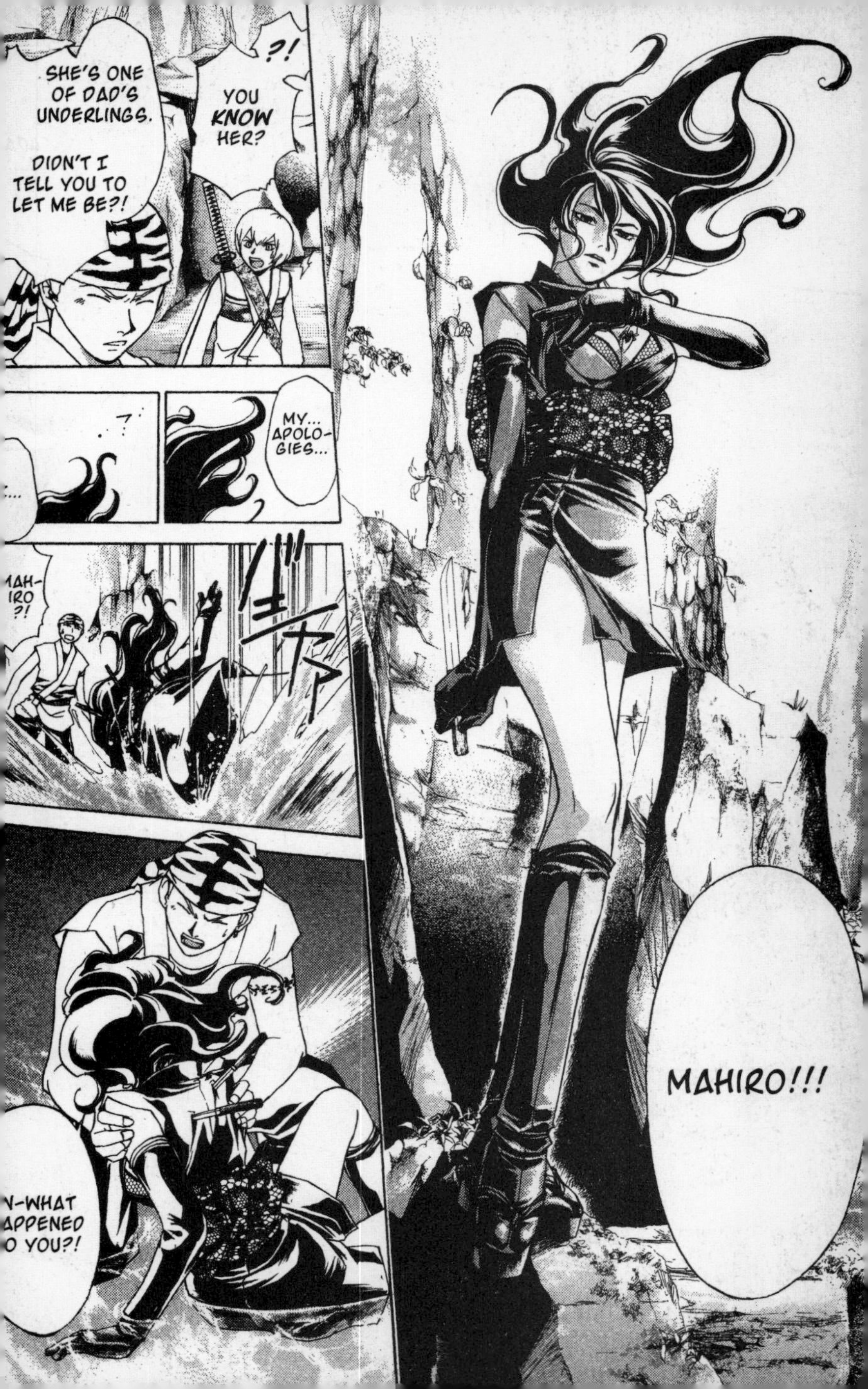
MAHIRO!!!
?!
YOU KNOW HER?
SHE'S ONE OF DAD'S UNDERLINGS.
DIDN'T I TELL YOU TO LET ME BE?!
MY... APOLOGIES...
...?
....
AH-IRO ?!
V-WHAT APPENED O YOU?!

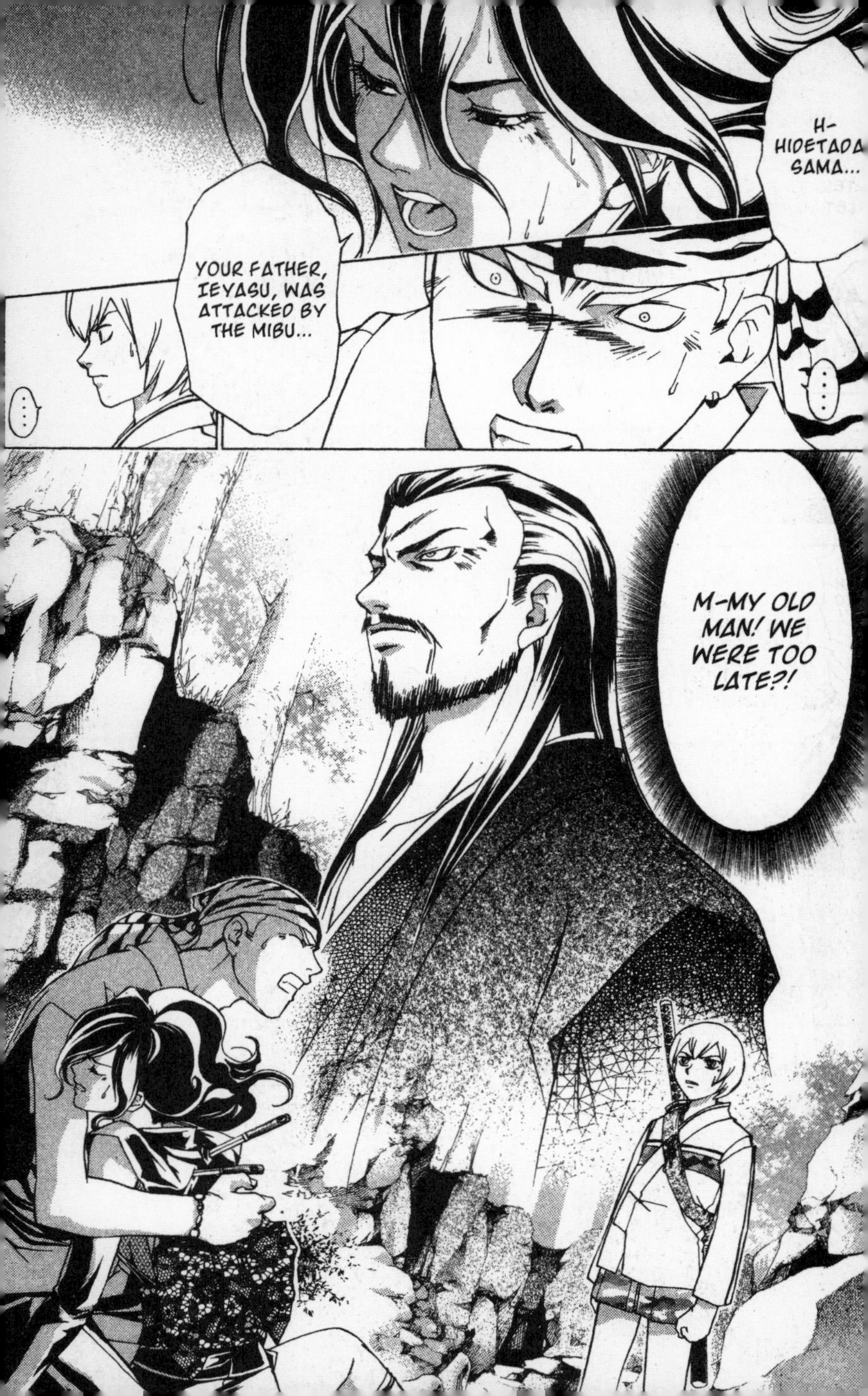
H-HIDETADA SAMA...
YOUR FATHER, IEYASU, WAS ATTACKED BY THE MIBU...
...
...
M-MY OLD MAN! WE WERE TOO LATE?!

Q&A CORNER

Q: WHEN IS YOUR BIRTHDAY?
A: SEPTEMBER 13.

Q: WHAT DO YOU LOOK LIKE? I KEEP SEEING THAT LITTLE PURPLE GUY IN MY DREAMS.
A: THAT'S EXACTLY WHAT I LOOK LIKE. I'M OFTEN ASKED TO SHOW MY FACE, BUT IT'S REALLY BEST KEPT UNSEEN.

Q: ARE YOU MARRIED?
A: NOPE. NOT UNLESS YOU COUNT SDK!

Q: IS SDK YOUR FIRST MANGA TITLE?
A: MY FIRST SERIOUS ONE, YES.

Q: DOES YOUR HAND EVER GO NUMB? WHAT DO YOU DO?
A: WHETHER MY HANDS DROOP, SEIZE UP, CRAMP, OR WELL, I WILL KEEP DRAWING!

Q: WHAT HAPPENS TO OUR FAN LETTERS AFTER YOU GET THEM?
A: I PUT THEM INTO BAGS DIVIDED BY DATE SO I KNOW WHEN THEY CAME, AND I SAVE THEM ALONG WITH MY MANGA SCRIPTS. CHECK OUT SOME OF THEM AT THE BACK OF THIS BOOK!

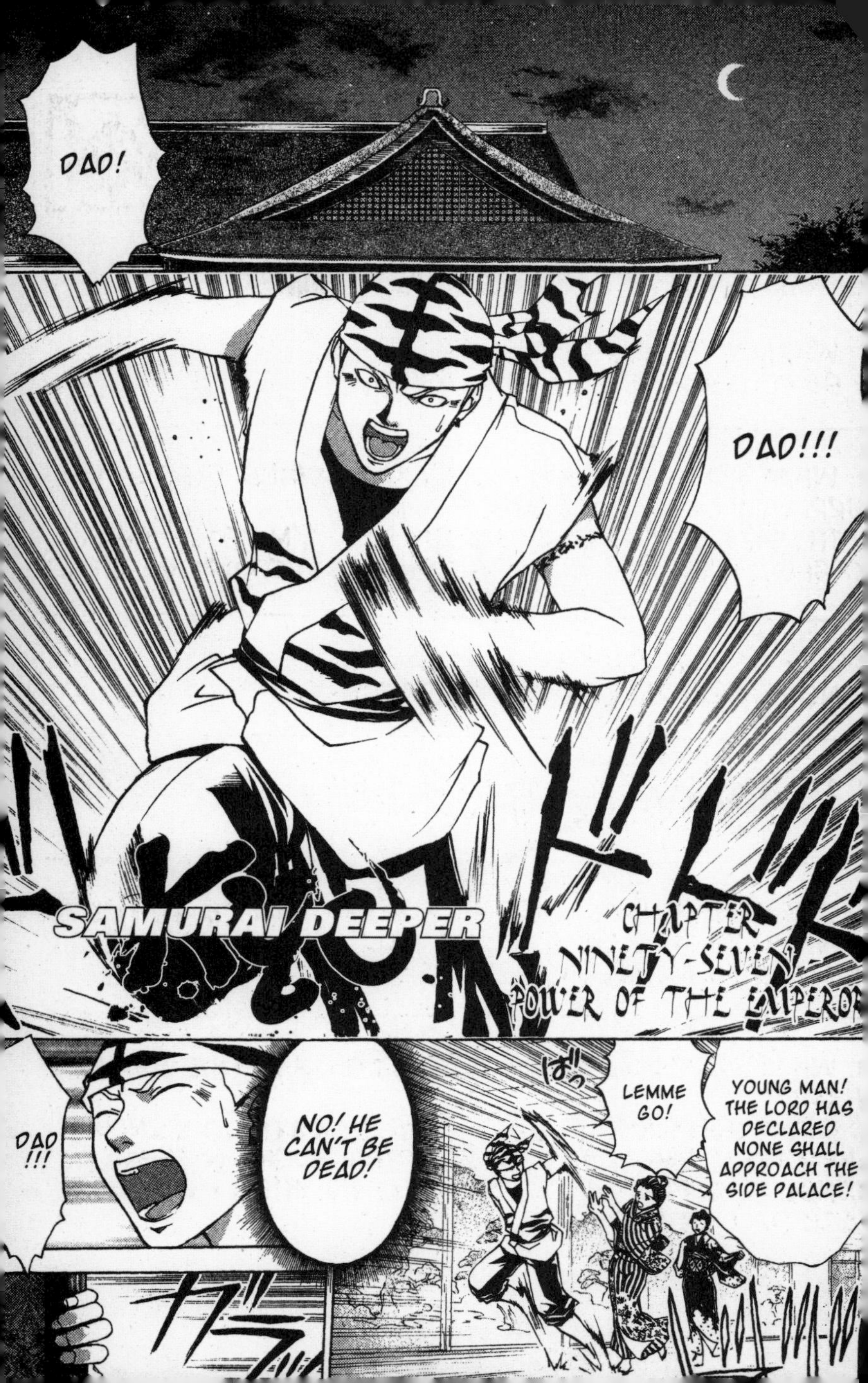
DAD!
DAD!!!
SAMURAI DEEPER
CHAPTER NINETY-SEVEN
POWER OF THE EMPEROR
YOUNG MAN! THE LORD HAS DECLARED NONE SHALL APPROACH THE SIDE PALACE!
LEMME GO!
ばっ
NO! HE CAN'T BE DEAD!
DAD !!!

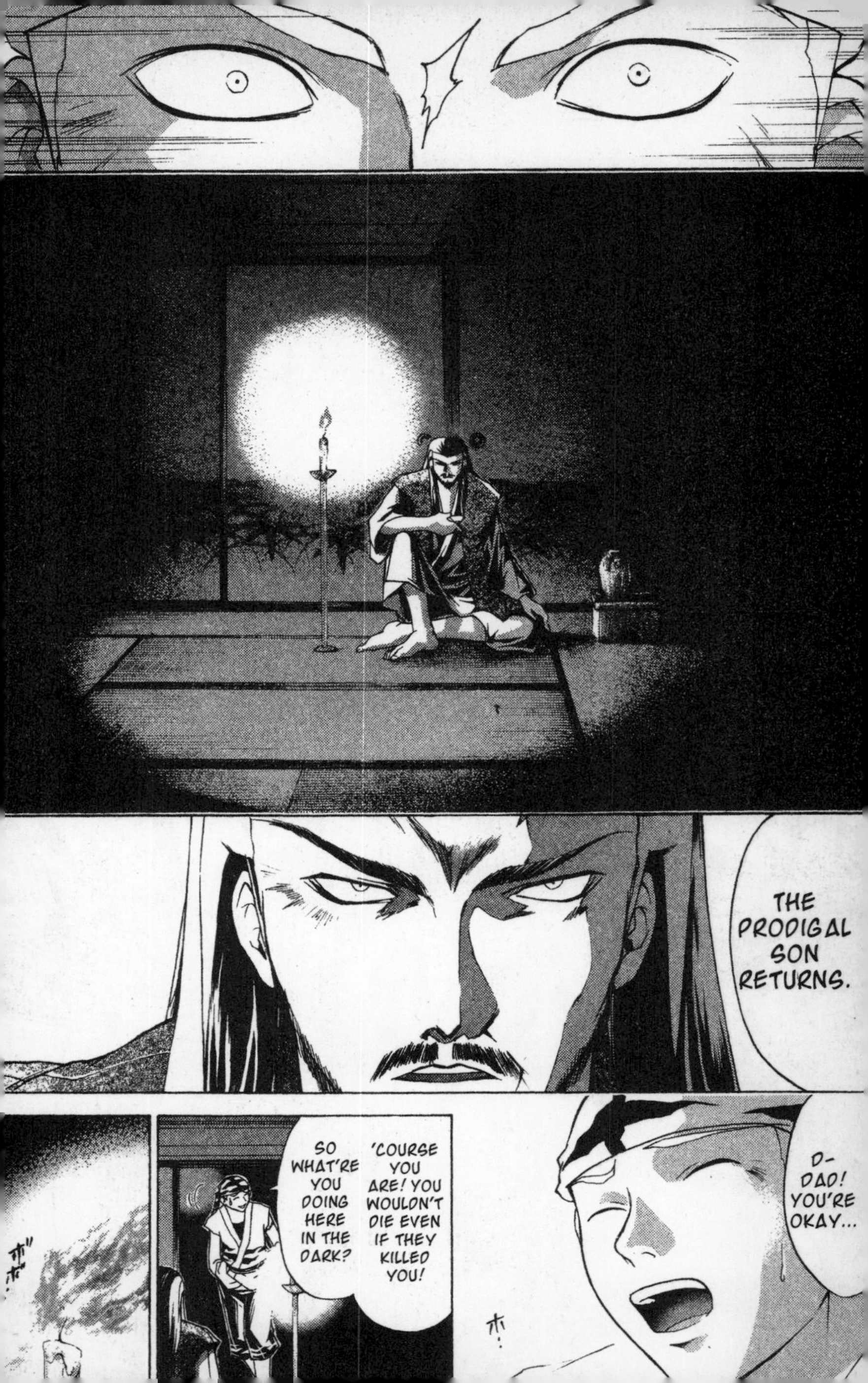
THE PRODIGAL SON RETURNS.
D-DAD! YOU'RE OKAY...
'COURSE YOU ARE! YOU WOULDN'T DIE EVEN IF THEY KILLED YOU!
SO WHAT'RE YOU DOING HERE IN THE DARK?

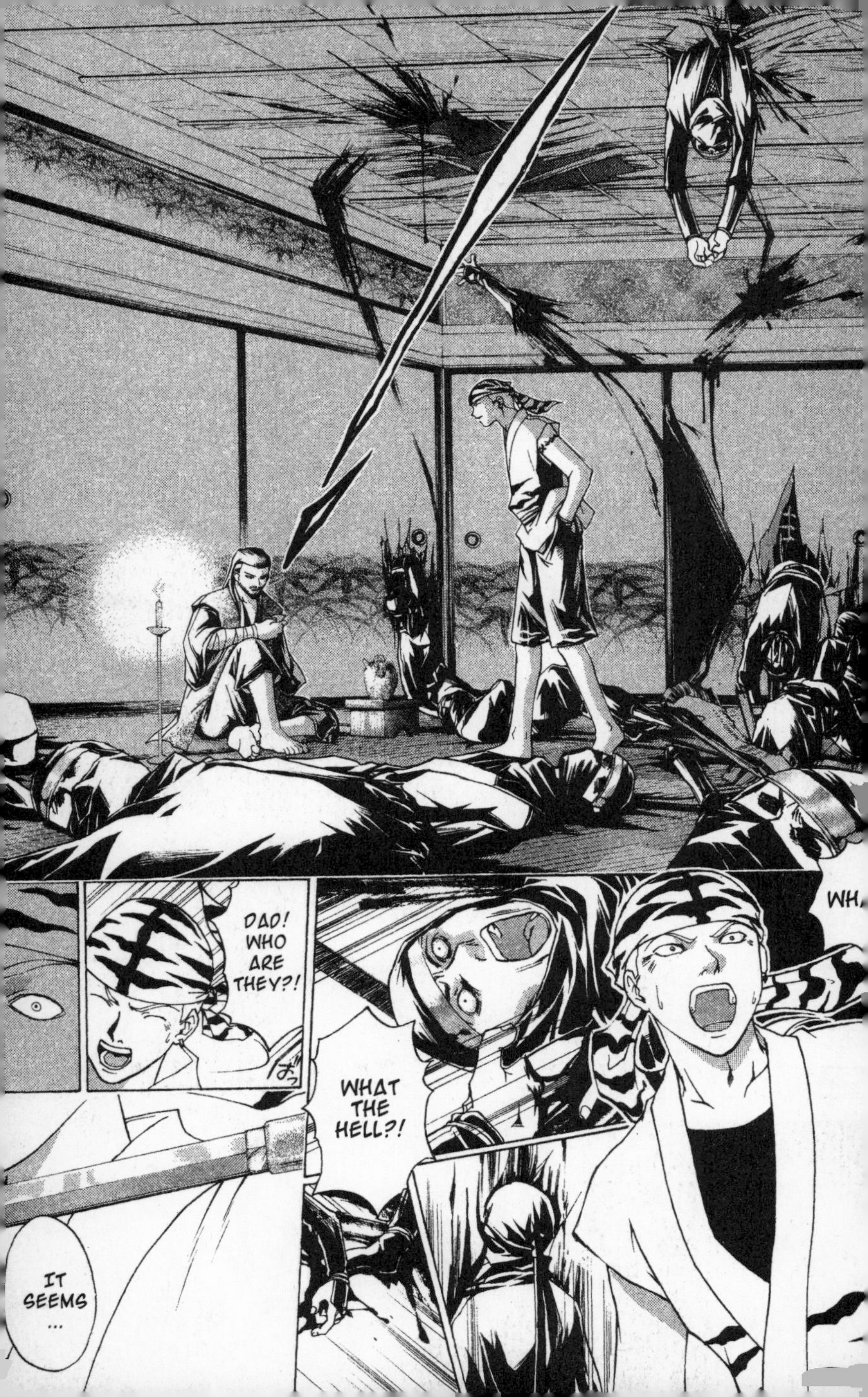
WH,
WHAT THE HELL?!
DAD! WHO ARE THEY?!
IT SEEMS ...

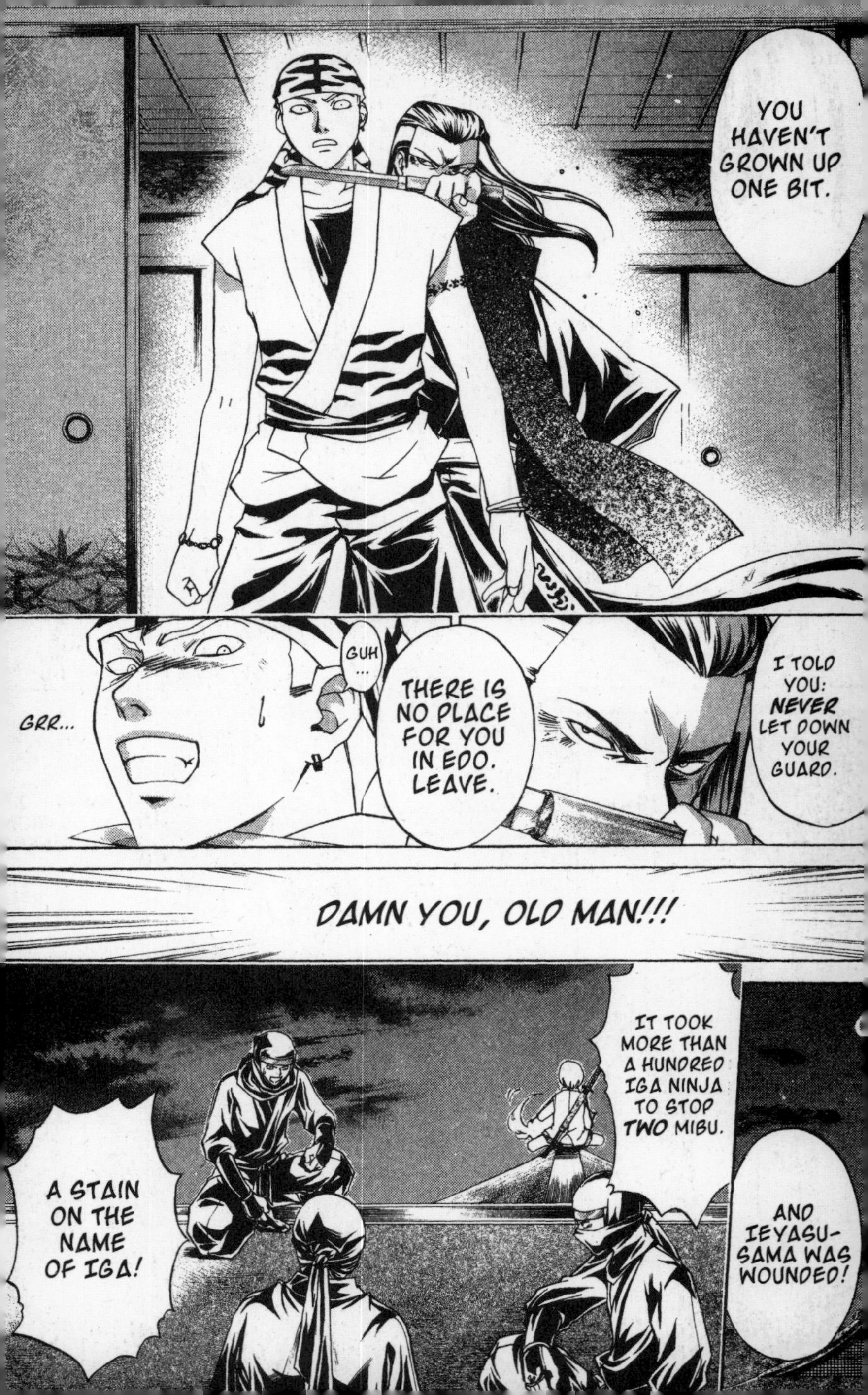
YOU HAVEN'T GROWN UP ONE BIT.
I TOLD YOU: NEVER LET DOWN YOUR GUARD.
THERE IS NO PLACE FOR YOU IN EDO. LEAVE.
GUH...
GRR...
DAMN YOU, OLD MAN!!!
AND IEYASU-SAMA WAS WOUNDED!
IT TOOK MORE THAN A HUNDRED IGA NINJA TO STOP TWO MIBU.
A STAIN ON THE NAME OF IGA!

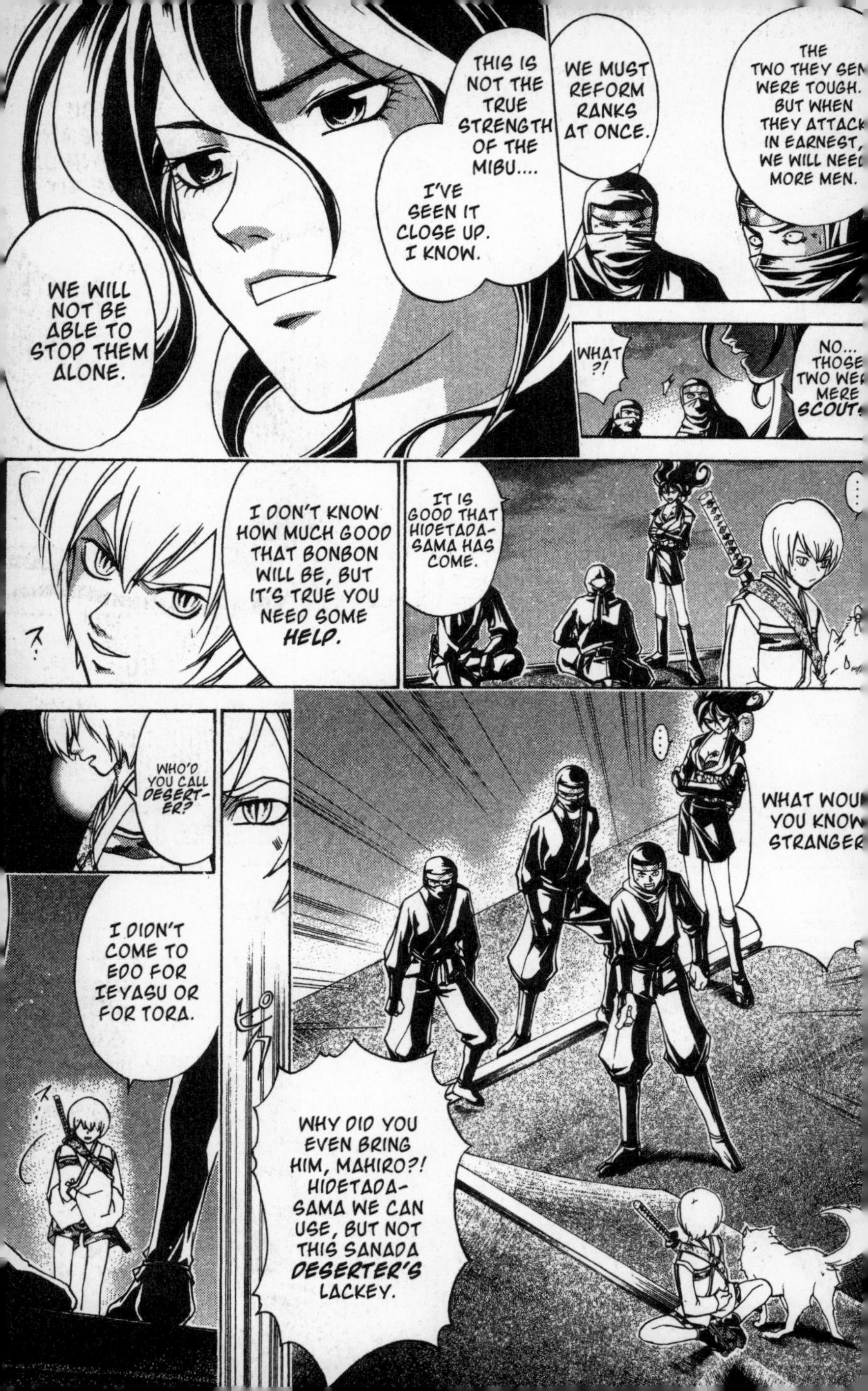
THE TWO THEY SEN WERE TOUGH. BUT WHEN THEY ATTACK IN EARNEST, WE WILL NEED MORE MEN.
WE MUST REFORM RANKS AT ONCE.
NO... THOSE TWO WE MERE SCOUT
WHAT ?!
THIS IS NOT THE TRUE STRENGTH OF THE MIBU....
I'VE SEEN IT CLOSE UP. I KNOW.
WE WILL NOT BE ABLE TO STOP THEM ALONE.
...
IT IS GOOD THAT HIDETADA-SAMA HAS COME.
I DON'T KNOW HOW MUCH GOOD THAT BONBON WILL BE, BUT IT'S TRUE YOU NEED SOME HELP.
WHAT WOU YOU KNOW STRANGER
...
WHY DID YOU EVEN BRING HIM, MAHIRO?! HIDETADA-SAMA WE CAN USE, BUT NOT THIS SANADA DESERTER'S LACKEY.
WHO'D YOU CALL DESERTER?
I DIDN'T COME TO EDO FOR IEYASU OR FOR TORA.

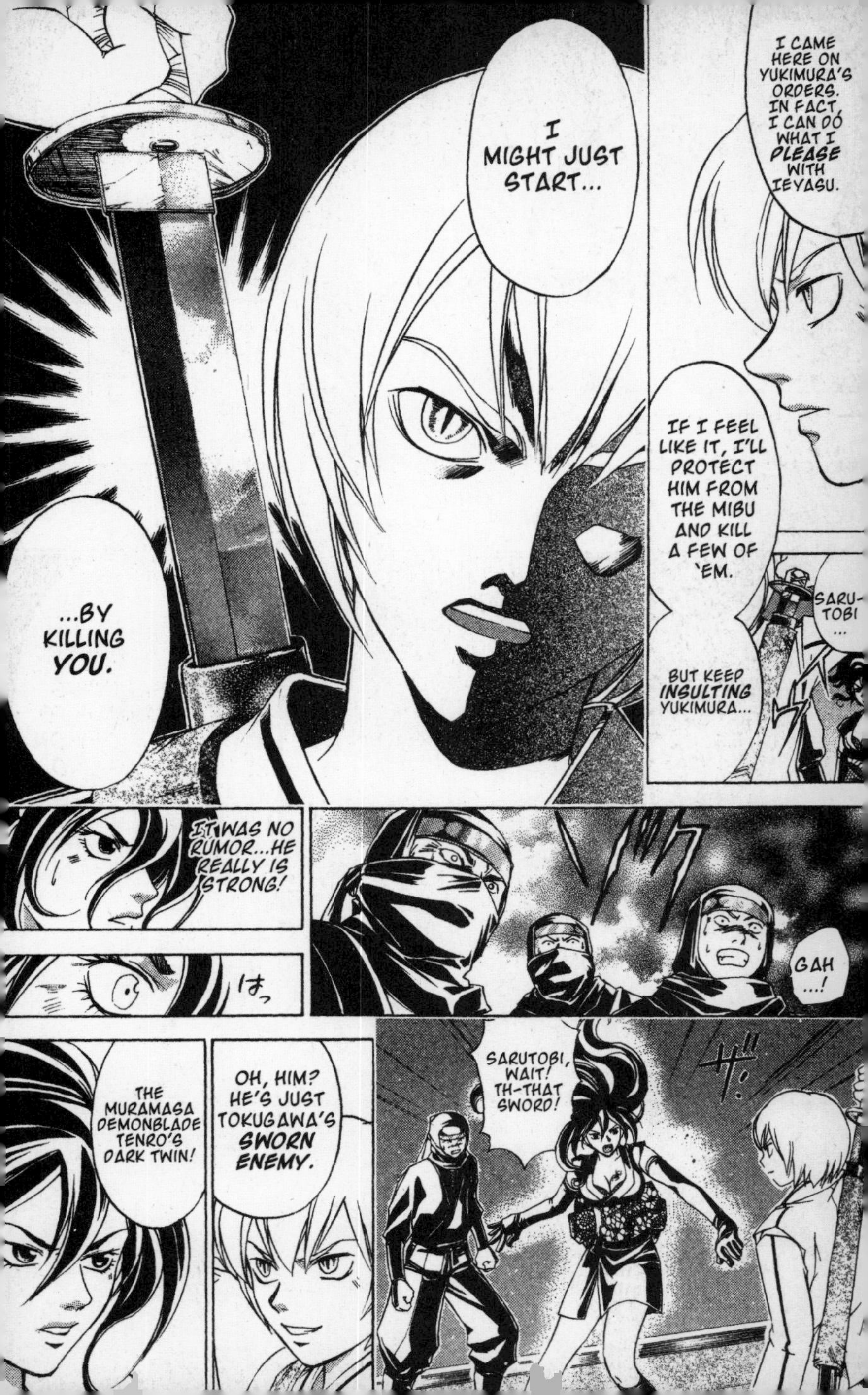
I CAME HERE ON YUKIMURA'S ORDERS. IN FACT, I CAN DO WHAT I PLEASE WITH IEYASU.
IF I FEEL LIKE IT, I'LL PROTECT HIM FROM THE MIBU AND KILL A FEW OF 'EM.
BUT KEEP INSULTING YUKIMURA...
SARU-TOBI...
I MIGHT JUST START...
...BY KILLING YOU.
GAH...!
IT WAS NO RUMOR...HE REALLY IS STRONG!
はっ
SARUTOBI, WAIT! TH-THAT SWORD!
OH, HIM? HE'S JUST TOKUGAWA'S SWORN ENEMY.
THE MURAMASA DEMONBLADE TENRO'S DARK TWIN!

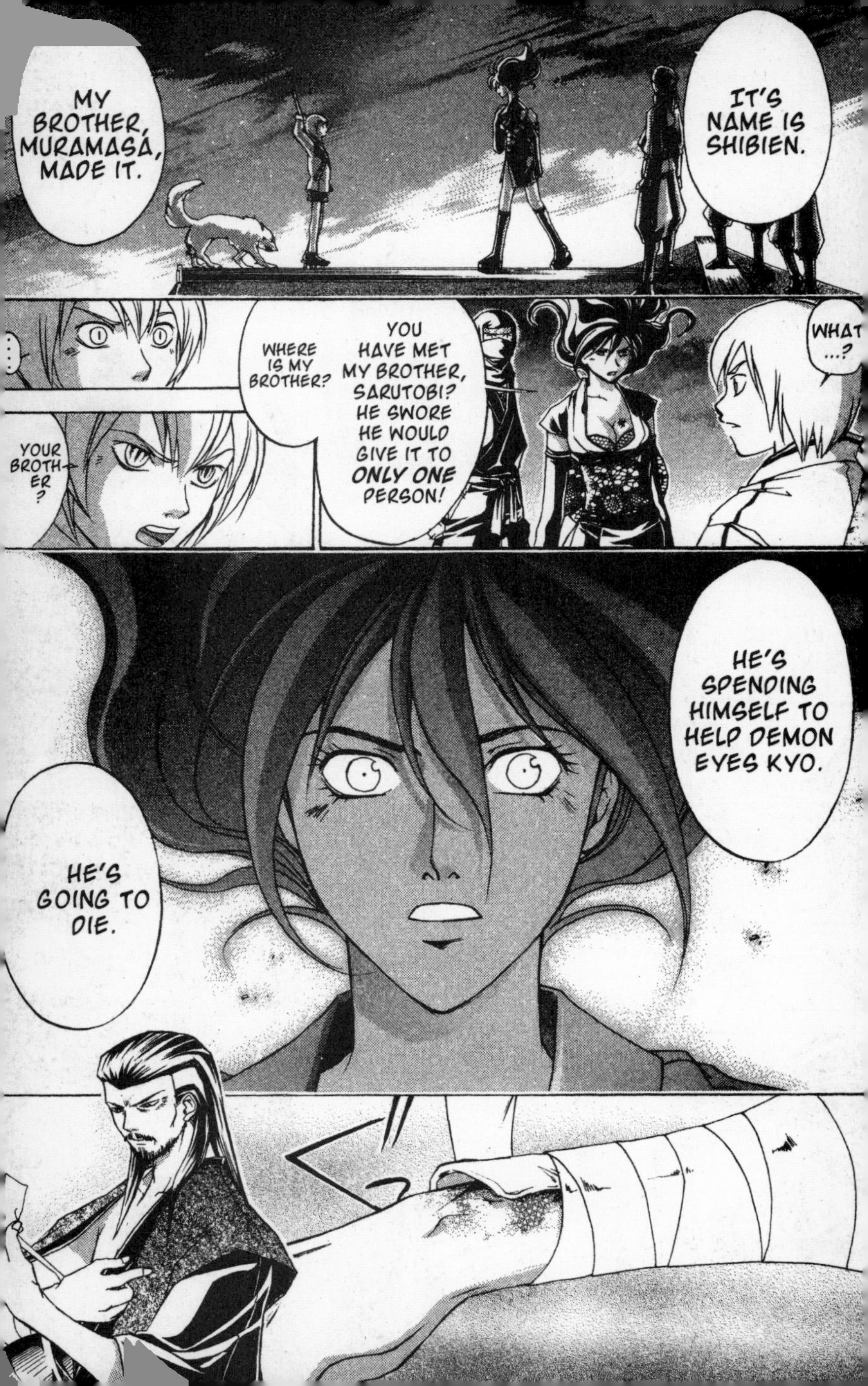
IT'S NAME IS SHIBIEN.
MY BROTHER, MURAMASA, MADE IT.
WHAT ...?
YOU HAVE MET MY BROTHER, SARUTOBI? HE SWORE HE WOULD GIVE IT TO ONLY ONE PERSON!
WHERE IS MY BROTHER?
...
YOUR BROTHER?
HE'S SPENDING HIMSELF TO HELP DEMON EYES KYO.
HE'S GOING TO DIE.

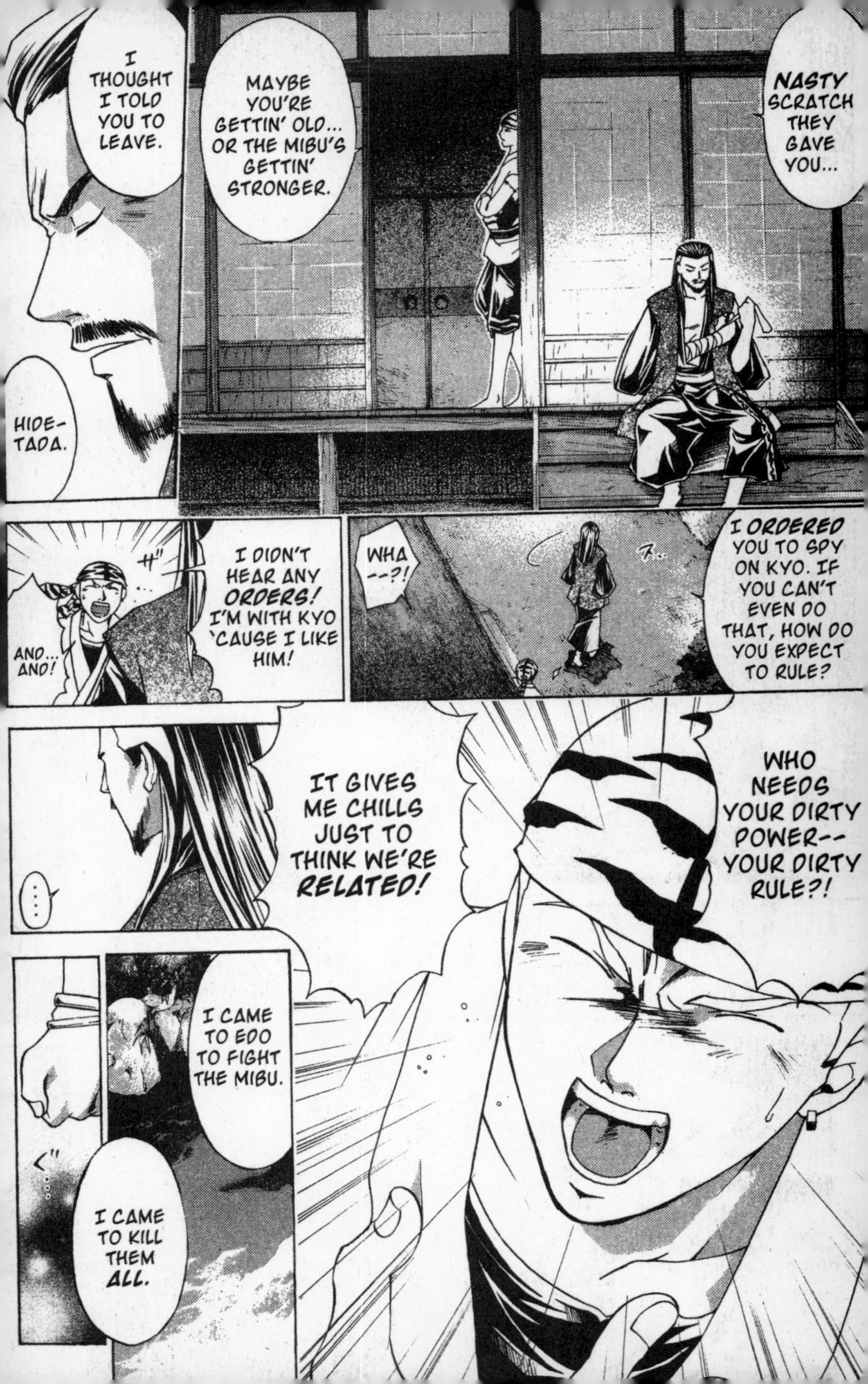
NASTY SCRATCH THEY GAVE YOU...
MAYBE YOU'RE GETTIN' OLD... OR THE MIBU'S GETTIN' STRONGER.
I THOUGHT I TOLD YOU TO LEAVE.
HIDE-TADA.
I ORDERED YOU TO SPY ON KYO. IF YOU CAN'T EVEN DO THAT, HOW DO YOU EXPECT TO RULE?
WHA--?!
I DIDN'T HEAR ANY ORDERS! I'M WITH KYO 'CAUSE I LIKE HIM!
AND... AND!
WHO NEEDS YOUR DIRTY POWER--YOUR DIRTY RULE?!
IT GIVES ME CHILLS JUST TO THINK WE'RE RELATED!
....
I CAME TO EDO TO FIGHT THE MIBU.
I CAME TO KILL THEM ALL.

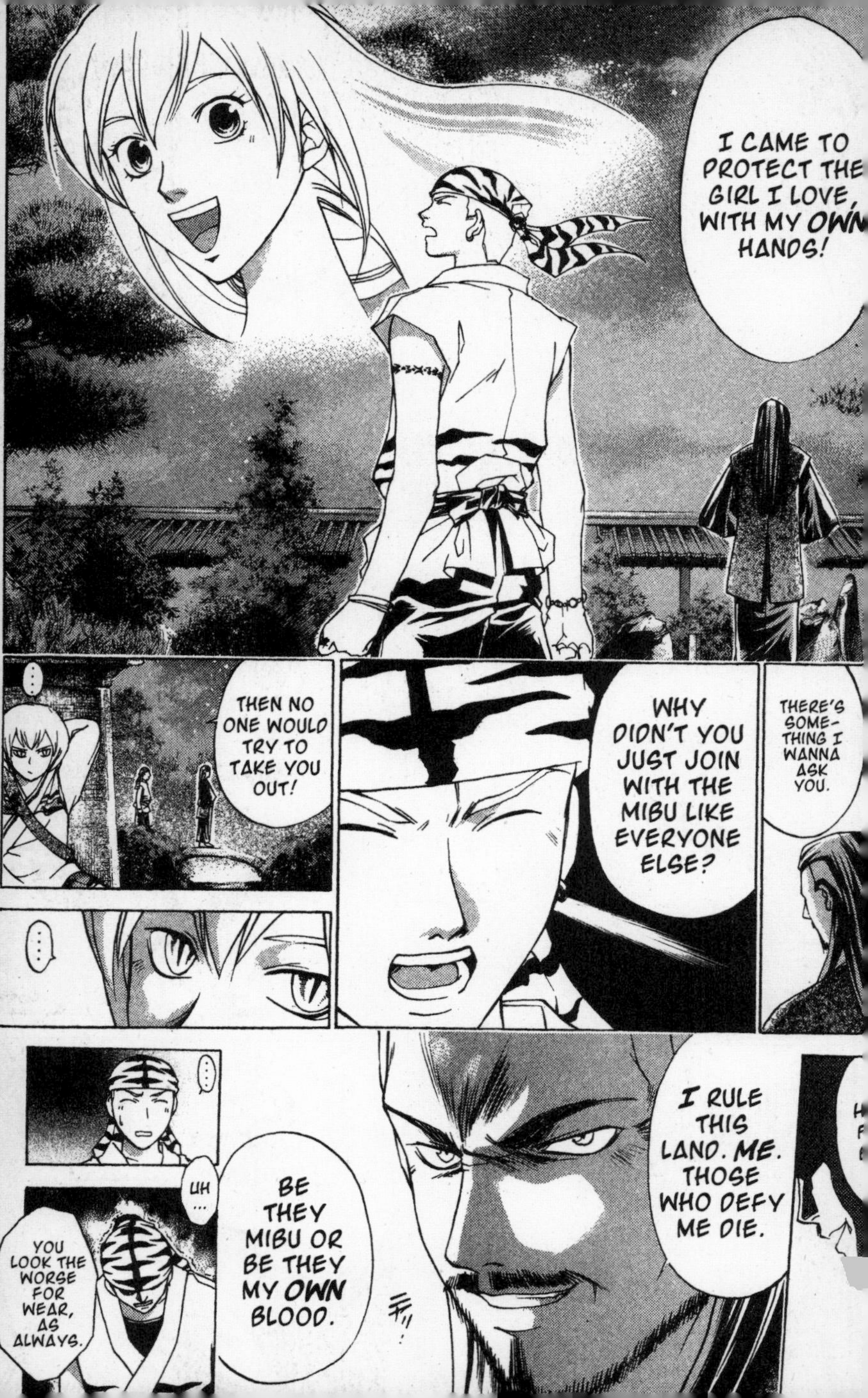
I CAME TO PROTECT THE GIRL I LOVE, WITH MY *OWN* HANDS!
THERE'S SOMETHING I WANNA ASK YOU.
WHY DIDN'T YOU JUST JOIN WITH THE MIBU LIKE EVERYONE ELSE?
...
THEN NO ONE WOULD TRY TO TAKE YOU OUT!
...
I RULE THIS LAND. *ME*. THOSE WHO DEFY ME DIE.
BE THEY MIBU OR BE THEY MY *OWN* BLOOD.
...
UH ...
YOU LOOK THE WORSE FOR WEAR, AS ALWAYS.

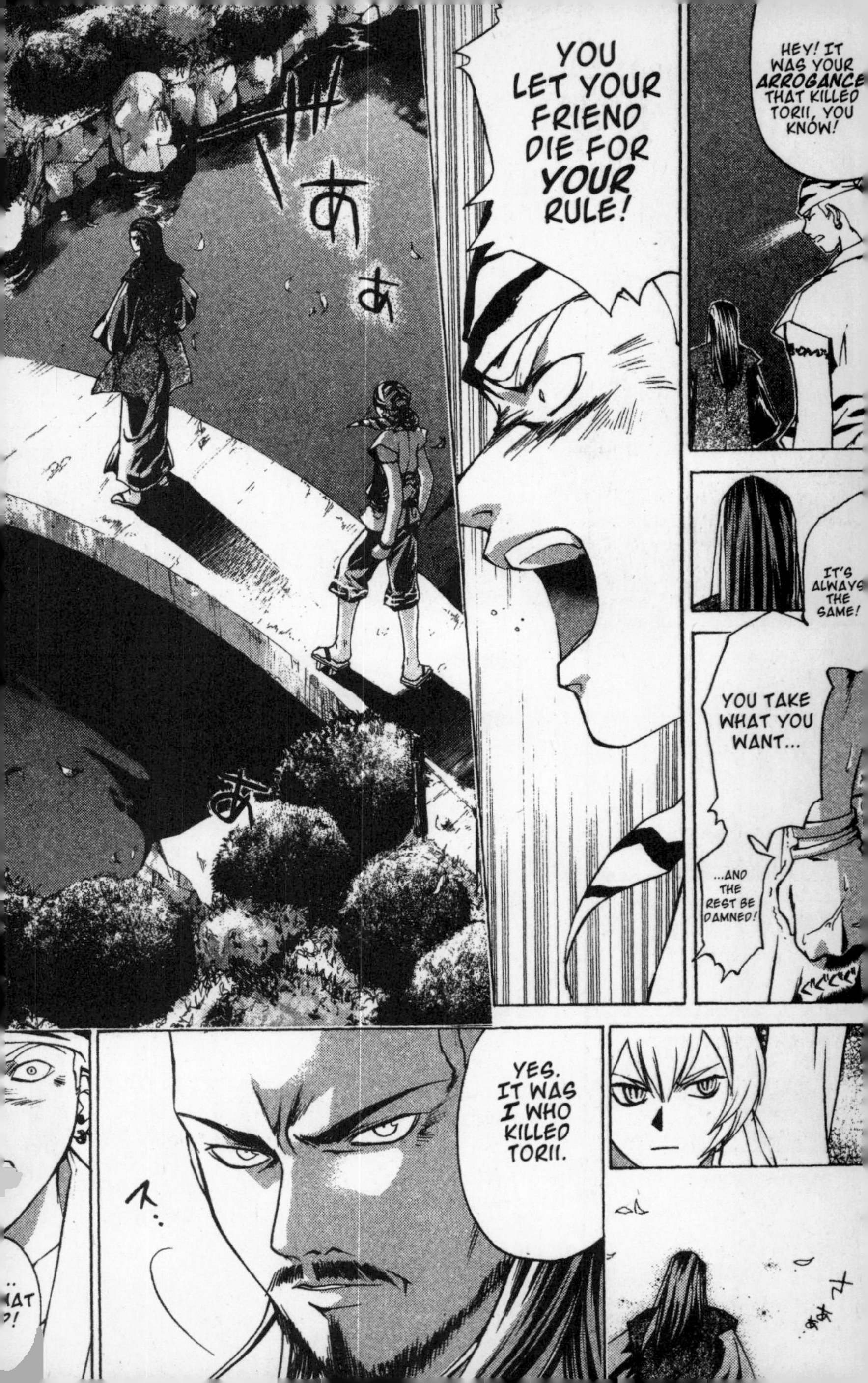
HEY! IT WAS YOUR ARROGANCE THAT KILLED TORII, YOU KNOW!
IT'S ALWAYS THE SAME!
YOU TAKE WHAT YOU WANT...
...AND THE REST BE DAMNED!
YOU LET YOUR FRIEND DIE FOR YOUR RULE!
あ
あ
あ
YES. IT WAS I WHO KILLED TORII.
ス...

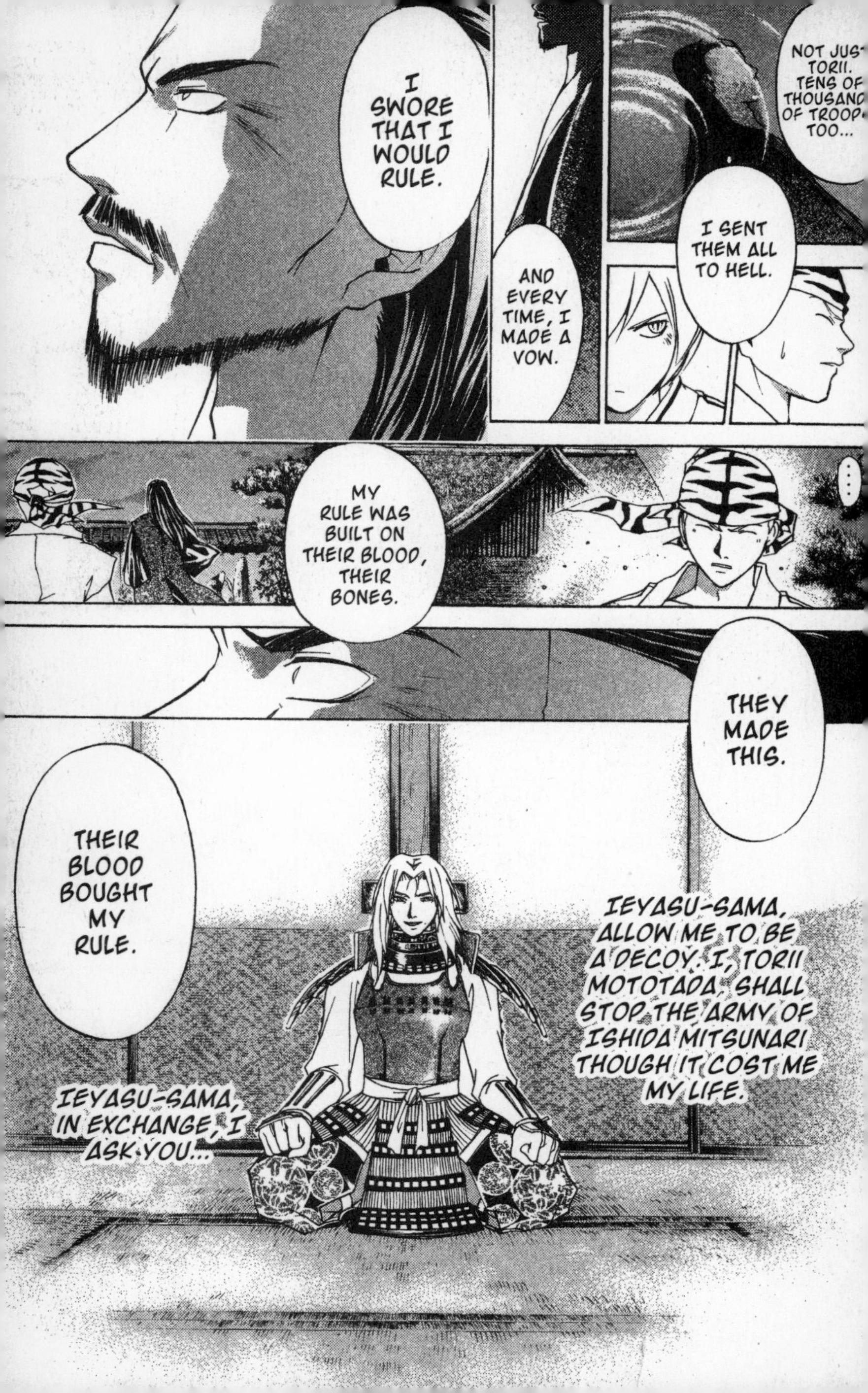
NOT JUST TORII. TENS OF THOUSANDS OF TROOPS TOO...
I SENT THEM ALL TO HELL.
AND EVERY TIME, I MADE A VOW.
I SWORE THAT I WOULD RULE.
...
MY RULE WAS BUILT ON THEIR BLOOD, THEIR BONES.
THEY MADE THIS.
THEIR BLOOD BOUGHT MY RULE.
IEYASU-SAMA, ALLOW ME TO BE A DECOY. I, TORII MOTOTADA, SHALL STOP THE ARMY OF ISHIDA MITSUNARI THOUGH IT COST ME MY LIFE.
IEYASU-SAMA, IN EXCHANGE, I ASK YOU...

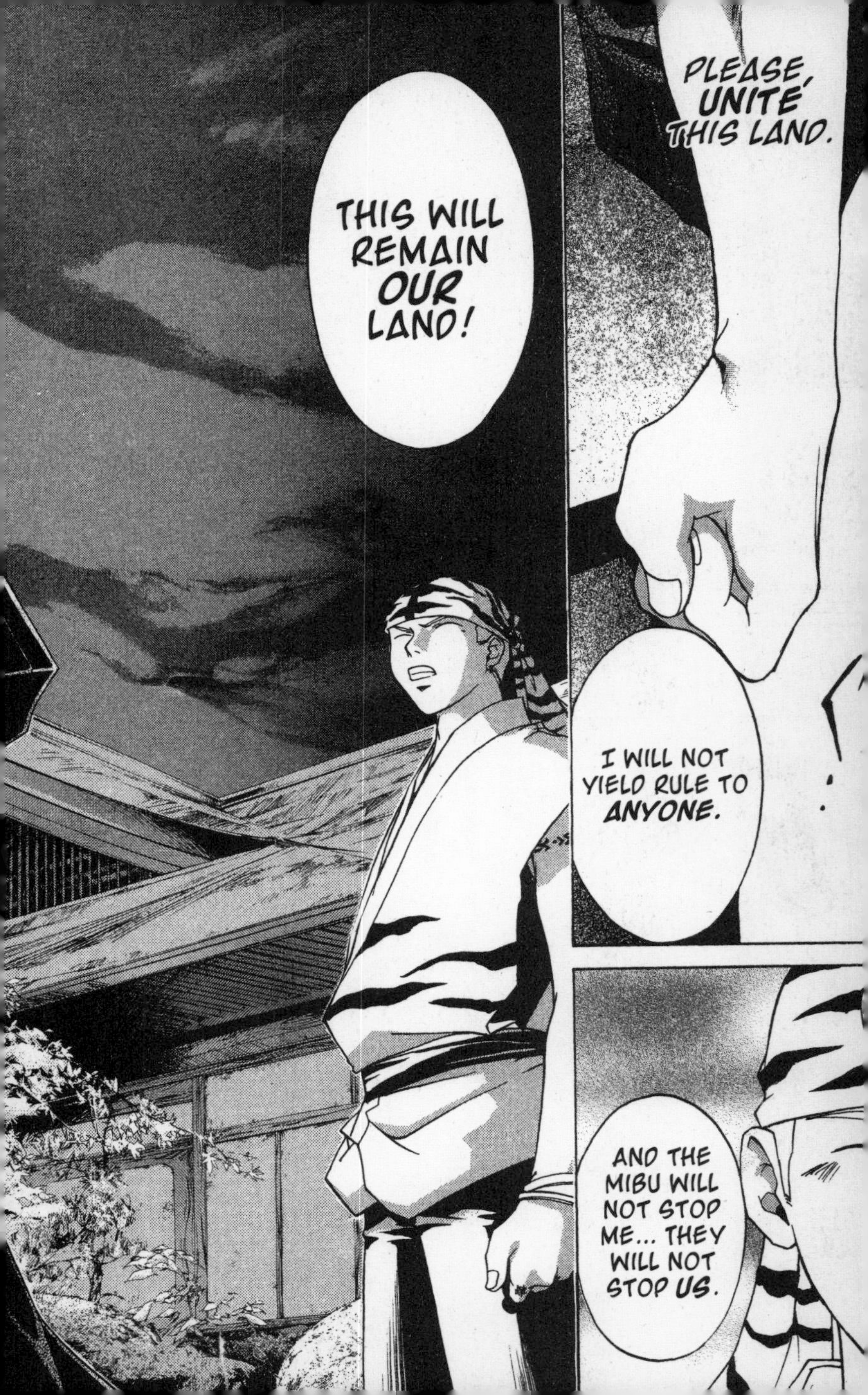
PLEASE, UNITE THIS LAND.
I WILL NOT YIELD RULE TO ANYONE.
AND THE MIBU WILL NOT STOP ME... THEY WILL NOT STOP US.
THIS WILL REMAIN OUR LAND!

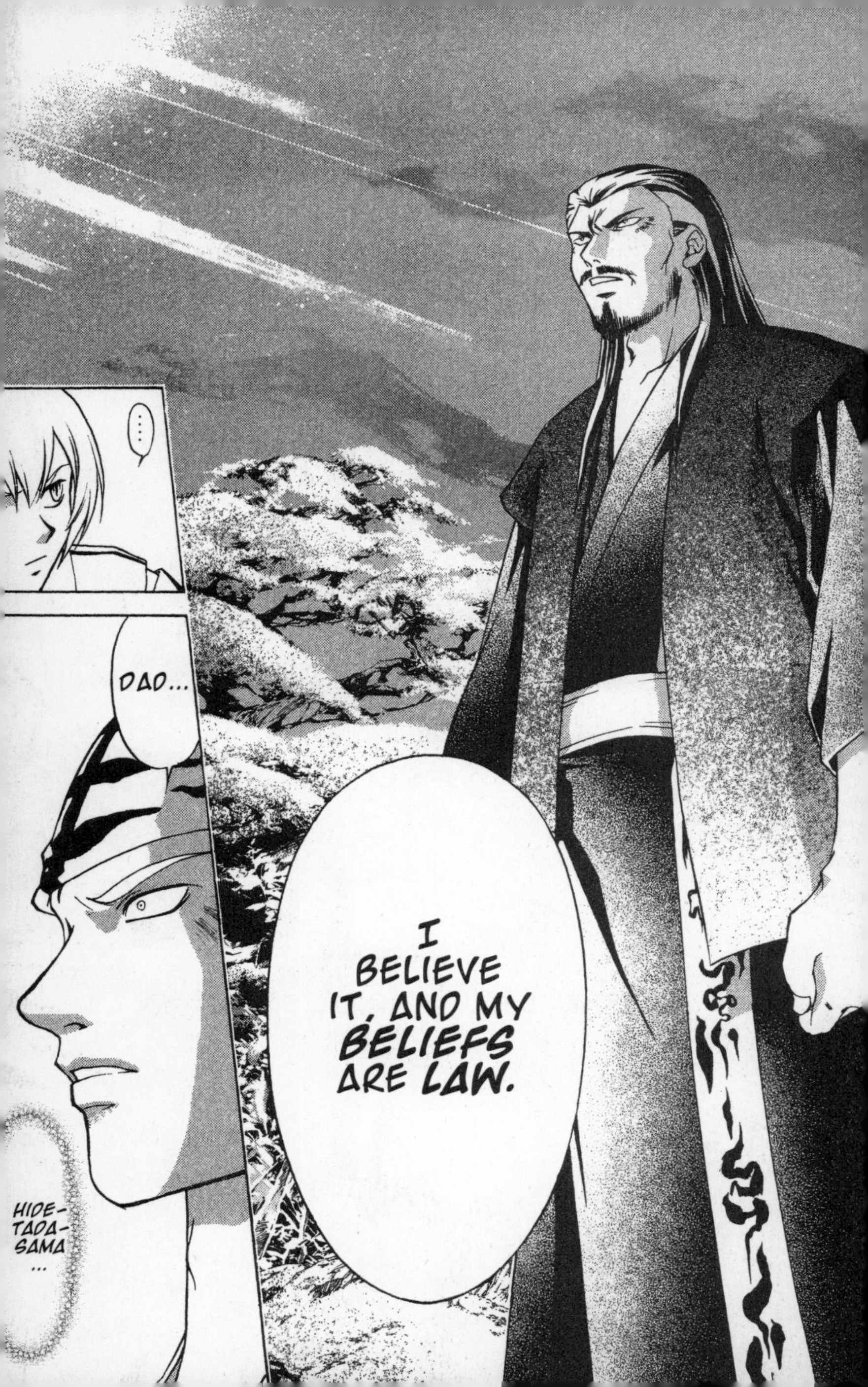
I BELIEVE IT, AND MY BELIEFS ARE LAW.
...
DAD...
HIDE-TADA-SAMA...

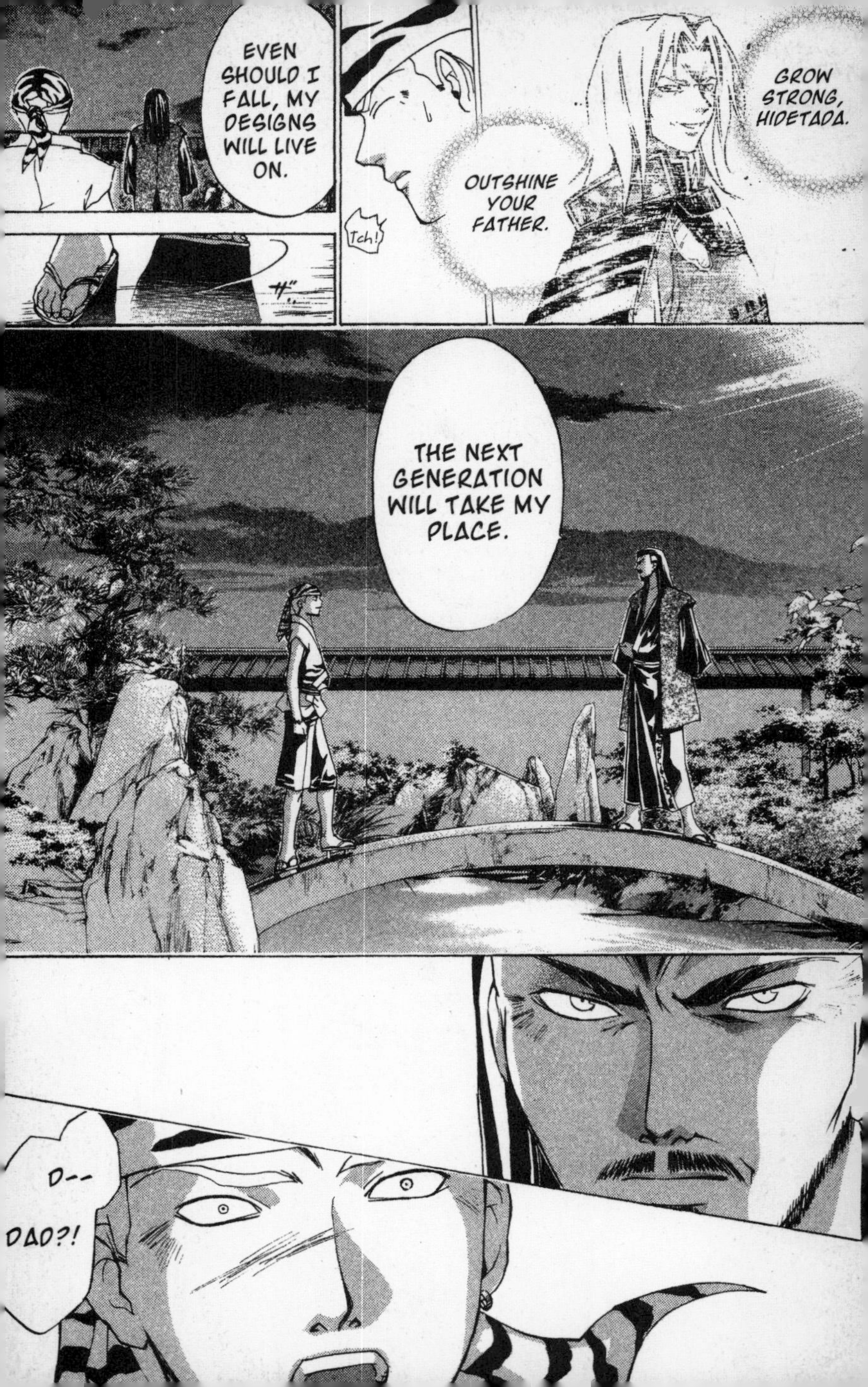
GROW STRONG, HIDETADA.
OUTSHINE YOUR FATHER.
Tch!
EVEN SHOULD I FALL, MY DESIGNS WILL LIVE ON.
ザ
THE NEXT GENERATION WILL TAKE MY PLACE.
D-- DAD?!

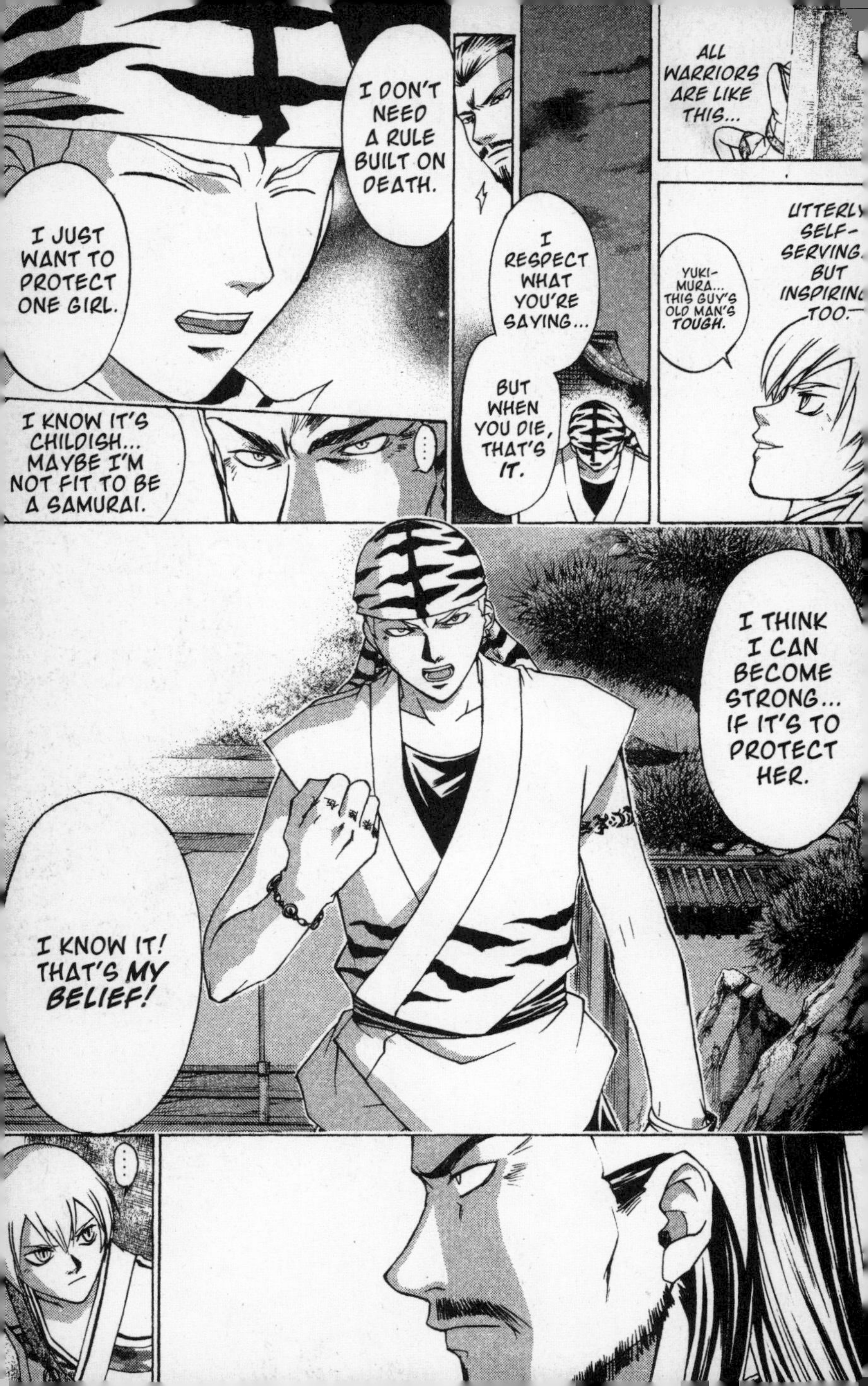
ALL WARRIORS ARE LIKE THIS...
UTTERLY SELF-SERVING. BUT INSPIRING TOO.
YUKI-MURA... THIS GUY'S OLD MAN'S TOUGH.
I RESPECT WHAT YOU'RE SAYING...
BUT WHEN YOU DIE, THAT'S IT.
I DON'T NEED A RULE BUILT ON DEATH.
I JUST WANT TO PROTECT ONE GIRL.
...
I KNOW IT'S CHILDISH... MAYBE I'M NOT FIT TO BE A SAMURAI.
I THINK I CAN BECOME STRONG... IF IT'S TO PROTECT HER.
I KNOW IT! THAT'S MY BELIEF!
...

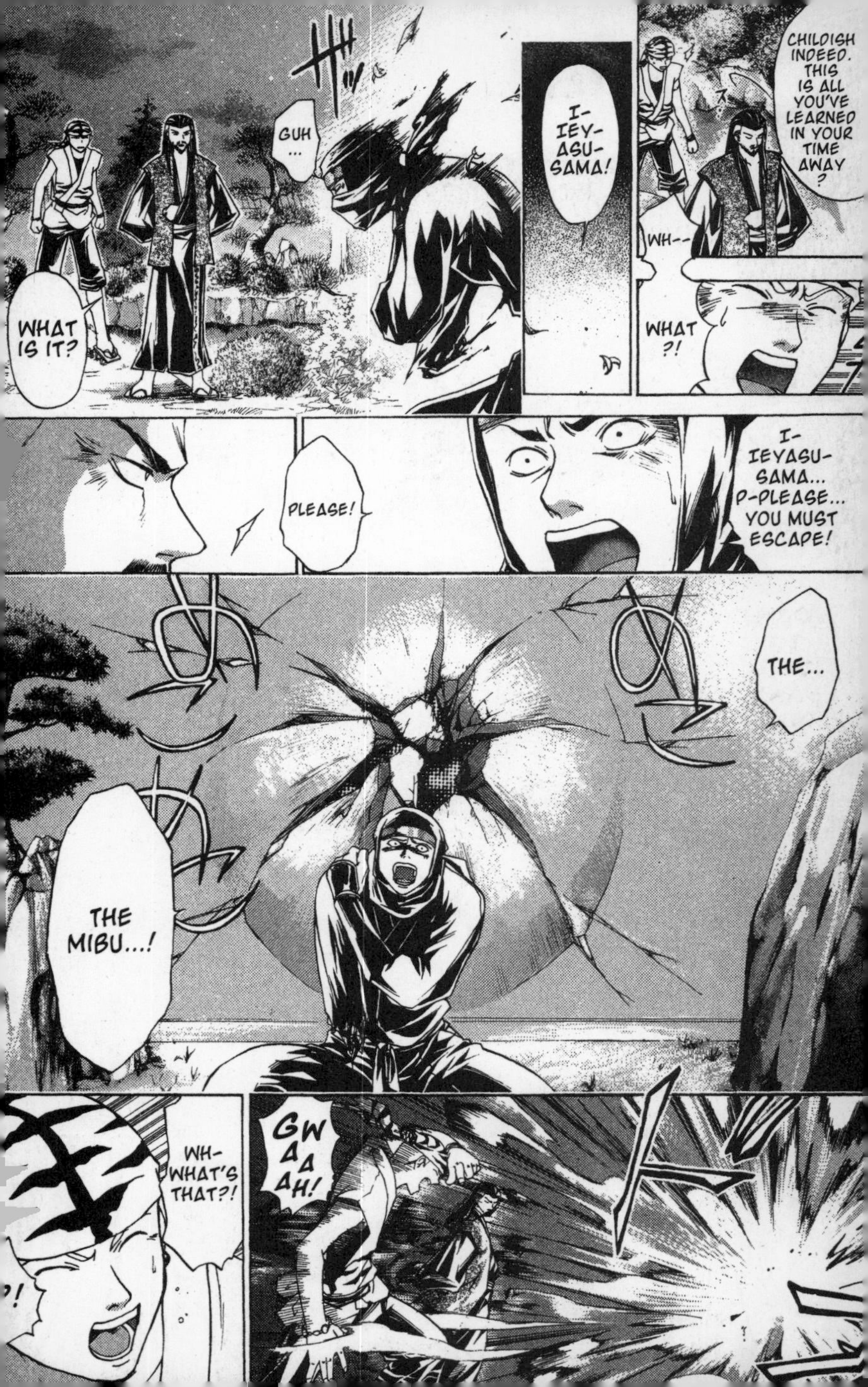
CHILDISH INDEED. THIS IS ALL YOU'VE LEARNED IN YOUR TIME AWAY?
WH--
WHAT ?!
I-IEYASU-SAMA!
GUH...
WHAT IS IT?
I-IEYASU-SAMA... P-PLEASE... YOU MUST ESCAPE!
PLEASE!
THE...
THE MIBU...!
GWAAAH!
WH-WHAT'S THAT?!

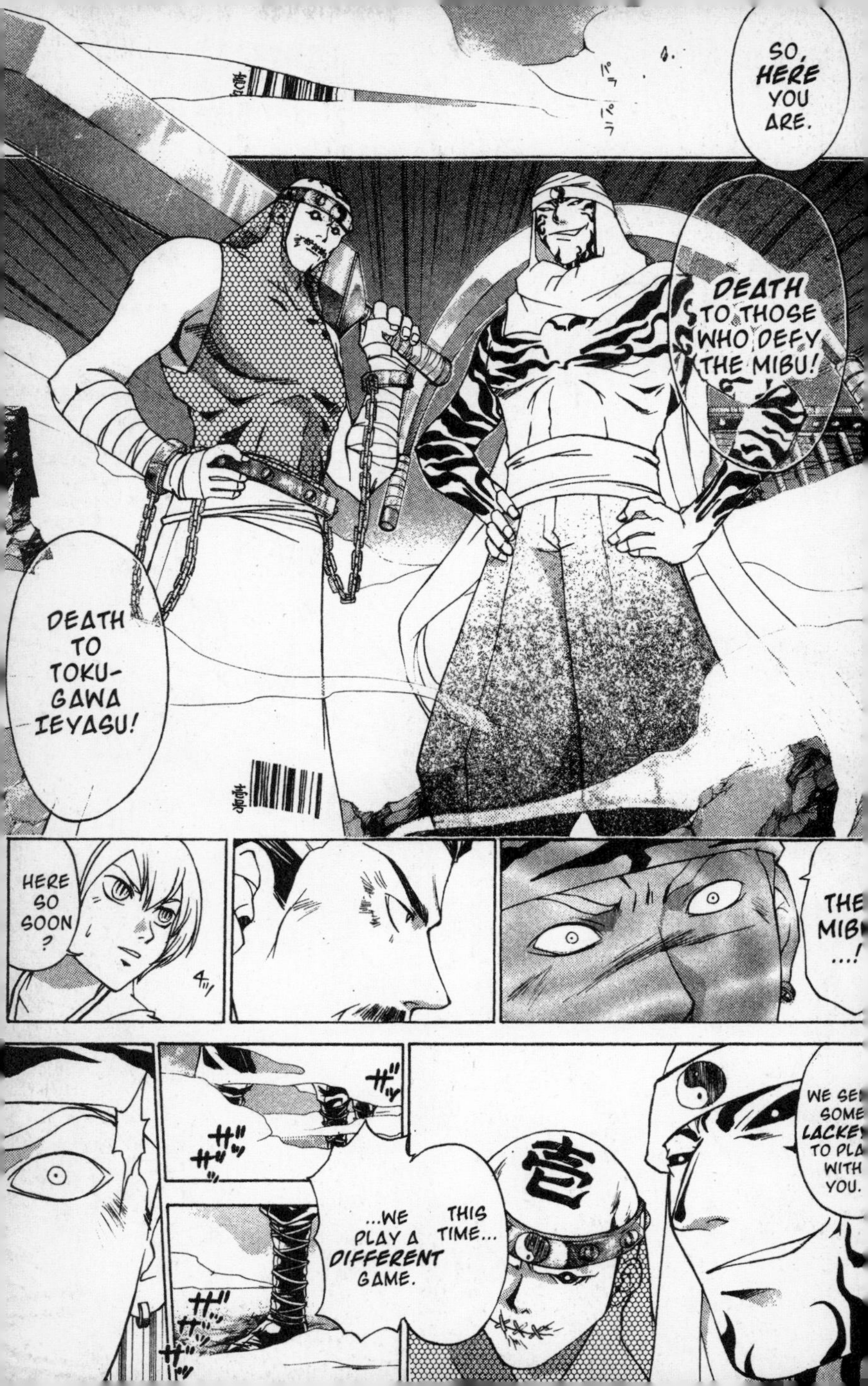
SO, **HERE** YOU ARE.
DEATH TO THOSE WHO DEFY THE MIBU!
DEATH TO TOKUGAWA IEYASU!
THE MIB ...!
HERE SO SOON?
WE SE SOME **LACKE** TO PLA WITH YOU.
THIS TIME...
...WE PLAY A **DIFFERENT** GAME.

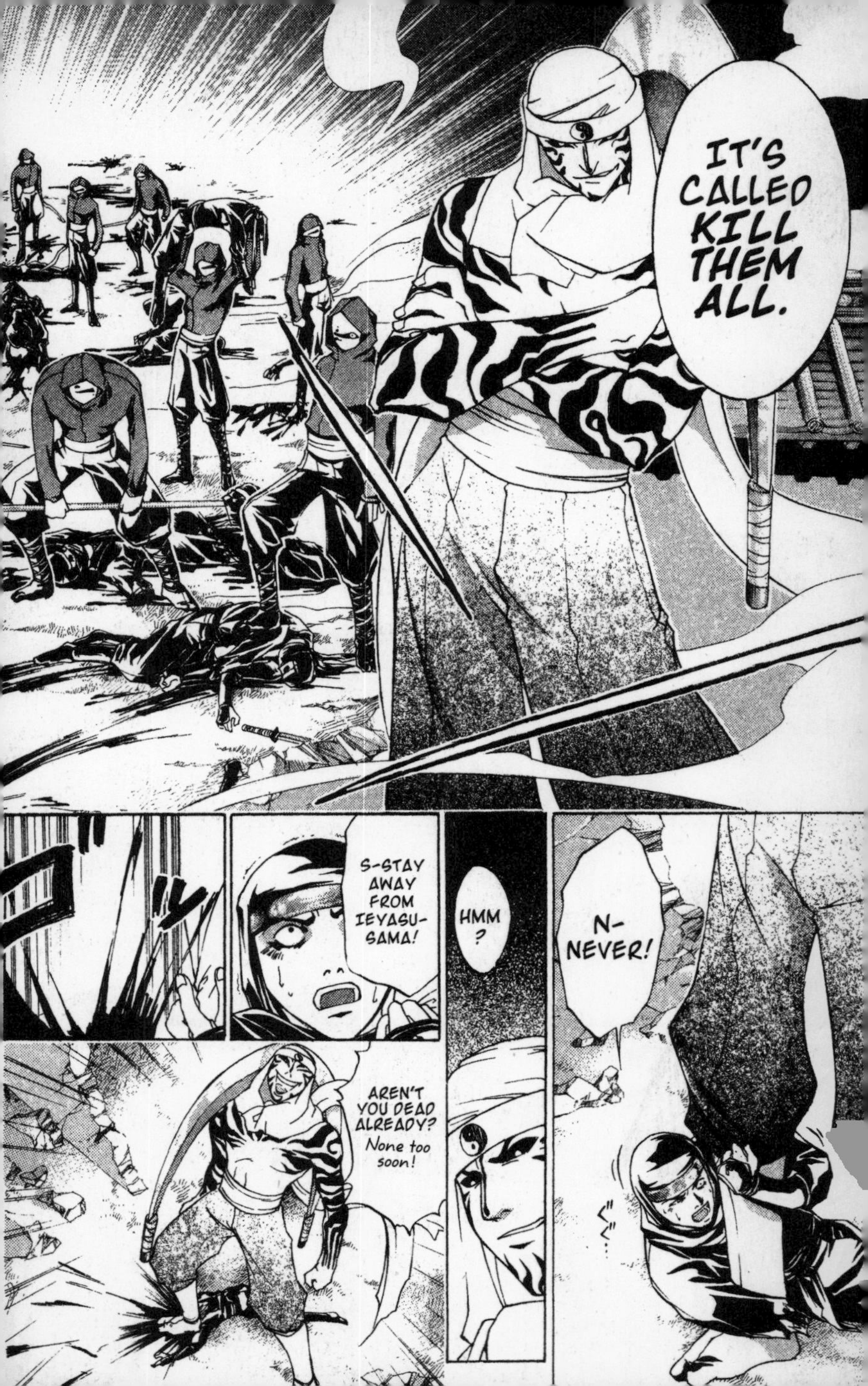
IT'S CALLED KILL THEM ALL.
N-NEVER!
ぐぐ…
HMM ?
S-STAY AWAY FROM IEYASU-SAMA!
AREN'T YOU DEAD ALREADY?
None too soon!

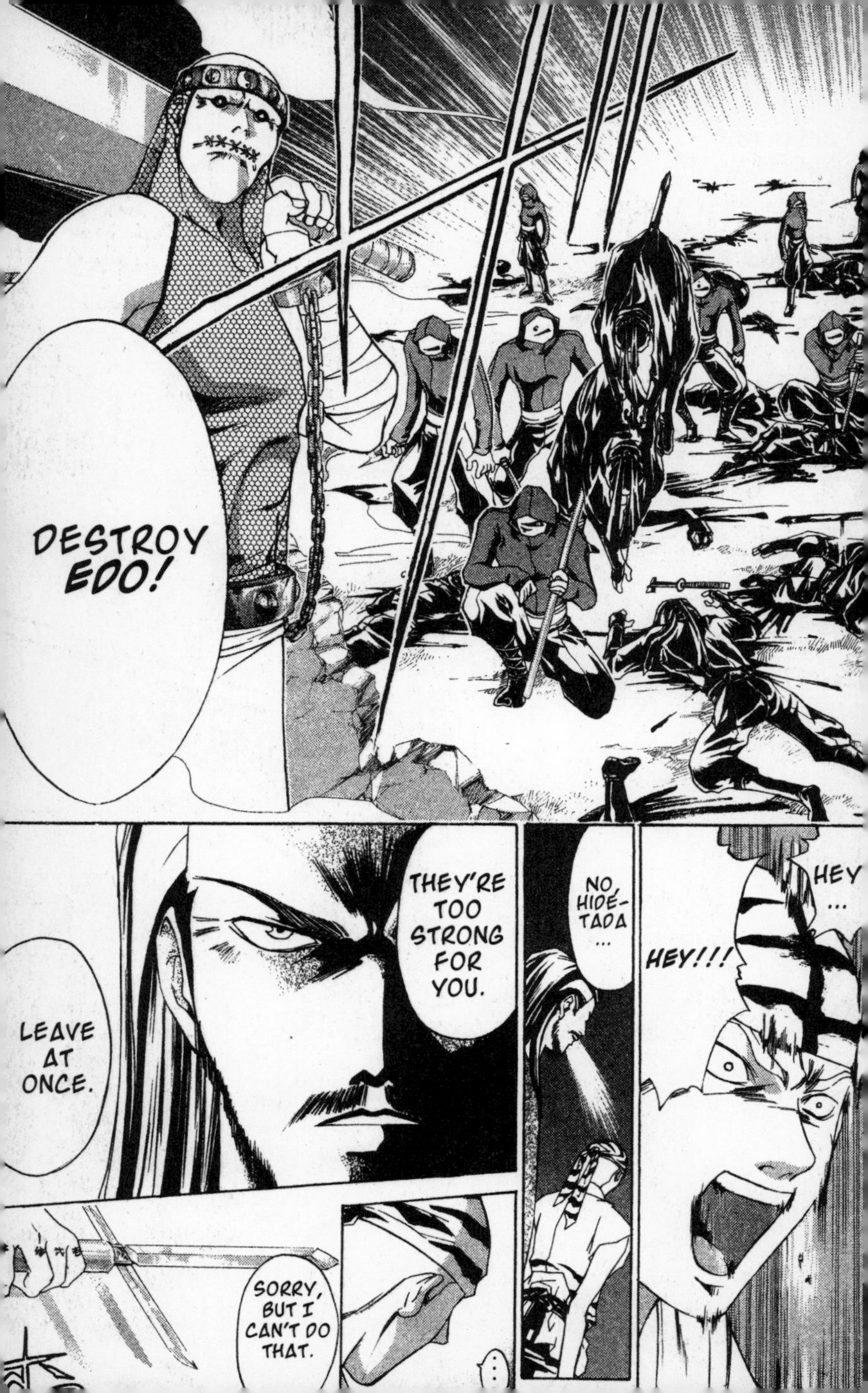

DESTROY EDO!
HEY ...
HEY!!!
NO, HIDE-TADA ...
THEY'RE TOO STRONG FOR YOU.
LEAVE AT ONCE.
...
SORRY, BUT I CAN'T DO THAT.

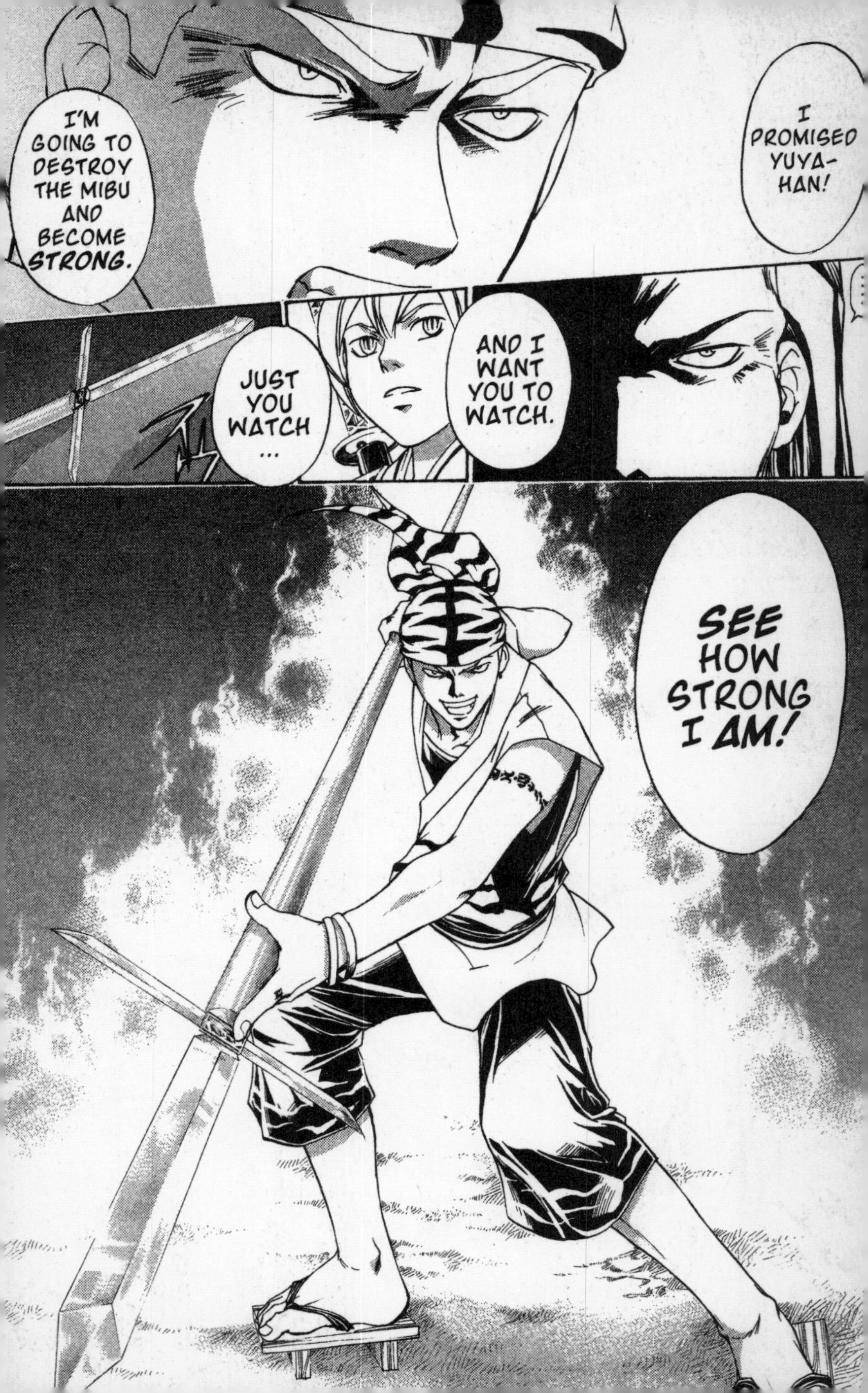
I PROMISED YUYA-HAN!
I'M GOING TO DESTROY THE MIBU AND BECOME STRONG.
AND I WANT YOU TO WATCH.
JUST YOU WATCH ...
SEE HOW STRONG I AM!

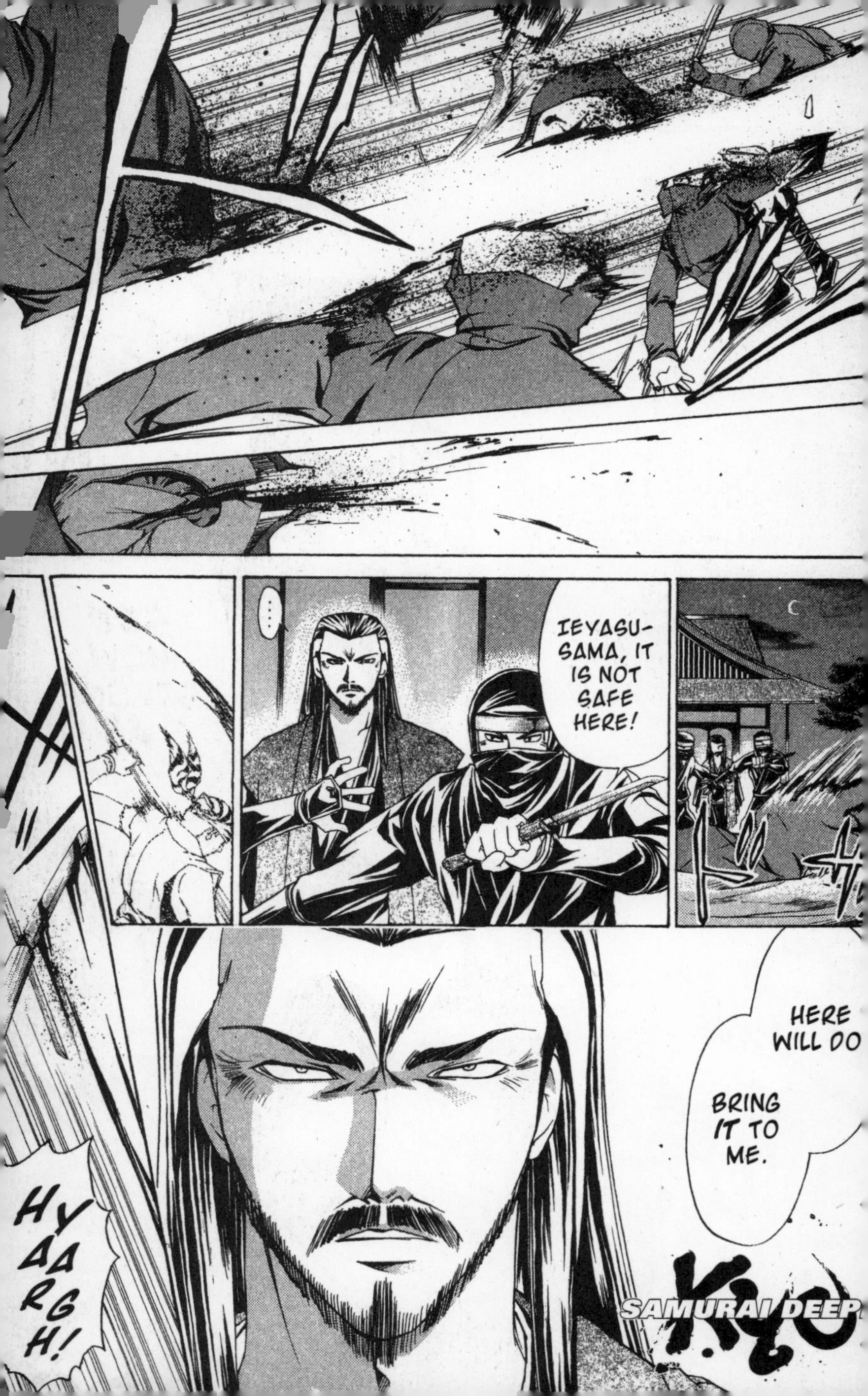
IEYASU-SAMA, IT IS NOT SAFE HERE!
...
HERE WILL DO
BRING IT TO ME.
HYAARGH!

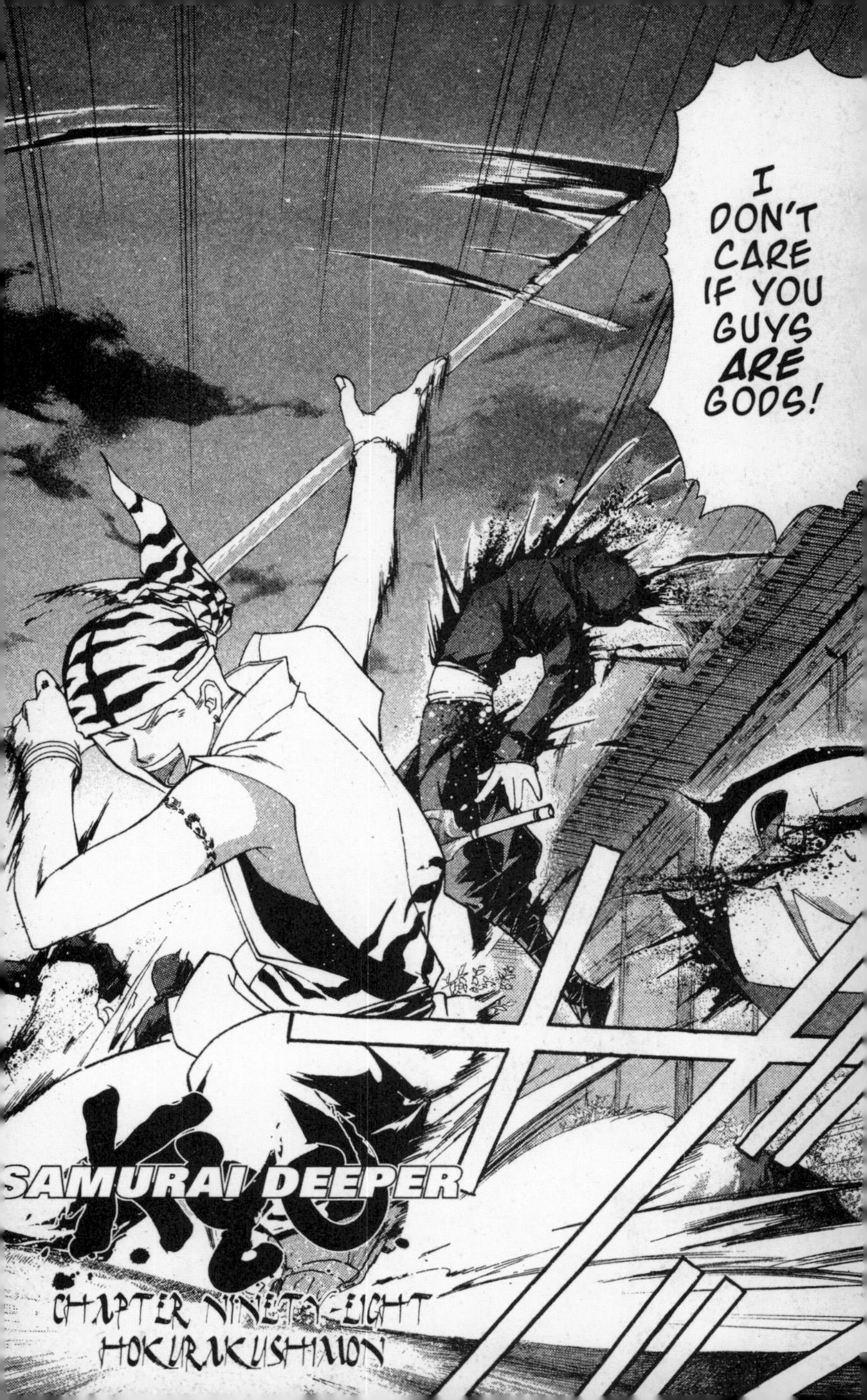
I DON'T CARE IF YOU GUYS ARE GODS!
SAMURAI DEEPER KYO
CHAPTER NINETY-EIGHT
HOKURAKUSHIMON

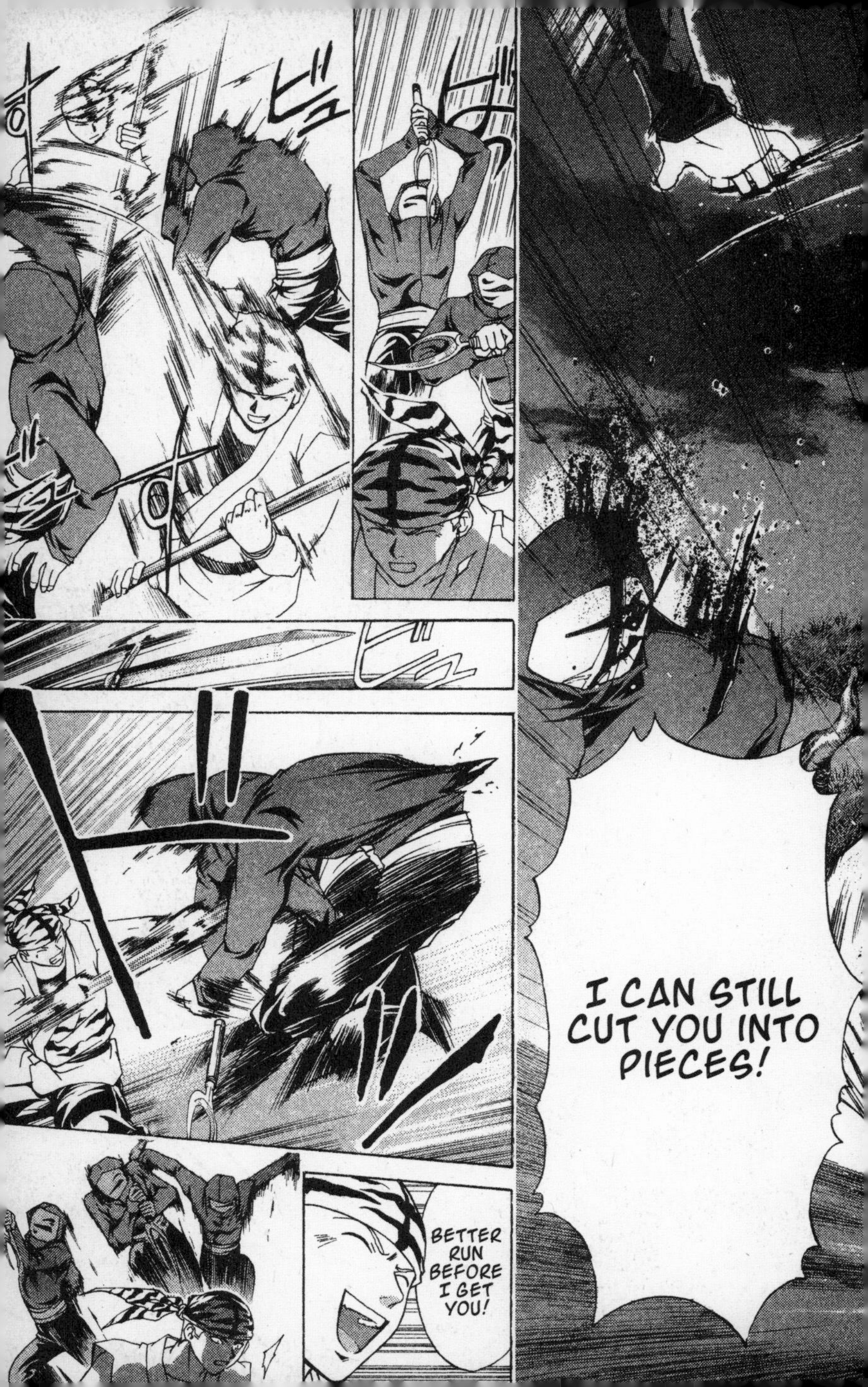
I CAN STILL CUT YOU INTO PIECES!
BETTER RUN BEFORE I GET YOU!

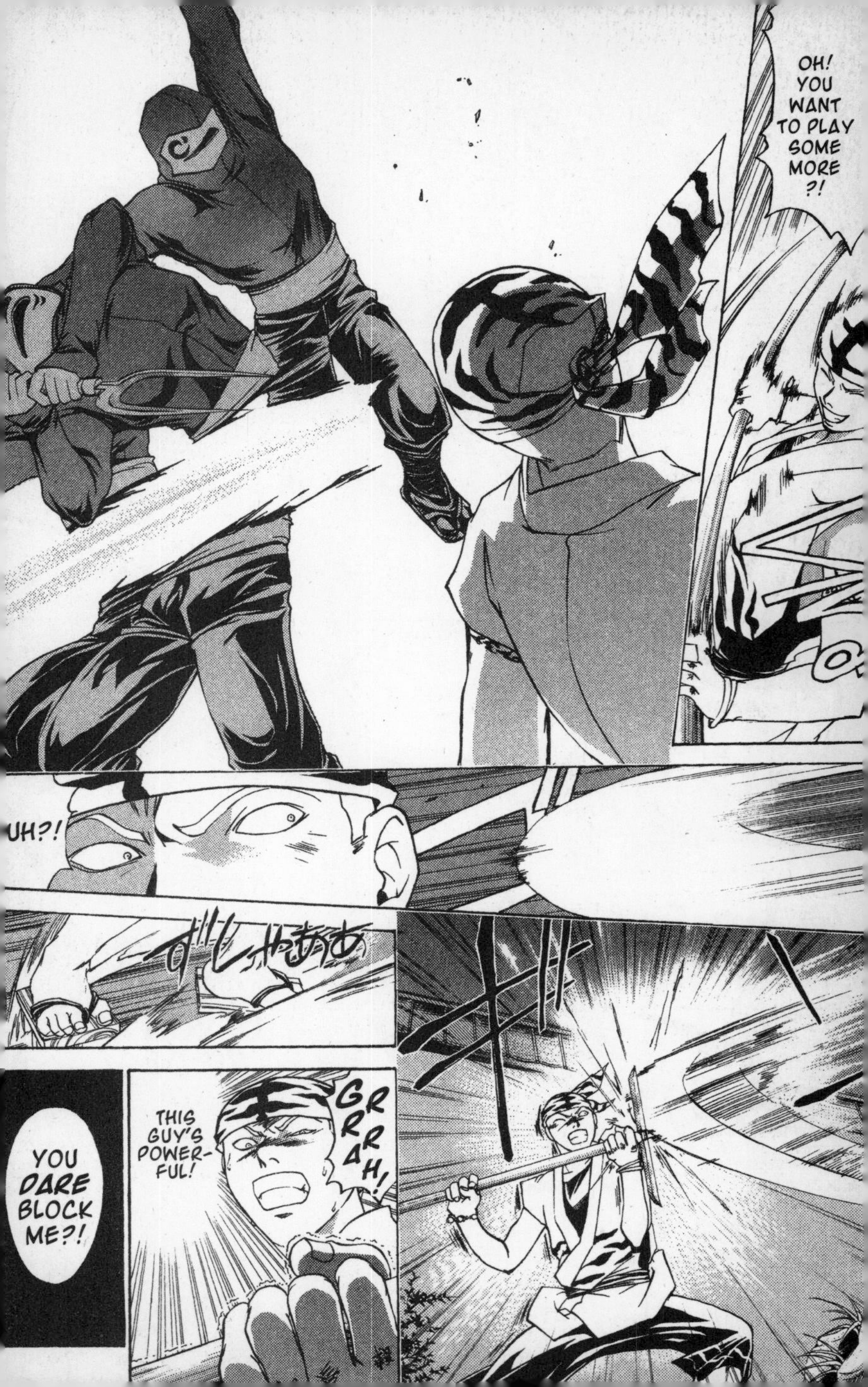
OH! YOU WANT TO PLAY SOME MORE ?!
UH?!
すしゃああ
GRRRAH!
THIS GUY'S POWER-FUL!
YOU DARE BLOCK ME?!

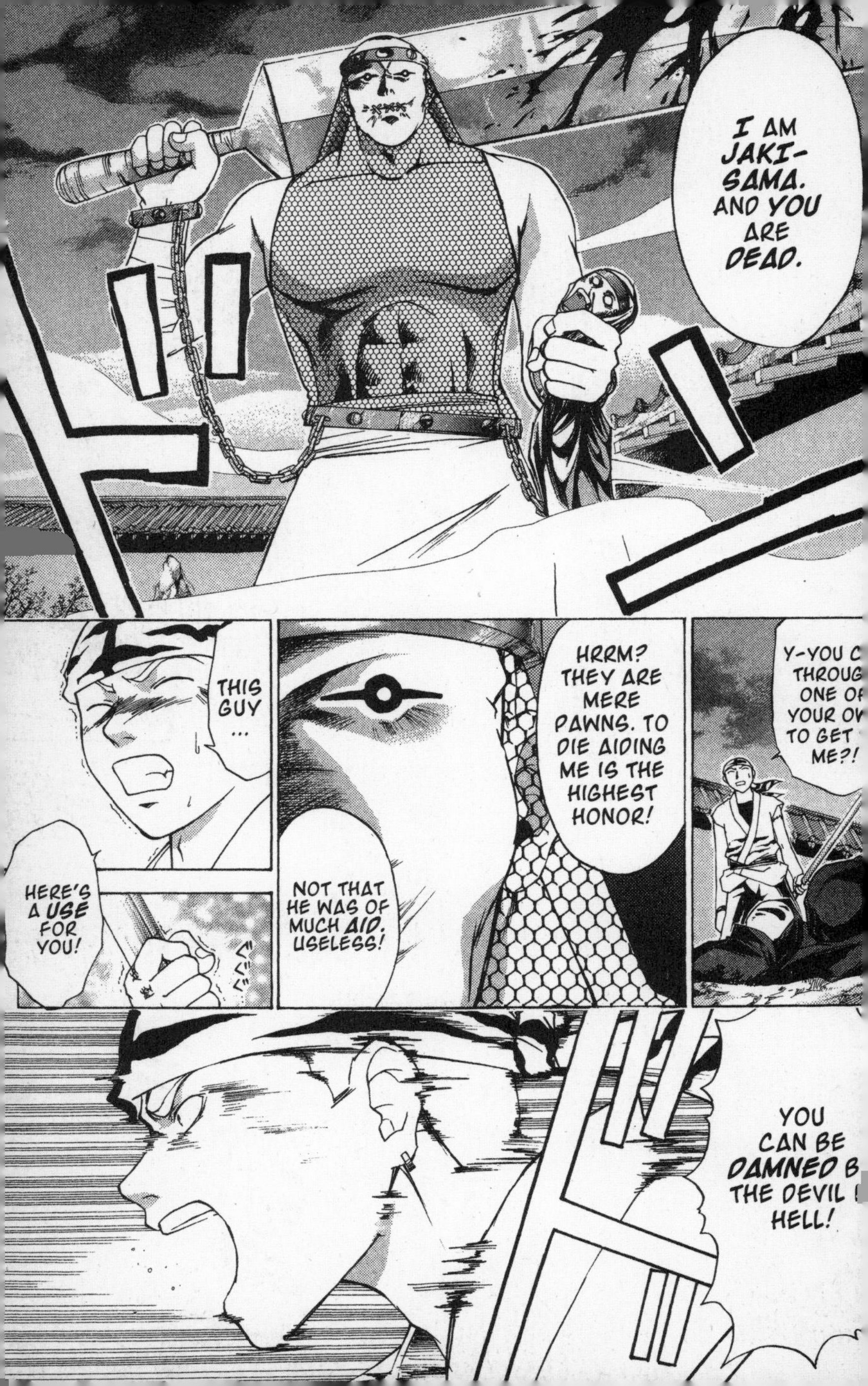
I AM JAKI-SAMA. AND YOU ARE DEAD.
Y-YOU C THROUG ONE OF YOUR OV TO GET ME?!
HRRM? THEY ARE MERE PAWNS. TO DIE AIDING ME IS THE HIGHEST HONOR!
NOT THAT HE WAS OF MUCH AID. USELESS!
THIS GUY ...
HERE'S A USE FOR YOU!
YOU CAN BE DAMNED B THE DEVIL HELL!

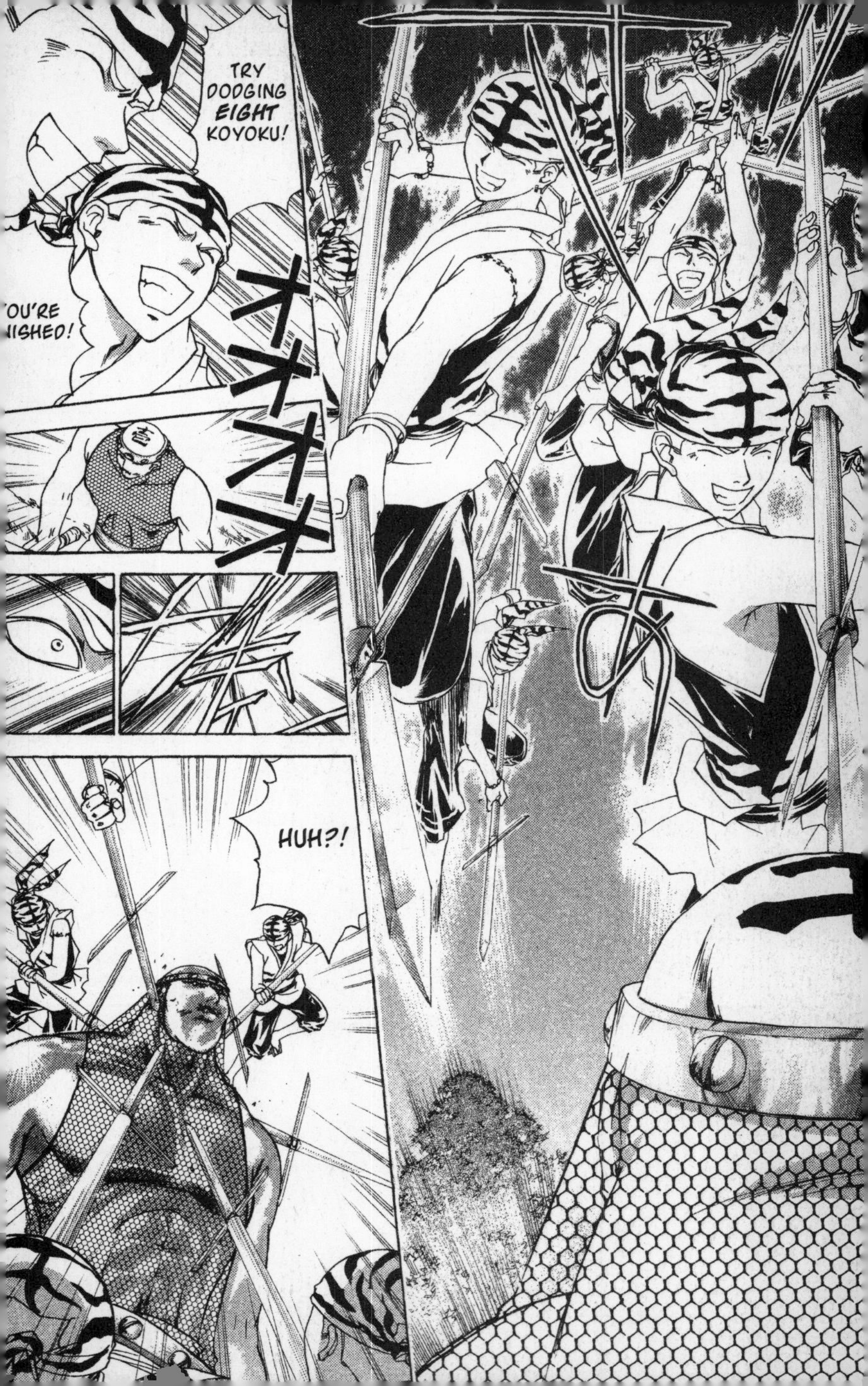
TRY DODGING EIGHT KOYOKU!
'OU'RE
IISHED!
オオオオ
HUH?!

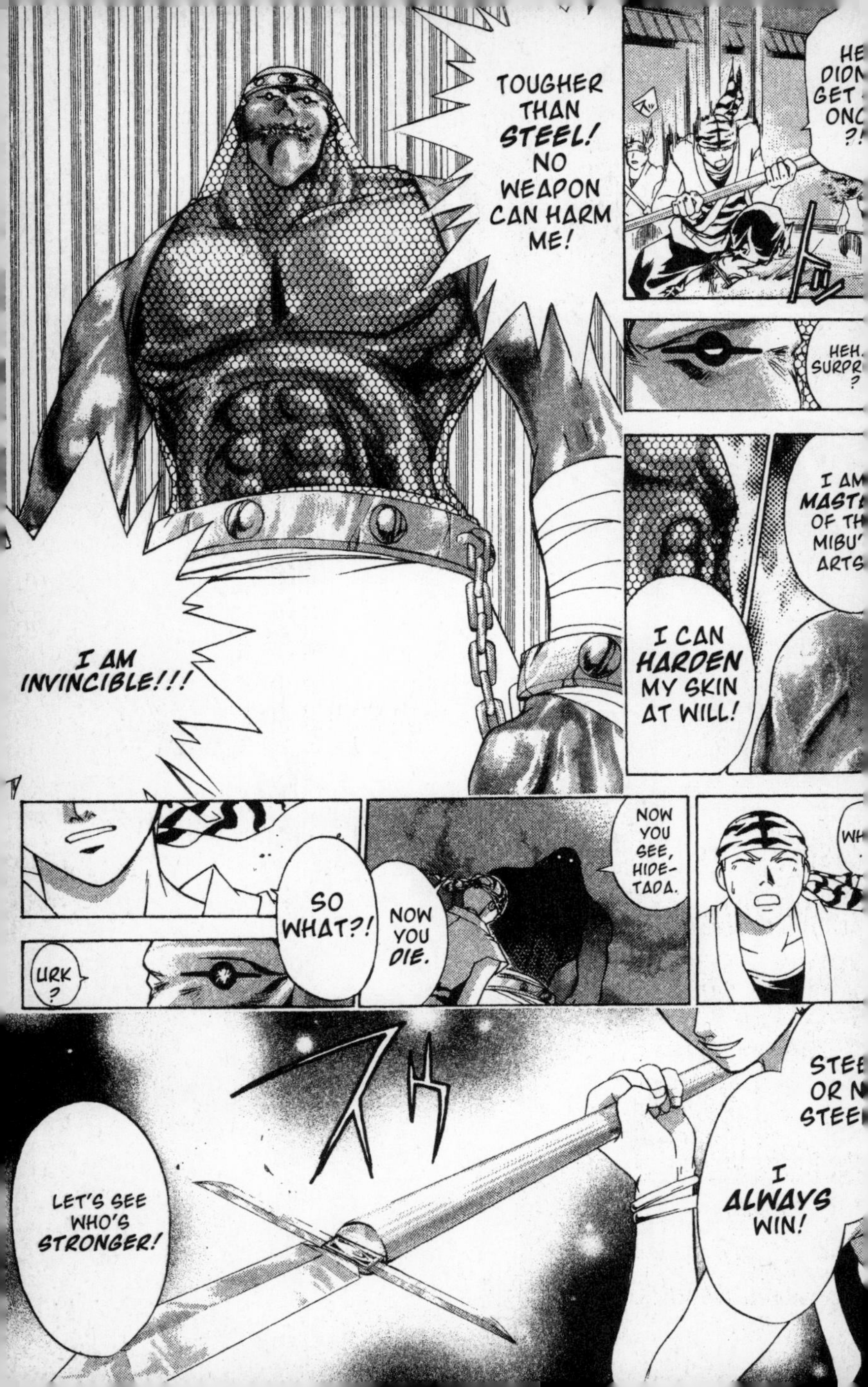
HE DIDN GET ONC ?!
HEH. SURPR ?
I AM MAST OF TH MIBU' ARTS
I CAN HARDEN MY SKIN AT WILL!
TOUGHER THAN STEEL! NO WEAPON CAN HARM ME!
I AM INVINCIBLE!!!
WH
NOW YOU SEE, HIDE-TADA.
NOW YOU DIE.
SO WHAT?!
URK ?
STEE OR N STEE
I ALWAYS WIN!
LET'S SEE WHO'S STRONGER!

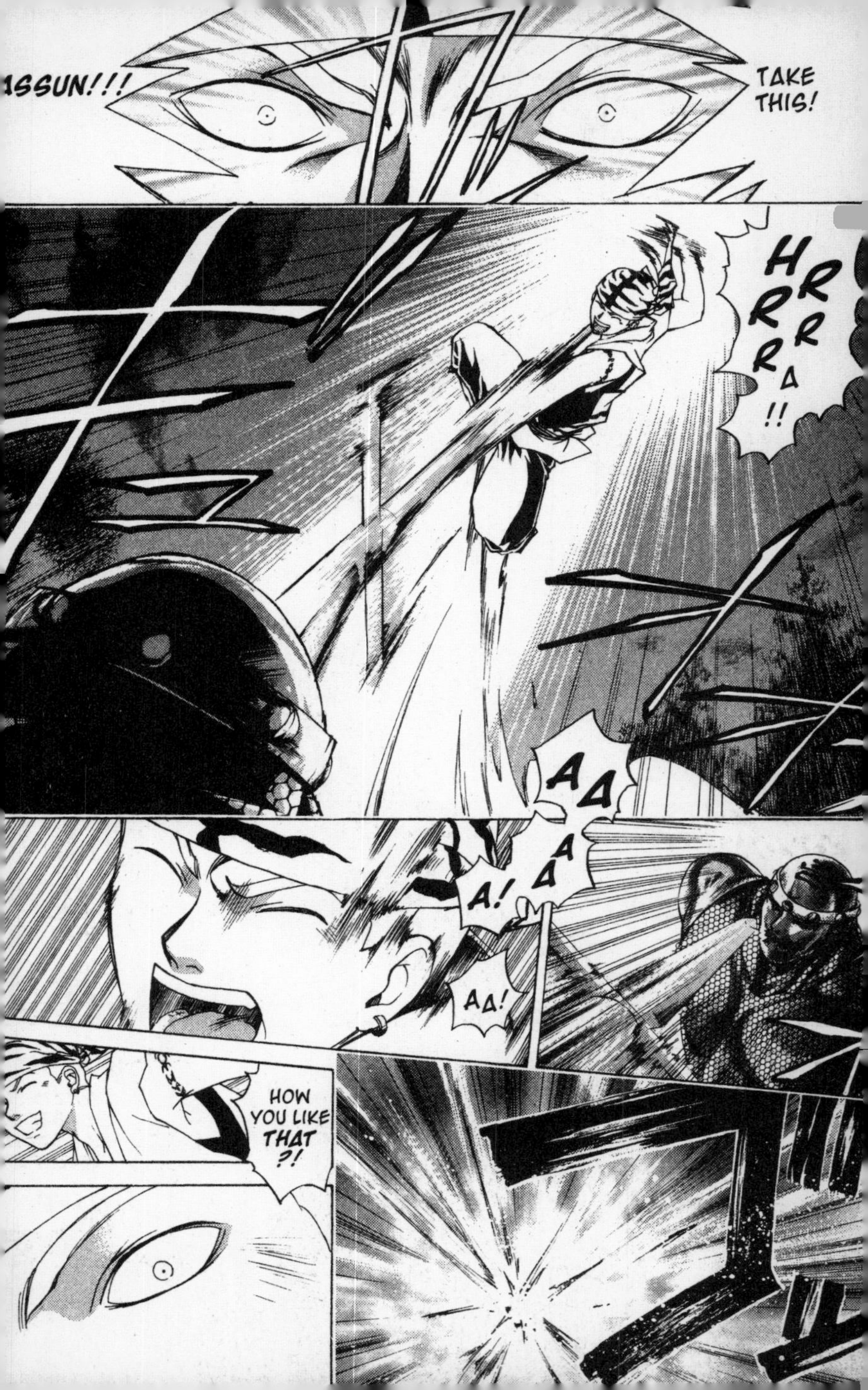
TAKE THIS!
ASSUN!!!
HRRRRA!!
AAAAA
A!
AA!
HOW YOU LIKE THAT?!

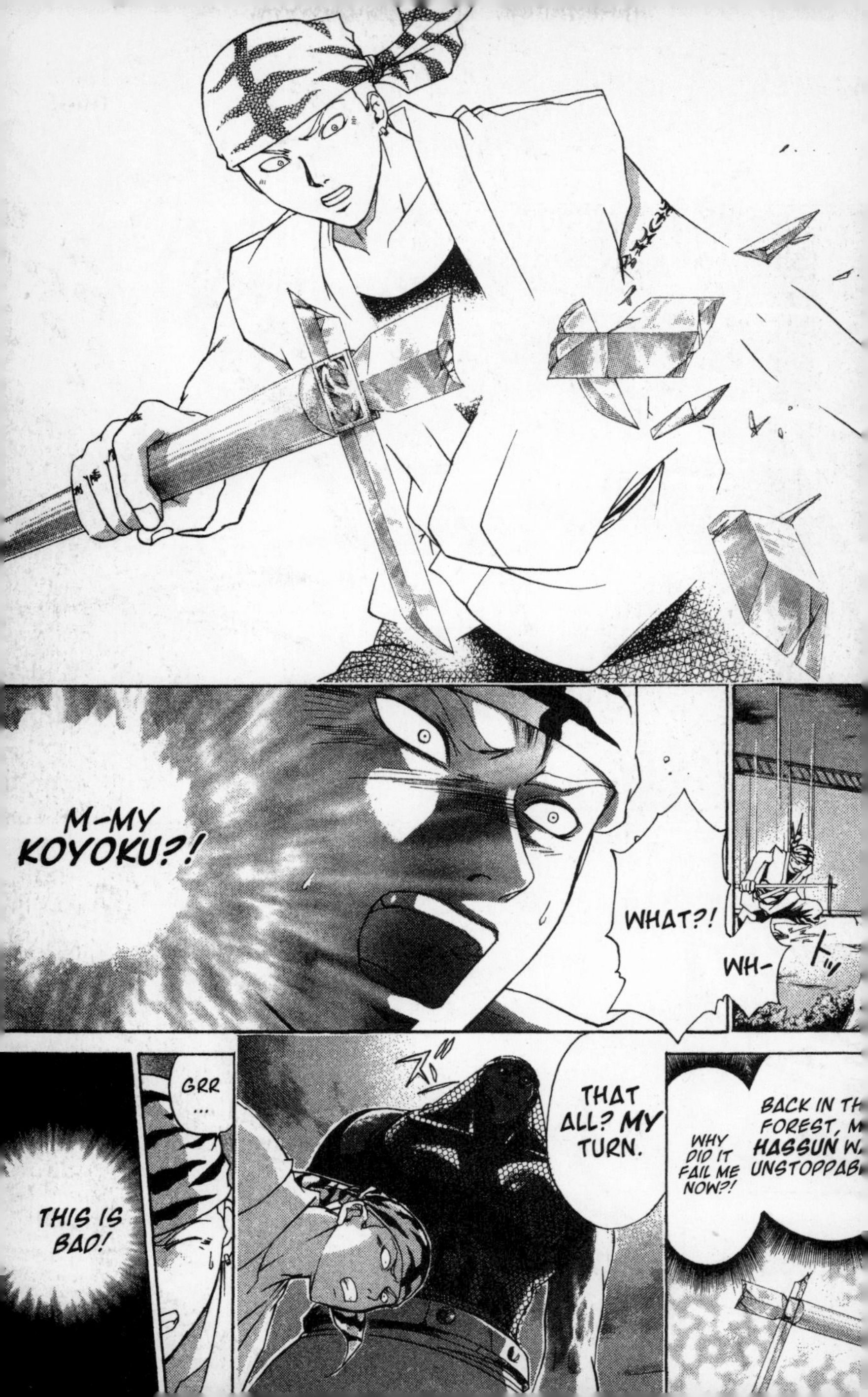
WH-
WHAT?!
M-MY KOYOKU?!
BACK IN TH FOREST, M HASSUN WA UNSTOPPAB
WHY DID IT FAIL ME NOW?!
THAT ALL? MY TURN.
GRR ...
THIS IS BAD!

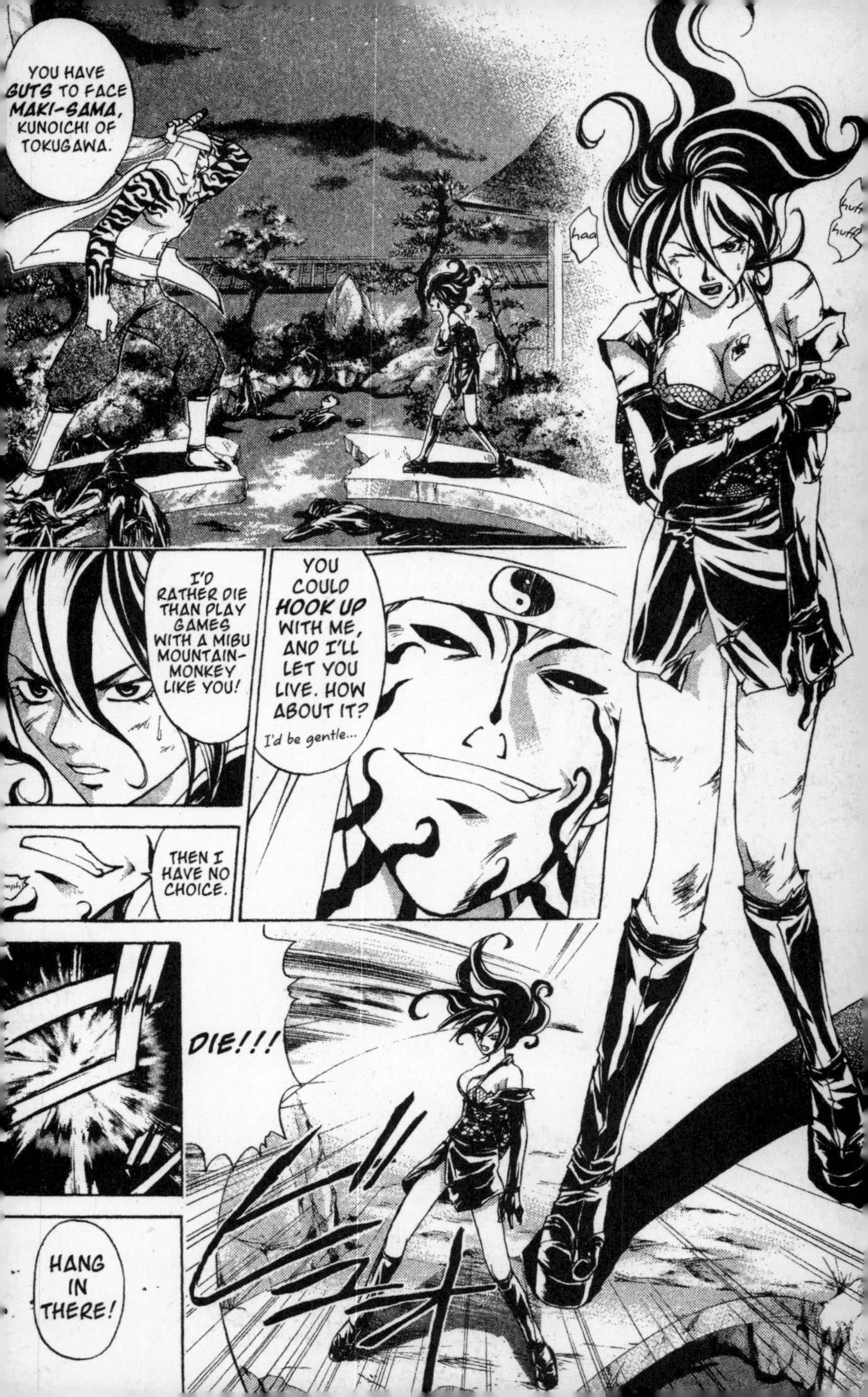
huff huff
haa
YOU HAVE GUTS TO FACE MAKI-SAMA, KUNOICHI OF TOKUGAWA.
YOU COULD HOOK UP WITH ME, AND I'LL LET YOU LIVE. HOW ABOUT IT?
I'd be gentle...
I'D RATHER DIE THAN PLAY GAMES WITH A MIBU MOUNTAIN-MONKEY LIKE YOU!
THEN I HAVE NO CHOICE.
DIE!!!
HANG IN THERE!

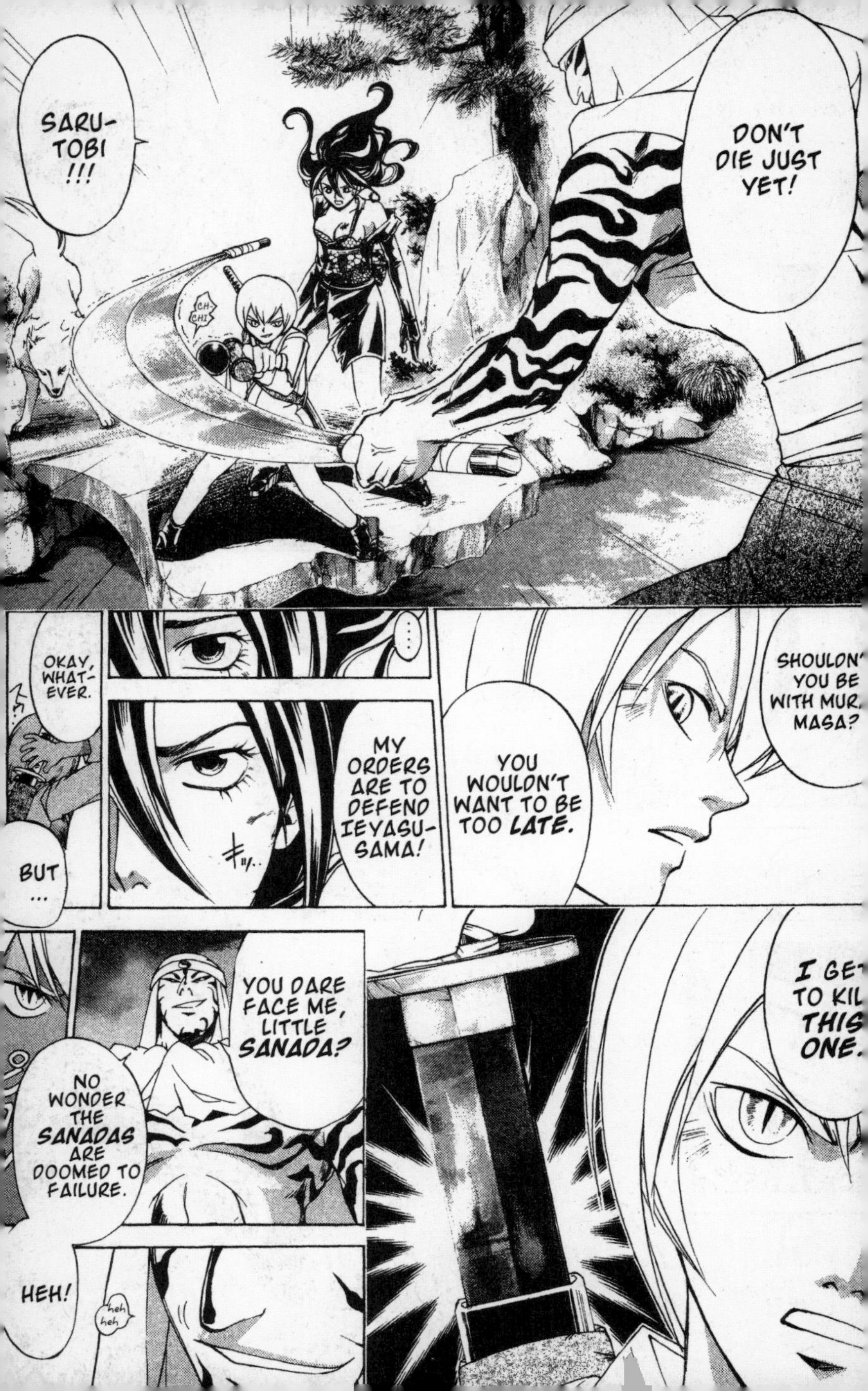
DON'T DIE JUST YET!
SARU-TOBI !!!
CH-CHI
SHOULDN' YOU BE WITH MUR, MASA?
YOU WOULDN'T WANT TO BE TOO LATE.
....
MY ORDERS ARE TO DEFEND IEYASU-SAMA!
OKAY, WHAT-EVER.
BUT ...
I GE TO KIL THIS ONE.
YOU DARE FACE ME, LITTLE SANADA?
NO WONDER THE SANADAS ARE DOOMED TO FAILURE.
HEH!
heh heh

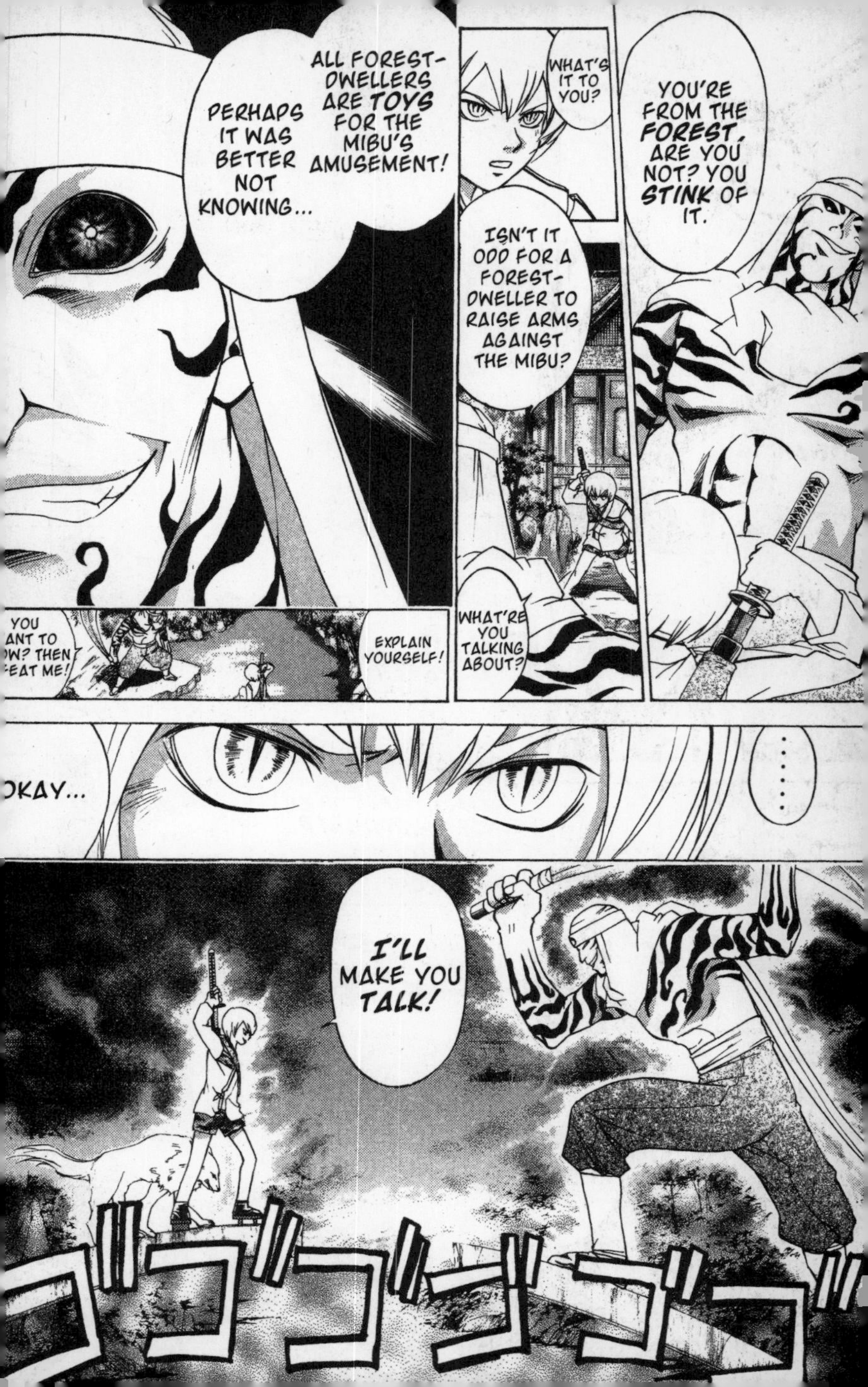
YOU'RE FROM THE FOREST, ARE YOU NOT? YOU STINK OF IT.
WHAT'S IT TO YOU?
ISN'T IT ODD FOR A FOREST-DWELLER TO RAISE ARMS AGAINST THE MIBU?
WHAT'RE YOU TALKING ABOUT?
EXPLAIN YOURSELF!
YOU ANT TO OW? THEN EAT ME!
ALL FOREST-DWELLERS ARE TOYS FOR THE MIBU'S AMUSEMENT!
PERHAPS IT WAS BETTER NOT KNOWING...
......
OKAY...
I'LL MAKE YOU TALK!
ゴゴゴゴ

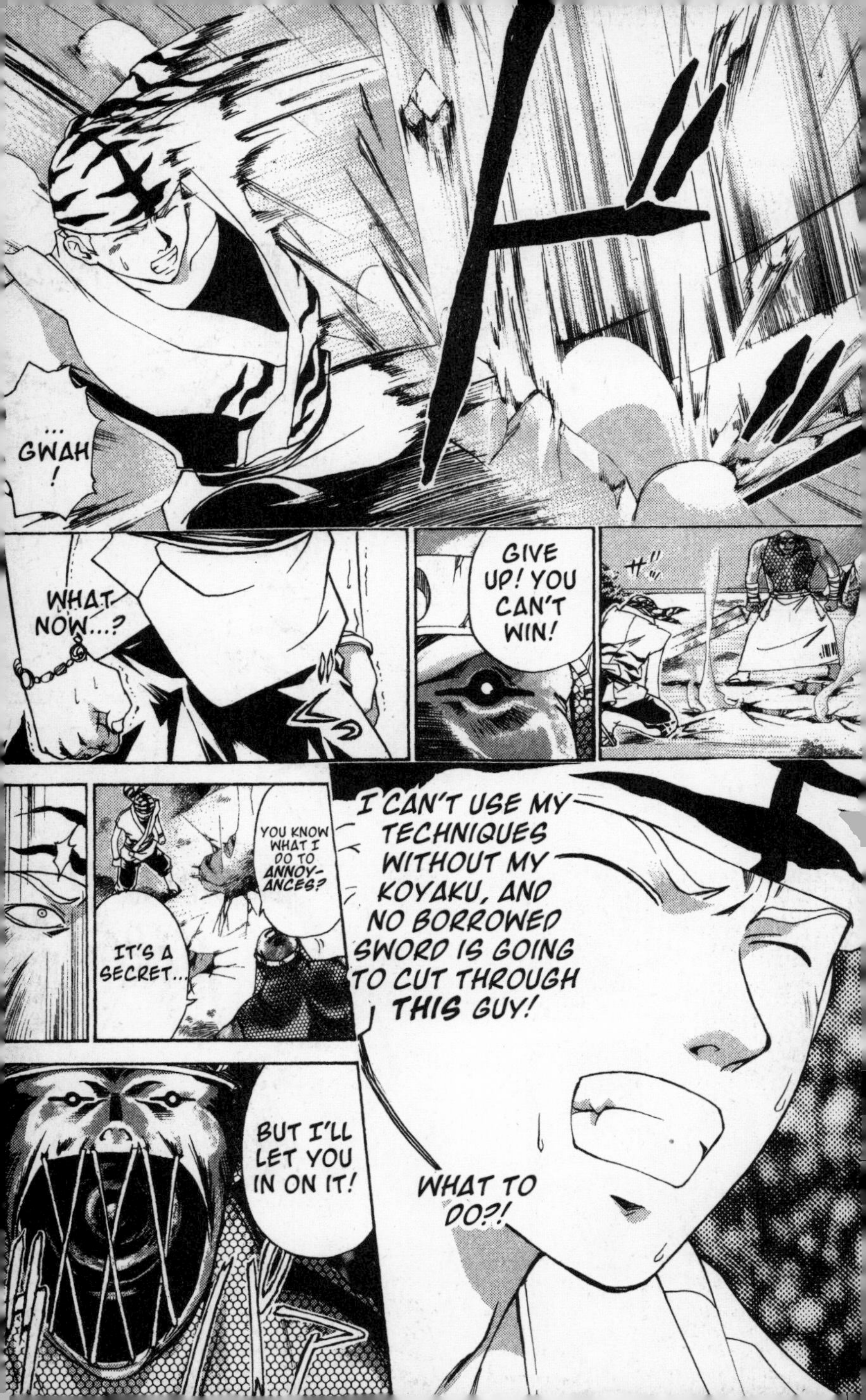

... GWAH!
GIVE UP! YOU CAN'T WIN!
WHAT NOW...?
I CAN'T USE MY TECHNIQUES WITHOUT MY KOYAKU, AND NO BORROWED SWORD IS GOING TO CUT THROUGH THIS GUY!
WHAT TO DO?!
YOU KNOW WHAT I DO TO ANNOYANCES?
IT'S A SECRET...
BUT I'LL LET YOU IN ON IT!

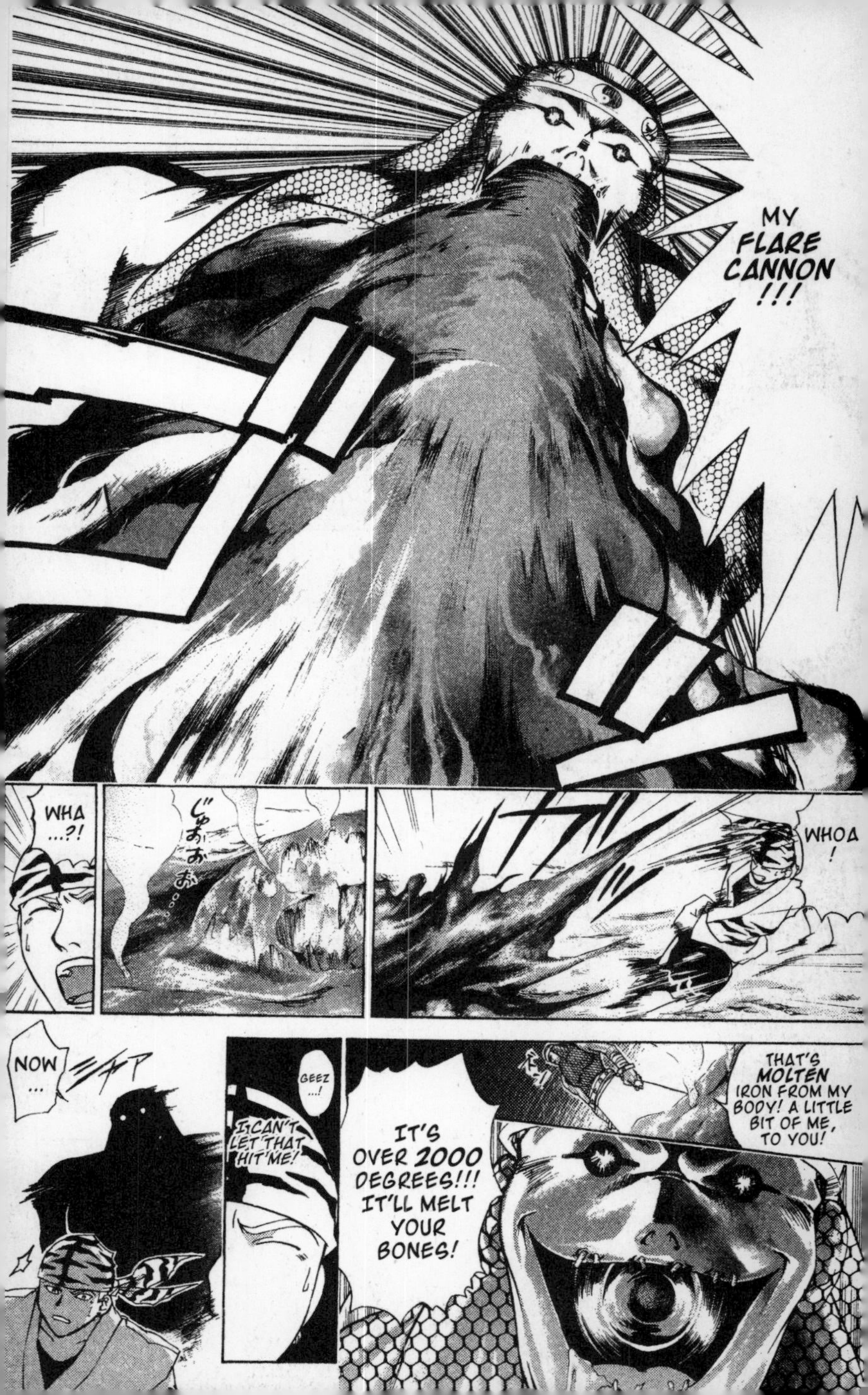
MY FLARE CANNON!!!
WHOA!
じゅおおお…
WHA...?!
THAT'S MOLTEN IRON FROM MY BODY! A LITTLE BIT OF ME, TO YOU!
IT'S OVER 2000 DEGREES!!! IT'LL MELT YOUR BONES!
GEEZ...!
I CAN'T LET THAT HIT ME!
NOW...

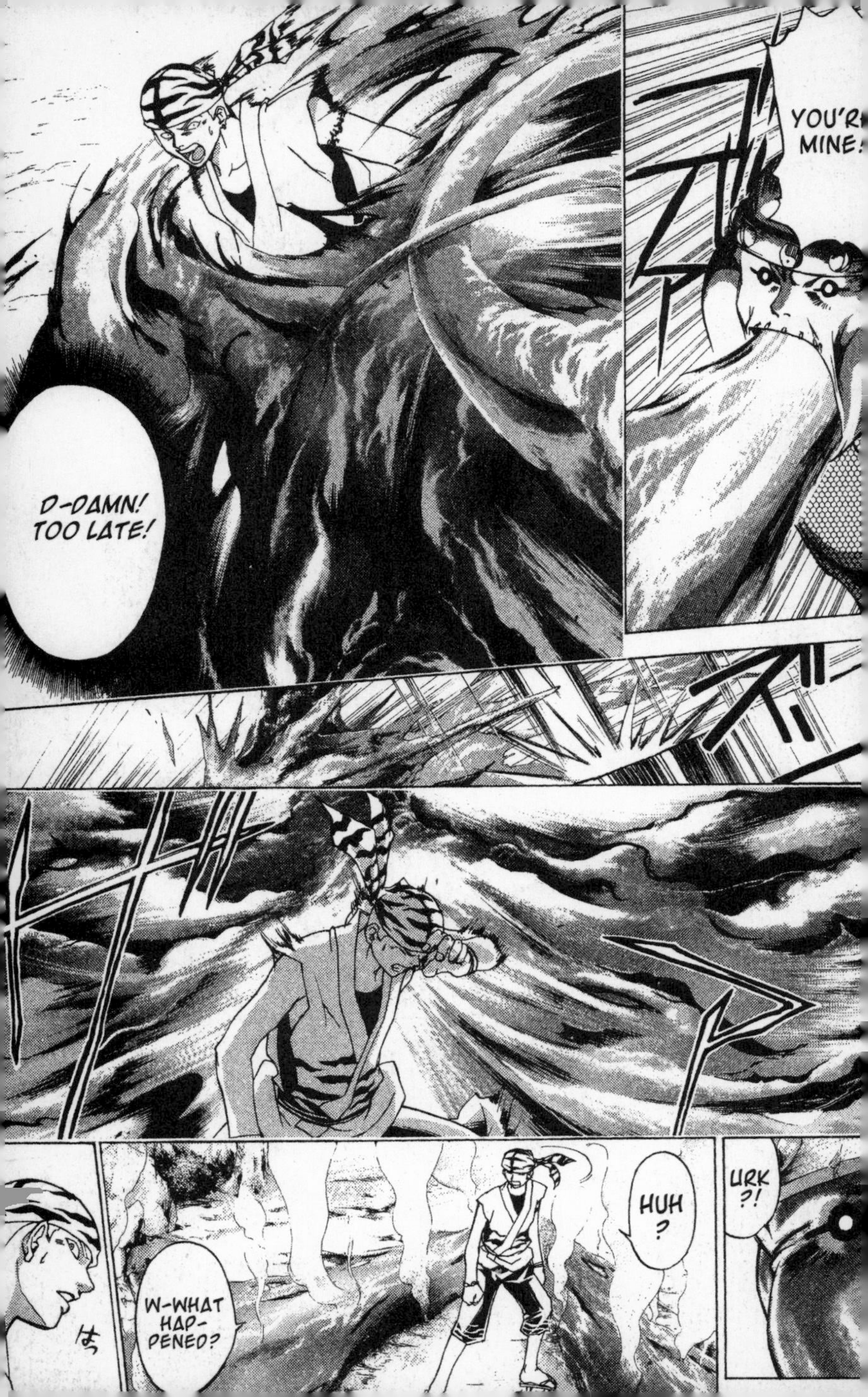
YOU'R
MINE!
D-DAMN! TOO LATE!
URK ?!
HUH ?
W-WHAT HAP-PENED?
は

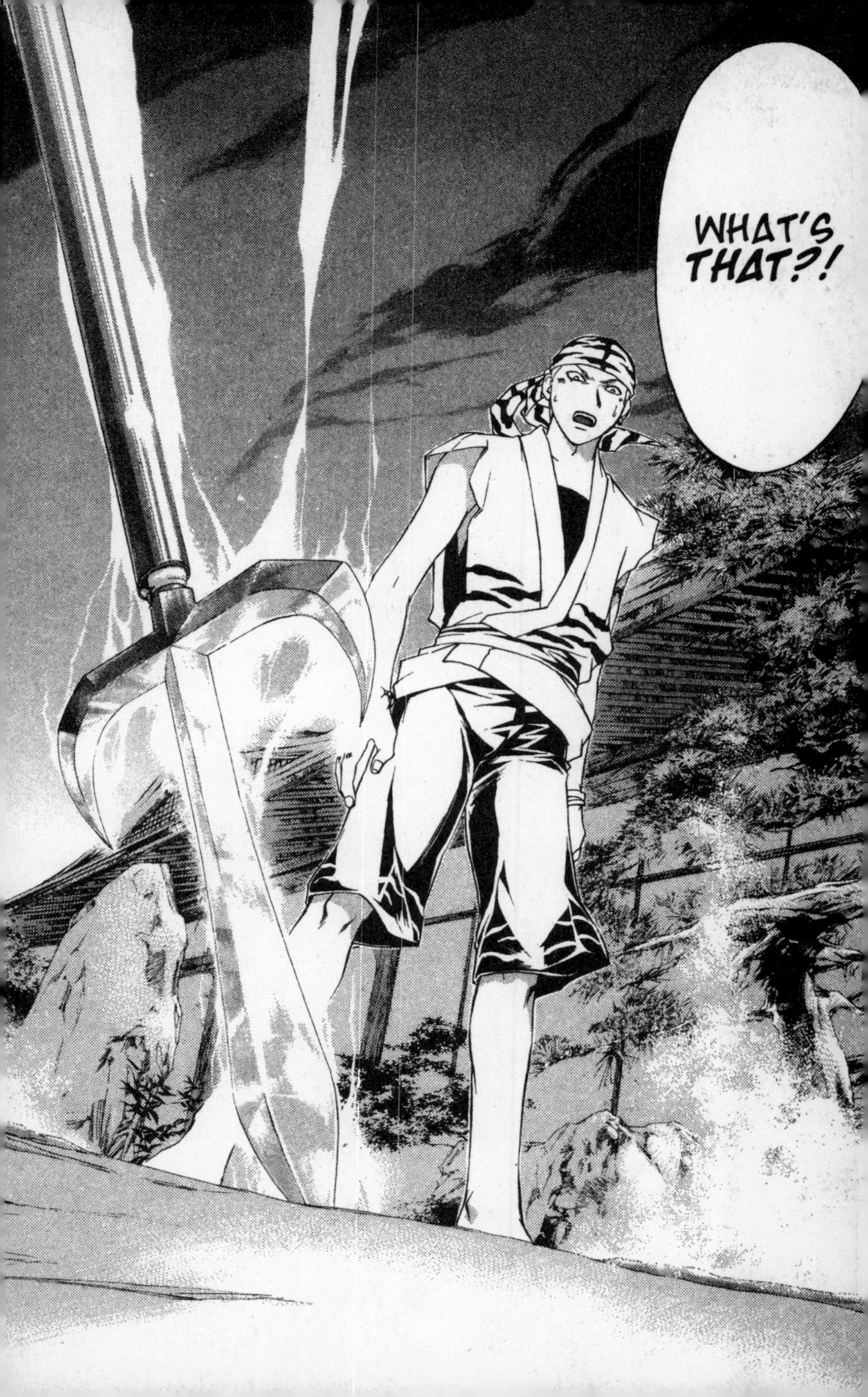
WHAT'S THAT?!

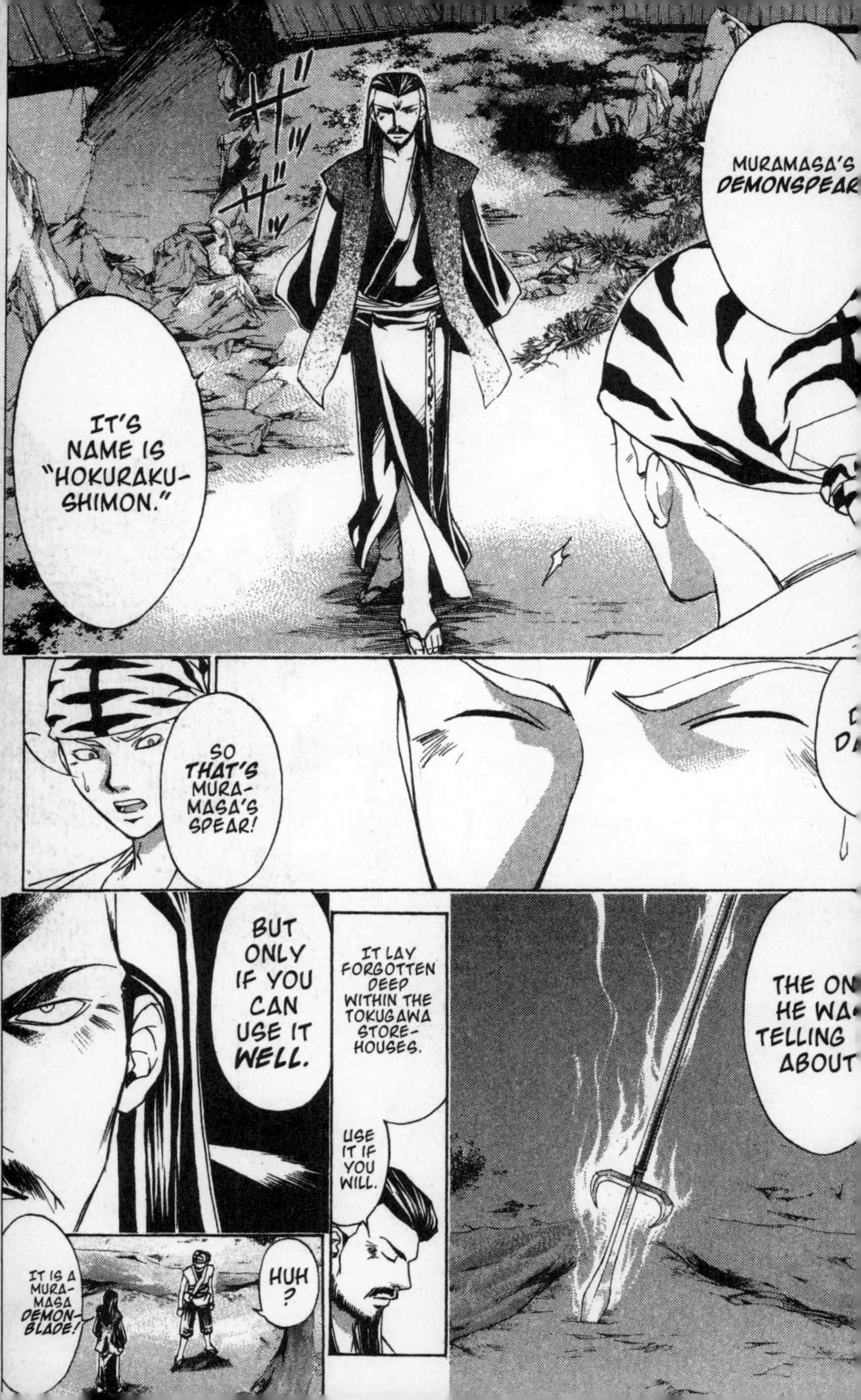
MURAMASA'S DEMONSPEAR
IT'S NAME IS "HOKURAKU-SHIMON."
SO THAT'S MURAMASA'S SPEAR!
THE ON HE WA TELLING ABOUT
IT LAY FORGOTTEN DEEP WITHIN THE TOKUGAWA STORE-HOUSES.
USE IT IF YOU WILL.
BUT ONLY IF YOU CAN USE IT WELL.
HUH?
IT IS A MURA-MASA DEMON-BLADE!

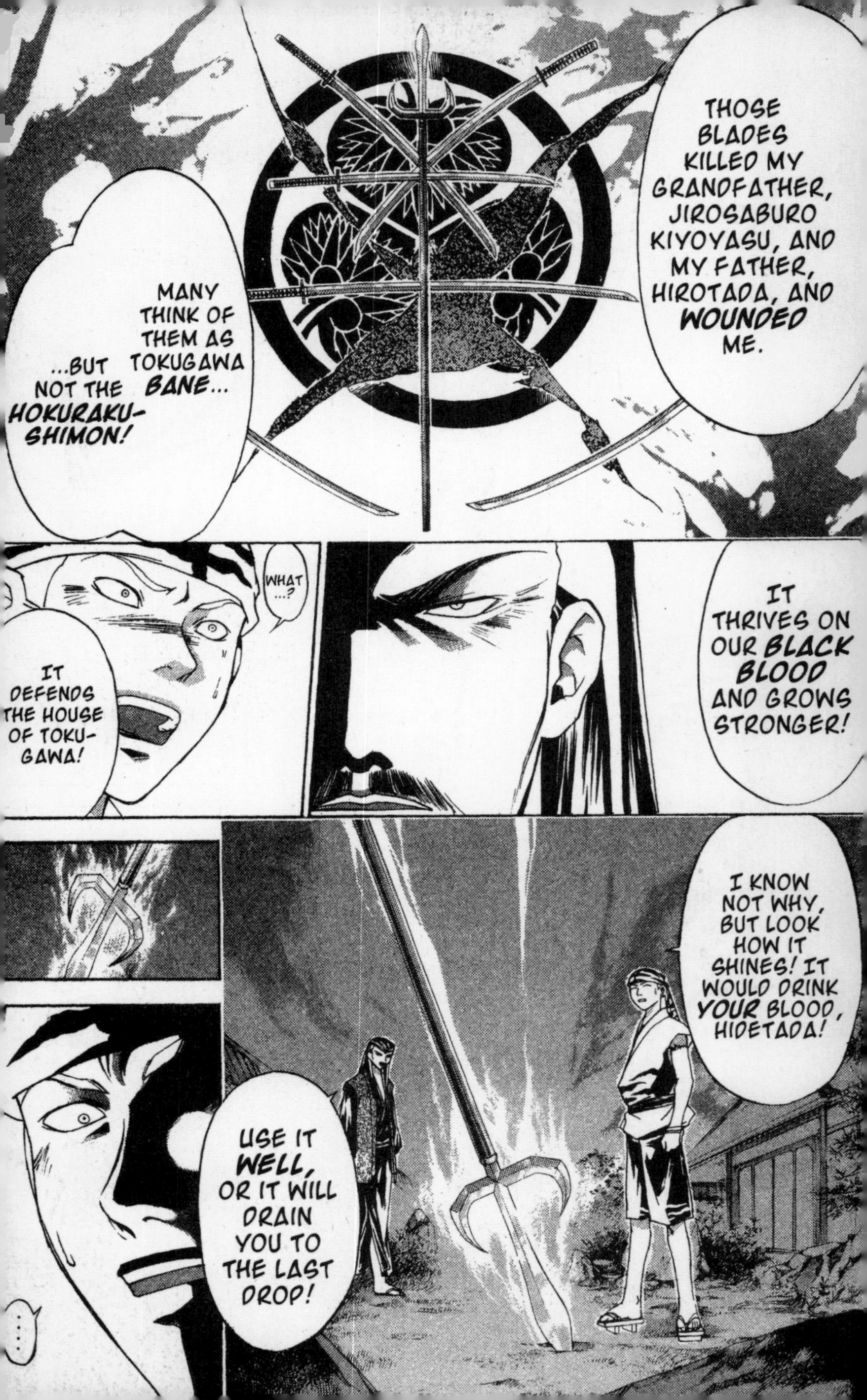
THOSE BLADES KILLED MY GRANDFATHER, JIROSABURO KIYOYASU, AND MY FATHER, HIROTADA, AND WOUNDED ME.
MANY THINK OF THEM AS TOKUGAWA BANE...
...BUT NOT THE HOKURAKU-SHIMON!
IT THRIVES ON OUR BLACK BLOOD AND GROWS STRONGER!
WHAT...?
IT DEFENDS THE HOUSE OF TOKU-GAWA!
I KNOW NOT WHY, BUT LOOK HOW IT SHINES! IT WOULD DRINK YOUR BLOOD, HIDETADA!
USE IT WELL, OR IT WILL DRAIN YOU TO THE LAST DROP!
.....

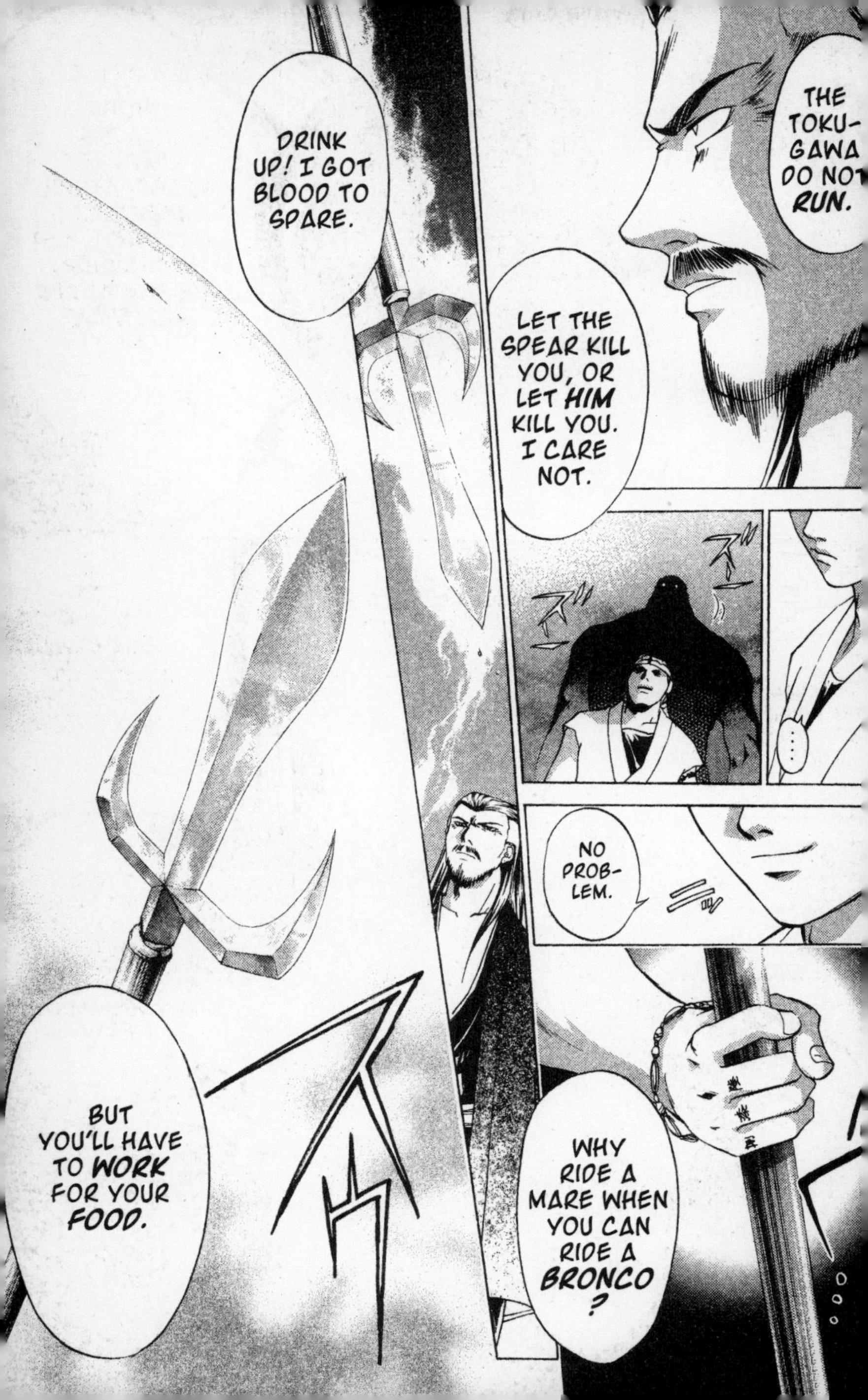
THE TOKU-GAWA DO NOT RUN.
LET THE SPEAR KILL YOU, OR LET HIM KILL YOU. I CARE NOT.
....
NO PROB-LEM.
WHY RIDE A MARE WHEN YOU CAN RIDE A BRONCO?
DRINK UP! I GOT BLOOD TO SPARE.
BUT YOU'LL HAVE TO WORK FOR YOUR FOOD.

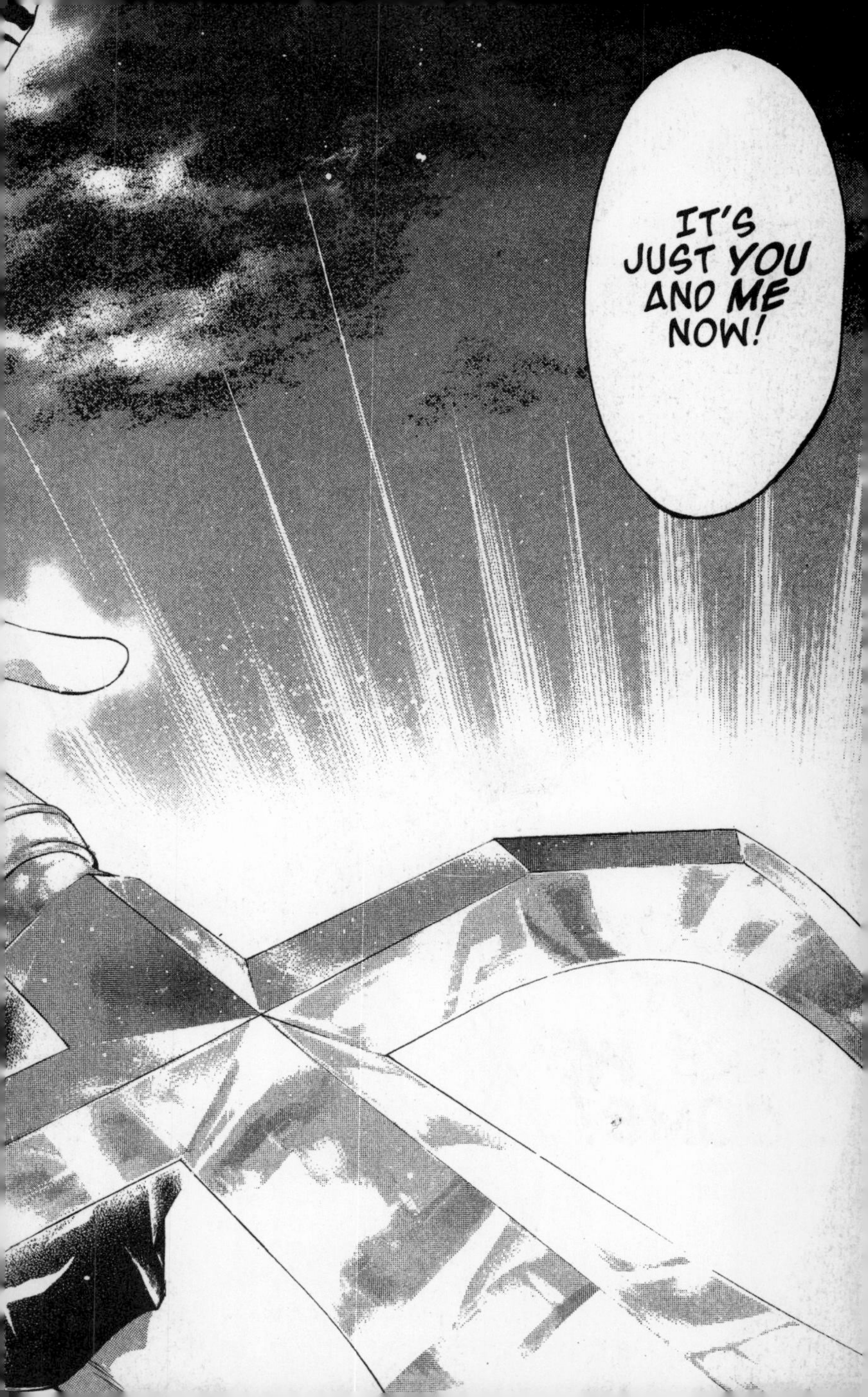
IT'S JUST YOU AND ME NOW!

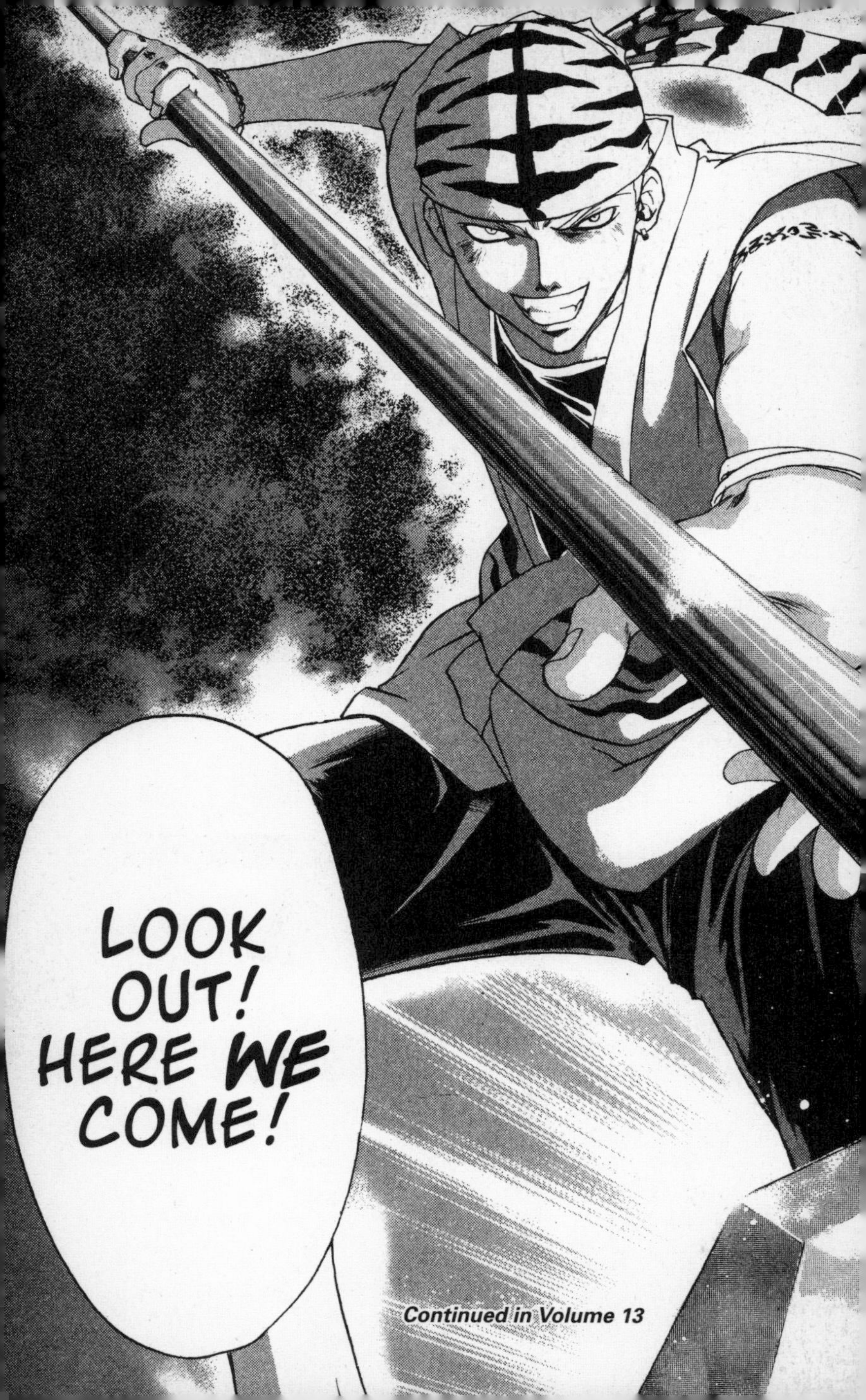
LOOK OUT! HERE WE COME!
Continued in Volume 13

■STAFFS■

Takaya Nagao (The Chief)
Hazuki Asami (The Sub-Chief)
Ken'ichi Suetake
Soma Akatsuki
The Gentleman Pumpkin
Shiba Tataoka

We would like to thank everyone who has helped make SDK, the family and friends who have supported us, and most of all, the readers!

(Don't worry! It's not over yet!)

Kamijyo-Sensei's IT-WASN'T-MY-IDEA

Really!

With Date-o-Meter!

WHAT'S YOUR SAMURAI DEEPER KYO HOROSCOPE?

Consultant: Izumo-no-Okuni

If you compared your personality to a character from SDK, who would you be? Get ready, Okuni-san is going to tell you your SDK Horoscope! Try not to get TOO upset if you get someone you weren't expecting...and have fun!

Historically speaking, I was a miko shaman. All the better to divine your horoscope! ♡

★ ★ How To Read Your Horoscope ★

(一) *(1) Look at Chart [1] on the next page and find the number that corresponds to the year and the month you were born.*

(二) *(2) Now, add the day you were born to the number you got in Step 1 above!*

(三) *(3) Now look at Chart [2] and find the number you got in Step 2 above! The name on the left of the row with your number in it is the character that best represents you! Who did you get, I wonder?*

Example: If you were born on 1/22/1975...

(1) On Chart [1], you look at Jan, 1975...and get "3."
(2) Now add your day of birth ("22") to the "3" from Step 1 and you get 22+3 = 25!

(3) Look up "25" on Chart [2]... and you're a "Benitora"!

CHART 1	JAN	FEB	MAR	APR	MAY	JUN	JUL	AUG	SEP	OCT	NOV	DEC

1961	0	3	3	6	1	4	6	2	5	0	3	5
1962	1	4	4	0	2	5	0	3	6	1	4	6
1963	2	5	5	1	3	6	1	4	0	2	5	0
1964	3	6	0	3	5	1	3	6	2	4	0	2
1965	5	1	1	4	6	2	4	0	3	5	1	3
1966	6	2	2	5	0	3	5	1	4	6	2	4
1967	0	3	3	6	1	4	6	2	5	0	3	5
1968	1	4	5	1	3	6	1	4	0	2	5	0
1969	3	6	6	2	4	0	2	5	1	3	6	1
1970	4	0	0	3	5	1	3	6	2	4	0	2
1971	5	1	1	4	6	2	4	0	3	5	1	3
1972	6	2	3	6	1	4	6	2	5	0	3	5
1973	1	4	4	0	2	5	0	3	6	1	4	6
1974	2	5	5	1	3	6	1	4	0	2	5	0
1975	3	6	6	2	4	0	2	5	1	3	6	1
1976	4	0	1	4	6	2	4	0	3	5	1	3
1977	6	2	2	5	0	3	5	1	4	6	2	4
1978	0	3	3	6	1	4	6	2	5	0	3	5
1979	1	4	4	0	2	5	0	3	6	1	4	6
1980	2	5	6	2	4	0	2	5	1	3	6	1
1981	4	0	0	3	5	1	3	6	2	4	0	2
1982	5	1	1	4	6	2	4	0	3	5	1	3
1983	6	2	2	5	0	3	5	1	4	6	2	4
1984	0	3	4	0	2	5	0	3	6	1	4	6
1985	2	5	5	1	3	6	1	4	0	2	5	0
1986	3	6	6	2	4	0	2	5	1	3	6	1
1987	4	0	0	3	5	1	3	6	2	4	0	2
1988	5	1	2	5	0	3	5	1	4	6	2	4
1989	0	3	3	6	1	4	6	2	5	0	3	5
1990	1	4	4	0	2	5	0	3	6	1	4	6
1991	2	5	5	1	3	6	1	4	0	2	5	0
1992	3	6	0	3	5	1	3	6	2	4	0	2
1993	5	1	1	4	6	2	4	0	3	5	1	3
1994	6	2	2	5	0	3	5	1	4	6	2	4
1995	0	3	3	6	1	4	6	2	5	0	3	5
1996	1	4	5	1	3	6	1	4	0	2	5	0
1997	3	6	6	2	4	0	2	5	1	3	6	1
1998	4	0	0	3	5	1	3	6	2	4	0	2
1999	5	1	1	4	6	2	4	0	3	5	1	3
2000	6	2	3	6	1	4	6	2	5	0	3	5

EACH DESCRIPTION HAS A "YANG" SIDE (THE GOOD STUFF) AND A "YIN" SIDE (THE NOT-SO-GOOD STUFF)!

CHART 2						
Nobunaga	1	8	15	22	29	36
Yuya	2	9	16	23	30	37
Kyo	3	10	17	24	31	
Benitora	4	11	18	25	32	
Akira	5	12	19	26	33	
Yukimura	6	13	20	27	34	
Kyoshiro	7	14	21	28	35	

POWERFUL AS A DEMON!

KYO

 YANG: Full of vitality, you're ready to take on any challenge, and you're at the top of your game when it comes to work and study. And you've got a special talent: no matter how selfish or naughty you might be, you aren't scolded--in fact, people like you even more! Amazing! ♡

 YIN: You're a lone wolf, hard on other people, and a little too aggressive. It's fine for Kyo, but shouldn't you think more about other people's feelings? There's a reason why Kyo has so many enemies!

THE LIFE OF THE PARTY!

YUKIMURA

 YANG: You're very social, with an excellent eye for what is beautiful. Your presentation is perfect, and you love making things fun for others. Not to mention you're gifted with empathy for other's feelings. All that, and you're loyal to your friends, too. You're as well-liked as they come!

 YIN: You tend to over-calculate situations, but watch out you don't write people off--nobody likes that. Also, take care not to just say what you think people want to hear. That can get out of control, and you won't know what you really want.

YUYA

KIND AND HARD-WORKING!

 YANG: You think of other people, and take care of your friends--and you can't si still when someone seems out of sorts, o is getting picked on. For all your caring, though, you have a will of steel, and once you set your mind on something you WILL do it. You're straightforward, yes, but you shine!

 YIN: Your steel-will has a way of turning into stubbornness. Try to open up and listen to other people even when you don't want to! You also have a problem giving a straight apology--at least you regret it afterwards.

LIFE IS SHORT, SO HAVE FUN!

BENITORA

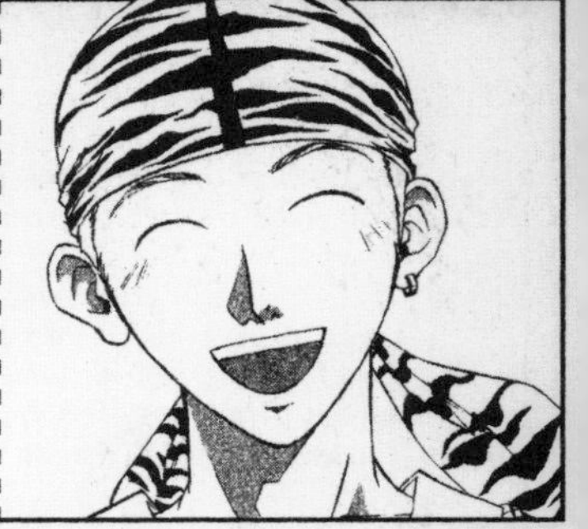

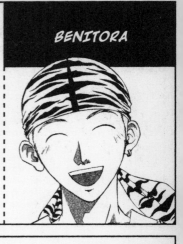

陽 **YANG:** *You're a born optimist. You love anything fun and anything wild. You've got a quick mind, and you're a positive thinker. You don't worry about things too much, and your curiosity and imagination are both top class! Who would have thought you were so creative?!*

陰 **YIN:** *It's all right to have fun, but sometimes you overdo it. You don't want people to take you lightly, or not trust you. Also, you've got curiosity aplenty, but you tend to lose interest in things quickly, too.*

AKIRA

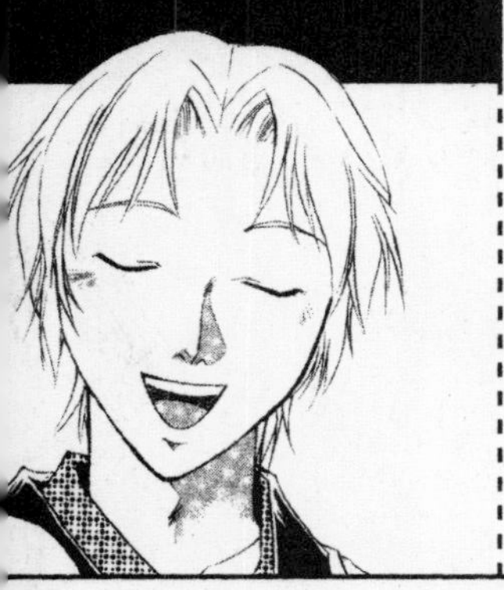

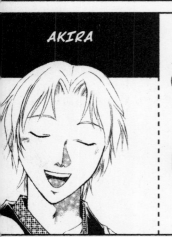

COOL, BUT SCARY WHEN MAD!

陽 **YANG:** *You're cool-headed with a strong sense of right and wrong. You won't tolerate misbehavior and always strive to follow the rules. Your sense of justice can earn you the steady trust of others. You're a bit of a genius, too: original, with lots of ideas.*

陰 **YIN:** *You have trouble letting faults or mistakes go. You tend to get too wrapped up in things, and see yourself as the victim. Try not to let your emotions get the better of you in tight situations!*

YOUR CHARISMA COULD BE YOUR WORST ENEMY!

NOBUNAGA

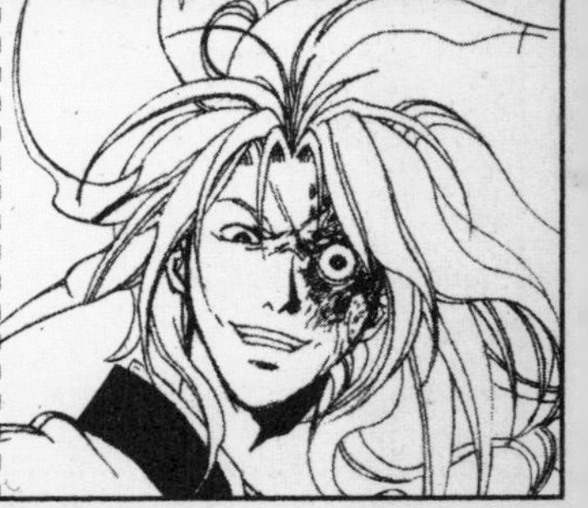

陽 **YANG:** *You're an individualist with a vision for the world. You're smart, and can make objective judgments. Still, people seem to gather around you wherever you go! You're a charisamatic, born leader.*

陰 **YIN:** *Your popularity has gone to your head, and you're a bit overconfident. Careful you don't get so happy with yourself that you become self-centered. You might find yourself losing some of those treasured friends!*

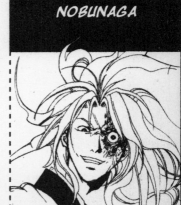

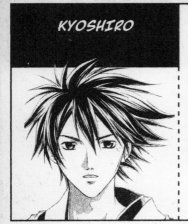

KYOSHIRO

A MAN OF PASSION?!

陽 *YANG: You're happy-go-lucky and laid ba on the surface, but limitless energy and passion churn in the depths! You're focus and stable, and once you set your eyes o something, you forge straight ahead and won't stop till you get it.*

陰 *YIN: While you think you're just being normal, other people might get irritated a your laid-back ways. You're not very goo at social situations, either. Be careful you don't end up hiding in your room all day. Get out there and meet people!*

BONUS!

How would you do on a date with another character?!

THE SDK DATE-O-METER!

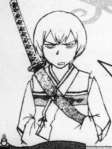

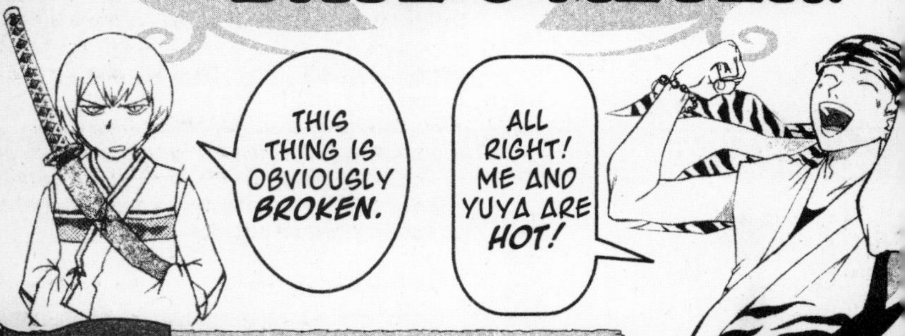

ALL RIGHT! ME AND YUYA ARE HOT!
THIS THING IS OBVIOUSLY BROKEN.

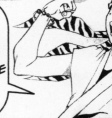

HOW TO READ

◎= *HOT!* ○= *Pretty Good!*

△= *Average.* ×= *Not so good.* ××= *TOTAL BOMB!*

	Nobunaga	Yuya	Kyo	Benitora	Akira	Yukimura	Kyoshi
Nobunaga	××	×	○	××	×	◎	△
Yuya	×	△	○	◎	×	△	△
Kyo	○	○	△	×	◎	△	××
Benitora	××	◎	×	△	××	×	◎
Akira	×	×	◎	××	△	○	××
Yukimura	◎	△	△	×	○	△	×
Kyoshiro	△	△	××	◎	××	×	○

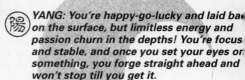

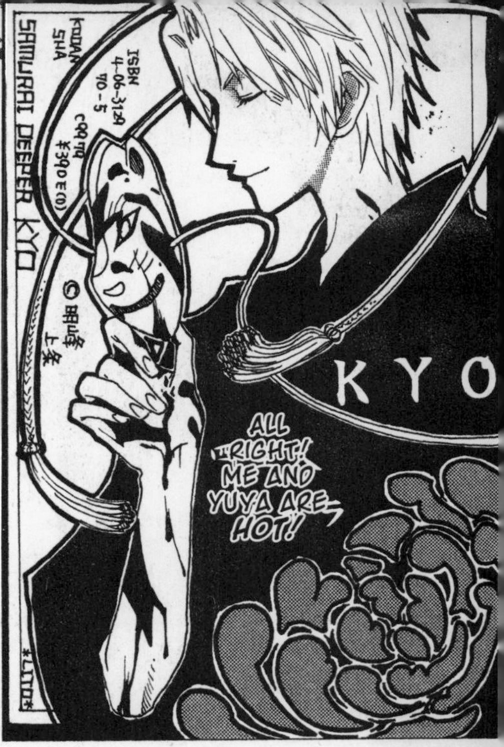
KODANSHA
SAMURAI DEEPER KYO
KYO
ALL RIGHT! ME AND YUYA ARE HOT!

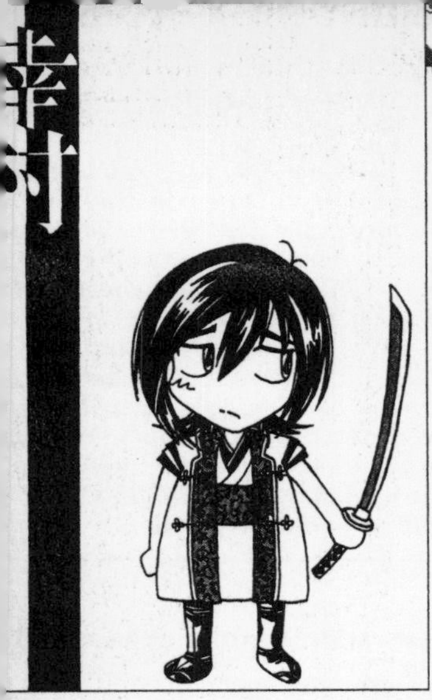
幸村

[Riji/Nagaoka Prefecture]
T-too good!

[Riji/Nagaoka Prefecture]
T-too good!

Challenge Akimine Kamijyo!

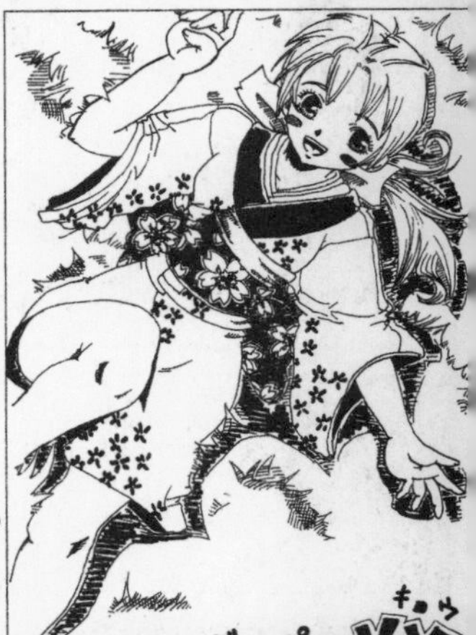
サムライディーパー
キョウ
SAMURAI DEEPER KYO

[Sakiko Ono / Miyagi Prefecture]
Ah, so gentle!

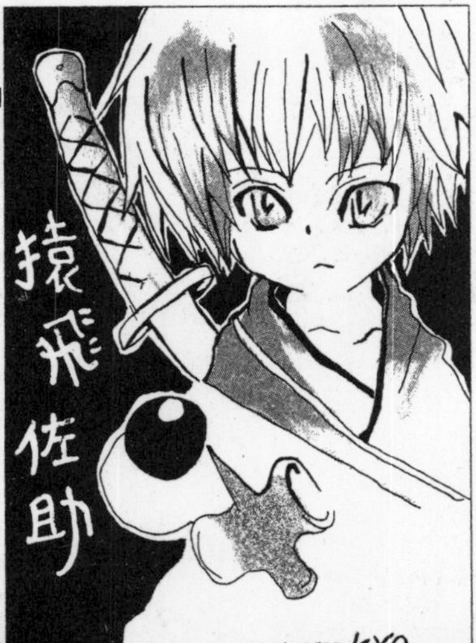
猿飛佐助
SAMURAI DEEPER KYO

UMI
Chiba
ecture]
have
nique
yle!

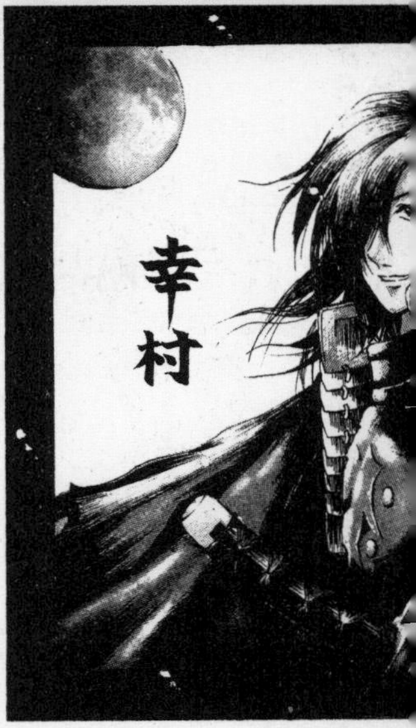
幸村

[Tomoya Hirose / Okaya
Prefecture]
Even his hair has persona

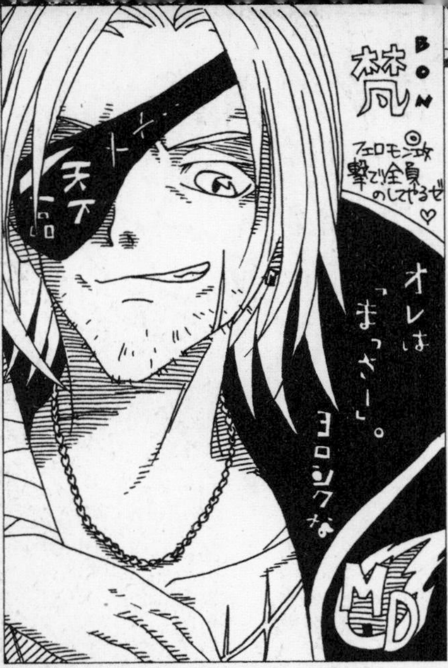
BON
梵
フェロモン攻撃で全員のしてやるぜ♡
オレは「まっさー」。
ヨロシクな
MD

[Ryoko Kaneya / Chiba
Prefecture]
Bet his pheromones
are stinky! :-)

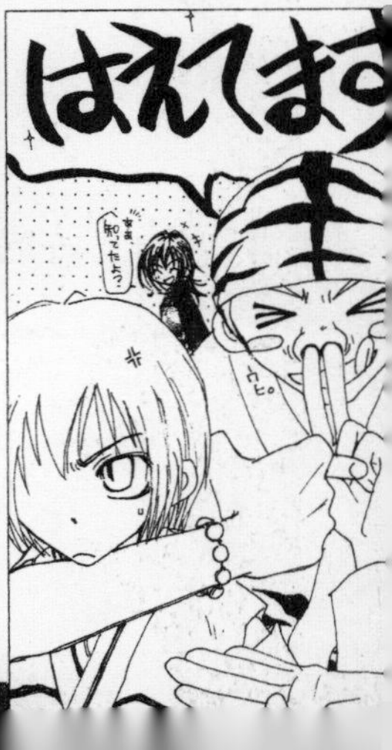
はえてます

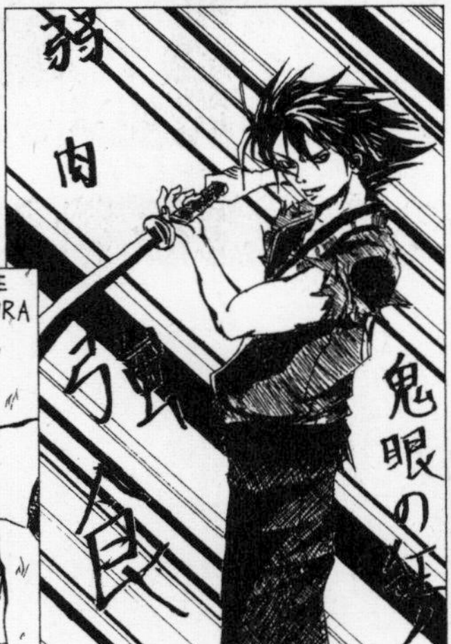
弱肉強食
鬼眼の狂

[Hitoshi Higuchi / Hokkaido]
Great feeling of speed!

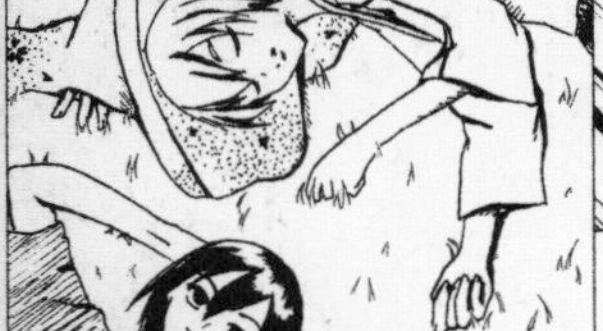
KOSUKE·SASUKE
YUKIMURA

[Lolita / Saitama Prefecture]
The warriors at rest!

[Hitoshi Higuchi /
Hokkaido]
Great feeling of speed!

More pages!
'hanks to you
the Kyoshiro
Gallery was a
! Next volume:
e Kyo Gallery!

A message from Akimine Kamijyo:
♡

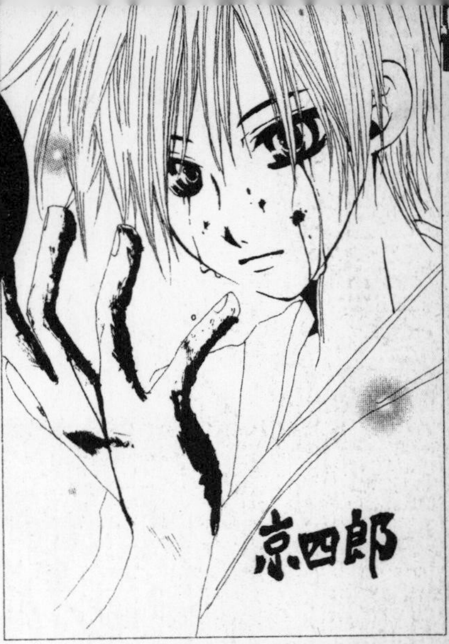
京四郎

[Larus Aotsuki / Akita Prefecture]
He looks teary eyed...

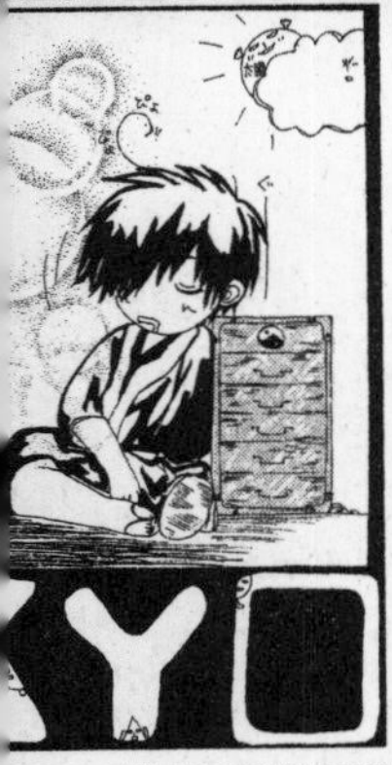

[Ryuki Sakuranojo / Osaka]
That's the way to be!

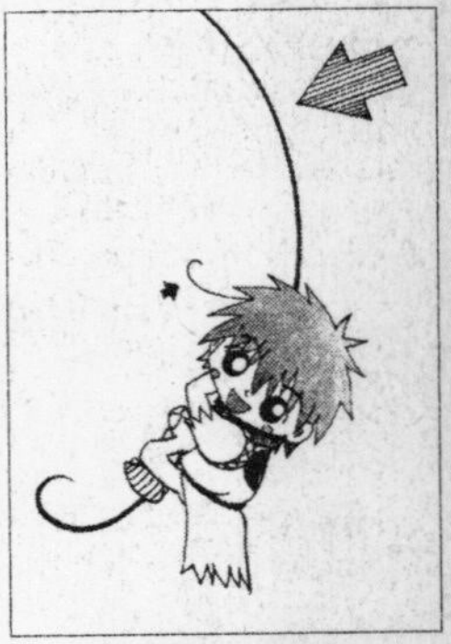

[Kei / Oita Prefecture]
Lil' Kyo?!

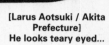

[Snow Elephant / Saitama Prefecture]
Hmm...the perfect punching bag? :-)

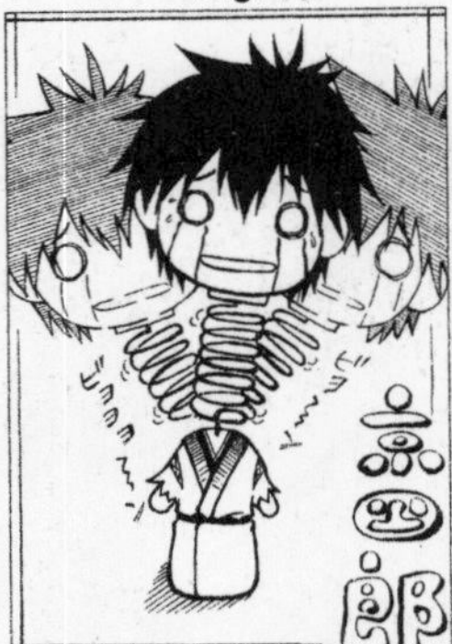
京四郎

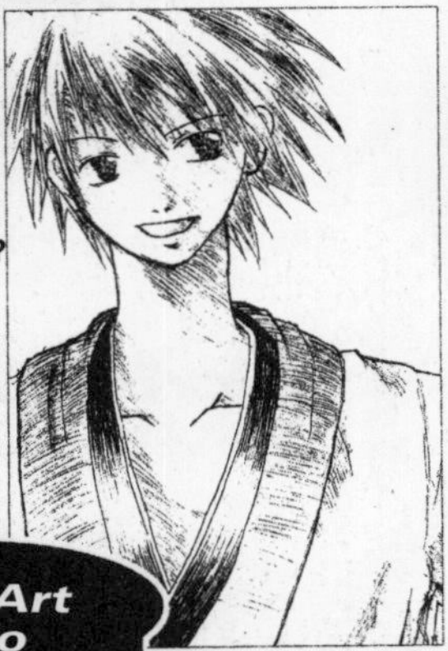

deru
uhara
vate
cture]
n will
ee him
again?

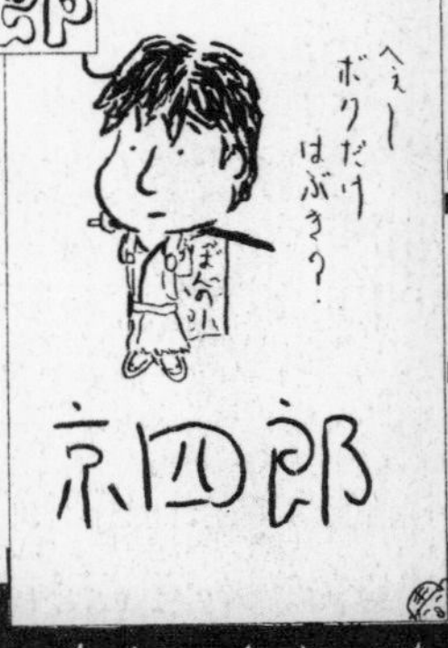
京四郎

[Black Tora-no-suke / Kanagawa Prefecture]
He may not show up much, but when he does...!

Fan Art Info

ubmission Info

How to submit:
1) Send your work via regular mail (NOT e-mail) to:

SAMURAI DEEPER KYO FAN MAIL
C/O TOKYOPOP
5900 WILSHIRE BLVD., SUITE 2000
LOS ANGELES, CA 90036

2) All work should be in black-and-white and no larger than 8.5"x11".(And try not to fold it too many times!) 3) Anything you send will not be returned. If you want to keep your original, it's fine to send us a copy. 4) Please include your full name, age, city and state for us to print with your work. If you'd rather us use a pen name, please include that too. 5) IMPORTANT: If you're under the age of 18, you must have your parent's permission in order for us to print your work. Any submissions without a signed note of parental consent will not be used. 6) For full details, please check out http://www.tokyopop.com/aboutus/fanart.php

SAMURAI DEEPER KYO ONE

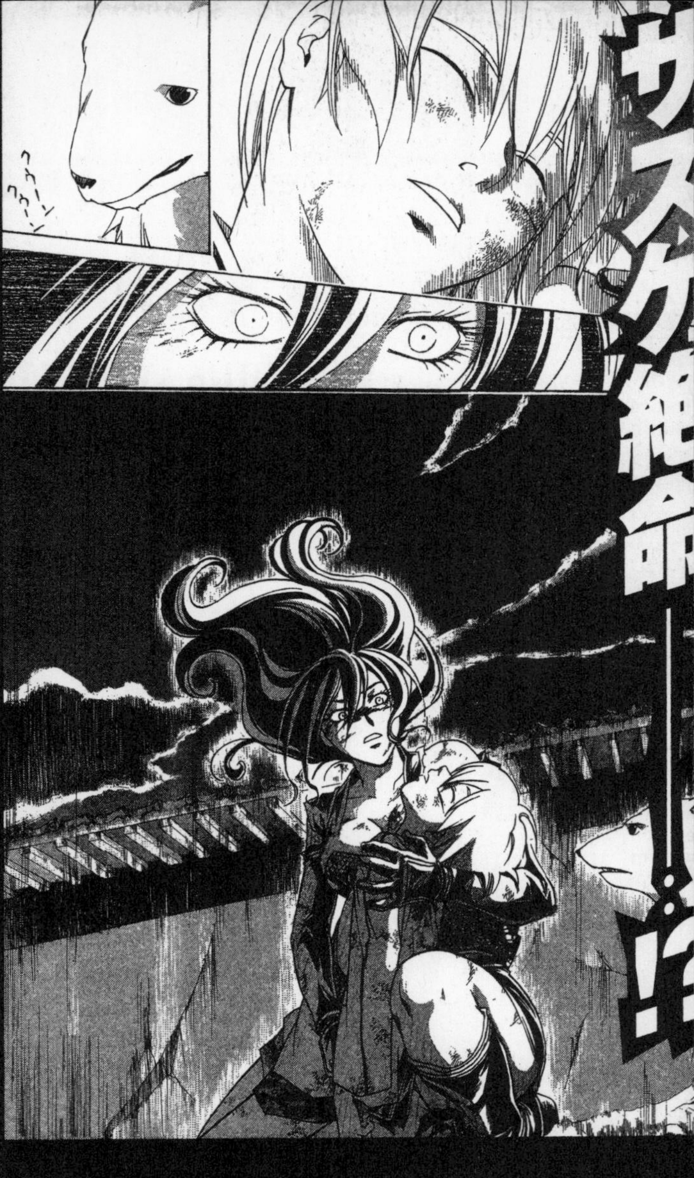
サスケ絶命――!?
クゥーン
クゥーン

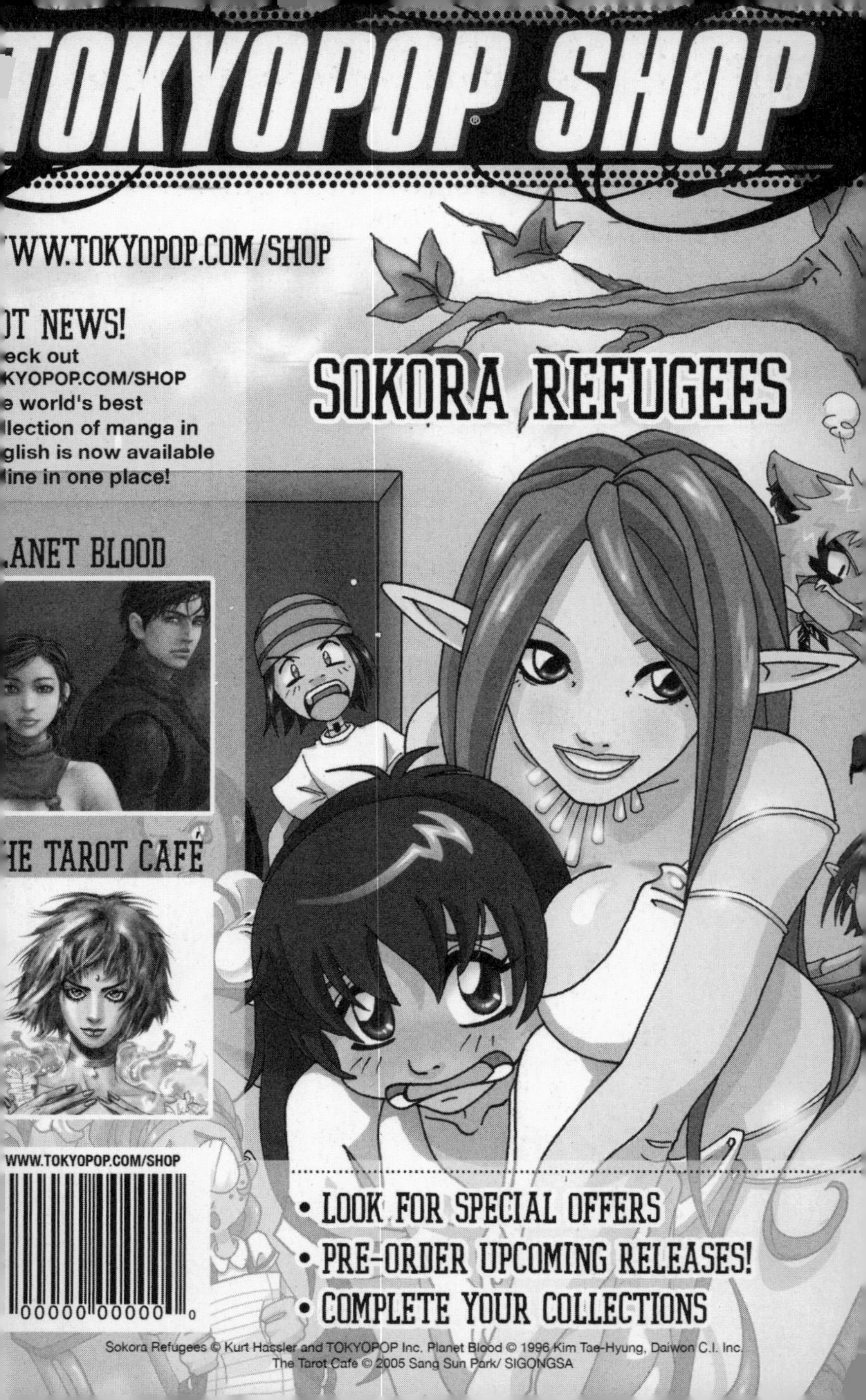
TOKYOPOP® SHOP
WWW.TOKYOPOP.COM/SHOP
OT NEWS!
eck out
KYOPOP.COM/SHOP
e world's best
llection of manga in
glish is now available
line in one place!
LANET BLOOD
HE TAROT CAFÉ
SOKORA REFUGEES
WWW.TOKYOPOP.COM/SHOP
00000 00000 0
• LOOK FOR SPECIAL OFFERS
• PRE-ORDER UPCOMING RELEASES!
• COMPLETE YOUR COLLECTIONS
Sokora Refugees © Kurt Hassler and TOKYOPOP Inc. Planet Blood © 1996 Kim Tae-Hyung, Daiwon C.I. Inc.
The Tarot Cafe © 2005 Sang Sun Park/ SIGONGSA

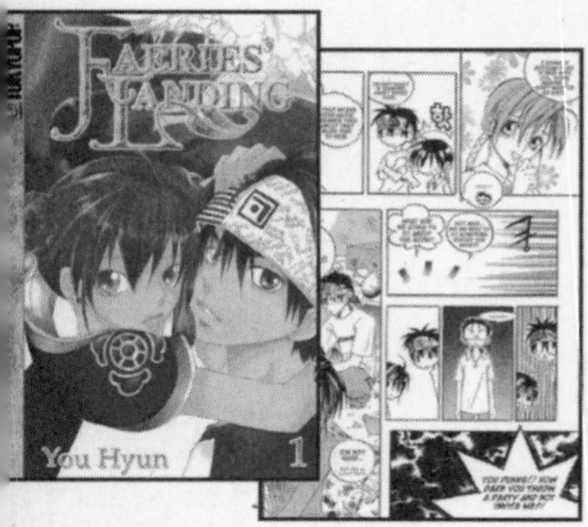
Faeries' Landing
You Hyun
1

BY YOU HYUN

FAERIES' LANDING

Following the misadventures of teenager Ryang Jegal and Fanta, a faerie who has fallen from the heavens straight into South Korea, *Faeries' Landing* is both a spoof of modern-day teen romance and a lighthearted fantasy epic. Imagine if Shakespeare's *A Midsummer Night's Dream* had come from the pen of Joss Whedon after about a dozen shots of espresso, and you have an idea of what to expect from You Hyun's funny little farce. Bursting with sharp wit, hip attitude and vibrant art, *Faeries' Landing* is guaranteed to get you giggling.
~Tim Beedle, Editor

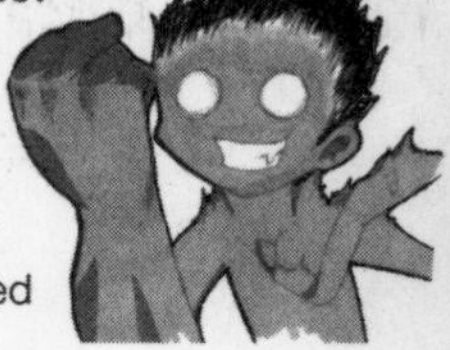

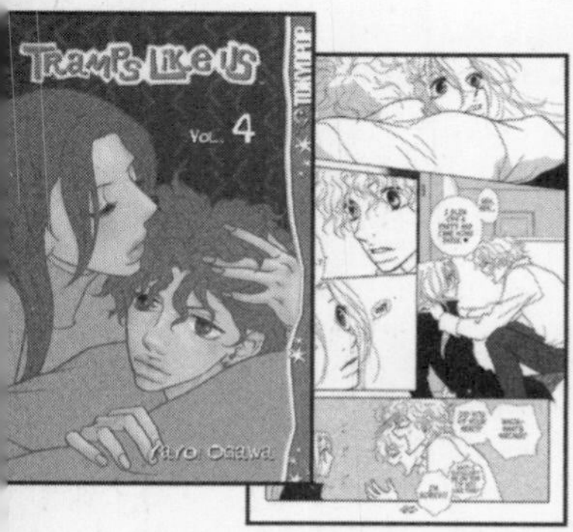
Tramps Like Us
Vol. 4
TOKYOPOP
Yayoi Ogawa

BY YAYOI OGAWA

TRAMPS LIKE US

Yayoi Ogawa's *Tramps Like Us*—known as *Kimi wa Pet* in Japan—is the touching and humorous story of Sumire, a woman whose striking looks and drive for success alienate her from her friends and co-workers...until she takes in Momo, a cute homeless boy, as her "pet." As sketchy as the situation sounds, it turns out to be the sanest thing in Sumire's hectic life. In his quiet way, Momo teaches Sumire how to care for another being while also caring for herself...in other words, how to love. And there ain't nothin' wrong with that.
~Carol Fox, Editor

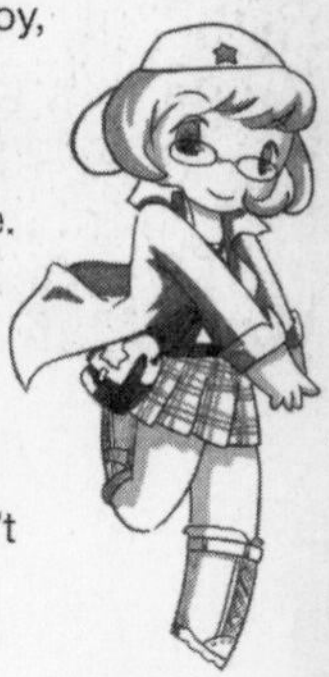

SGT FROG

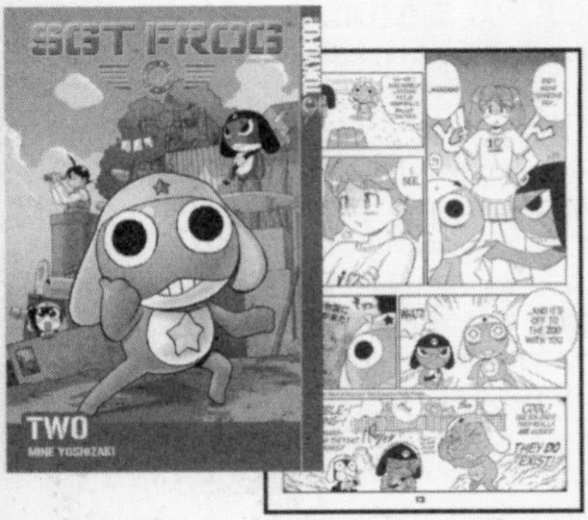
SGT. FROG
TOKYOPOP
TWO
MINE YOSHIZAKI

BY MINE YOSHIZAKI

Sgt. Frog is so absurdly comical, it has me in stitches every time I edit it. Mine Yoshizaki's clever sci-fi spoof showcases the hijinks of Sergeant Keroro, a cuddly looking alien, diabolically determined to oppress our planet! While some E.T.s phone home, this otherworldly menace has your number! Abandoned on Earth, Keroro takes refuge in the Hinata home, whose residents quickly take advantage of his stellar cleaning skills. But between scrubbing, vacuuming and an unhealthy obsession with Gundam models, Keroro still finds time to plot the subjugation of humankind!

~ Paul Morrissey, Editor

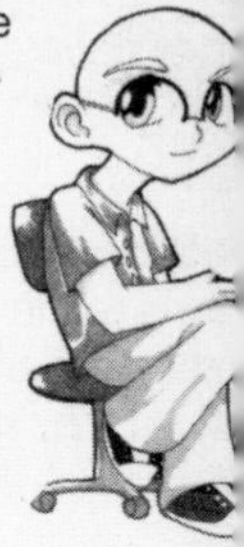

@LARGE

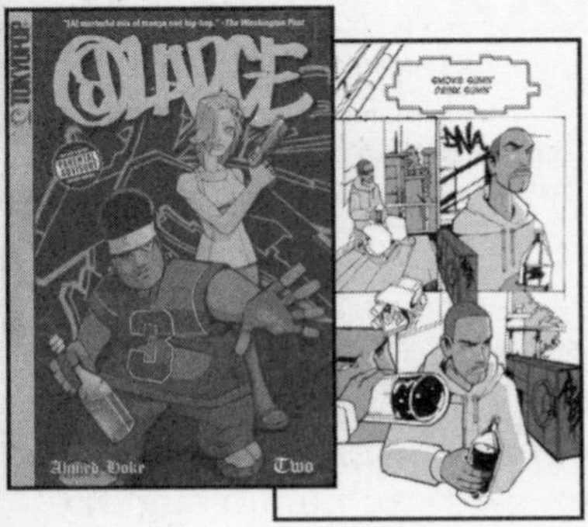
TOKYOPOP
Ahmed Hoke
Two

BY AHMED HOKE

Ahmed Hoke's revolutionary hip-hop manga is a groundbreaking graphic novel. While at first glace this series may seem like a dramatic departure from traditional manga styles, on a deeper level one will find a rich, lyrical world full of wildly imaginative characters, intense action and heartfelt human emotions. This is a truly unique manga series that needs to be read by everyone—whether they are fans of hip-hop or not.

~Rob Valois, Editor

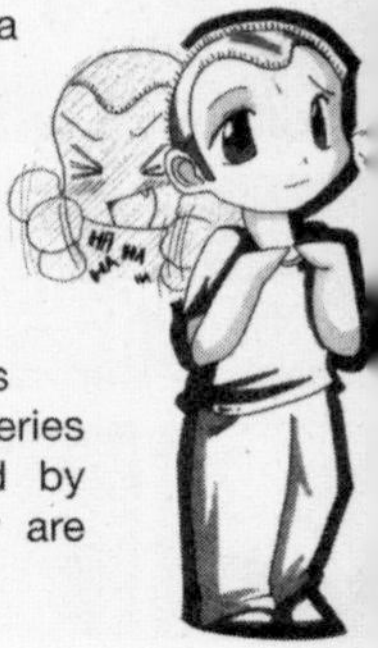

STOP!

This is the back of the book.
You wouldn't want to spoil a great ending!

This book is printed "manga-style," in the authentic Japanese right-to-left format. Since none of the artwork has been flipped or altered, readers get to experience the story just as the creator intended. You've been asking for it, so TOKYOPOP® delivered: authentic, hot-off-the-press, and far more fun!

DIRECTIONS

If this is your first time reading manga-style, here's a quick guide to help you understand how it works.

It's easy... just start in the top right panel and follow the numbers. Have fun, and look for more 100% authentic manga from TOKYOPOP®!